A·N·N·U·A·L E·D·I·T·I·O·N·S

Global Issues 01/02

Seventeenth Edition

EDITOR

Robert M. Jackson
California State University, Chico

Robert M. Jackson is a professor of political science and dean of the School of Graduate, International, and Sponsored Programs at California State University, Chico. In addition to teaching, he has published articles on the international political economy, international relations simulations, and political behavior. His special research interest is in the way northern California is becoming increasingly linked to the Pacific Basin. His travels include China, Japan, Hong Kong, Taiwan, Singapore, Malaysia, Portugal, Spain, Morocco, Costa Rica, El Salvador, Honduras, Guatemala, Mexico, Germany, Belgium, the Netherlands, Russia, and Czechoslovakia.

McGraw-Hill/Dushkin
530 Old Whitfield Street, Guilford, Connecticut 06437

Visit us on the Internet
http://www.dushkin.com

Credits

1. Global Issues in the Twenty-First Century: An Overview
Unit photo—Courtesy of NASA.
2. Population and Food Production
Unit photo—United Nations photo by J. P. Laffont.
3. The Global Environment and Natural Resources Utilization
Unit photo—United Nations photo.
4. Political Economy
Unit photo—United Nations/Pendl.
5. Conflict
Unit photo—AP/Wide World Photos.
6. Cooperation
Unit photo—United Nations photo.
7. Values and Visions
Unit photo—United Nations photo by John Isaac.

Copyright

Cataloging in Publication Data
Main entry under title: Annual Editions: Global Issues. 2001/2002.
1. Civilization, Modern—20th century—Periodicals. 2. Social prediction—Periodicals. 3. Social problems—20th century—Periodicals. I. Jackson, Robert, *comp.* II. Title: Global issues.
ISBN 0-07-243375-2 909.82′05 85-658006 ISSN 1093-278X

Seventeenth Edition

Printed in the United States of America 1234567890BAHBAH54321 Printed on Recycled Paper

Editors/Advisory Board Staff

Members of the Advisory Board are instrumental in the final selection of articles for each edition of ANNUAL EDITIONS. Their review of articles for content, level, currentness, and appropriateness provides critical direction to the editor and staff. We think that you will find their careful consideration well reflected in this volume.

EDITOR

Robert M. Jackson
California State University, Chico

ADVISORY BOARD

Peter K. Angstadt
Wesley College

Thomas E. Arcaro
Elon College

Diane N. Barnes
University of Southern Maine

Eric N. Budd
Fitchburg State College

H. Thomas Collins
George Washington University

E. Gene DeFelice
Purdue University Calumet

Dennis R. Gordon
Santa Clara University

Elizabeth Crump Hanson
University of Connecticut Storrs

James E. Harf
Ohio State University

Fayyaz Hussain
Michigan State University

Sadat Kazi
Vanier College

Sondra King
Northern Illinois University

Steven L. Lamy
University of Southern California

T. David Mason
University of Memphis

Louis L. Ortmayer
Davidson College

Guy Poitras
Trinity University

Helen E. Purkitt
U.S. Naval Academy

Christian Søe
California State University Long Beach

John H. P. Williams
East Carolina University

Kenneth L. Wise
Creighton University

Rodger Yeager
West Virginia University

EDITORIAL STAFF

Ian A. Nielsen, Publisher
Roberta Monaco, Senior Developmental Editor
Dorothy Fink, Associate Developmental Editor
Addie Raucci, Senior Administrative Editor
Robin Zarnetske, Permissions Editor
Joseph Offredi, Permissions Assistant
Diane Barker, Proofreader
Lisa Holmes-Doebrick, Senior Program Coordinator

TECHNOLOGY STAFF

Richard Tietjen, Senior Publishing Technologist
Jonathan Stowe, Director of Technology
Janice Ward, Software Support Analyst
Ciro Parente, Editorial Assistant

PRODUCTION STAFF

Brenda S. Filley, Director of Production
Charles Vitelli, Designer
Laura Levine, Graphics
Mike Campbell, Graphics
Tom Goddard, Graphics
Eldis Lima, Graphics
Nancy Norton, Graphics
Juliana Arbo, Typesetting Supervisor
Marie Lazauskas, Typesetter
Karen Roberts, Typesetter
Jocelyn Proto, Typesetter
Larry Killian, Copier Coordinator

To the Reader

In publishing ANNUAL EDITIONS we recognize the enormous role played by the magazines, newspapers, and journals of the public press in providing current, first-rate educational information in a broad spectrum of interest areas. Many of these articles are appropriate for students, researchers, and professionals seeking accurate, current material to help bridge the gap between principles and theories and the real world. These articles, however, become more useful for study when those of lasting value are carefully collected, organized, indexed, and reproduced in a low-cost format, which provides easy and permanent access when the material is needed. That is the role played by ANNUAL EDITIONS.

The beginning of the new millennium was celebrated with considerable fanfare. While there is indeed much for which to congratulate ourselves, it is equally true that the issues confronting humanity are uniquely complex and diverse. While the mass media may focus on the latest crisis for a few days or weeks, the broad forces that are shaping the world are seldom given the in-depth analysis that they warrant. Scholarly research about these historic change factors can be found in a wide variety of publications, but these are not readily accessible. In addition, students just beginning to study global issues can be discouraged by the terminology and abstract concepts that characterize much of the scholarly literature. In selecting and organizing the materials for this book, we have been mindful of the needs of beginning students and have, thus, selected articles that invite the student into the subject matter.

Each unit begins with an introductory article providing a broad overview of the area to be explored. The remaining articles examine in more detail some of the issues presented. The unit then concludes with an article (or two) that not only identifies a problem but suggests positive steps that are being taken to improve the situation. The world faces many serious issues, the magnitude of which would discourage even the most stouthearted individual. Though identifying problems is easier than solving them, it is encouraging to know that many of the issues are being successfully addressed.

Perhaps the most striking feature of the study of contemporary global issues is the absence of any single, widely held theory that explains what is taking place. Therefore, we have made a conscious effort to present a wide variety of ideologies and theories. The most important consideration has been to present global issues from an international perspective, rather than from a purely American or Western point of view. By encompassing materials originally published in many different countries and written by authors of various nationalities, the anthology represents the great diversity of opinions that people hold on important global issues. Two writers examining the same phenomenon may reach very different conclusions. It is not a question of who is right and who is wrong. What is important to understand is that people from different vantage points have differing perceptions of issues.

Another major consideration when organizing these materials was to explore the complex interrelationship of factors that produce social problems such as poverty. Too often, discussions of this problem (and others like it) are reduced to arguments about the fallacies of not following the correct economic policy or not having the correct form of government. As a result, many people overlook the interplay of historic, cultural, environmental, economic, and political factors that form complex webs that bring about many different problems. Every effort has been made to select materials that illustrate this complex interaction of factors, stimulating the beginning student to consider realistic rather than overly simplistic approaches to the pressing problems that threaten the existence of civilization.

Included in this edition of *Annual Editions: Global Issues* are *World Wide Web* sites that can be used to further explore topics addressed in the articles. These sites are cross-referenced in the *topic guide.*

Finally, we selected the materials in this book for both their intellectual insights and their readability. Timely and well-written materials should stimulate good classroom lectures and discussions. We hope that students and teachers will enjoy using this book. Readers can have input into the next edition by completing and returning the postage-paid *article rating form* in the back of the book.

I would like to acknowledge the help and support of Ian Nielsen. I am grateful for his encouragement and helpful suggestions in the selection of materials for *Annual Editions: Global Issues 01/02.* It is my continuing goal to encourage the readers of this book to have a greater appreciation of the world in which we live. I hope each of you will be motivated to further explore the complex issues faced by the world as we enter the twenty-first century.

Robert M. Jackson
Editor

Contents

To the Reader iv
Topic Guide 2
Selected World Wide Web Sites 4

Overview 6

1. **A Special Moment in History,** Bill McKibben, *The Atlantic Monthly,* May 1998. 8
The interconnected dangers of ***overpopulation, climate change, and pollution*** have been in the headlines for years, but doomsday has not yet arrived. Bill McKibben examines two important questions: What if we already have inflicted serious damage on the planet? and, What if there are only a few decades left to salvage a stable environment?

2. **The Many Faces of the Future,** Samuel P. Huntington, *Utne Reader,* May/June 1997. 13
The most important distinctions among people are not ideological or political. Samuel Huntington asserts that, contrary to what some argue, there is little likelihood of a universal civilization emerging. Rather, the factors that define the nine major ***cultures*** of the world—religion, ancestry, language, customs, and so on—will continue to define ***international politics.***

3. **World Prisms: The Future of Sovereign States and International Order,** Richard Falk, *Harvard International Review,* Summer 1999. 17
Richard Falk examines ***the future of the sovereign nation-state.*** He identifies a number of forces that are diminishing the power of the nation-state but observes that these factors are often contradictory. There are also transnational forces creating regional arrangements while, at the same time, other forces are fragmenting the current state-centered system.

4. **The American Way of Victory: A Twentieth-Century Trilogy,** James Kurth, *The National Interest,* Summer 2000. 22
James Kurth provides a panoramic view of the twentieth century and of the successful as well as the flawed "victory strategies" the United States and other major political powers implemented after the two ***world wars.*** He draws lessons about these ***military and economic strategies*** to evaluate United States policy following its victory in the cold war. He concludes, "Living with China is the single most important challenge facing a United States still living with victory."

Global Issues in the Twenty-First Century: An Overview

Four articles in this section present distinct views on the present and future state of life on Earth.

The concepts in bold italics are developed in the article. For further expansion please refer to the Topic Guide, the Glossary, and the Index.

UNIT 2

Population and Food Production

Four selections in this section discuss the contributing factors to the world's population growth and the challenge of providing food for this added strain on the world's capacity.

Overview 30

5. The Big Crunch, Jeffrey Kluger, *Time,* April/May 2000. **32**
A general overview is offered of the changing global ***demographic trends*** of fewer children and increased longevity. Jeffrey Kluger describes variations between different geographic regions and the varying patterns of consumption among the world's ***rich and poor.***

6. Breaking *Out* or Breaking *Down,* Lester R. Brown and Brian Halweil, *World Watch,* September/October 1999. **35**
The spread of the HIV virus, aquifer depletion, and shrinking cropland have been growing trends for years. The magnitude of these problems now threatens to increase ***death rates*** in many of the ***world's poorest regions,*** raising ***the specter of social unrest*** and increased poverty.

7. The Misery Behind the Statistics: Women Suffer Most, Diana Brown, *Free Inquiry,* Spring 1999. **43**
Diana Brown focuses on the widespread abuses of ***women,*** with a special emphasis on policies that relate to the control of ***population growth.***

8. Grains of Hope, J. Madeleine Nash, *Time,* July 31, 2000. **46**
Genetically engineered crops could revolutionize farming. Protesters fear they could destroy the ***ecosystem.*** Madeleine Nash provides an overview of this growing debate.

UNIT 3

The Global Environment and Natural Resources Utilization

Five articles in this section discuss natural resources and their effects on the world's environment.

Overview 56

9. The Global Challenge, Michael H. Glantz, *The World & I,* April 1997. **56**
Circulating freely around the planet, the atmosphere and oceans are shared resources whose resiliency is being tested by ever-growing human demands. Michael Glantz examines a number of specific ***issues that affect the so-called global commons*** and raises questions about the ability of people to respond to these environmental issues.

10. Climatic Changes That Make the World Flip, Robert Mathews, *The UNESCO Courier,* November 1999. **60**
The impact of global warming on the ***environment*** is not necessarily a drawn-out affair. Recent evidence indicates that rapid changes, or "climate flips," could occur virtually overnight. This hypothesis is supported by a variety of historical case studies.

11. The Energy Question, Again, Vaclav Smil, *Current History,* December 2000. **65**
Abundant, cheap ***energy*** is taken for granted by citizens of the ***rich*** countries. The ***future*** of this fundamental component of the global ***economy,*** however, is uncertain. The author describes both ***environmental*** and supply issues that threaten the energy future.

The concepts in bold italics are developed in the article. For further expansion please refer to the Topic Guide, the Glossary, and the Index.

12. Invasive Species: Pathogens of Globalization, Christopher Bright, *Foreign Policy,* Fall 1999. **70**
World trade has become a primary source of the most dangerous forms of ***environmental decline***: Thousands of invasive species are hitchhiking through the global trading network of ships, planes, and railroads. The negative impact of this bioinvasion is visible on all landmasses and in most coastal waters.

13. We *Can* Build a Sustainable Economy, Lester R. Brown, *The Futurist,* July/August 1996. **77**
The world is faced with an enormous need for change in a short period of time. Human behavior and ***values,*** and national priorities that reflect them, change in response to either new information or new experiences. Lester Brown asserts that regaining control of our destiny depends on stabilizing ***population*** as well as ***climate.***

Political Economy

Eight articles present various views on economic and social development in the nonindustrial and industrial nations.

Overview **82**

A. GLOBALIZATION DEBATE

14. The Complexities and Contradictions of Globalization, James N. Rosenau, *Current History,* November 1997. **84**
Globalization is a complex concept that means different things to different people. James Rosenau first defines the concept and then ***contrasts the process of globalization with localization.*** Rather than conclude that one force will prevail over the other, Rosenau argues that the two forces will contradictorily and simultaneously accommodate each other.

15. Dueling Globalizations: A Debate Between Thomas L. Friedman and Ignacio Ramonet, Thomas L. Friedman and Ignacio Ramonet, *Foreign Policy,* Fall 1999. **89**
Proponents of two distinct perspectives on the trends and challenges of the global ***political economy*** offer a spirited debate. The authors challenge each other's assumptions, raising interesting questions about the distribution of ***wealth,*** the power of ***governments,*** and the ***quality of life*** in the future.

16. The Crisis of Globalization, James K. Galbraith, *Dissent,* Summer 1999. **100**
James Galbraith critically evaluates the basic ***economic assumptions*** of globalization; that is, that markets are efficient, states are unnecessary, and the ***rich and poor*** have no conflicting interests. He argues that the exceptions to these assumptions outnumber examples of where they have successfully worked. This has resulted in a situation where the economic ***prospects*** for millions of the world's poorest have been undermined.

The concepts in bold italics are developed in the article. For further expansion please refer to the Topic Guide, the Glossary, and the Index.

17. **Globalization and American Power,** Kenneth N. Waltz, *The National Interest,* Spring 2000. **104**
Kenneth Waltz challenges the assumption that markets increasingly rule the world. He argues that the growing ***inequality in power*** is the dominant theme of the post–cold war era, not increased ***interdependence.*** He concludes, "Politics prevails over economics."

18. **Reality Check: The WTO and Globalization After Seattle,** Peter D. Sutherland, *Harvard International Review,* Winter/Spring 2000. **111**
The former director-general of the GATT and the WTO responds to critics of globalization. He argues that the ***legal structure*** governing the global ***trading system*** has resulted in broadly shared ***economic benefits.*** A system of managing trade is not equated with other globalization trends such as the Internet, travel, and the media.

B. CASE STUDIES

19. **Where Have All the Farmers Gone?** Brian Halweil, *World Watch,* September/October 2000. **115**
The globalization of ***agriculture*** is critically evaluated in this abridged version of the orginal article. In an economic system that is integrated from farm to market, the small, independent farmer is being forced out of business. Many interesting ***environmental*** and ***public policy*** issues are raised by author Brian Halweil.

20. **Beyond the Transition: China's Economy at Century's End,** Edward S. Steinfeld, *Current History,* September 1999. **127**
Edward Steinfeld reviews 20 years of Chinese ***economic reform*** along with the dramatic policy shifts associated with the ***government's*** desire to join the World Trade Organization. Steinfeld comes to the interesting conclusion that "China is not scrambling to dismantle socialism; it is scrambling to regulate a market system."

21. **What Pacific Century?** Louis Kraar, *Fortune,* November 22, 1999. **132**
For years futurists have declared that Asia would rule the world economy of the twenty-first century. The author concludes that it isn't likely to happen. He argues that traditional Asian values are getting in the way.

The concepts in bold italics are developed in the article. For further expansion please refer to the Topic Guide, the Glossary, and the Index.

Overview 134

22. Life After Pax Americana, Charles A. Kupchan, *World Policy Journal,* Fall 1999. 136
Charles Kupchan argues that the structure of ***international politics*** will undergo profound changes as the dominant role of the United States begins to recede. The main challenge is weaning Europe and East Asia from their dependence on the United States while at the same time minimizing rivalries within those two regions.

23. An Anachronistic Policy: The Strategic Obsolescence of the "Rogue Doctrine," Michael T. Klare, *Harvard International Review,* Summer 2000. 141
United States' ***military policy*** since the early 1990s has been guided by the so-called "Rogue Doctrine." The author examines its basic assumptions and identifies a number of changing circumstances such as the proliferation of ***nuclear weapons*** in India and Pakistan that challenge the doctrine's underlying assumptions.

24. Europe at Century's End: The Challenge Ahead, Richard N. Haass, *Brookings Review,* Summer 1999. 146
Richard Haass offers a broad overview of the ***strategic challenges*** facing Europe, including a discussion of their ***economic*** underpinnings. He provides a special focus on the changing role of NATO, including the uncertain role of Russia in European affairs.

25. Ethnic Conflict: Think Again, Yahya Sadowski, *Foreign Policy,* Summer 1998. 150
Some observers have predicted that ***ethnic conflicts*** are likely to become a worldwide political epidemic. Based on an analysis of recent historical trends, Yahya Sadowski rejects this forecast. He concludes that while ethnic conflicts are a serious problem, today's prophets of anarchy suffer from a simplistic view of ethnicity.

26. The Nuclear Agenda, James M. Lindsay, *Brookings Review,* Fall 2000. 156
In the final years of the Clinton administration, a number of important nuclear weapons issues were left unresolved. The Bush administration is now faced with a complex set of interrelated issues of ***arms control*** and ***missile defense.*** These nuclear age challenges will be a test of diplomatic and ***policymaking*** skills.

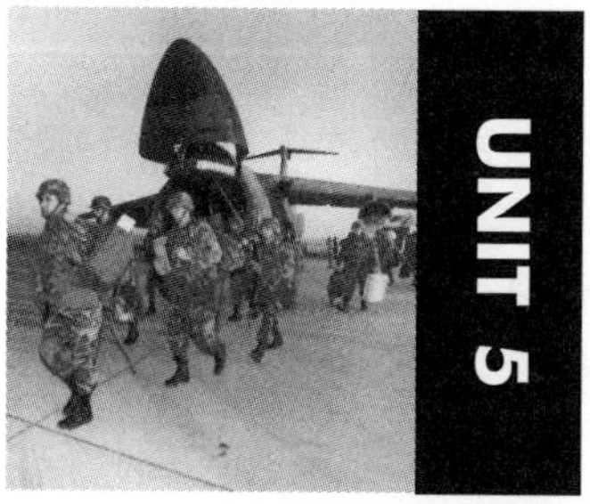

Conflict

Five articles in this section discuss the basis for world conflict and the current state of peace in the international community.

Overview 160

27. Justice Goes Global, *Time,* July 27, 1998. 162
The fact that the International Criminal Court, which has genuine power, has been created is an unprecedented move by the world community to make the ***rule of law*** finally prevail over brute force. The treaty, signed by 160 countries, creates a global tribunal to judge ***war criminals.*** However, the refusal of the United States to sign the accord leaves many questions about what will be the future of the new court.

28. Enforcing Human Rights, Karl E. Meyer, *World Policy Journal,* Fall 1999. 164
The history of the ***Universal Declaration of Human Rights*** is reviewed. Three alternative ***U.S. foreign policies*** are evaluated. The author argues that instead of unilateral U.S. action, the United Nations should have a multinational standby force that could be quickly deployed when the human rights of a group of people are threatened.

Cooperation

Five selections in this section examine patterns of international cooperation and the social structures that support this cooperation.

The concepts in bold italics are developed in the article. For further expansion please refer to the Topic Guide, the Glossary, and the Index.

29. Ecotourism Without Tears, Sylvie Blangy, *UNESCO Courier*, July/August 1999. **169**
This case study of ***global tourism*** describes how ***indigenous communities*** are developing partnerships with tour operators to promote tourism that generates ***revenue*** while protecting the culture of these communities as well as the surrounding ***natural environment.***

30. Tribes Under the Microscope, Vida Foubister, *The Rotarian*, December 2000. **172**
Genetic ***researchers*** view the world's indigenous cultures as "living laboratories." But what happens when new science clashes with ancient ***beliefs***? This question is examined and creative solutions are described.

31. Child Labour: Rights, Risks, and Realities, Carol Bellamy, *The Rotarian*, September 1997. **176**
Carol Bellamy, executive director of UNICEF, describes the ***exploitation of children*** and the international efforts to mobilize society to combat this denial of basic ***human rights.***

UNIT 7

Values and Visions

Seven articles discuss human rights, ethics, values, and new ideas.

Overview **180**

32. Are Human Rights Universal? Shashi Tharoor, *World Policy Journal*, Winter 1999/2000. **182**
The author, who works in the Office of the Secretary General of the United Nations, responds to criticisms of the Universal Declaration of Human Rights. Contrary to those who argue that the Declaration is an attempt to impose alien, Western ***values*** on the rest of the world, the author examines a variety of ***cultural*** and ethical issues and concludes that "a universal idea of human rights can help make the world safe for diversity."

33. The Grameen Bank, Muhammad Yunus, *Scientific American*, November 1999. **187**
A small experiment, begun in Bangladesh to loan money to poor people as a way of helping them become more productive, has turned into ***a major new concept in the eradication of poverty.***

34. Why Environmental Ethics Matters to International Relations, John Barkdull, *Current History*, November 2000. **192**
The dominant worldviews of ***Western culture*** do not have core assumptions that are defined in terms of an ***"environmental ethic."*** After examining alternative environmental ethics and then applying them to "realism" and "liberal institutionalism," the author calls for a new political dialogue that only a more "authentic democracy" can generate in order to better integrate social choices with a vision of the "natural" world we create.

The concepts in bold italics are developed in the article. For further expansion please refer to the Topic Guide, the Glossary, and the Index.

35. Will Globalization Make You Happy? Robert Wright, *Foreign Policy,* September/October 2000. **197**
The psychological dimensions of ***globalization*** are explored in light of the changing relative and absolute gap between ***rich and poor.*** The speed of economic change and the impact of new global ***telecommunication technologies*** are additional factors explored by the author.

36. A Fourth Way? The Latin American Alternative to Neoliberalism, Lucy Conger, *Current History,* November 1998. **204**
The growing ***inequality between rich and poor*** is especially pronounced in Latin America. A group of intellectuals and politicians is determined to chart ***a new policy*** that promotes productive investment and a democratized economy by ***investing in human resources.***

37. Democracy in Russia: How Free Is Free? *The Economist,* November 25, 2000. **209**
The institutional roots of Russian ***democracy*** are shallow. When compared to the Soviet era, there are now many freedoms. At the same time, there are trends that suggest that political ***corruption*** and ***racism*** are increasing. This paradox of conflicting trends is examined.

38. One Battle After Another, Sophie Bessis, *UNESCO Courier,* June 2000. **213**
Women have fought for their ***rights*** throughout the twentieth century. Sophie Bessis offers an overview of the issues and trends along with a description of how the struggle varies from country to country.

World Map **216**
Glossary **218**
Index **226**
Test Your Knowledge Form **228**
Article Rating Form **229**

The concepts in bold italics are developed in the article. For further expansion please refer to the Topic Guide, the Glossary, and the Index.

Topic Guide

This topic guide suggests how the selections in this book relate to the subjects covered in your course.

The Web icon (●) under the topic articles easily identifies the relevant Web sites, which are numbered and annotated on the next two pages. By linking the articles and the Web sites by topic, this ANNUAL EDITIONS reader becomes a powerful learning and research tool.

TOPIC AREA	TREATED IN
Agriculture Food, and Hunger	1. Special Moment in History 6. Breaking *Out* or Breaking *Down* 8. Grains of Hope 13. We *Can* Build a Sustainable Economy 19. Where Have All the Farmers Gone? ● ***2, 7, 8, 9, 10, 19***
Communications	2. Many Faces of the Future 14. Complexities and Contradictions of Globalization ● ***1, 18, 20, 24, 25, 26***
Cultural Customs and Values	2. Many Faces of the Future 3. World Prisms 7. Misery Behind the Statistics 13. We *Can* Build a Sustainable Economy 14. Complexities and Contradictions of Globalization 15. Dueling Globalizations 19. Where Have All the Farmers Gone? 21. What Pacific Century? 25. Ethnic Conflict 27. Justice Goes Global 28. Enforcing Human Rights 29. Ecotourism Without Tears 30. Tribes Under the Microscope 31. Child Labour: Rights, Risks, and Realities 32. Are Human Rights Universal? 33. Grameen Bank 34. Why Environmental Ethics Matters 35. Will Globalization Make You Happy? 37. Democracy in Russia 38. One Battle After Another ● ***1, 8, 12, 15, 20, 31, 32***
Development: Economic and Social	5. Big Crunch 6. Breaking *Out* or Breaking *Down* 7. Misery Behind the Statistics 8. Grains of Hope 9. Global Challenge 13. We *Can* Build a Sustainable Economy 14. Complexities and Contradictions of Globalization 15. Dueling Globalizations 16. Crisis of Globalization 17. Globalization and American Power 18. Reality Check 19. Where Have All the Farmers Gone? 20. Beyond the Transition: China's Economy 29. Ecotourism Without Tears 30. Tribes Under the Microscope 31. Child Labour: Rights, Risks, and Realities 32. Are Human Rights Universal? 33. Grameen Bank 36. Fourth Way? The Latin American Alternative to Neoliberalism 38. One Battle After Another ● ***2, 5, 6, 17, 18, 19, 20, 21, 29, 32***
Economics	1. Special Moment in History 4. American Way of Victory 6. Breaking *Out* or Breaking *Down* 10. Climatic Changes That Make the World Flip 11. Energy Question Again 13. We *Can* Build a Sustainable Economy 14. Complexities and Contradictions of Globalization 15. Dueling Globalizations 16. Crisis of Globalization 17. Globalization and American Power 18. Reality Check 19. Where Have All the Farmers Gone? 20. Beyond the Transition: China's Economy 29. Ecotourism Without Tears 31. Child Labour: Rights, Risks, and Realities 33. Grameen Bank 34. Why Environmental Ethics Matters 36. Fourth Way? The Latin American Alternative to Neoliberalism ● ***1, 2, 17, 18, 19, 20, 21, 29***
Energy: Exploration, Production, Research, and Politics	11. Energy Question, Again 13. We *Can* Build a Sustainable Economy ● ***11, 12, 13, 14, 15, 16, 18, 20***
Environment, Ecology, and Conservation	1. Special Moment in History 6. Breaking *Out* or Breaking *Down* 8. Grains of Hope 9. Global Challenge 10. Climatic Changes That Make the World Flip 11. Energy Question, Again 12. Invasive Species 13. We *Can* Build a Sustainable Economy 19. Where Have All the Farmers Gone? 29. Ecotourism Without Tears 34. Why Environmental Ethics Matters ● ***11, 12, 13, 14, 15, 16***

TOPIC AREA	TREATED IN
The Future	1. Special Moment in History 2. Many Faces of the Future 3. World Prisms 4. American Way of Victory 5. Big Crunch 6. Breaking *Out* or Breaking *Down* 7. Misery Behind the Statistics 8. Grains of Hope 9. Global Challenge 10. Climatic Changes That Make the World Flip 11. Energy Question, Again 12. Invasive Species 13. We *Can* Build a Sustainable Economy 14. Complexities and Contradictions of Globalization 19. Where Have All the Farmers Gone? 22. Life After Pax Americana 23. Anachronistic Policy 24. Europe at Century's End 26. Nuclear Age 34. Why Environmental Ethics Matters 35. Will Globalization Make You Happy? 37. Democracy in Russia 38. One Battle After Another ● ***3, 4, 5, 6, 7, 8, 9, 10, 11, 13, 15, 16, 18, 19, 20, 29, 30, 31, 32***
International Economics, Trade, Aid, and Dependencies	4. American Way of Victory 11. Energy Question, Again 12. 14. Complexities and Contradictions of Globalization 15. Dueling Globalizations 16. Crisis of Globalization 17. Globalization and American Power 18. Reality Check 19. Where Have All the Farmers Gone? 21. What Pacific Century? 33. Grameen Bank 36. Fourth Way? The Latin American Alternative to Neoliberalism ● ***1, 2, 5, 6, 17, 18, 19, 20, 21, 29***
Military: Warfare and Terrorism	4. American Way of Victory 22. Life After Pax Americana 23. Anachronistic Policy 24. Europe at Century's End 25. Ethnic Conflict 26. Nuclear Age 27. Justice Goes Global 28. Enforcing Human Rights ● ***22, 23, 24, 25***
Natural Resources	6. Breaking *Out* or Breaking *Down* 9. Global Challenge 11. Energy Question, Again 12. Invasive Species 13. We *Can* Build a Sustainable Economy 34. Why Environmental Ethics Matters ● ***11, 12, 13, 14, 15, 16, 31***
Political and Legal Global Issues	9. Global Challenge 18. Reality Check 19. Where Have All the Farmers Gone? 27. Justice Goes Global 28. Enforcing Human Rights 30. Tribes Under the Microscope 31. Child Labour: Rights, Risks, and Realities 32. Are Human Rights Universal? ● ***18, 19, 20, 26, 27***
Population and Demographics (Quality of Life Indicators)	1. Special Moment in History 5. Big Crunch 6. Breaking *Out* or Breaking *Down* 7. Misery Behind the Statistics 35. Will Globalization Make You Happy? ● ***5, 6, 8, 10, 20***
Science, Technology, and Research and Development	1. Special Moment in History 8. Grains of Hope 13. We *Can* Build a Sustainable Economy 26. Nuclear Age 30. Tribes Under the Microscope ● ***1, 2, 9, 11, 12, 13, 14, 17, 18***
Underdeveloped Countries	5. Big Crunch 6. Breaking *Out* or Breaking *Down* 7. Misery Behind the Statistics 8. Grains of Hope 15. Dueling Globalizations 16. Crisis of Globalization 18. Reality Check 19. Where Have All the Farmers Gone? 20. Beyond the Transistion: China's Economy 29. Ecotourism Without Tears 30. Tribes Under the Microscope 31. Child Labour: Rights, Risks, and Realities 33. Grameen Bank 36. Fourth Way? The Latin American Alternative to Neoliberalism ● ***2, 5, 6, 7, 8, 9, 10, 12, 15, 16, 19, 20, 21, 28, 31***

AE: Global Issues

The following World Wide Web sites have been carefully researched and selected to support the articles found in this reader. The sites are cross-referenced by number and the Web icon ( ) in the topic guide. In addition, it is possible to link directly to these Web sites through our DUSHKIN ONLINE support site at *http://www.dushkin.com/online/*.

The following sites were available at the time of publication. Visit our Web site—we update DUSHKIN ONLINE regularly to reflect any changes.

General Sources

1. U.S. Information Agency (USIA)

http://www.usinfo.state.gov

USIA'S home page provides definitions, related documentation, and discussions of topics of concern to students of global issues. The site addresses today's Hot Topics as well as ongoing issues that form the foundation of the field.

2. World Wide Web Virtual Library: International Affairs Resources

http://www.etown.edu/vl/

Surf this site and its extensive links to learn about specific countries and regions, to research various think tanks and international organizations, and to study such vital topics as international law, development, the international economy, human rights, and peacekeeping.

Global Issues in the Twenty-First Century: An Overview

3. The Henry L. Stimson Center

http://www.stimson.org

The Stimson Center, a nonpartisan organization, focuses on issues where policy, technology, and politics intersect. Use this site to find varying assessments of U.S. foreign policy in the post–cold war world and to research other topics.

4. The Heritage Foundation

http://www.heritage.org

This page offers discussion about and links to many sites having to do with foreign policy and foreign affairs, including news and commentary, policy review, events, and a resource bank.

5. IISDnet

http://iisd1.iisd.ca

The International Institute for Sustainable Development presents information through links to business, sustainable development, and developing ideas. "Linkages" is its multimedia resource for policymakers.

6. The North-South Institute

http://www.nsi-ins.ca/ensi/index.html

Searching this site of the North-South Institute, which works to strengthen international development cooperation and enhance gender and social equity, will help you find information and debates on a variety of global issues.

Population and Food Production

7. The Hunger Project

http://www.thp.org

Browse through this nonprofit organization's site, whose goal is the end to global hunger through leadership at all levels of society. The Hunger Project contends that the persistence of hunger is at the heart of the major security issues threatening our planet.

8. Penn Library: Resources by Subject

http://www.library.upenn.edu/resources/websitest.html

This vast site is rich in links to information about subjects of interest to students of global issues. Its extensive population and demography resources address such concerns as migration, family planning, and health and nutrition in various world regions.

9. World Health Organization

http://www.who.int

This home page of the World Health Organization will provide you with links to a wealth of statistical and analytical information about health and the environment in the developing world.

10. WWW Virtual Library: Demography & Population Studies

http://demography.anu.edu.au/VirtualLibrary/

A definitive guide to demography and population studies can be found at this site. It contains a multitude of important links to information about global poverty and hunger.

The Global Environment and Natural Resources Utilization

11. Friends of the Earth

http://www.foe.co.uk/index.html

This nonprofit organization pursues a number of campaigns to protect Earth and its living creatures. This site has links to many important environmental sites, covering such broad topics as ozone depletion, soil erosion, and biodiversity.

12. National Geographic Society

http://www.nationalgeographic.com

This site provides links to material related to the atmosphere, the oceans, and other environmental topics.

13. National Oceanic and Atmospheric Administration (NOAA)

http://www.noaa.gov

Through this home page of NOAA, part of the U.S. Department of Commerce, you can find information about coastal issues, fisheries, climate, and more. The site provides many links to research materials and to other Web resources.

14. Public Utilities Commission of Ohio (PUCO)

http://www.puc.state.oh.us/consumer/gcc/index.html

PUCO's site serves as a clearinghouse of information about global climate change. Its links explain the science and chronology of global climate change.

15. SocioSite: Sociological Subject Areas

http://www.pscw.uva.nl/sociosite/TOPICS/

This huge site provides many references of interest to those interested in global issues, such as links to information on ecology and the impact of consumerism.

16. United Nations Environment Programme (UNEP)

http://www.unep.ch

Consult this home page of UNEP for links to critical topics of concern to students of global issues, including desertification, migratory species, and the impact of trade on the environment.

Political Economy

17. Belfer Center for Science and International Affairs (BCSIA)

http://ksgwww.harvard.edu/csia/

BCSIA is the hub of Harvard University's John F. Kennedy School of Government's research, teaching, and training in international affairs related to security, environment, and technology.

18. Communications for a Sustainable Future

http://csf.colorado.edu

Information on topics in international environmental sustainability is available on this Gopher site. It pays particular attention to the political economics of protecting the environment.

19. U.S. Agency for International Development

http://www.info.usaid.gov

Broad and overlapping issues such as democracy, population and health, economic growth, and development are covered on this Web site. It provides specific information about different regions and countries.

20. Virtual Seminar in Global Political Economy/Global Cities & Social Movements

http://csf.colorado.edu/gpe/gpe95b/resources.html

This site of Internet resources is rich in links to subjects of interest in regional environmental studies, covering topics such as sustainable cities, megacities, and urban planning. Links to many international nongovernmental organizations are included.

21. World Bank

http://www.worldbank.org

News, press releases, summaries of new projects, speeches, publications, and coverage of numerous topics regarding development, countries, and regions are provided at this World Bank site. It also contains links to other important global financial organizations.

Conflict

22. DefenseLINK

http://www.defenselink.mil

Learn about security news and research-related publications at this U.S. Department of Defense site. Links to related sites of interest are provided. The information systems BosniaLINK and GulfLINK can also be found here. Use the search function to investigate such issues as land mines.

23. Federation of American Scientists (FAS)

http://www.fas.org

FAS, a nonprofit policy organization, maintains this site to provide coverage of and links to such topics as global security, peace, and governance in the post–cold war world. It notes a variety of resources of value to students of global issues.

24. ISN International Relations and Security Network

http://www.isn.ethz.ch

This site, maintained by the Center for Security Studies and Conflict Research, is a clearinghouse for information on international relations and security policy. Topics are listed by category (Traditional Dimensions of Security, New Dimensions of Security, and Related Fields) and by major world region.

25. The NATO Integrated Data Service (NIDS)

http://www.nato.int/structur/nids/nids.htm

NIDS was created to bring information on security-related matters to within easy reach of the widest possible audience. Check out this Web site to review North Atlantic Treaty Organization documentation of all kinds, to read *NATO Review,* and to explore key issues in the field of European security and transatlantic cooperation.

Cooperation

26. American Foreign Service Association

http://www.afsa.org/related.html

The AFSA offers this page of related sites as part of its Web presence. Useful sites include DiploNet, Public Diplomacy, and InterAction. Aso click on Diplomacy and Diplomats and other sites on the sidebar.

27. Carnegie Endowment for International Peace

http://www.ceip.org

An important goal of this organization is to stimulate discussion and learning among both experts and the public at large on a wide range of international issues. The site provides links to *Foreign Policy,* to the Moscow Center, to descriptions of various programs, and much more.

28. Commission on Global Governance

http://www.cgg.ch

This site provides access to *The Report of the Commission on Global Governance,* produced by an international group of leaders who want to find ways in which the global community can better manage its affairs.

29. OECD/FDI Statistics

http://www.oecd.org/statistics/

Explore world trade and investment trends and statistics on this site from the Organization for Economic Cooperation and Development. It provides links to many related topics and addresses the issues on a country-by-country basis.

30. U.S. Institute of Peace

http://www.usip.org

USIP, which was created by the U.S. Congress to promote peaceful resolution of international conflicts, seeks to educate people and to disseminate information on how to achieve peace. Click on Highlights, Publications, Events, Research Areas, and Library and Links.

Values and Visions

31. Human Rights Web

http://www.hrweb.org

The history of the human rights movement, text on seminal figures, landmark legal and political documents, and ideas on how individuals can get involved in helping to protect human rights around the world can be found in this valuable site.

32. InterAction

http://www.interaction.org

InterAction encourages grassroots action and engages government policymakers on advocacy issues. The organization's Advocacy Committee provides this site to inform people on its initiatives to expand international humanitarian relief, refugee, and development-assistance programs.

We highly recommend that you review our Web site for expanded information and our other product lines. We are continually updating and adding links to our Web site in order to offer you the most usable and useful information that will support and expand the value of your Annual Editions. You can reach us at: *http://www.dushkin.com/annualeditions/*.

Unit 1

Unit Selections

1. **A Special Moment in History,** Bill McKibben
2. **The Many Faces of the Future,** Samuel P. Huntington
3. **World Prisms: The Future of Sovereign States and International Order,** Richard Falk
4. **The American Way of Victory: A Twentieth-Century Trilogy,** James Kurth

Key Points to Consider

❖ Do the analyses of any of the authors in this section employ the assumptions implicit in the allegory of the balloon? If so, how? If not, how are the assumptions of the authors different?

❖ All the authors point to interactions among different factors. What are some of the relationships that they cite? How do the authors differ in terms of the relationships they emphasize?

❖ What assets that did not exist 100 years ago do people have now to solve problems?

❖ What events during the twentieth century have had the greatest impact on shaping the realities of contemporary international affairs?

❖ What do you consider to be the five most pressing global problems of today? How do your answers compare to those of your family, friends, and classmates?

DUSHKINONLINE Links www.dushkin.com/online/

3. **The Henry L. Stimson Center**
   http://www.stimson.org
4. **The Heritage Foundation**
   http://www.heritage.org
5. **IISDnet**
   http://iisd1.iisd.ca
6. **The North-South Institute**
   http://www.nsi-ins.ca/ensi/index.html

These sites are annotated on pages 4 and 5.

Global Issues in the Twenty-First Century: An Overview

Imagine a clear, round, inflated balloon. Now imagine that a person begins to brush yellow paint onto this miniature globe; symbolically, the color yellow represents *people*. In many ways the study of global issues is ultimately the study of people. Today, there are more people occupying Earth than ever before. In addition, the world is in the midst of a period of unprecedented population growth. Not only are there many countries where the majority of people are under age 16, but because of improved health care, there are also more older people alive than ever before. The effect of a growing global population, however, goes beyond sheer numbers, for a growing population has unprecedented impacts on natural resources and social services. Population issues, then, are an appropriate place to begin the study of global issues.

Imagine that our fictional artist dips the brush into a container of blue paint to represent the world of *nature*. The natural world plays an important role in setting the international agenda. Shortages of raw materials, drought and crop failures, and pollution of waterways are just a few examples of how natural resources can have global implications.

Adding blue paint to the balloon also reveals one of the most important concepts found in this book of readings. Although the balloon originally was covered by yellow and blue paint (people and nature as separate conceptual entities), the two combined produce an entirely different color: green. Talking about nature as a separate entity or about people as though they were somehow removed from the forces of the natural world is a serious intellectual error. The people-nature relationship is one of the keys to understanding many of today's most important global issues.

The third color added to the balloon is red. It represents the *meta component* (i.e., those qualities that make human beings different from animals). These include new ideas and inventions, culture and values, religion and spirituality, and art and literature. The addition of the red paint immediately changes the color green to brown, again emphasizing the relationship among all three factors.

The fourth and final color added is white. This color represents *social structures*. Factors such as whether a society is urban or rural, industrial or agrarian, planned or decentralized, and consumer-oriented or dedicated to the needs of the state fall into this category. The relationship between this component and the others is extremely important. The impact of political decisions on the environment, for example, is one of the most unusual features of the contemporary world. Historically, the forces of nature determined which species survived or perished. Today, survival depends on political decisions—or indecision. Will the whales or bald eagles survive? The answer to this question will often depend on governmental activities, not evolutionary forces.

Understanding this relationship between social structure and nature (known as "ecopolitics") is important to the study of global issues. If the painter continues to ply the paintbrush over the miniature globe, a marbling effect will become evident. In some areas, the shading will vary because one element is greater than another. The miniature system appears dynamic. Nothing is static; relationships are continually changing. This leads to a number of theoretical insights: (1) there is no such thing as separate elements, only connections or relationships; (2) changes in one area (such as the weather) will result in changes in all other areas; and (3) complex relationships make it difficult to predict events accurately, so observers are often surprised by unexpected processes and outcomes.

This book is organized along the basic lines of the balloon allegory. The first unit explores a variety of perspectives on the forces that are shaping the world of the twenty-first century. Unit 2 focuses on population and food production. Unit 3 examines the environment and related issues. The next three units look at different aspects of the world's social structures. They explore issues of economics, national security, conflict, and international cooperation. In the final unit, a number of "meta" factors are discussed.

The reader should be aware that, just as it was impossible to keep the individual colors from blending into new colors on the balloon, it is also impossible to separate global issues into discrete chapters in a book. Any discussion of agriculture, for example, must take into account the impact of a growing population on soil and water resources, as well as new scientific breakthroughs in food production. Therefore, the organization of this book focuses attention on issue areas; it does not mean to imply that these factors are somehow separate.

With the collapse of the Soviet empire and the end of the cold war, the outlines of a new global agenda are beginning to emerge. Rather than being based on the ideology and interests of the two superpowers, new political, economic, and environmental factors are interacting in an unprecedented fashion. Rapid population growth, environmental decline, and uneven economic growth are all parts of a complex situation for which there is no historic parallel. As we begin the twenty-first century, signs abound that we are entering a new era. In the words of Abraham Lincoln, "As our case is new, so we must think anew." Compounding this situation, however, is a whole series of old problems such as ethnic and religious rivalries.

The authors in this first unit provide a variety of perspectives on the trends that they believe are the most important to understanding the historic changes at work at the global level. This discussion is then pursued in greater detail in the following units.

It is important for the reader to note that although the authors look at the same world, they often come to different conclusions. This raises an important issue of values and beliefs, for it can be argued that there really is no objective reality, only differing perspectives. In short, the study of global issues will challenge each thoughtful reader to examine her or his own values and beliefs.

A Special Moment in History

Bill McKibben

We may live in the strangest, most thoroughly different moment since human beings took up farming, 10,000 years ago, and time more or less commenced. Since then time has flowed in one direction—toward *more,* which we have taken to be progress. At first the momentum was gradual, almost imperceptible, checked by wars and the Dark Ages and plagues and taboos; but in recent centuries it has accelerated, the curve of every graph steepening like the Himalayas rising from the Asian steppe. . . .

But now—now may be the special time. So special that in the Western world we might each of us consider, among many other things, having only one child—that is, reproducing at a rate as low as that at which human beings have ever voluntarily reproduced. Is this really necessary? Are we finally running up against some limits?

To try to answer this question, we need to ask another: *How many of us will there be in the near future?* Here is a piece of news that may alter the way we see the planet—an indication that we live at a special moment. At least at first blush the news is hopeful. *New demographic evidence shows that it is at least possible that a child born today will live long enough to see the peak of human population.*

Around the world people are choosing to have fewer and fewer children—not just in China, where the government forces it on them, but in almost every nation outside the poorest parts of Africa. . . . If this keeps up, the population of the world will not quite double again; United Nations analysts offer as their mid-range projection that it will top out at 10 to 11 billion, up from just under six billion at the moment. . . .

The good news is that we won't grow forever. The bad news is that there are six billion of us already, a number the world strains to support. One more near-doubling—four or five billion more people—will nearly double that strain. Will these be the five billion straws that break the camel's back? . . .

LOOKING AT LIMITS

The case that the next doubling, the one we're now experiencing, might be the difficult one can begin as readily with the Stanford biologist Peter Vitousek as with anyone else. In 1986 Vitousek decided to calculate how much of the earth's "primary productivity" went to support human beings. He added together the grain we ate, the corn we fed our cows, and the forests we cut for timber and paper; he added the losses in food as we overgrazed grassland and turned it into desert. And when he was finished adding, the number he came up with was 38.8 percent. We use 38.8 percent of everything the world's plants don't need to keep themselves alive; directly or indirectly, we consume 38.8 percent of what it is possible to eat. "That's a relatively large number," Vitousek says. "It should give pause to people who think we are far from any limits." Though he never drops the measured tone of an academic, Vitousek speaks with considerable emphasis: "There's a sense among some economists that we're *so* far from any biophysical limits. I think that's not supported by the evidence."

For another antidote to the good cheer of someone like Julian Simon, sit down with the Cornell biologist David Pimentel. He believes that we're in big trouble. Odd facts stud his conversation—for example, a nice head of iceberg lettuce is 95 percent water and contains just fifty calories of energy, but it takes 400 calories of energy to grow that head of lettuce in California's Central Valley, and another 1,800 to ship it east. ("There's practically no nutrition in the damn stuff anyway," Pimentel says. "Cabbage is a lot better, and we can grow it in upstate New York.") Pimentel has devoted the past three decades to tracking the planet's capacity, and he believes that we're already too crowded—that the earth can support only two billion people over the long run at a middle-class standard of living, and that trying to support more is doing damage. He has spent considerable time studying soil erosion, for instance. Every raindrop that hits exposed ground is like a small explosion, launching soil particles into the air. On a slope, more than half of the soil contained in those splashes is carried downhill. If crop residue—cornstalks, say—is left in the field after harvest, it helps to shield the soil: the raindrop doesn't hit hard. But in the developing world, where firewood is scarce, peasants burn those cornstalks for cooking fuel. About 60 percent of crop residues in China and 90 percent in Bangladesh are removed and burned, Pimentel says. When planting season comes, dry soils simply blow away. "Our measuring stations pick up African soils in the wind when they start to plough."

The very things that made the Green Revolution so stunning—that made the last doubling possible—now cause trouble. Irrigation ditches, for instance, water 27 percent of all arable land and help to produce a third of all crops. But when flooded soils are baked by the sun, the water evaporates and the minerals in the irrigation water are deposited on the land. A hectare (2.47 acres) can accumulate two to five tons of salt annually, and eventually plants won't grow there. Maybe 10 percent of all irrigated land is affected.

. . . [F]ood production grew even faster than population after the Second World War. Year after year the yield of wheat and corn and rice rocketed up about three percent annually. It's a favorite statistic of the eternal optimists. In Julian Simon's book *The Ultimate Resource* (1981) charts show just how fast the growth was, and how it continually cut the cost of food. Simon wrote, "The obvious implication of this historical trend toward cheaper food—a trend that probably extends back to the beginning of agriculture—is that real prices for food will continue to drop. . . . It is a fact that portends more drops in price and even less scarcity in the future."

A few years after Simon's book was published, however, the data curve began to change. That rocketing growth in grain production ceased; now the gains were coming in tiny increments, too small to keep pace with population growth. The world reaped its largest harvest of grain per capita in 1984; since then the amount of corn and wheat and rice per person has fallen by six percent. Grain stockpiles have shrunk to less than two months' supply.

No one knows quite why. The collapse of the Soviet Union contributed to the trend—cooperative farms suddenly found the fertilizer supply shut off and spare parts for the tractor hard to come by. But there were other causes, too, all around the world—the salinization of irrigated fields, the erosion of topsoil, and all the other things that environmentalists had been warning about for years. It's possible that we'll still turn production around and start it rocketing again. Charles C. Mann, writing in *Science,* quotes experts who believe that in the future a "gigantic, multi-year, multi-billion-dollar scientific effort, a kind of agricultural 'person-on the-moon project,' " might do the trick. The next great hope of the optimists is genetic engineering, and scientists have indeed managed to induce resistance to pests and disease in some plants. To get more yield, though, a cornstalk must be made to put out another ear, and conventional breeding may have exhausted the possibilities. There's a sense that we're running into walls.

. . . What we are running out of is what the scientists call "sinks"—places to put the by-products of our large appetites. Not garbage dumps (we could go on using Pampers till the end of time and still have empty space left to toss them away) but the atmospheric equivalent of garbage dumps.

It wasn't hard to figure out that there were limits on how much coal smoke we could pour into the air of a single city. It took a while longer to figure out that building ever higher smokestacks merely lofted the haze farther afield, raining down acid on whatever mountain range lay to the east. Even that, however, we are slowly fixing, with scrubbers and different mixtures of fuel. We can't so easily repair the new kinds of pollution. These do not come from something going wrong—some engine without a catalytic converter, some waste-water pipe without a filter, some smokestack without a scrubber. New kinds of pollution come instead from things going as they're supposed to go—but at such a high volume that they overwhelm the planet. They come from normal human life—but there are so many of us living those normal lives that something abnormal is happening. And that something is different from the old forms of pollution that it confuses the issue even to use the word.

Consider nitrogen, for instance. But before plants can absorb it, it must become "fixed"—bonded with carbon, hydrogen, or oxygen. Nature does this trick with certain kinds of algae and soil bacteria, and with lightning. Before human beings began to alter the nitrogen cycle, these mechanisms provided 90–150 million metric tons of nitrogen a year. Now human activity adds 130–150 million more tons. Nitrogen isn't pollution—it's essential. And we are using more of it all the time. Half the industrial nitrogen fertilizer used in human history has been applied since 1984. As a result, coastal waters and estuaries bloom with toxic algae while oxygen concentrations dwindle, killing fish; as a result, nitrous oxide traps solar heat. And once the gas is in the air, it stays there for a century or more.

Or consider methane, which comes out of the back of a cow or the top of a termite mound or the bottom of a rice paddy. As a result of our determination to raise more cattle, cut down more tropical forest (thereby causing termite populations to explode), and grow more rice, methane concentrations in the atmosphere are more than twice as high as they have been for most of the past 160,000 years. And methane traps heat—very efficiently.

Or consider carbon dioxide. In fact, concentrate on carbon dioxide. If we had to pick one problem to obsess about over the next fifty years, we'd do well to make it CO_2—which is not pollution either. Carbon *mon*oxide is pollution: it kills you if you breathe enough of it. But carbon *di*oxide, carbon with two oxygen atoms, can't do a blessed thing to you. If you're reading this indoors, you're breathing more CO_2 than you'll ever get outside. For generations, in fact, engineers said that an engine burned clean if it produced only water vapor and carbon dioxide.

Here's the catch: that engine produces a *lot* of CO_2. A gallon of gas weighs about eight pounds. When it's burned in a car, about five and a half pounds of carbon, in the form of carbon dioxide, come spewing out the back. It doesn't matter if the car is a 1958 Chevy or a 1998 Saab. And no filter can reduce that flow—it's an inevitable by-product of fossil-fuel combustion, which is why CO_2 has been piling up in the atmosphere ever since the Industrial Revolution. Before we started burning oil and coal and gas, the atmosphere contained about 280 parts CO_2 per million. Now the figure is about 360. Unless we do everything we can think of to eliminate fossil fuels from our diet, the air will test out at more than 500 parts per million fifty or sixty years from now, whether it's sampled in the South Bronx or at the South Pole.

This matters because, as we all know by now, the molecular structure of this clean, natural, common element that we are adding to every cubic foot of the atmosphere surrounding us traps heat that would otherwise radiate back out to space. Far more than even methane and nitrous oxide, CO_2 causes global warming—the greenhouse effect—and climate change. Far more than any other single factor, it is turning the earth we were born on into a new planet.

. . . For ten years, with heavy funding from governments around the world, scientists launched satellites, monitored weather balloons, studied clouds. Their work culminated in a long-awaited report from the UN's Intergovernmental Panel on Climate Change, released in the fall of 1995. The panel's 2,000 scientists, from every corner of the globe, summed up their findings in this dry but historic bit of understatement: "The balance of evidence suggests that there is a discernible human influence on global climate." That is to say, we are heating up the planet—substantially. If we don't reduce emissions of carbon dioxide and other gases, the panel warned, temperatures will probably rise 3.6° Fahrenheit by 2100, and perhaps as much as 6.3°.

You may think you've already heard a lot about global warming. But most of our sense of the problem is behind the curve. Here's the current news: the changes are already well under way. When politicians and businessmen talk about "future risks," their rhetoric is outdated. This is not a problem for the distant future, or even for the near future. The planet has already heated up by a degree or more. We are perhaps a quarter of the way into the greenhouse era, and the effects are already being felt. From a new heaven, filled with nitrogen, methane, and carbon, a new earth is being born. If some alien astronomer is watching us, she's doubtless puzzled. This is the most obvious effect of our numbers and our appetites, and the key to understanding why the size of our population suddenly poses such a risk.

STORMY AND WARM

What does this new world feel like? For one thing, it's stormier than the old one. Data analyzed last year by Thomas Karl, of the National Oceanic and Atmospheric Administration, showed that total winter precipitation in the United States has increased by 10 percent since 1900 and that "extreme precipitation events"—rainstorms that dumped more than two inches of water in twenty-four hours and blizzards—had increased by 20 percent. That's because warmer air holds more water vapor than the colder atmosphere of the old earth; more water evaporates from the ocean, meaning more clouds, more rain, more snow. Engineers designing storm sewers, bridges, and culverts used to plan for what they called the "hundred-year storm." That is, they built to withstand the worst flooding or wind that history led them to expect in the course of a century. Since that history no longer applies, Karl says, "there isn't really a hundred-year event anymore . . . we seem to be getting these storms of the century every couple of years." When Grand Forks, North Dakota, disappeared beneath the Red River in the spring of last year, some meteorologists referred to it as "a 500-year flood"—meaning, essentially, that all bets are off. Meaning that these aren't acts of God. "If you look out your window, part of what you see in terms of weather is produced by ourselves," Karl says. "If you look out the window fifty years from now, we're going to be responsible for more of it."

Twenty percent more bad storms, 10 percent more winter precipitation—these are enormous numbers. It's like opening the newspaper to read that the average American is smarter by 30 IQ points. And the same data showed increases in drought, too. With more water in the atmosphere, there's less in the soil, according to Kevin Trenberth, of the National Center for Atmospheric Research. Those parts of the continent that are normally dry—the eastern sides of mountains, the plains and deserts—are even drier, as the higher average temperatures evaporate more of what rain does fall. "You get wilting plants and eventually drought faster than you would otherwise," Trenberth says. And when the rain does come, it's often so intense that much of it runs off before it can soak into the soil.

So—wetter and drier. *Different*. . . .

The effects of . . . warming can be found in the largest phenomena. The oceans that cover most of the planet's surface are clearly rising, both because of melting glaciers and because water expands as it warms. As a result, low-lying Pacific islands already report surges of water washing across the atolls. "It's nice weather and all of a sudden water is pouring into your living room," one Marshall Islands resident told a newspaper reporter. "It's very clear that something is happening in the Pacific, and these islands are feeling it." Global warming will be like a much more powerful version of El Niño that covers the entire globe and lasts forever, or at least until the next big asteroid strikes.

If you want to scare yourself with guesses about what might happen in the near future, there's no shortage of possibilities. Scientists have already observed large-scale shifts in the duration of the El Niño ocean warming, for instance. The Arctic tundra has warmed so much that in some places it now gives off more carbon dioxide than it absorbs—a switch that could trigger a potent feedback loop, making warming ever worse. And researchers studying glacial cores from the Greenland Ice Sheet recently concluded that local climate shifts have occurred with incredible rapidity in the past—18° in one three-year stretch. Other scientists worry that such a shift might be enough to flood the oceans with fresh water and reroute or shut off currents like the Gulf Stream and the North Atlantic, which keep Europe far warmer than it would otherwise be. (See "The Great Climate Flip-flop," by William H. Calvin, January *Atlantic*.) In the words of Wallace Broecker, of Columbia University, a pioneer in the field, "Climate is an angry beast, and we are poking it with sticks."

But we don't need worst-case scenarios: best-case scenarios make the point. The population of the earth is going to nearly double one more time. That will bring it to a level that even the reliable old earth we were born on would be hard-pressed to support. Just at the moment when we need everything to be working as smoothly as possible, we find ourselves inhabiting a new planet, whose carrying capacity we cannot conceivably estimate. We have no idea how much wheat this planet can grow. We don't know what its politics will be like: not if there are going to be heat waves like the one that killed more than 700 Chicagoans in 1995; not if rising sea levels and other effects of climate change create tens of millions of environmental refugees; not if a 1.5° jump in India's temperature could reduce the country's wheat crop by 10 percent or divert its monsoons. . . .

We have gotten very large and very powerful, and for the foreseeable future we're stuck with the results. The glaciers won't grow back again anytime soon; the oceans won't drop. We've already done deep and systemic damage. To use a human analogy, we've already said the angry and unforgivable words that will haunt our marriage till its end. And yet we can't simply walk out the door. There's no place to go. We have to salvage what we can of our relationship with the earth, to keep things from getting any worse than they have to be.

If we can bring our various emissions quickly and sharply under control, we *can* limit the damage, reduce dramatically the chance of horrible surprises, preserve more of the biology we were born into. But do not underestimate the task. The UN's Intergovernmental Panel on Climate Change projects that an immediate 60 percent reduction in fossil-fuel use is necessary just to stabilize climate at the current level of disruption. Nature may still meet us halfway, but halfway is a long way from where we are now. What's more, we can't delay. If we wait a few decades to get started, we may as well not even begin. It's not like poverty, a concern that's always there for civilizations to address. This is a timed test, like the SAT: two or three decades, and we lay our pencils down. It's *the* test for our generations, and population is a part of the answer. . . .

The numbers are so daunting that they're almost unimaginable. Say, just for argument's sake, that we decided to cut world fossil-fuel use by 60 percent—the amount that the UN panel says would stabilize world climate. And then say that we shared the remaining fossil fuel equally. Each human being would get to produce 1.69 metric tons of carbon dioxide annually—which would allow you to drive an average American car nine miles a day. By the time the population increased to 8.5 billion, in about 2025, you'd be down to six miles a day. If you carpooled, you'd have about three pounds of CO_2 left in your daily ration—enough to run a highly efficient refrigerator. Forget your computer, your TV, your stereo, your stove, your dishwasher, your water heater, your microwave, your water pump, your clock. Forget your light bulbs, compact fluorescent or not.

I'm not trying to say that conservation, efficiency, and new technology won't help. They will—but the help will be slow and expensive. The tremendous momentum of growth will work against it. Say that someone invented a new furnace tomorrow that used half as much oil as old furnaces. How many years would it be before a substantial number of American homes had the new device? And what if it cost more? And if oil stays cheaper per gallon than bottled water? Changing basic fuels—to hydrogen, say—would be even more expensive. It's not like running out of white wine and switching to red. Yes, we'll get new technologies. One day last fall *The New*

York Times ran a special section on energy, featuring many up-and-coming improvements: solar shingles, basement fuel cells. But the same day, on the front page, William K. Stevens reported that international negotiators had all but given up on preventing a doubling of the atmospheric concentration of CO_2. The momentum of growth was so great, the negotiators said, that making the changes required to slow global warming significantly would be like "trying to turn a supertanker in a sea of syrup."

There are no silver bullets to take care of a problem like this. Electric cars won't by themselves save us, though they would help. We simply won't live efficiently enough soon enough to solve the problem. Vegetarianism won't cure our ills, though it would help. We simply won't live simply enough soon enough to solve the problem.

Reducing the birth rate won't end all our troubles either. That, too, is no silver bullet. But it would help. There's no more practical decision than how many children to have. (And no more mystical decision, either.)

The bottom-line argument goes like this: The next fifty years are a special time. They will decide how strong and healthy the planet will be for centuries to come. Between now and 2050 we'll see the zenith, or very nearly, of human population. With luck we'll never see any greater production of carbon dioxide or toxic chemicals. We'll never see more species extinction or soil erosion. Greenpeace recently announced a campaign to phase out fossil fuels entirely by mid-century, which sounds utterly quixotic but could—if everything went just right—happen.

So it's the task of those of us alive right now to deal with this special phase, to squeeze us through these next fifty years. That's not fair—any more than it was fair that earlier generations had to deal with the Second World War or the Civil War or the Revolution or the Depression or slavery. It's just reality. We need in these fifty years to be working simultaneously on all parts of the equation—on our ways of life, on our technologies, and on our population.

As Gregg Easterbrook pointed out in his book *A Moment on the Earth* (1995), if the planet does manage to reduce its fertility, "the period in which human numbers threaten the biosphere on a general scale will turn out to have been much, much more brief" than periods of natural threats like the Ice Ages. True enough. But the period in question happens to be our time. That's what makes this moment special, and what makes this moment hard.

Bill McKibben is the author of several books about the environment, including *The End of Nature* (1989) and *Hope, Human and Wild* (1995). His article in this issue will appear in somewhat different form in his book *Maybe One: A Personal and Environmental Argument for Single-Child Families,* published in 1998 by Simon & Schuster.

THE MANY FACES OF the Future

Why we'll never have a universal civilization

By Samuel P. Huntington

Conventional Wisdom tells us that we are witnessing the emergence of what V.S. Naipaul called a "universal civilization," the cultural coming together of humanity and the increasing acceptance of common values, beliefs, and institutions by people throughout the world. Critics of this trend point to the global domination of Western-style capitalism and culture (*Baywatch,* many note with alarm, is the most popular television show in the world), and the gradual erosion of distinct cultures—especially in the developing world. But there's more to universal civilization than GATT and David Hasselhoff's pecs.

If what we mean by universal culture are the assumptions, values, and doctrines currently held by the many elites who travel in international circles, that's not a viable "one world" scenario. Consider the "Davos culture." Each year about a thousand business executives, government officials, intellectuals, and journalists from scores of countries meet at the World Economic Forum in Davos, Switzerland. Almost all of them hold degrees in the physical sciences, social sciences, business, or law; are reasonably fluent in English; are employed by governments, corporations, and academic institutions with extensive international connections; and travel frequently outside of their own countries. They also generally share beliefs in individualism, market economies, and political democracy,

From *Utne Reader,* May/June 1997, pp. 75–77, 102–103. Adapted from *The Clash of Civilizations and Remaking of World Order* by Samuel P. Huntington. © 1997 by Samuel P. Huntington. Reprinted by permission of Simon & Schuster.

which are also common among people in Western civilization. This core group of people controls virtually all international institutions, many of the world's governments, and the bulk of the world's economic and military organizations. As a result, the Davos culture is tremendously important, but it is far from a universal civilization. Outside the West, these values are shared by perhaps 1 percent of the world's population.

If a universal civilization is emerging, there should be signs of a universal language and religion. Nothing of the sort is occurring.

The argument that the spread of Western consumption patterns and popular culture around the world is creating a universal civilization is also not especially profound. Innovations have been transmitted from one civilization to another throughout history. But they are usually techniques lacking in significant cultural consequences or fads that come and go without altering the underlying culture of the recipient civilization. The essence of Western civilization is the Magna Carta, not the Magna Mac. The fact that non-Westerners may bite into the latter does not necessarily mean they are more likely to accept the former. During the '70s and '80s Americans bought millions of Japanese cars and electronic gadgets without being "Japanized," and, in fact, became considerably more antagonistic toward Japan. Only naive arrogance can lead Westerners to assume that non-Westerners will become "Westernized" by acquiring Western goods.

A slightly more sophisticated version of the universal popular culture argument focuses on the media rather than consumer goods in general. Eighty-eight of the world's hundred most popular films in 1993 were produced in the United States, and four organizations based in the United States and Europe—the Associated Press, CNN, Reuters, and the French Press Agency—dominate the dissemination of news worldwide. This situation simply reflects the universality of human interest in love, sex, violence, mystery, heroism, and wealth, and the ability of profit-motivated companies, primarily American, to exploit those interests to their own advantage. Little or no evidence exists, however, to support the assumption that the emergence of pervasive global communications is producing significant convergence in attitudes and beliefs around the world. Indeed, this Western hegemony encourages populist politicians in non-Western societies to denounce Western cultural imperialism and to rally their constituents to preserve their indigenous cultures. The extent to which global communications are dominated by the West is, thus, a major source of the resentment non-Western peoples have toward the West. In addition, rapid economic development in non-Western societies is leading to the emergence of local and regional media industries catering to the distinctive tastes of those societies.

The central elements of any civilization are language and religion. If a universal civilization is emerging, there should be signs of a universal language and a universal religion developing. Nothing of the sort is occurring. Despite claims from Western business leaders that the world's language is English, no evidence exists to support this proposition, and the most reliable evidence that does exist shows just the opposite. English speakers dropped from 9.8 percent of the world's population in 1958 to 7.6 percent in 1992. Still, one can argue that English has become the world's lingua franca, or in linguistic terms, the principal language of wider communication. Diplomats, business executives, tourists, and the service professionals catering to them need some means of efficient communication, and right now that is largely in English. But this is a form of *intercultural* communication; it presupposes the existence of separate cultures. Adopting a lingua franca is a way of coping with linguistic and cultural differences, not a way of eliminating them. It is a tool for communication, not a source of identity and community.

The linguistic scholar Joshua Fishman has observed that a language is more likely to be accepted as a lingua franca if it is not identified with a particular ethnic group, religion, or ideology. In the past, English carried many of those associations. But more recently, Fishman says, it has been "de-ethnicized (or minimally ethnicized)," much like what happened to Akkadian, Aramaic, Greek, and Latin before it. As he puts it, "It is part of the relative good fortune of English as an additional language that neither its British nor its American fountainheads have been widely or deeply viewed in an ethnic or ideological context for the past quarter century or so." Resorting to English for intercultural communication helps maintain—and, indeed, reinforce—separate cultural identities. Precisely because people want to preserve their own culture, they use English to communicate with people of other cultures.

A universal religion is only slightly more likely to emerge than a universal language. The late 20th century has seen a resurgence of religions around the world, including the rise of fundamentalist movements. This trend has reinforced the differences among religions, and has not necessarily resulted in significant shifts in the distribution of religions worldwide.

Of course, there have been increases during the past century in the percentage of people practicing the two major proselytizing religions, Islam and Christianity. Western Christians accounted for 26.9 percent of the world's population in 1900 and peaked at about 30 percent in 1980, while the Muslim population increased from 12.4 percent in 1900 to as much as 18 percent in 1980. The percentage of Christians in the world will probably decline to about 25 percent by 2025. Meanwhile, because of extremely high rates of population growth, the proportion of Muslims in the world will continue to increase dramatically and represent about 30 percent of the world's population by 2025. Neither, however, qualifies as a universal religion.

The argument that some sort of universal civilization is emerging rests on one or more of three assumptions: that the collapse of Soviet communism meant the end of history and the universal victory of liberal democracy; that increased interaction among peoples through trade, investment, tourism, media, and electronic communications is creating a common world culture; and that a universal civilization is the logical result of the process of global modernization that has been going on since the 18th century.

The first assumption is rooted in the Cold War perspective that the only alternative to communism is liberal democracy, and the demise of the first inevitably produces the second. But there are many alternatives to liberal democracy—including authoritarianism, nationalism, corporatism, and market communism (as in China)—that are alive and well in today's world. And, more significantly, there are all the religious alternatives that lie outside the world of secular ideologies. In the modern world, religion is a central, perhaps *the* central, force that motivates and mobilizes people. It is sheer hubris to think that because Soviet communism has collapsed, the West has conquered the world for all time and that non-Western peoples are going to rush to embrace Western liberalism as the only alternative. The Cold War division of humanity is over. The more fundamental divisions of ethnicity, religions, and civilizations remain and will spawn new conflicts.

The Real World

The civilizations shaping the new global order

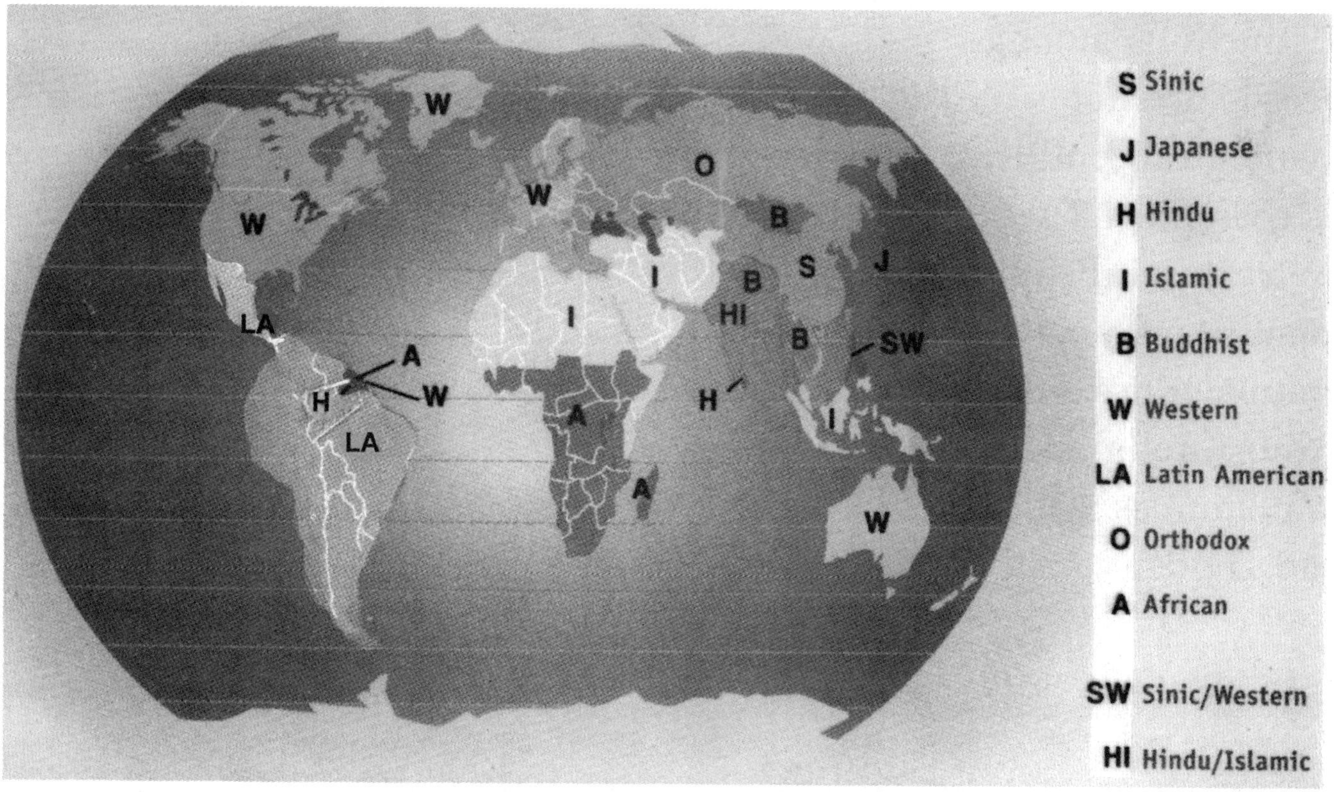

The new global economy is a reality. Improvements in transportation and communications technology have indeed made it easier and cheaper to move money, goods, knowledge, ideas, and images around the world. But what will be the impact of this increased economic interaction? In social psychology, distinctiveness theory holds that people define themselves by what makes them different from others in a particular context: People define their identity by what they are not. As advanced communications, trade, and travel multiply the interactions among civilizations, people will increasingly accord greater relevance to identity based on their own civilization.

Those who argue that a universal civilization is an inevitable product of modernization assume that all modern societies must become Westernized. As the first civilization to modernize, the West leads in the acquisition of the culture of modernity. And as other societies acquire similar patterns of education, work, wealth, and class structure—the argument runs—this modern Western culture will become the universal culture of the world. That significant differences exist between modern and traditional cultures is beyond dispute. It doesn't necessarily follow, however, that societies with modern cultures resemble each other more than do societies with traditional cultures. As historian Fernand Braudel writes, "Ming China . . . was assuredly closer to the France of the Valois than the China of Mao Tse-tung is to the France of the Fifth Republic."

Yet modern societies could resemble each other more than do traditional societies for two reasons. First, the increased interaction among modern societies may not generate a common culture, but it does facilitate the transfer of techniques, inventions, and practices from one society to another with a speed and to a degree that were impossible in the traditional world. Second, traditional society was based on agriculture; modern society is based on industry. Patterns of agriculture and the social structure that goes with them are much more dependent on the natural environment than are patterns of industry. Differences in industrial organization are likely to derive from differences in culture and social structure rather than geography, and the former conceivably can converge while the latter cannot.

Modern societies thus have much in common. But do they necessarily merge into homogeneity? The argument that they do rests on the assumption that modern society must approximate a single type, the Western type. This is a totally false assumption. Western civilization emerged in the 8th and 9th centuries. It did not begin to modernize until the 17th and 18th centuries. The West was the West long before it was modern. The central characteristics of the West—the classical legacy, the mix of Catholicism and Protestantism, and the separation of spiritual and temporal authority—distinguish it from other civilizations and antedate the modernization of the West.

In the post–Cold War world, the most important distinctions among people are not ideological, political, or economic. They are

In today's world, the most important distinctions among people are not ideological, political, or economic. They are cultural. People identify with cultural groups: tribes, ethnic groups, religious communities, nations, and civilizations.

cultural. People and nations are attempting to answer a basic human question: Who are we? And they are answering that question in the traditional way, by reference to the things that mean the most to them: ancestry, religion, language, history, values, customs, and institutions. People identify with cultural groups: tribes, ethnic groups, religious communities, nations, and, at the broadest level, civilizations. They use politics not just to advance their interests but also to define their identity. We know who we are only when we know who we are not, and often only when we know who we are against.

Nation-states remain the principal actors in world affairs. Their behavior is shaped, as in the past, by the pursuit of power and wealth, but it is also shaped by cultural preferences and differences. The most important groupings are no longer the three blocs of the Cold War but rather the world's major civilizations *(See* map):

S Sinic
All scholars recognize the existence of either a single distinct Chinese civilization dating back at least to 1500 B.C., or of two civilizations—one succeeding the other—in the early centuries of the Christian epoch.

J Japanese
Some scholars combine Japanese and Chinese culture, but most recognize Japan as a distinct civilization, the offspring of Chinese civilization, that emerged between A.D. 100 and 400.

H Hindu
A civilization—or successive civilizations—has existed on the Indian subcontinent since at least 1500 B.C. In one form or another, Hinduism has been central to the culture of India since the second millennium B.C.

I Islamic
Originating on the Arabian peninsula in the 7th century A.D., Islam spread rapidly across North Africa and the Iberian Peninsula and also eastward into central Asia, the Indian subcontinent, and Southeast Asia. Many distinct cultures—including Arab, Turkic, Persian, and Malay—exist within Islam.

W Western
The emergence of Western civilization—what used to be called Western Christendom—is usually dated at about 700 A.D. It has two main components, in Europe and North America.

LA Latin American
Latin America, often considered part of the West, has a distinct identity. It has had a corporatist, authoritarian culture, which Europe had to a much lesser degree and North America did not have at all. Europe and North America both felt the effects of the Reformation and have combined Catholic and Protestant cultures, while Latin America has been primarily Catholic. Latin American civilization also incorporates indigenous cultures, which were wiped out in North America.

O Orthodox
This civilization, which combines the Orthodox tradition of Christianity with the Slav cultures of Eastern Europe and Russia, has resurfaced since the demise of the Soviet Union.

A African
There may be some argument about whether there is a distinct African civilization. North Africa and the east coast belong to Islamic civilization. (Historically, Ethiopia constituted a civilization of its own.) Elsewhere, imperialism brought elements of Western civilization. Tribal identities are pervasive throughout Africa, but Africans are also increasingly developing a sense of African identity. Sub-Saharan Africa conceivably could cohere into a distinct civilization, with South Africa as its core.

B Buddhist
Beginning in the first century A.D., Buddhism was exported from India to China, Korea, Vietnam, and Japan, where it was assimilated by the indigenous cultures and/or suppressed. What can legitimately be described as a Buddhist civilization, however, does exist in Sri Lanka, Burma, Thailand, Laos, Cambodia; and Tibet, Mongolia, and Bhutan. Overall, however, the virtual extinction of Buddhism in India and its incorporation into existing cultures in other major countries means that it has not been the basis of a major civilization. (Modern India represents a mix of Hindu and Islamic civilizations, while the Philippines is a unique Sinic-Western hybrid by virtue of its history of Spanish, then American rule.)

As Asian and Muslim civilizations begin to assert the universal relevance of *their* cultures, Westerners will see the connection between universalism and imperialism and appreciate the virtues of a pluralistic world. In order to preserve Western civilization, the West needs greater unity of purpose. It should incorporate into the European Union and NATO the western states of central Europe; encourage the Westernization of Latin America; slow the drift of Japan away from the West and toward accommodation with China; and accept Russia as the core state of Orthodoxy and a power with legitimate interests.

The main responsibility of Western leaders is to recognize that intervention in the affairs of other civilizations is the single most dangerous source of instability in the world.

The main responsibility of Western leaders is to recognize that intervention in the affairs of other civilizations is the single most dangerous source of instability in the world. The West should attempt not to reshape other civilizations in its own image, but to preserve and renew the unique qualities of its own civilization.

Samuel P. Huntington is Albert J. Weatherhead III University Professor at Harvard University.

World Prisms

The Future of Sovereign States and International Order

As this century closes, the contradictory organizational energies associated with globalization and fragmentation are mounting concerted attacks on the primacy of the sovereign, territorial state as the sole building block of world order. To begin with, transnational social forces seem on the verge of forming some kind of global civil society over the course of the next several decades, providing a foundation for the project of "global democracy." Also significant is the resurgence of religion, and closely linked, the rise of civilizational consciousness.

BY RICHARD FALK

At the same time, the resilience of the state and its twin, the ideology of nationalism, strongly suggest that we have yet to experience the definitive waning of the state system, which is the form of world order that has dominated political imagination and history books for several centuries. And let us not overlook, in this preliminary examination of the world order, the potential of regionalism, which is often underestimated. Our dualistic mental habits lead many of us to think only of "states" and "the world," which involves comparing the most familiar part of our experience to an imagined whole while excluding from consideration all other possibilities.

Several salient issues warrant attention. Given the potent dynamic of economic globalization, how can market forces become effectively regulated in the future? The mobility of capital and the relative immobility of labor will challenge governments to balance their interest in promoting trade and profits against their concern with the well-being of their citizenry. At the same time, economic globalization and the information revolution, with their accompanying compression of time and space, could encourage an emerging political globalization; the processes and institutional and ethical consequences associated with this transformation have many ramifications for the future of a globalized international community. Within this changing global milieu, world cities are becoming political actors that form their own networks of transnational relationships that are producing a new layer of world order.

Other lines of inquiry point to the uncertain nature of international institutions in today's world. Is there a crucial role for regional institutions as a halfway house between utopian globalism and outmoded statism? Also at issue is whether the current eclipse of the United Nations is merely a temporary phenomenon associated with the high incidence of civic violence, or rather a more durable development that reflects the peculiarities of the current phase of peace and security issues dominated by civil wars and ethnic strife. Are the main political actors, especially states, adapting their roles in response to new challenges and realities, or are they being superseded and outflanked by alternative problem-solving and institutional frameworks? What is the impact of the particular style and substance of global leadership provided by the United States, and is this likely to change due to internal developments, lessons learned, and external challenges?

Building Pressures

These trends will exert pressure on existing institutions, creating receptivity and resistance to various proposals for institutional innovation, as well as encouraging a variety of regressive withdrawals from interstate cooperation. Perhaps the most ominous of these trends relates to the pressure of an expected population increase of more than two billion over the next two decades, more than 90 percent of which will be concentrated in developing countries. Such a pattern will impact many political arrangements and will challenge the adequacy of food and freshwater supplies in many settings that are already economically disadvantaged. Comparably serious concerns relate to the impacts of greenhouse gas emissions on climate change, deforestation and desertification, the extinction of species, ozone depletion, and the further spread, development, and retention of weapons of mass destruction. Such trends suggest that existing managerial and adaptive capacities will be badly overstretched, thresholds of ecological and social balance will likely be crossed, and tensions and conflicts will abound. The increased incidence of conflicts will prompt contradictory forms of reliance on hyper-modern and primitive types of coercion—that is, on super-smart weaponry of great technical sophistication and on terrorist violence. Both types of violence deeply challenge basic assumptions about legal, moral, and political limits on conflict.

Against such an ominous background, it is important to identify several potentially promising developments that could mitigate, if not overcome, these mounting dangers.

None of these developments is free of ambiguity, and the overall prospect of the future is embedded in the fluidity of the historical present.

The Eclipse of the UN

Ever since its founding in 1945, many of the hopes for a more peaceful and benign world have reflected confidence in the United Nations. The United Nations was created as a response to World War II in a climate of resolve to erase the memories of failure associated with the League of Nations. The new organization was promoted as embodying a new approach to world order based on the commitment of leading states to establish and enact "collective security." With the onset of the Cold War, this undertaking by leading states to ground global security upon the collective mechanisms of the United Nations became untenable, and balance-of-power politics was retrofitted to serve the security needs of bipolar conflict in the nuclear age. Although the United Nations managed to accomplish many useful tasks on behalf of the peoples of the world, including a variety of peace-keeping ventures at the edges of world politics, it was sidelined in relation to its central peace-and-security mission by the effects of East-West gridlock. When Mikhail Gorbachev came to power in Moscow in the mid-1980s, a flurry of UN activity ensued, enabling the organization to play a leading role in the resolution of a series of regional conflicts, including those in Afghanistan, El Salvador, Angola, Cambodia, Iran, and Iraq. This suggested a bright future for the organization when and if the superpowers tempered their opposition to each other.

After the surprisingly abrupt end of the Cold War in 1989, there emerged a strong expectation that a golden age for the United Nations lay just beyond the horizon. The Gulf War of 1991 confirmed this optimistic view for many observers of the global scene, demonstrating for the first time that the Security Council could organize an effective collective response to aggression, precisely along the lines envisaged by the drafters of the UN Charter so long ago. It should be noted, however, that this reinvigorated United Nations also aroused concern in some quarters, as some argued that the Security Council was becoming a geopolitical instrument in the hands of the United States and its allies. With the restoration of Kuwaiti sovereignty, the debate about the benefits and burdens of UN potency reached its climax, and was soon over-shadowed in the mid-1990s by a revived sense of futility, initially in reaction to Somalia, but most definitively with respect to ethnic cleansing in Bosnia and genocide in Rwanda. It then became evident that the United Nations had been used as a convenient mobilizing arena in the specific setting of strategic interests at risk in the Gulf Crisis. In contrast, where strategic interests were trivial or not present—as was the case in Somalia, Rwanda, and Bosnia—the political will of the Permanent Five was far too weak to support effective forms of humanitarian intervention under UN auspices.

File Photo

Alternatives to the United Nations as a global security organization may be needed.

Arguably, the United Nation's military role had been carefully confined, reflecting considerations of prudence and legal doctrine, to addressing warfare between states. When established, the organization was endowed with neither the competence nor the capability to respond to matters of civil strife. Nevertheless, neither governments nor the media made such a distinction in the early 1990s. Unable to meet these new demands, the United Nations was seriously discredited and once again sidelined in matters of peace and security. The new approach to global security at the end of the 1990s seems to be a mixture of old-fashioned geopolitics—that is, unilateralism by the leading military power—and coalition diplomacy under the aegis of NATO, as seen in this year's Kosovo intervention. If collective action on a world community scale has been seen as a world-order goal since World War I, then it would seem that the century is ending on a regressive note; a retreat to traditional methods of maintaining international order that depend on the strong-arm tactics of dominant states and their allies with little or no attention to international law.

The future of the United Nations as the basis of global security is not currently bright, but such an outlook could change rapidly. Memories are short, and if there are setbacks associated with US-NATO initiatives, a revived reliance on an augmented UN Security Council could materialize quickly. Even a change in the form and substance of US political leadership in the White House and Congress could rather abruptly confer upon the United Nations a new opportunity to play an important global security role. From the present vantage point, however, this outcome is not too likely. If the main security challenges continue to arise from intrastate violence, it seems unlikely that the United Nations, as presently constituted, could respond in a consistently useful manner. Also, the US approach to global leadership, given such recently hyped challenges as biowar and international terrorism, seems likely to avoid being constrained by the collective procedures of the United Nations.

Prospects for Reform

For these reasons, it seems appropriate not to expect too much from the United Nations in the peace-and-security area over the course of the next decade. At the same time, the United Nations remains a vital actor in relation to a wide range of global concerns: environment, food, health, humanitarian relief, human rights, refugees, lawmaking, and development.

It is also helpful to keep in mind that the United Nations was established by states to serve states—that it was international in conception and operation, and not supranational or intranational. As such, it has been difficult for the United Nations to accommodate the various strands of transnational activity that together compose the phenomenon of "globalization." Neither the private sector nor global civil society can gain meaningful access to the main arenas of the United Nations, an exclusion that has resulted in high-profile activity engaging grassroots participation beyond the normal arenas of the United Nations. If the United Nations were

European regionalism remains the most dramatic challenge to the state system. The historical irony is evident: the region that invented the modern state and its diplomacy is taking the lead in establishing a form of world order that is sufficiently different to qualify as a sequel.

constitutionally recreated in the year 2000, it would not likely resemble the organization set up in 1945. The awareness of such a discrepancy between what was done then and what is needed now is made even more serious due to the inability to reform the organization in even minimal respects. It has not been possible to agree on how to alter the composition of the Security Council to take account of the enormous changes in the makeup of international society over the course of the last half-century. It is evident to even casual observers that to retain permanent seats on the Security Council for both Great Britain and France, while denying such a presence to India and Brazil, or Japan and Germany, is to mock the current distribution of influence in world politics. The legitimacy of the United Nations, and its credibility as an actor, depends on its own structures of authority more or less mirroring the structure of relations among states and regions.

It is far too soon to write off the United Nations as a viable global security organization, but there are few reasons to believe that it will play a central role in peace, security, and development activity over the course of the next decade or so. Fortunately, there are more promising alternatives.

Learning from Europe

The most daring world-order experiment of this century had undoubtedly been the European regional movement. It has encroached on the sovereign rights of territorial states far more than anything attempted by the United Nations, even though regional organizations are formally subordinated to the UN Security Council with respect to the use of force. The European Union has used its authority structures, its institutional implementing procedures, and the integrative political will of government leaders to put a variety of supranational moves into operation: the supremacy of European Community Law; the external accountability of governments in relation to human-rights claims; the minimalization of obstacles to intra-regional trade, investment, customs, immigration, and travel controls; the existence of a common currency and central bank; and a directly elected regional parliament. The cumulative effect of these developments over the course of more than 50 years has been to bring into existence a distinctive European entity that is far from being either a single European superstate or merely a collaborative framework for a collection of states in Europe. Europe continues to evolve. Its final shape will not be known for several more decades.

The European Union is something quite new and different; it is likely to keep changing. If it is perceived outside of Europe as a success in these latest supranationalizing moves, it will provide Asia, Africa, and Latin America, or portions thereof, with positive models that they will be tempted to imitate and adapt to their regional conditions. The regional model is so promising that by 2025 and 2030 it might become natural to speak of "a world of regions" as an overarching successor metaphor to "a world of states."

At the same time, there are uncertainties associated with these European developments. The present turmoil in the Balkans could spread beyond the former Yugoslavia—and even if it does not, it could stimulate some drastic rethinking concerning the security implications of a regional approach, especially if linked, as in the Cold War, to US leadership. The NATO operation in Kosovo, besides suggesting the abandonment of the United Nations in the setting of global security, may discourage any further transfers of sovereignty by European states or contrarily provide momentum for the creation of an all-European security system. The Kosovo ordeal may also be regarded outside Europe as an indirect reaffirmation of the state as the basic ordering framework for most peoples in the world. It is also possible that Europeans will reevaluate NATO itself, since it is increasingly perceived as an alliance arrangement that belongs anachronistically to an era of old geopolitics—it is neither regional in orientation, nor collective in operation, nor responsive to the historical

File Photo

The effectiveness of the United Nations as an international actor remains in doubt.

File Photo

Cities are becoming transnational actors with their own worldviews, interests, and networks.

realities of Europe after the Cold War. If this type of revisionist thinking takes hold, a pooling of European security resources and at least a partial disengagement from dependence on the United States will follow, clarifying for a time the character of European regionalism.

However the Balkan crisis is eventually resolved, European regionalism remains the most fundamental challenge to the state system. The historical irony is that Europe, as the region that invented the modern state and its diplomacy, is taking the lead in establishing a form of world order that may soon turn out to be sufficiently different as to qualify as a sequel. Non-European forms of regionalism have also been moving ahead in this period, and need to be brought much more explicitly into our thinking about order, security, development, and justice as aspects of an emergent system of global governance.

The Re-empowered State

As I explained in greater detail in my work *Predatory Globalization: A Critique,* the effects of neo-liberal globalization have been to disempower the state with respect to solving both internal social and cultural problems. This generalization pertains to such external challenges as those arising from environmental deterioration, scarcity of renewable resources, and protection of the global commons for future generations. The idea of capital mobility on a regional and global scale in response to market factors offers the main insight into the disempowerment of the state, converting governments into capital facilitators and limiting the space for responsible political debate and party rivalry. Other important sources of this phenomenon of disempowerment have resulted from the weakening of organized labor as a source of societal pressure and the revolutionary impacts of information technology, the computer, and the internet, all tendencies that alter the role and identity of the state and weaken its disposition toward innovation and problem-solving.

Re-empowerment of the state implies reversing these trends, especially finding ways to offset the presiding influence of global market forces on the outlook and behavior of governing elites. Such a rebalancing of contending social force could result from the further mobilization of civil society in relation to such shared objectives as environmental quality, human rights, demilitarization, labor and welfare policy, and regulation of global capital flows. The Asian financial crisis which began in 1997, combined with the troubles in a series of other important countries such as Japan, Russia, and Brazil, has already caused a partial ideological retreat from extreme versions of neoliberal globalization. Further retreat could be prompted by instability generated in part by a spreading sense that the benefits of economic globalization are being unfairly distributed, with a steady increase in income and wealth disparities (a pattern clearly documented in the annual volumes of the *Human Development Report*).

Another reason for re-empowerment might arise from a growing anxiety, including among business elites, of backlash threats ranging from extremist religions, micro-nationalisms, and neo-fascist political movements. It may come to be appreciated by economic elites that the global economy needs to be steered with a greater attentiveness to social concerns and to the global public good, as well as in relation to efficiency of returns on capital. Otherwise, a new round of dangerous and costly revolutionary struggles looms menacingly on the horizon. A further supportive tendency is the appearance of "a new internationalism" in the form of various coalitions among many "normal" governments (those without extraregional global claims) and large numbers of transnational civic associations. This type of coalition was integral to the campaigns to ban anti-personnel landmines, to establish an international criminal court, and to call into question the legality and possession of nuclear weaponry. This set of initiatives put many governments in an activist mode and in opposition to the policy positions taken by the geopolitical leadership of the world, mainly the US government.

There is another somewhat silent re-empowerment taking place in the form of an extension of the authority of the state to manage the world's ocean's and outer space. The 1982 Law of the Sea Treaty, for example, validated an enormous expansion of coastal authority in the form of a 200-mile Exclusive Economic Zone. The magnitude of this re-empowerment can be appreciated when it is realized that 95 percent of the beneficial use of the ocean lies within these coastal waters.

The re-empowerment of the state is not meant to negate the benefits or reality of economic globalization. It is instead a matter of making the state more of a regulative mechanism in relation to market forces, and less of a facilitative force. Out of such re-empowerment might yet emerge an informal global social contract that could help provide the world economy with the sort of political and social stability that will be needed if "sustainable development" is to become a credible future reality.

Coordinating World Cities

It is not possible to do more than highlight this formidable frontier for ordering relations among peoples in ways that elude traditional and familiar frameworks. With an increasing proportion of wealth, culture, people, and innovation concentrated in or appropriated by world cities, these entities are more and more self-consciously becoming transnational actors with their own agendas, worldviews, and networks. The economic and political success of such city-states as Singapore and Hong Kong is also suggestive of the possibility that world order need not be premised on territorial dominion in the future. Whether states will successfully contain this disempowering trend or appropriate it for their own goals remains largely uncertain, as is the impact of deepening European-style regionalism. China's relationship to Hong Kong will be a test of whether the city as a political actor can withstand the challenges to its autonomy being posed by Beijing. In any event, the role and future of city-states in the next century is definitely an idea worth including on any chart depicting emergent forms of world order.

Creeping Functionalism

Among the most evident world-order trends is the impulse of governmental and other bureaucracies to coordinate specialist activities across state boundaries by way of consultation, periodic meetings, and informal codes of conduct. Through banking, shipping, and insurance specialists, an enormous proliferation of ad hoc functional arrangements are being negotiated and implemented in a wide variety of international arenas. Some interpreters of the global scene have identified the proliferation of such undertakings as the wave of the future, as a disaggregating response of sovereign states to the complexity of a highly interconnected world. Anne-Marie Slaughter articulates this position and gives it a positive spin in the 75th Anniversary Issue of *Foreign Affairs.* In a basic sense, this extension of functional modes of coordination to address a dazzling array of technical and commercial issues represents a series of practical adjustments to the growing complexity of international life. The role of the state is being tailored to work more on behalf of common economic interests associated with globalization and to be less preoccupied with the promotion of exclusively national economic interests.

In some circles, this devolution and dispersion of authority, with more direct rulemaking participation by private-sector representatives, along with the overall erosion of public-private sector distinctions, is sometimes referred to as "the new medievalism." Such a terminology deliberately recalls the world order of feudal Europe with its overlapping patterns of authority and the importance of both local and universal institutional actors. It was the territorial consolidation of this confusing reality that gave rise initially to the absolute state ruled by a monarch, and later to a constitutional government legitimized by the consent of the governed. The postmodern state is in the process of formation, and is as varied in character and orientation as are the circumstances of differing cultures, stages of development, degrees of integration, and respect for human rights that exist around the world.

A New World Order?

It is evident that in the institutional ferment of the moment, several trends and counter-trends make it impossible to depict the future shape of the world order with any confidence. Central to this future is the uncertain degree to which the sovereign state can adapt its behavior and role to a series of deterritorializing forces associated with markets, transnational social forces, cyberspace, demographic and environmental pressures, and urbanism. Also critical to the future is the fate of the European Union and the way in which it is reflected in non-European opinion. Seemingly less crucial, but still of interest, is whether the United Nations can find ways to retrieve its reputation as relevant to peace and security while continuing to engineer a myriad of useful activities beyond the gaze of the media. At issue, finally, is the sort of global leadership provided by the United States, and the nature of leadership alternatives, if any exist. Crossing the millennial threshold is likely to clarify the mix of these developments, but probably not in a definitive enough pattern to be worthy of being labeled "a new world order," at least for several decades.

RICHARD FALK is Albert G. Milbank Professor of International Law and Practice at Princeton University.

The American Way of Victory

A Twentieth-Century Trilogy

James Kurth

THE TWENTIETH century, the first American century, was also the century of three world wars. The United States was not only victorious in the First World War, the Second World War and the Cold War, but it was more victorious than any of the other victor powers. As the pre-eminent victor power, the subsequent strategies of the United States did much to shape the three postwar worlds. They therefore also did much to prepare the ground for the second and third world wars in the sequence. Now, ten years after the American victory in that third, cold, world war, it is time to evaluate the U.S. victor strategies of the 1990s and to consider if they will make the twenty-first century a second American century, this time one of world peace and prosperity, or if they could lead, sometime in the next few decades, to a fourth world war.

The First and Second British Centuries

LIKE America at the beginning of the twenty-first century, Britain in the early nineteenth century had passed through a century of three wars that were worldwide in scope—the War of the Spanish Succession (1702–13), the Seven Years' War (1756–63) and the successive Wars of the French Revolution and Napoleonic Wars (1792–1815). Britain had been victorious in each of these wars, making the eighteenth century something of a British one. The victor strategy that Britain pursued after the Napoleonic Wars laid the foundations for what has been called "the Hundred Years Peace" (1815–1914), making the second British century as peaceful as the first one had been warlike.[1]

The central elements of the British victor strategy were four; two involved international security and two involved the international economy.[2] The security elements were established immediately after the victory over Napoleon. They were, first, a British-managed balance of power system on the European continent, and, second, British naval supremacy in the rest of the world. The economic elements were established about a generation later. They involved, third, British industrial supremacy operating in an open international economy (Britain serving as "the workshop of the world"), and, fourth, British financial supremacy, also operating in an open international economy (the City of London serving as "the world's central bank").

By the beginning of the twentieth century, however, British naval and industrial supremacy were threatened by the spectacular growth of German military and economic power. When in August 1914 it appeared that Germany was about to destroy the Continental balance of power system with its invasion of Belgium and France, Britain went to war to stop it. The Hundred Years Peace and the second British century came to a crashing and catastrophic end with the First World War.

Victory therefore presents a profound challenge to a victor power, especially to a pre-eminent one: it must create a victor strategy to order the postwar world in a way that does not lead to a new major war. The British victor strategy after the Napoleonic Wars was successful in meeting this challenge for almost a century. But even this sophisticated strategy ultimately proved inadequate to the task of managing the problems posed by the rise of a new and very assertive power. As shall be discussed below, the American victor strategies after the First and Second World Wars were similar to the earlier British one in their efforts to combine several different dimensions of international security and economy; indeed, the American strategies relied upon some of the same elements, particularly naval, industrial and financial supremacy. They did not, however, succeed in preventing the Second World War and the Cold War. The fundamental question for our time is whether the American victor strategies after the Cold War will succeed in preventing some kind of a new world war in the next century.

As it happens, the Spring 2000 issue of *The National Interest* contained an array of articles that can help us

© The National Interest, Summer 2000, No. 60, Washington, D.C. Reprinted by permission.

address this question. In considering the lessons that can be drawn from the earlier American experiences of living with victory, I shall be making use of them. In particular, these lessons underline the importance of managing the rise of Chinese military and economic power and of doing so in ways similar to those that Zbigniew Brzezinski advocates in his "Living With China." They also underline the danger but potential relevance of the arguments that Robert Kagan and William Kristol advance in their essay, "The Present Danger."

Living With Victory After the First World War

IT TOOK FOUR years of war and the massive engagement of the United States before, in November 1918, the Western Allies succeeded in defeating Germany. But even in defeat, the nation whose rise to military and economic power Britain had failed to manage still retained most of its inherent strengths. The German problem, which had been at the center of international relations before the war, was redefined by the Allied victory, but it was still there, and Western victory still had to focus upon the German reality.

Germany remained the central nation on the European continent. Demographically, it had the largest and best educated population in Europe. (Russia, although it had a larger population, was convulsed by revolution and civil war.) Economically, it had the largest and most advanced industry in Europe. Strategically, it faced formidable powers to the west (France and Britain), but to the east lay only new and weak states (Poland and Czechoslovakia). In this sense, Germany's strategic position was actually better after its defeat in the First World War than it had been before the war began, when to the east it had faced Russia as a great power. It would only be a matter of time before Germany recovered its political unity, gathered up its inherent strengths, and once again converted these into military and economic power. This was the long-term reality that the victorious Allies had to consider as they composed their victor strategies.

There were four basic strategies that different allies employed at different times: territorial dismemberment, military containment, security cooperation and economic engagement. These were not new inventions; they derived from the strategies employed by victor powers after earlier wars. The first two derived from territorial annexations and frontier fortifications, strategies that the Continental powers had used against each other in the eighteenth and nineteenth centuries. The last two derived from the "concert of Europe", or balance of power system, and the open international economy that Britain had managed in the nineteenth century. But these strategies were not obsolescent conceptions; the latter three prefigured the victor strategies that the United States would employ after the Second World War and after the Cold War.

Territorial dismemberment and military containment.

One apparent solution to the German problem was territorial dismemberment. This was the strategy preferred by France. The dismemberment of a defeated enemy can sometimes be carried out by victorious powers, and the Allies did so with that other Central Power in World War I, the Austro-Hungarian monarchy. But while this division destroyed a former adversary, it unleashed a sort of international anarchy in southeastern Europe that still reverberates today. Dismemberment is also what happened to the Soviet Union after the Cold War. Here too, while this division greatly diminished a former adversary, it has unleashed internal and international anarchy in the Caucasus and Central Asia.

Whatever might be the advantages of dismemberment as a victor strategy, they were not applicable to Germany in 1919. By that time, the German nation had become a solid reality with a solid identity; it could not be permanently undone by artificial territorial divisions, unless these were enforced by military occupation (which is how the division of Germany was to be enforced after the Second World War). There are today a few international analysts who argue that the United States should encourage the territorial division of troublesome powers, particularly Russia and China. There are, however, hardly any specialists on China or even Russia who believe that a permanent division of these nations is possible.

An alternative but closely related solution to the German problem was military containment. This was the objective of the Treaty of Versailles, which set up what was known as the Versailles system to carry it out. Military containment was another victor strategy chosen by France, and in the early 1920s the French were quite active at implementing it, as in their military occupation of the Ruhr in 1923.

The Democratic administration of President Woodrow Wilson advanced a kinder, gentler version of the Versailles system in its proposals for a League of Nations and a U.S. security guarantee to France and Britain. The military containment of Germany embodied in the security guarantee would be institutionalized and legitimatized in a collective security system embodied in the League. But, of course, the Republican-controlled U.S. Senate rejected these proposals, and the United States never again considered the strategy of military containment as a solution to the German problem.

Economic engagement and security cooperation.

Instead, a few years later, the United States addressed the German problem (now accentuated by the unstable French occupation of the Ruhr) with a strategy of economic engagement. This took the form of the Dawes Plan, an ingenious project for financial recycling, in which American banks loaned capital to Germany, Germany paid war reparations to France and Britain, and France and Britain repaid war debts to the American banks. The Dawes Plan thus encouraged an open international economy among the most advanced economies, and it sought to integrate Germany into this mutually beneficial system.[3]

The Dawes Plan succeeded very well from 1924 to 1929. It formed the basis for Germany's reintegration not only into the international economic system but into the international security system as well. It encouraged France and Britain to develop a new strategy of security cooperation toward Germany. In 1925 they signed the Lucarno security treaty with Germany, and in 1926 Germany entered the League of Nations. The new American strategy of economic engagement seemed to be working far better than the earlier French strategy of military containment.

But as Charles Kindleberger famously demonstrated in his 1973 book, *The World in Depression 1929–1939*, an open international economic system requires an "economic hegemon" to keep it running, in bad times as well as good. The economic hegemon performs three essential functions: (1) providing long-term loans and investments (as in the Dawes Plan); (2) providing short-term credits and foreign exchange in times of currency crises; and (3) opening its markets to receive the exports of economies that are passing through recession. Britain had performed these functions before the First World War, and they in turn had provided the economic foundations for the Hundred Years Peace. After the war, however, Britain no longer had the economic strength to play the hegemon role, even though it still had the will. Conversely, the United States now had the economic strength but had not yet developed the will. The Dawes Plan was only one step in the right direction, and it was a step in only one dimension. Still, for a few years in the prosperous 1920s, the international economy seemed to be operating well enough without an economic hegemon.

The prosperous and open international economic system of the 1920s allowed the victor powers to engage in a strategy of security cooperation (or even appeasement, then still an innocuous term). Given the success of the strategies of economic engagement and security cooperation, the strategy of military containment appeared unnecessary or even counterproductive, and it was largely abandoned even by France. But, with the exception of the Dawes Plan, neither Britain nor the United States stepped forward to assume leadership in managing either the German problem or the international economy, in good times or bad.

With the beginning of the Great Depression (which Kindleberger ascribed to the failure of the United States to act as an economic hegemon), the prosperous and open economic system of the 1920s collapsed and was replaced with the impoverished and closed economic system of the 1930s. Whereas the prosperity system had permitted a strategy of appeasement, the poverty system required a strategy of containment. But for political reasons (polarization between the Left and the Right), France in the 1930s no longer had the political will to provide leadership for such a strategy.

Leadership in managing the German problem fell by default to Britain, which had never been a strong believer in the strategy of military containment. It chose instead a modest version of the strategy of economic engagement, at a time when the conditions of the Depression made this no longer adequate and attractive for Germany. Further, economic engagement seemed to imply a strategy of security appeasement, which was now even less appropriate for Germany. As for the United States, with the collapse of the Dawes Plan it gave up on any effort to manage the German problem at all.

Thus, by the early 1930s, none of the three victor powers from World War I—France, Britain and the United States—was pursuing a coherent and consistent strategy to preserve its victory. With the coming to power of the National Socialist regime, Germany decided to manage the German problem in its own way. The Second World War was the result.

ON THE OTHER side of the world in East Asia, the United States pursued a quite different strategy. Here it faced the rising power of Japan, which had been an ally of Britain since 1902 and which was one of the victor powers in the First World War. Japan's growing military and economic strengths and its ambitions in China presented a serious challenge to the dominant powers in East Asia in the early 1920s, the United States and Britain.

The Republican administration of President Warren G. Harding, and particularly his secretary of state, Charles Evans Hughes, took the lead in designing an innovative strategy of security cooperation to deal with Japan.[4] It convened a conference in Washington in 1921–22, out of which came the following security elements: the Washington Naval Treaty, an agreement between the United States, Britain and Japan to limit the numbers of their battleships; the Four-Power Treaty, which provided for consultations on security issues among these three powers plus France; and the Nine-Power Treaty, which provided for common principles and cooperation in regard to China. These arrangements, which were later called "the Washington system", were an elaboration of the U.S. strategy of security cooperation. However, the United States did not develop a comparable strategy of economic engagement for Japan, to serve as the basis for this security strategy. Instead, it largely relied on conventional international trade between the two nations, which seemed sufficient in the prosperous and open international economy of the 1920s. But with the beginning of the Great Depression, this international trade largely collapsed, and the collapse of the Washington system of security cooperation soon followed.

Thus by the mid-1920s, the United States had conceived of some important elements for a victor strategy. In Europe, the Dawes Plan echoed the nineteenth-century British use of financial power in an open international economy. In East Asia, the Washington system echoed the nineteenth-century British use of naval power and balance of power management. But there was not much of a U.S. security strategy in Europe or of a U.S. economic strategy in East Asia. The U.S. victor strategies after the First World War had not added up to a grand design. They failed to prevent the Great Depression and the ensuing Second World War.

Why did the United States fail to adopt a coherent and consistent victor strategy after World War I? The traditional explanation blames American immaturity and "idealism", and the resulting "isolationism." A related explanation blames the isolationism and protectionism of the Republican Party. However, the Dawes Plan and the Washington system were quite sophisticated projects (even by British standards) that can hardly be described as isolationist—and these were projects advanced by Republican administrations.

The main reason why the United States did not have a coherent and consistent victor strategy was that its victory in 1918 was *too* complete. As a result, in the 1920s the United States faced no obvious great power adversary or "peer competitor", which could have concentrated the American mind and provided the desirable coherence and consistency. Conversely, in the 1930s the Great Depression produced a real American isolationism. It also produced real great power adversaries (Germany and Japan), but these posed quite different strategic threats in quite different regions. This too made it difficult for the United States to compose a coherent and consistent strategy.

Living With Victory After the Second World War

THE UNITED States learned profound lessons from the failure of the Versailles and Washington systems to manage the German and Japanese problems and to prevent the Second World War. As it turned out, these lessons were largely expanded versions of the lessons that the Wilson administration, the Harding administration and the American bankers had already learned from the First World War. As World War II was drawing to a close, the United States took the lead in establishing a number of international institutions that would complete the first but abortive steps taken after the previous war.

Security cooperation and economic engagement. On the security dimension, the United Nations was to succeed and perfect the League of Nations. On the economic dimension, three organizations were to help the United States perform the role of economic hegemon, one for each of the three functions identified by Kindleberger. The task of long-term lending would be promoted by the International Bank for Reconstruction and Development (the World Bank); the task of short-term currency support would be promoted by the International Monetary Fund; and the task of opening trade would be promoted by an International Trade Organization (ITO). Together, the three organizations were known as the Bretton Woods system. As it happened, the Republican-controlled U.S. Senate rejected the ITO treaty in 1947, but a less institutionalized arrangement, the General Agreement on Tariffs and Trade, took its place. (Almost fifty years later, the World Trade Organization was established, and this at last completed the original grand design.) The overall victor strategy of the United States was one of security cooperation based upon economic engagement.

This strategy—and its elaborate United Nations and Bretton Woods systems—might have been perfect for dealing with the German and Japanese problems that existed after the First World War. But the problems that now existed were altogether different. Whereas after the first war Germany was not defeated enough, after the second it was defeated too much. The victorious allies, including the United States, could easily, and almost automatically, impose the alternative and simpler victor strategy of territorial division and military occupation, and at first they did so.

Conversely, whereas after the first war Russia was in a sense doubly defeated (first by the German army and then by the chaos of the Russian Revolution and Civil War), after the second it was doubly victorious (first by defeating Germany and then by occupying or annexing—along with its soon-to-be involuntary allies, Poland and Czechoslovakia—the eastern half of it). The German problem suddenly ceased to be the central problem of international security and instead became a subordinate part of the new central problem, which was the Russian one.

The United States initially tried to apply its overall strategy of security cooperation and economic engagement to this new Russian problem. But it was crucial to this strategy that it be implemented through international institutions led by the United States, i.e., the United Nations and the Bretton Woods system. Both the strategy and its systems were incompatible with the interests of the Soviet Union, as those were defined by Stalin. Security cooperation and economic engagement required some degree of an open society and a free market, and these contradicted the closed society and command economy that characterized the Soviet Union. Instead, the worldwide reach of the American system was aborted by the Cold War and the establishment of the Soviet bloc.

The United States therefore was only able to apply its strategy and system to the Free World, especially the

First World. In Europe, the United Nations was replaced by NATO, and the Bretton Woods system was reinforced by the Marshall Plan. NATO represented a sort of second coming of Wilson's abortive security guarantee to France and Britain, as was the Marshall Plan a second coming of the Dawes Plan. In East Asia, the United States concluded a series of bilateral security treaties and bilateral economic aid programs (including the Dodge Plan for Japan). The ensemble of security treaties echoed the earlier Washington system, and since it was based upon U.S. naval supremacy in the Pacific, it also echoed earlier British strategies based upon naval supremacy.

This American strategy and this system, whose prototypes had been aborted after the First World War and whose applications were confined to only half the world after the Second World War, were extraordinarily successful where they did operate. They certainly helped to solve a good part of the old German and Japanese problems. However, they could not solve the new Russian problem (some historians think that they even accentuated it). The result was the Cold War.

Military containment.

The Russian problem was addressed by a version of the alternative victor strategy, military containment—in this case, containment not of the recently defeated enemy but of the victorious ally. By 1948 there had already been the sudden reversal of the alliance between the Western Allies (Britain and the United States) and the Soviet Union against Germany into an emerging alliance between the Western Allies and Germany against the Soviet Union. The rapidity of the transformation was quite breathtaking, but it was readily accepted by the American public. (In his famous novel, *1984*, written in 1948 as this transformation was being completed, George Orwell portrayed the sudden reversal of the alliance between Oceania and Eastasia against Eurasia into an alliance between Oceania and Eurasia against Eastasia.)

When the communists came to power on the Chinese mainland in 1949, they presented a new security problem. For a brief time, the Truman administration was inclined to hope that some version of the strategy of security cooperation (perhaps based upon traditional Chinese suspicions of Russia) and economic engagement would work to solve this new Chinese problem, but this hope was aborted by Mao's alliance with Stalin in January 1950, the Chinese entry into the Korean War in November 1950, and the closed society and command economy that characterized communist China.

The prosperous and open international economic system of the 1920s had permitted a strategy of security cooperation or appeasement toward Germany and Japan. But this was because these two nations had capitalist economies and were willing to engage with a prosperous and open international economy. When the international economy ceased to be so, the basis for a strategy of security appeasement disappeared; the only effective alternative would have been a strategy of military containment.

The Soviet Union and communist China in the 1940s–50s, on the other hand, were command economies. Because of this, they were not willing to engage with an open international economy, even one that was prosperous. Consequently, there was no basis for a strategy of security cooperation (or appeasement). The alternative strategy of military containment therefore became necessary. But although containment of the Soviet Union and communist China was necessary, it did present problems of its own. Military containment once led to defeat for the United States (the Vietnam War) and once led to near disaster for the world (the Cuban Missile Crisis). And military containment by itself was not sufficient to defeat the Soviet Union, to reform communist China, and to bring about a U.S. victory in the Cold War. The successful and sustained operation of the free market and open international economy in the First or Free World, in contrast with the gradual but steady exhaustion of the command and closed economic systems in the Second or Communist World, exerted a magnetic force upon the Soviet Union and China, and drove them by the 1980s, each in its own way, to reform their economies and to engage in the American-led international economic system. But of course this did not happen quickly or easily. Forty years of Cold War and military containment were the price.

Why did the United States succeed in adopting a generally coherent and consistent victor strategy after the Second World War? The main reason was that its victory was in some sense a Pyrrhic one. The German enemy was replaced almost immediately by the Russian one, and the Japanese enemy was soon replaced by the Chinese one. Even more, since both enemies were communist and initially were in alliance, they could easily be seen as one enormous enemy. This wonderfully concentrated the American mind into a generally coherent and consistent strategy in the late 1940s and 1950s.

Living With Victory After the Cold War

THE circumstances of victory and defeat after the Cold War had more in common with those pertaining after the First World War than those after the Second.

The redefined Russian problem.

Russia was more defeated after the Cold War than Germany after the First World War (but less defeated than Germany after the Second). As the Soviet Union was reinvented as Russia, it lost a quarter of its territory and half of its population. The Russian economy in the 1990s was beset both by deep depression and by high inflation, and the Russian military was beset by weakness and incompetence, with only an arsenal of nuclear weapons remaining as the legacy from the era of Soviet power. The strategic position of Russia was removed from the center to the periphery of the European continent, and it remained the central nation only in the emptiness of Central Asia. The Russian problem was redefined from being one of organized power into one of organized crime. Only in 2000—with a new president, Vladimir Putin, modest economic recovery and ambiguous military success in the Chechnya war—are there signs that Russia may have begun a revival to the degree that Germany did in the mid-1920s.

The U.S. victor strategy toward this "Weimar Russia" has been a variation of that adopted toward Weimar Germany, a new version of the strategy of security cooperation and economic engagement. Russia's generally positive role in the United Nations echoes Germany's role in the League. However, the enlargement of NATO into Eastern Europe (really a form of military containment of Russia) echoes Wilson's abortive security guarantee to Western Europe (really a form of military containment of Germany). The extensive U.S. and international economic aid to Russia echoes the Dawes Plan (although it has not been nearly as extensive and effective as the Marshall Plan). But just as the U.S. victor strategy toward Germany in the 1920s depended upon integrating that nation into an international economy that remained open and prosperous, so too does the contemporary U.S. victor strategy toward Russia. It would fail if either the international economy collapsed into one that was closed and depressed (like the 1930s), or if the Russian economy reverted into one that was closed and command (like the 1940s–70s).

The new Chinese problem.

In East Asia, the United States faces the rising power of China, a situation not unlike that it faced with Japan after the First World War. China's growing economic and military strengths, and its goals regarding Taiwan and the South China Sea, have presented a serious challenge. Indeed, the Chinese problem after the Cold War has been an even greater challenge for the United States than the Japanese problem was after the First World War (although it is not nearly as threatening as the Russian problem was after the Second).

The U.S. strategy toward China that evolved in the 1990s has in some sense been an inversion of the U.S. strategy toward Japan in the 1920s (and an expansion of the U.S. strategy toward Weimar Germany). Whereas the strategy toward Japan provided for an elaborate system of security cooperation (the Washington system) but only for relatively simple economic engagement (conventional international trade), the strategy toward China provides for an elaborate system of economic engagement ("the Washington consensus", including the admission of China into the World Trade Organization), but for relatively simple security cooperation (conventional military visits). In a more important sense, however, the U.S. strategy involves an innovative combination of economic engagement and military containment (particularly in respect to Taiwan and the South China Sea). But since China thinks of Taiwan as being properly part of China, what the United States perceives as its strategy of military containment, China perceives as a strategy of territorial dismemberment.

Probably the most difficult single challenge facing the contemporary U.S. victor strategy is how to sustain this innovative and complex combination of economic engagement and military containment in regard to China. The article by Zbigniew Brzezinski, "Living With China", is a sustained and eminently sensible analysis of this problem. In essence, he hopes that the Taiwan independence question can be dissolved into the World Trade Organization, that the tensions from military containment can themselves be contained by the rewards of economic engagement. His proposals are thus very different from those of Robert Kagan and William Kristol in "The Present Danger", who hardly consider the international economy at all. Consequently, they advocate a pure strategy of military containment toward China, including U.S. efforts to bring about a "regime change."

We have seen that the U.S. strategies toward Germany and Japan in the 1920s depended upon integrating those nations into an open and prosperous international economy, and that the U.S. contemporary strategy toward Russia depends upon the same. To an even greater extent, the U.S. strategy toward China has as its foundation the integration of that giant nation—one with more and more of a nationalist mentality—into such a global economy. If the global economy were to exclude China from its benefits, or if it were to become a closed and depressed one, the entire complex U.S. strategy toward China would collapse. The United States would be driven, at best, to the classic alternative, a simple strategy of military containment, or, at worst, as was the case in the 1930s in regard to both Germany and Japan, to no strategy at all. At that point, the proposals of Brzezinski would become obsolete, and the proposals of Kagan and Kristol could appear to be necessary. The management of the new China problem therefore depends upon the management of the new global economy, and the development of any real Sino-American security cooperation depends upon the performance of the United States as the global economic hegemon.

Challenges to the Victor

The culminating point of victory.

EVEN when a victor power conceives a victor strategy that is sound and appropriate to the military and economic realities of the time, there will be challenges that arise from how it is implemented. The first of these challenges is to determine what is, in Clausewitz's phrase, "the culminating point of victory", and to not go beyond it. Victor powers are prone to succumb to "the victory disease"; they continue to pursue the strategies that brought them victory in the utterly new and inappropriate circumstances that the victory has created. Concentration in war becomes compulsion in victory. The most famous example of the twentieth century was Hitler following his successful blitzkriegs of Poland and France with his disastrous invasion of the Soviet Union. The most familiar American example was MacArthur following his successful landing at Inchon and recovery of South Korea with his disastrous drive to the Yalu River and the Chinese border, resulting in China's entry into the war.

A contemporary American example of going beyond the culminating point of victory could be the enlargement of NATO. Although the admission of Poland, the Czech Republic and Hungary may not have passed that point, a "second round of enlargement" including the Baltic states and reaching the most sensitive borders of Russia probably would do so. This kind of victory disorder may also be developing with the U.S. promotion of human rights over national sovereignty, and especially with the use of military force for the purpose of humanitarian intervention. The 1995 U.S.-led humanitarian intervention in Bosnia was accepted by all of the other major powers. The 1999 U.S.-led humanitarian intervention in Kosovo was greatly resented, and in some measure rejected, by Russia and China. A third such intervention anytime soon, especially in a country traditionally in the sphere of influence of Russia (e.g., the Caucasus and Central Asia) or of China (e.g., the South China Sea), very likely would go beyond the culminating point of victory; it would represent a humanitarian disease.

The realistic range of opportunities.

The second challenge for the victor power is in some sense the opposite of the first. It is to determine what is the realistic range of opportunities resulting from victory. The victor power is suddenly in a position where all things seem possible, where there are too many options. It may erratically pursue this objective, then that, and then another. Versatility in war becomes diffusion, even dissipation, in victory. This is an error to which pluralist democracies, with their different interest groups, are especially prone.

It has often been argued that Britain succumbed to this victory disorder in the nineteenth century. The British continued to expand their colonial empire, one of the opportunities that came with their victory in the Napoleonic Wars, until they entered into the condition of "imperial overstretch." One result was that Britain had to undertake numerous and continuous military operations on "the turbulent frontier." Another result, more serious in its long-run consequences, was that the ample British investment capital was diffused across a wide range of colonies and foreign countries, rather than concentrated upon the development of new technologies and industries within Britain itself. Such new technologies and industries would have better suited Britain for its competition with Germany.

A contemporary American example of the error of diffusion or dissipation seems to be developing with the U.S. promotion of every aspect of the American way of life in every part of the world. The promotion of economic globalization may be inherent in the U.S. performance as economic hegemon, but it does weaken the economic conditions and social bonds of many Americans. Even more, the promotion of social and cultural globalization—of the American way of expressive individualism, popular culture and the dysfunctional family—has generated resentment and resistance in a wide arc of countries in the Middle East, South Asia and East Asia. This, it seems, is the American way of producing a turbulent frontier.

The balancing effect.

The third challenge is the most familiar and the most fundamental, although Americans are inclined to think that they are exempt from it. It is derived from the well-known balancing effect. Victory brings the pre-eminent victor power hegemony, which in turn can initiate a realignment of the lesser victor powers against it (perhaps joined by the defeated one). The balancing effect was always especially pronounced among the continental powers of Europe. However, since Britain was an offshore power with no ambitions for territorial acquisitions on the continent, its victories did not initiate this balancing process. Indeed, its role as an "offshore balancer" helped it on occasion to exercise a sort of offshore hegemony.

The United States has served as an offshore or rather overseas balancer for Europe and also for East Asia. Even more than Britain, its remote position has permitted it to exercise an overseas hegemony over the nations of Western Europe (while balancing against the Soviet Union) and over those of East Asia (while balancing against China). Indeed, the United States continues to exercise this overseas hegemony, now over all of Europe, even with the collapse of the Soviet Union and with no other power to balance at all. By historical comparison with the European past, this hegemonic security system is an extraordinary achievement on the part of the United States. Were America located on the continent where France is, or even thirty miles offshore where Britain is, it probably would not have occurred; it can exist because the United States is located an ocean away and in another hemisphere. The U.S. hegemonic security system in East Asia continues to include Japan, South Korea, the Philippines and the problematic Taiwan; it provides the basis for any strategy of military containment of China.

The overseas location of the United States thus enables it to avoid the balancing effect and instead to perform the role of security hegemon in Europe, parts of East Asia and, in more complicated conditions, parts of the Middle East (as in the Gulf War and the continuing air strikes against Iraq). Of course, the United States also acts as the security hegemon in Latin America, where there is no prospect of a balancing effect against "the colossus of the North" (a case of an opposite phenomenon, which international relations specialists call the "bandwagoning effect").

Hegemony versus hyper-victory.

The U.S. role as the security hegemon in several regions of the globe complements the U.S. role as the economic hegemon in the global economy. America's security hegemony is acceptable because of its unique overseas location and the sustained peace that it has provided. Its economic hegemony is acceptable because of the unique economic functions that it performs and the sustained prosperity that it has produced. The United States has operated the security and economic dimensions of hegemony together to consolidate and preserve its great victory after the Cold War. It does so in ways reminiscent of Britain coordinating the security and economic dimensions of its supremacy to consolidate and preserve its great victory after the Napoleonic Wars.

This splendid achievement of the United States could be undermined, however, by its own actions. The victory disorders of compulsion and dissipation could eventually overcome even the powerful U.S. advantages of overseas position and economic performance, and drive some major powers—most obviously China and Russia—into the balancing effect and even into a sort of containment policy directed at the United States. This was the prospect put forward by Samuel Huntington in his famous argument about the "clash of civilizations." Huntington was concerned that American excesses could bring about a Sino-Islamic alliance or even "the West versus the Rest." These prospects would become even more likely if the prosperous and open international economy should turn into a poor and closed one—if the "New Economy" of the 1990s, based upon the computer and the Internet, should suddenly collapse, as the "New Era" economy of the 1920s, based upon the automobile and the radio, had done.

Whatever form a balancing effect or containment coalition might take, however, at its core would be China. It would be the new Central Power on the Eurasian land mass, just as it was once the Middle Kingdom. The arrival of this coalition on the international scene would mean that the U.S. victory after the first cold war would have been followed by a second cold war (or worse), and this in turn would mean another war on a global scale. This alone makes living with China the single most important challenge facing a United States that is still living with victory, and which is still expecting to do so for decades to come.

Notes

1. Karl Polanyi, *The Great Transformation: The Political and Economic Origins of Our Time* (Boston: Beacon Press, 1957), chapter 1.
2. Realist theories of international relations focus on international security; liberal theories focus on the international economy. In practice, however, successful strategies have combined both, e.g., the British strategy of the nineteenth century and the American strategy during the Cold War. At its best, the Anglo-American tradition in international relations has been *both* realist and liberal. See my "Inside the Cave: The Banality of I.R. Studies", *The National Interest* (Fall 1998).
3. P.M.H. Bell, *The Origins of the Second World War in Europe*, second edition (New York: Longman, 1997), chapter 3.
4. Akira Iriye, *The Origins of the Second World War in Asia and the Pacific* (New York: Longman, 1987), chapter 1.

James Kurth is Claude Smith Professor of Political Science at Swarthmore College.

Unit 2

Unit Selections

Key Points to Consider

- What are the basic characteristics of the global population situation? How many people are there? How long do people typically live?
- How fast is the world's population growing? What are the reasons for this growth? How do population dynamics vary from one region to the next?
- How does rapid population growth affect the quality of the environment, social structures, and the ways in which humanity views itself?
- How does a rapidly growing population affect a poor country's ability to plan its economic development?
- How can economic and social policies be changed in order to reduce the impact of population growth on environmental quality?
- In an era of global interdependence, how much impact can individual governments have on demographic changes?

DUSHKINONLINE Links — www.dushkin.com/online/

7. **The Hunger Project**
   http://www.thp.org
8. **Penn Library: Resources by Subject**
   http://www.library.upenn.edu/resources/websitest.html
9. **World Health Organization**
   http://www.who.int
10. **WWW Virtual Library: Demography & Population Studies**
    http://demography.anu.edu.au/VirtualLibrary/

These sites are annotated on pages 4 and 5.

Population and Food Production

After World War II, the world's population reached an estimated 2 billion people. It had taken 250 years to triple to that level. In the 55 years since the end of World War II, the population has tripled again to 6 billion. When the typical reader of this book reaches the age of 50, experts estimate that the global population will have reached 8½ billion! By 2050, or about 100 years after World War II, some experts forecast that the world may be populated by 10 to 12 billion people. A person born in 1946 (a so-called baby boomer) who lives to be 100 could see a six-fold increase in population.

Nothing like this has ever occurred before. To state this in a different way: In the next 50 years there will have to be twice as much food grown, twice as many schools and hospitals available, and twice as much of everything else just to maintain the current and rather uneven standard of living. We live in an unprecedented time in human history.

One of the most interesting aspects of this population growth is that there is little agreement about whether this situation is good or bad. The government of China, for example, has a policy that encourages couples to have only one child. In contrast, there are a few governments that use various financial incentives to promote large families.

Some experts view population growth as the major problem facing the world, while others see it as secondary to social, economic, and political problems. The theme of conflicting views, in short, has been carried forward from the introductory unit of this book to the more specific discussion of population.

As the world celebrates the new millennium, there are many population issues that transcend numerical or economic considerations. The disappearance of indigenous cultures is a good example of the pressures of population growth on people who live on the margins of modern society. Finally, while demographers develop various scenarios forecasting population growth, it is important to remember that there are circumstances that could lead not to growth but to a significant decline in global population. The spread of AIDS and other infectious diseases reveals that confidence in modern medicine's ability to control these scourges may be premature. Nature has its own checks and balances to the population dynamic that are not policy instruments of some international organization. This factor is often overlooked in an age of technological optimism.

The lead article in this section provides an overview of the general demographic trends of the contemporary world. The unit continues with a more focused discussion of a few regions in the world that are experiencing a sudden reversal in the general trend to longer life. The discussion of population continues with a special focus on women.

There is no greater check on population growth than the ability to produce an adequate food supply. Some experts question whether current technologies are sustainable over the long run. How much food are we going to need in the decades to come, and how are farmers and fishermen going to produce it?

Making predictions about the future of the world's population is a complicated task, for there are a variety of forces at work and considerable variation from region to region.

The danger of oversimplification must be overcome if governments and international organizations are going to respond with meaningful policies. Perhaps one could say that there is not a global population problem but rather many challenges that vary from country to country and region to region.

THE BIG CRUNCH

Birthrates are falling, but it may be a half-century before the number of people—and their impact—reaches a peak

By Jeffrey Kluger

ODDS ARE YOU'LL NEVER MEET ANY OF THE ESTIMATED 247 HUMAN BEINGS WHO WERE BORN IN THE PAST MINUTE. IN A POPULATION OF 6 BILLION, 247 IS A DEMOGRAPHIC HICCUP. IN THE MINUTE BEFORE LAST, HOWEVER, THERE WERE ANOTHER 247. IN THE MINUTES TO COME THERE WILL be another, then another, then another. By next year at this time, all those minutes will have produced nearly 130 million newcomers to the great human mosh pit. That kind of crowd is awfully hard to miss.

For folks inclined to fret that the earth is heading for the environmental abyss, the population problem has always been one of the biggest causes for worry—and with good reason. The last time humanity celebrated a new century there were 1.6 billion people here for the party—or a quarter as many as this time. In 1900 the average life expectancy was, in some places, as low as 23 years; now it's 65, meaning the extra billions are staying around longer and demanding more from the planet. The 130 million or so births registered annually—even after subtracting the 52 million deaths—is still the equivalent of adding nearly one new Germany to the world's population each year.

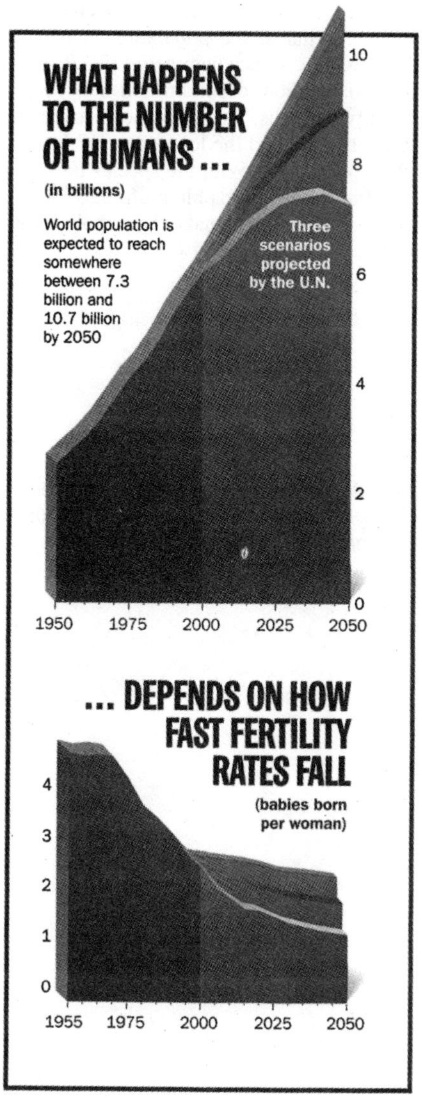

Source: United Nations

But things may not be as bleak as they seem. Lately demographers have come to the conclusion that the population locomotive—while still cannonballing ahead—may be chugging toward a stop. In country after country, birthrates are easing, and the population growth rate is falling.

To be sure, this kind of success is uneven. For every region in the world that has brought its population under control, there's another where things are still exploding. For every country that has figured out the art of sustainable agriculture, there are others that have worked their land to exhaustion. The population bomb may yet go off before governments can snuff the fuse, but for now, the news is better than it's been in a long time. "We could have an end in sight to population growth in the next century," says Carl Haub, a demographer with the nonprofit Population Research Bureau. "That's a major change."

Cheering as the population reports are becoming today, for much of the past 50 years, demographers were bearers of mostly bad tidings. In census after census, they reported that humanity was not just settling the planet but smothering it. It was not until the century was nearly two-thirds over that scientists and governments finally bestirred themselves to do something about it. The first great brake on population growth came in the early 1960s, with the development of the birth-control pill, a magic pharmacological bullet that made contraception easier—not to mention tidier—than it had ever been before. In 1969 the United Nations got in on the population game, creating the U.N. Population Fund, a global organization dedicated to bringing family-planning techniques to women who would not otherwise have them. In the decades that followed, the U.N. increased its commitment, sponsoring numerous global symposiums to address the population problem further. The most significant was the 1994 Cairo conference, where attendees pledged $5.7 billion to reduce birthrates in the developing world and acknowledged that giving women more education and reproductive freedom was the key to accomplishing that goal. Even a global calamity like AIDS has yielded unexpected dividends, with international campaigns to promote condom use and abstinence helping to prevent not only disease transmission but also conception.

Such efforts have paid off in a big way. According to U.N. head counters, the average number of children produced per couple in the developing world—a figure that reached a whopping 4.9 earlier this century—has plunged to just 2.7. In many countries, including Spain, Slovenia, Greece and Germany, the fertility rate is well below 1.5, meaning parents are producing 25% fewer offspring than would be needed to replace themselves—in effect, throwing the census into reverse. A little more than 30 years ago, global population growth was 2.04% a year, the highest in human history. Today it's just 1.3%. "It was a remarkable century," says Joseph Chamie of the U.N. Population Division. "We quadrupled the population in 100 years, but that's not going to happen again."

Sunny as the global averages look, however, things get a lot darker when you break them down by region. Even the best family-planning programs do no good if there is neither the money nor governmental expertise to carry them out, and in less-developed countries—which currently account for a staggering 96% of the annual population increase—both are sorely lacking. In parts of the Middle East and Africa, the fertility rate exceeds seven babies per woman. In India, nearly 16 million births are registered each year, for a growth rate of 1.8%. While Europe's population was three times that of Africa in 1950, today the two continents have about the same count. At the current rate, Africa will triple Europe in another 50 years.

Many of the countries in the deepest demographic trouble have imposed aggressive family-planning programs, only to see them go badly—even criminally—awry. In the 1970s, Indian Prime Minister Indira Gandhi tried to reduce the national birthrate by offering men cash and transistor radios if they would undergo vasectomies. In the communities in which those sweeteners failed, the government resorted to coercion, putting millions of males—from teenage boys to elderly men—on the operating table. Amid the popular backlash that followed, Gandhi's government was turned out of office, and the public rejected family planning.

China's similarly notorious one-child policy has done a better job of slowing population growth but not without problems. In a country that values boys over girls, one-child rules have led to abandonments, abortions and infanticides, as couples limited to a single offspring keep spinning the reproductive wheel until it comes up male. "We've learned that there is no such thing as 'population control,' " says Alex Marshall of the U.N. Population Fund. "You don't control it. You allow people to make up their own mind."

That strategy has worked in many countries that once had runaway population growth. Mexico, one of Latin America's population success stories, has made government-subsidized contraception widely available and at the same time launched public-information campaigns to teach people the value of using it. A recent series of ads aimed at men makes the powerful point that there is more machismo in clothing and feeding offspring than in conceiving and leaving them. In the past 30 years, the average number of children born to a Mexican woman has plunged from seven to just 2.5. Many developing nations are starting to recognize the importance of educating women and letting them—not just their husbands—have a say in how many children they will have.

But bringing down birthrates loses some of its effectiveness as mortality rates also fall. At the same time Mexico reduced its children-per-mother figure, for example, it also boosted its average life expectancy from 50 years to 72—a wonderful accomplishment, but one that offsets part of the gain achieved by reducing the number of births.

When people live longer, populations grow not just bigger but also older and frailer. In the U.S. there has been no end of hand wringing over what will happen when baby boomers—who owe their very existence to the procreative free-for-all that followed World War II—retire, leaving themselves to be supported by the much smaller generation they produced. In Germany there are currently four workers for every retired person. Before long that ratio will be down to just 2 to 1.

For now, the only answer may be to tough things out for a while, waiting for the billions of people born during the great

STATE OF THE PLANET

Humans already use 54% of Earth's rainfall, says the U.N. report, and 70% of that goes to agriculture

population booms to live out their long life, while at the same time continuing to reduce birthrates further so that things don't get thrown so far out of kilter again. But there's no telling if the earth—already worked to exhaustion feeding the 6 billion people currently here—can take much more. People in the richest countries consume a disproportionate share of the world's resources, and as poorer nations push to catch up, pressure on the planet will keep growing. "An ecologist looks at the population size relative to the carrying capacity of Earth," says Lester Brown, president of the Worldwatch Institute. "Looking at it that way, things are much worse than we expected them to be 20 years ago."

How much better they'll get will be decided in the next half-century (*see chart*). According to three scenarios published by the U.N., the global population in the year 2050 will be somewhere between 7.3 billion and 10.7 billion, depending on how fast the fertility rate falls. The difference between the high scenario and the low scenario? Just one child per couple. With the species poised on that kind of demographic knife edge, it pays for those couples to make their choices carefully.

—Reported by William Dowell/New York, Meenakshi Ganguly/New Delhi and Dick Thompson/ Washington

Breaking *Out* or Breaking *Down*

In some parts of the world, the historic trend toward longer life has been abruptly reversed.

by Lester R. Brown and Brian Halweil

On October 12 of this year, the world's human population is projected to pass 6 billion. The day will be soberly observed by population and development experts, but media attention will do nothing to immediately slow the expansion. During that day, the global total will swell by another 214,000—enough people to fill two of the world's largest sports stadiums.

Even as world population continues to climb, it is becoming clear that the several billion additional people projected for the next half century are not likely to materialize. What is not clear is how the growth will be curtailed. Unfortunately, in some countries, a slowing of the growth is taking place only partly because of success in bringing birth rates down—and increasingly because of newly emergent conditions that are raising death rates.

Evidence of this shift became apparent in late October, 1998, when U.N. demographers released their biennial update of world population projections, revising the projected global population for 2050. Instead of rising in the next 50 years by more than half, to 9.4 billion (as computed in 1996), the 1998 projection rose only to 8.9 billion. The good news was that two-thirds of this anticipated slow-down was expected to be the result of falling fertility—of the decisions of more couples to have fewer children. But the other third was due to rising death rates, largely as a result of rising mortality from AIDS.

This rather sudden reversal in the human death rate trend marks a tragic new development in world demography, which is dividing the developing countries into two groups. When these countries embarked on the development journey a half century or so ago, they followed one of two paths. In the first, illustrated by the East Asian nations of South Korea, Taiwan, and Thailand, early efforts to shift to smaller families set in motion a positive cycle of rising living standards and falling fertility. Those countries are now moving toward population stability.

In the second category, which prevails in sub-Saharan Africa (770 million people) and the Indian subcontinent (1.3 billion), fertility has remained high or fallen very little, setting the stage for a vicious downward spiral in which rapid population growth reinforces poverty, and in which some segments of society eventually are deprived of the resources needed even to survive. In Ethiopia, Nigeria, and Pakistan, for example, demographers estimate that the next half-century will bring a doubling or near-tripling of populations. Even now, people in these regions each day awaken to a range of daunting conditions that threatens to drop their living standards below the level at which humans can survive.

We now see three clearly identifiable trends that either are already raising death rates or are likely to do so in these regions: the spread of the HIV virus that causes AIDS, the depletion of aquifers, and the shrinking amount of cropland available to support each person. The HIV epidemic is spiraling out of control in sub-Saharan Africa. The depletion of aquifers has become a major threat to India, where water tables are falling almost everywhere. The shrinkage in cropland per person threatens to force reductions in food consumed per person, increasing malnutrition—and threatening lives—in many parts of these regions.

Containing one-third of the world's people, these two regions now face a potentially dramatic shortening of life expectancy. In sub-Saharan Africa, mortality rates are already rising, and in the Indian subcontinent they could begin rising soon. Without clearly defined national strategies for quickly lowering birth rates in these countries, and without a commitment by the international community to support them in their efforts, one-third of humanity could slide into a demographic black hole.

From *World Watch,* September/October 1999, pp. 20-29.

Birth and Death

Since 1950, we have witnessed more growth in world population than during the preceding 4 million years since our human ancestors first stood upright. This post-1950 explosion can be attributed, in part, to several developments that reduced death rates throughout the developing world. The wider availability of safe drinking water, childhood immunization programs, antibiotics, and expanding food production sharply reduced the number of people dying of hunger and from infectious diseases. Together these trends dramatically lowered mortality levels.

But while death rates fell, birth rates remained high. As a result, in many countries, population growth rose to 3 percent or more per year—rates for which there was no historical precedent. A 3 percent annual increase in population leads to a twenty-fold increase within a century. Ecologists have long known that such rates of population growth—which have now been sustained for close to half a century in many countries—could not be sustained indefinitely. At some point, if birth rates did not come down, disease, hunger, or conflict would force death rates up.

Although most of the world has succeeded in reducing birth rates to some degree, only some 32 countries—containing a mere 12 percent of the world's people—have achieved population stability. In these countries, growth rates range between 0.4 percent per year and minus 0.6 percent per year. With the exception of Japan, all of the 32 countries are in Europe, and all are industrial. Although other industrial countries, such as the United States, are still experiencing some population growth as a result of a persistent excess of births over deaths, the population of the industrial world as a whole is not projected to grow at all in the next century—unless, perhaps, through the arrival of migrants from more crowded regions.

Within the developing world, the most impressive progress in reducing fertility has come in East Asia. South Korea, Taiwan, and Thailand have all reduced their population growth rates to roughly one percent per year and are approaching stability. (See table, this page.) The biggest country in Latin America—Brazil—has reduced its population growth to 1.4 percent per year. Most other countries in Latin America are also making progress on this front. In contrast, the countries of sub-Saharan Africa and the Indian subcontinent have lagged in lowering growth rates, and populations are still rising ominously—at rates of 2 to 3 percent or more per year.

Graphically illustrating this contrast are Thailand and Ethiopia, each with 61 million people. Thailand is projected to add 13 million people over the next half century for a gain of 21 percent. Ethiopia, meanwhile, is projected to add 108 million for a gain of 177 percent. (The U.N.'s projections are based on such factors as the number of children per woman, infant mortality, and average life span in each country—factors that could change in time, but meanwhile differ sharply in the two countries.) The deep poverty among those living in sub-Saharan Africa and the Indian subcontinent has been a principal factor in their rapid population growth, as couples lack access to the kinds of basic social services and education that allow control over reproductive choices. Yet, the population growth, in turn, has only worsened their poverty—perpetuating a vicious cycle in which hopes of breaking out become dimmer with each passing year.

After several decades of rapid population growth, governments of many developing countries are simply being overwhelmed by their crowding—and are suffering from what we term "demographic fatigue." The simultaneous challenges of educating growing numbers of children, creating jobs for the swelling numbers of young people coming into the job market, and confronting such environmental consequences of rapid population growth as deforestation, soil erosion, and falling water tables, are undermining the capacity of governments to cope. When a major new threat arises, as has happened with the HIV virus, governments often cannot muster the leadership energy and fiscal resources to mobilize effectively. Social problems that are easily contained in industrial societies can become humanitarian disasters in many developing ones. As a result, some of the latter may soon see their population growth curves abruptly flattered, or even thrown into decline, not because of falling birth rates but because of fast-rising death rates. In some countries, that process has already begun.

Projected Population Growth in Selected Developing Countries, 1999 to 2050

	1999 (millions)	2050 (millions)	Growth From 1999 to 2050 (millions)	Growth From 1999 to 2050 (percent)
Developing Countries That Have Slowed Population Growth:				
South Korea	46	51	5	+11
Taiwan	22	25	3	+14
Thailand	61	74	13	+21
Developing Countries Where Rapid Population Growth Continues:				
Ethiopia	61	169	108	+177
Nigeria	109	244	135	+124
Pakistan	152	345	193	+127

Source: *United Nations, Global Population Projections, 1998.*

Shades of the Black Death

Industrial countries have held HIV infection rates under 1 percent of the adult population, but in many sub-Saharan African countries, they are spiraling upward, out of control. In Zimbabwe, 26 percent of the adult population is infected; in Botswana, the rate is 25 percent. In South Africa, a country of 43 million people, 22 percent are infected. In Namibia, Swaziland, and Zambia, 18 to 20 percent are. (See table, this page.) In these countries, there is little to suggest that these rates will not continue to climb.

In other African nations, including some with large populations, the rates are lower but climbing fast. In both Tanzania, with 32 million people, and Ethiopia, with its 61 million, the race is now 9 percent. In Nigeria, the continent's largest country with 111 million people, the latest estimate now puts the infection rate also at 9 percent and rising.

What makes this picture even more disturbing is that most Africans carrying the virus do not yet know they are infected, which means the disease can gain enormous momentum in areas where it is still largely invisible. This, combined with the social taboo that surrounds HIV/AIDS in Africa, has made it extremely difficult to mount an effective control effort.

Barring a medical miracle, countries such as Zimbabwe, Botswana, and South Africa will lose at least 20 percent of their adult populations to AIDS within the next decade, simply because few of those now infected with the virus can afford treatment with the costly antiviral drugs now used in industrial countries. To find a precedent for such a devastating region-wide loss of life from an infectious disease, we have to go back to the decimation of Native American communities by the introduction of small pox in the sixteenth century from Europe or to the bubonic plaque that claimed roughly a third of Europe's population in the fourteenth century (see table, next page).

Countries Where HIV Infection Rate Among Adults Is Greater Than Ten Percent

Country	Population (millions)	Share of Adult Population Infected (percent)
Zimbabwe	11.7	26
Botswana	1.5	25
South Africa	43.3	22
Namibia	1.6	20
Zambia	8.5	19
Swaziland	0.9	18
Malawi	10.1	15
Mozambique	18.3	14
Rwanda	5.9	13
Kenya	28.4	12
Central African Republic	3.4	11
Cote d'Ivoire	14.3	10

Reversing Progress

The burden of HIV is not limited to those infected, or even to their generation. Like a powerful storm or war that lays waste to a nation's physical infrastructure, a growing HIV epidemic damages a nation's social infrastructure, with lingering demographic and economic effects. A viral epidemic that grows out of control is likely to reinforce many of the very conditions—poverty, illiteracy, malnutrition—that gave it an opening in the first place.

Using life expectancy—the sentinel indicator of development—as a measure, we can see that the HIV virus is reversing the gains of the last several decades. For example, in Botswana life expectancy has fallen from 61 years in 1990 to 44 years in 1999. By 2010, it is projected to drop to 39 years—a life expectancy more characteristic of medieval times than of what we had hoped for in the twenty-first century.

Beyond its impact on mortality, HIV also reduced fertility. For women, who live on average scarcely 10 years after becoming infected, many will die long before they have reached the end of their reproductive years. As the symptoms of AIDS begin to develop, women are less likely to conceive. For those who do conceive, the likelihood of spontaneous abortion rises. And among the reduced number who do give birth, an estimated 30 percent of the infants born are infected and an additional 20 percent are likely to be infected before they are weaned. For babies born with the virus, life expectancy is less than 2 years. The rate of population growth falls, but not in the way any family-planning group wants to see.

One of the most disturbing social consequences of the HIV epidemic is the number of orphans that it produces. Conjugal sex is one of the surest ways to spread AIDS, so if one parent dies, there is a good change the other will as well. By the end of 1997, there were already 7.8 million AIDS orphans in Africa—a new and rapidly growing social subset. The burden of raising these AIDS orphans falls first on the extended family, and then on society at large. Mortality rates for these orphans are likely to be much higher than the rates for children whose parents are still with them.

As the epidemic progresses and the symptoms become visible, health care systems in developing countries are being overwhelmed. The estimated cost of providing antiviral treatment (the standard regimen used to reduce symptoms, improve life quality, and postpone death) to all

Profiles of Major Epidemics Throughout Human History

Epidemic and Date	Mode of Introduction and Spread	Description of Plague and Its Effects on Population
Black Death in Europe, 14th century	Originating in Asia, the plague bacteria moved westward via trade routes, entering Europe in 1347; transmitted via rats as well as coughing and sneezing.	One fourth of the population of Europe was wiped out (an estimated 25 million deaths); old, young, and poor hit hardest.
Smallpox in the New World, 16th century	Spanish conquistadors and European colonists introduced virus into the Americas, where it spread through respiratory channels and physical contact.	Decimated Aztec, Incan, and native American civilizations, killing 10 to 20 million.
HIV/AIDS, worldwide, 1980 to present	Thought to have originated in Africa; a primate virus that mutated and spread to infect humans; transmitted by the exchange of bodily fluids, including blood, semen, and breast milk.	More than 14 million deaths worldwide thus far; an additional 33 million infected; one-fifth of adult population infected in several African nations; strikes economically active populations hardest.

Source: Jared Diamond, *Guns, Germs, and Steel: The Fates of Human Societies,* 1997; UNAIDS.

infected individuals in Malawi, Mozambique, Uganda, and Tanzania would be larger than the GNPs of those countries. In some hospitals in South Africa, 70 percent of the beds are occupied by AIDS patients. In Zimbabwe, half the health care budget now goes to deal with AIDS. As AIDS patients increasingly monopolize nurses' and doctors' schedules, and drain funds from health care budgets, the capacity to provide basic health care to the general population—including the immunizations and treatments for routine illnesses that have underpinned the decline in mortality and the rise in life expectancy in developing countries—begins to falter.

Worldwide, more than half of all new HIV infections occur in people between the ages of 15 and 24—an atypical pattern for an infectious disease. Human scourges have historically spread through respiratory exposure to coughing or sneezing, or through physical contact via shaking hands, food handling, and so on. Since nearly everyone is vulnerable to such exposure, the victims of most infectious diseases are simply those among society at large who have the weakest immune systems—generally the very young and the elderly. But with HIV, because the primary means of transmission is unprotected sexual activity, the ones who are most vulnerable to infection are those who are most sexually active—young, healthy adults in the prime of their lives. According to a UNAIDS report, "the bulk of the increase in adult death is in the younger adult ages—a pattern that is common in wartime and has become a signature of the AIDS epidemic, but that is otherwise rarely seen."

One consequence of this adult die-off is an increase in the number of children and elderly who are dependent on each economically productive adult. This makes it more difficult for societies to save and, therefore, to make the investments needed to improve living conditions. To make matters worse, in Africa it is often the better educated, more socially mobile populations who have the highest infection rate. Africa is losing the agronomists, the engineers, and the teachers it needs to sustain its economic development. In South Africa, for example, at the University of Durban-Westville, where many of the country's future leaders are trained, 25 percent of the students are HIV positive.

Countries where labor forces have such high infection levels will find it increasingly difficult to attract foreign investment. Companies operating in countries with high infection rates face a doubling, tripling, or even quadrupling of their health insurance costs. Firms once operating in the black suddenly find themselves in the red. What has begun as an unprecedented social tragedy is beginning to translate into an economic disaster. Municipalities throughout South Africa have been hesitant to publicize the extent of their local epidemics or scale up control efforts for fear of deterring outside investment and tourism.

The feedback loops launched by AIDS may be quite predictable in some cases, but could also destabilize societies in unanticipated ways. For example, where levels of unemployment are already high—the present situation in most African nations—a growing population of orphans and displaced youths could exacerbate crime. Moreover, a country in which a substantial share of the population suffers from impaired immune systems as a result of AIDS is much more vulnerable to the spread of other infectious diseases, such as tuberculosis, and waterborne illness. In

Zimbabwe, the last few years have brought a rapid rise in deaths due to tuberculosis, malaria, and even the bubonic plague—even among those who are not HIV positive. Even without such synergies, in the early years of the next century, the HIV epidemic is poised to claim more lives than did World War II.

Sinking Water Tables

While AIDS is already raising death rates in sub-Saharan Africa, the emergence of acute water shortages could have the same effect in India. As population grows, so does the need for water. Home to only 358 million people in 1950, India will pass the one-billion mark later this year. It is projected to overtake China as the most populous nation around the year 2037, and to reach 1.5 billion by 2050.

As India's population has soared, its demand for water for irrigation, industry, and domestic use has climbed far beyond the sustainable yield of the country's aquifers. According to the International Water Management Institute (IWMI), water is being pumped from India's aquifers at twice the rate the aquifers are recharged by rainfall. As a result, water tables are falling by one to three meters per year almost everywhere in the country. In thousands of villages, wells are running dry.

In some cases, wells are simply drilled deeper—if there is a deeper aquifer within reach. But many villages now depend on trucks to bring in water for household use. Other villages cannot afford such deliveries, and have entered a purgatory of declining options—lacking enough water even for basic hygiene. In India's western state of Gujarat, water tables are falling by as much as five meters per year, and farmers now have to drill their wells down to between 700 and 1200 feet to reach the receding supply. Only the more affluent can afford to drill to such depths.

Although irrigation goes back some 6,000 years, aquifer depletion is a rather recent phenomenon. It is only within the last half century or so that the availability of powerful diesel and electric pumps has made it possible to extract water at rates that exceed recharge rates. Little is known about the total capacity of India's underground supply, but the unsustainability of the current consumption is clear. If the country is currently pumping water at double the rate at which its aquifers recharge, for example, we know that when the aquifers are eventually depleted, the rate of pumping will necessarily have to be reduced to the recharge rate—which would mean that the amount of water pumped would be cut in half. With at least 55 percent of India's grain production now coming from irrigated lands, IWMI speculates that aquifer depletion could reduce India's harvest by one-fourth. Such a massive cutback could prove catastrophic for a nation where 53 percent of the children are already undernourished and underweight.

Impending aquifer depletion is not unique to India. It is also evident in China, North Africa and the Middle East, as well as in large tracts of the United States. However, in wealthy Kuwait or Saudi Arabia, precariously low water availability per person is not life-threatening because these countries can easily afford to import the food that they cannot produce domestically. Since it takes 1,000 tons of water to produce a ton of grain, the ability to import food is in effect an ability to import water. But in poor nations, like India, where people are immediately dependent on the natural-resource base for subsistence and often lack money to buy food, they are limited to the water they can obtain from their immediate surroundings—and are much more endangered if it disappears.

In India—as in other nations—poorer farmers are thus disproportionately affected by water scarcity, since they often cannot get the capital or credit to obtain bigger pumps necessary to extract water from ever-greater depths. Those farmers who can no longer deepen their wells often shift their cropping patterns to include more water-efficient—but lower-yielding—crops, such as mustard, sorghum, or millet. Some have abandoned irrigated farming altogether, resigning themselves to the diminished productivity that comes with depending only on rainfall.

When production drops, of course, poverty deepens. When that happens, experience shows that most people, before succumbing to hunger or starvation, will migrate. On Gujarat's western coast, for example, the overpumping of underground water has led to rapid salt-water intrusion as seawater seeps in to fill the vacuum left by the freshwater. The groundwater has become so saline that farming with it is impossible, and this has driven a massive migration of farmers inland in search of work.

Village communities in India tend to be rather insular, so that these migrants—uprooted from their homes—cannot take advantage of the social safety net that comes with community and family bonds. Local housing restrictions force them to camp in the fields, and their access to village clinics, schools, and other social services is restricted. But while attempting to flee, the migrants also bring some of their troubles along with them. Navroz Dubash, a researcher at the World Resources Institute who examined some of the effects of the water scarcity in Gujarat, notes that the flood of migrants depresses the local labor markets, driving down wages and diminishing the bargaining power of all landless laborers in the region.

In the web of feedback loops linking health and water supply, another entanglement is that when the *quantity* of available water declines, the *quality* of the water, too, may decline, because shrinking bodies of water lose their efficacy in diluting salts or pollutants. In Gujarat, water pumped from more than 700 feet down tends to have an unhealthy concentration of some inorganic elements, such as fluoride. As villagers drink and irrigate with this contaminated water, the degeneration of teeth and bones known as fluorosis has emerged as a major health threat. Similarly, in both West Bengal, India and Bangladesh, receding water tables have exposed arsenic-laden sediments to oxygen, converting them to a water-soluble form. According to UNDP estimates, at least 30 million people are exposed to health-impairing levels of arsenic in their drinking water.

As poverty deepens in the rural regions of India—and is driven deeper by mutually exacerbating health threats and water scarcities—migration from rural to urban areas is likely to increase. But for those who leave the farms, conditions in the cities may be no better. If water is scarce in the countryside, it is also likely to be scarce in the squatter settlements or other urban areas accessible to the poor. And where water is scarce, access to adequate sanitation and health services is poor. In most developing nations, the incidence of infectious diseases, including waterborne microbes, tuberculosis, and HIV/AIDS, is considerably higher in urban slums—where poverty and compromised health define the way of life—than in the rest of the city.

AIDS attacks whole communities, but unlike other scourges it takes its heaviest toll on teenagers and young adults—the people most needed to care for children and keep the economy productive.

In India, with so many of the children undernourished, even a modest decline in the country's ability to produce or purchase food is likely to increase child mortality. With India's population expected to increase by 100 million people per decade over the next half century, the potential losses of irrigation water pose an ominous specter not only to the Indian people now living but to the hundreds of millions more yet to come.

Shrinking Cropland Per Person

The third threat that hangs over the future of nearly all the countries where rapid population growth continues is the steady decline in the amount of cropland remaining per person—a threat both of rising population and of the conversion of cropland to other uses. In this analysis, we use grainland per person as a surrogate for cropland, because in most developing countries the bulk of land is used to produce grain, and the data are much more reliable. Among the more populous countries where this trend threatens future food security as Nigeria, Ethiopia, and Pakistan—all countries with weak family-planning programs.

As a limited amount of arable land continues to be divided among larger numbers of people, the average amount of cropland available for each person inexorably shrinks. Eventually, it drops below the point where people can feed themselves. Below 600 square meters of grainland per person (about the area of a basketball court), nations typically begin to depend heavily on imported grain. Cropland scarcity, like, water scarcity, can easily be translated into increased food imports in countries that can afford to import grain. But in the poorer nations of sub-Saharan Africa and the Indian subcontinent, subsistence farmers may not have access to imports. For them, land scarcity readily translates into malnutrition, hunger, rising mortality, and migration—and sometimes conflict. While most experts agree that resource scarcity alone is rarely the cause of violent conflict, resource scarcity has often compounded socioeconomic and political disruptions enough to drive unstable situations over the edge.

Thomas Homer-Dixon, director of the Project on Environment, Population, and Security at the University of Toronto, notes that "environmental scarcity is, without doubt, a significant cause of today's unprecedented levels of internal and international migration around the world." He has examined two cases in South Asia—a region plagued by land and water scarcity—in which resource constraints were underlying factors in mass migration and resulting conflict.

In the first case, Homer-Dixon finds that over the last few decades, land scarcity has caused millions of Bangladeshis to migrate to the Indian states of Assam, Tripura, and West Bengal. These movements expanded in the late 1970s after several years of flooding in Bangladesh, when population growth had reduced the grainland per person in Bangladesh to less than 0.08 hectares. As the average person's share of cropland began to shrink below the survival level, the lure of somewhat less densely populated land across the border in the Indian state of Assam became irresistible. By 1990, more than 7 million Bangladeshis had crossed the border, pushing Assam's population from 15 million to 22 million. The new immigrants in turn exacerbated land shortages in the Indian states, setting off a string of ethnic conflicts that have so far killed more than 5,000 people.

In the second case, Homer-Dixon and a colleague, Peter Gizewski, studied the massive rural-to-urban migration that has taken place in recent years in Pakistan. This migration, combined with population growth within the cities, has resulted in staggering urban growth rates of roughly 15 percent a year. Karachi, Pakistan's coastal capital, has seen its population balloon to 11 million. Urban services have been unable to keep pace with growth, especially for low-income dwellers. Shortages of water, sanitation, health services and jobs have become especially acute, leading to deteriorating public health and growing impoverishment.

"This migration . . . aggravates tensions and violence among diverse ethnic groups," according to Homer-Dixon and Gizewski. "This violence, in turn, threatens the general stability of Pakistani society." The cities of Karachi,

Hyderabad, Islamabad, and Rawalpindi, in particular, have become highly volatile, so that "an isolated, seemingly chance incident—such as a traffic accident or short-term breakdown in services—ignites explosive violence." In 1994, water shortages in Islamabad provoked widespread protest and violent confrontation with police in hard-hit poorer districts.

When people of parenting age die, the elderly are often left alone to care for the children. Meanwhile, poverty worsens with the loss of wage-earners. In other situations, poverty is worsened by declines in the amounts of productive land or fresh water available to each person and here, too, death may take an unnatural toll.

Without efforts to step up family planning in Pakistan, these patterns are likely to be magnified. Population is projected to grow from 146 million today to 345 million in 2050, shrinking the grainland area per person in Pakistan to a miniscule 0.036 hectares by 2050—less than half of what it is today. A family of six will then have to produce its food on roughly one-fifth of a hectare, or half an acre—the equivalent of a small suburban building lot in the United States.

Similar prospects are in the offing for Nigeria, where population is projected to double to 244 million over the next half century, and in Ethiopia, where population is projected to nearly triple. In both, of course, the area of grainland per person will shrink dramatically. In Ethiopia, if the projected population growth materializes, it will cut the amount of cropland per person to one-third of its current 0.12 hectares per person—a level at which already more than half of the country's children are undernourished. And even as its per capita land shrinks, its long-term water supply is jeopardized by the demands of nine other rapidly growing, water-scarce nations throughout the Nile River basin. But even these projections may underestimate the problem, because they assume an equitable distribution of land among all people. In reality, the inequalities in land distribution that exist in many African and South Asian nations mean that as the competition for declining resources becomes more intense, the poorer and more marginal groups face even harsher deprivations than the averages imply.

Moreover, in these projections we have assumed that the total grainland area over the next half-century will not change. In reality this may be overly optimistic simply because of the ongoing conversion of cropland to nonfarm uses and the loss of cropland from degradation. A steadily growing population generates a need for more homes, schools, and factories, many of which will be built on once-productive farmland. Degradation, which may take the form of soil erosion or of the waterlogging and salinization of irrigated land, is also claiming cropland.

Epidemics, resource scarcity, and other societal stresses thus do not operate in isolation. Several disruptive trends will often intersect synergistically, compounding their effects on public health, the environment, the economy, and the society. Such combinations can happen anywhere, but the effects are likely to be especially pernicious—and sometimes dangerously unpredictable—in such places as Bombay and Lagos, where HIV prevalence is on the rise, and where fresh water and good land are increasingly beyond the reach of the poor.

Regaining Control of Our Destiny

The threats from HIV, aquifer depletion, and shrinking cropland are not new or unexpected. We have known for at least 15 years that the HIV virus could decimate human populations if it is not controlled. In each of the last 18 years, the annual number of new HIV infections has risen, climbing from an estimated 200,000 new infections in 1981 to nearly 6 million in 1998. Of the 47 million people infected thus far, 14 million have died. In the absence of a low-cost cure, most of the remaining 33 million will be dead by 2005.

It may seem hard to believe, given the advanced medical knowledge of the late twentieth century, that a controllable disease is decimating human populations in so many countries. Similarly, it is hard to understand how falling water tables, which may prove an even greater threat to future economic progress, could be so widely ignored.

The arithmetic of emerging resource shortages is not difficult. The mystery is not in the numbers, but in our failure to do what is needed to prevent such threats from spiraling out of control.

Today's political leaders show few signs of comprehending the long-term consequences of persistent environmental and social trends, or of the interconnectedness of these trends. Despite advances in our understanding of the complex—often chaotic—nature of biological, ecological, and climatological systems, political thought continues to be dominated by reductionist thinking that fails to target the root causes of problems. As a result, political action focuses on responses to crises rather than prevention.

Leaders who are prepared to meet the challenges of the next century will need to understand that universal access to family planning not only is essential to coping with resource scarcity and the spread of HIV/AIDS, but is likely to improve the quality of life for the citizens they serve. Family planning comprises wide availability of contraception and reproductive healthcare, as well as improved access to educational opportunities for young women and men. Lower birth rates generally allow greater investment in each child, as has occurred in East Asia.

Leaders all over the world—not just in Africa and Asia—now need to realize that the adverse effects of global population growth will affect those living in nations such as the United States or Germany, that seem at first glance to be relatively protected from the ravages now looming in Zimbabwe or Ethiopia. Economist Herman Daly observes that whereas in the past surplus labor in one nation had the effect of driving down wages only in that nation, "global economic integration will be the means by which the consequences of overpopulation in the Third World are generalized to the globe as a whole." Large infusions of job-seekers into Brazil's or India's work force that may lower wages there may now also mean large infusions into the global workforce, with potentially similar consequences.

> Overwhelmed by multiple attacks on its health, the society falls deeper into poverty and as the cycle continues, more of its people die prematurely.

As the recent Asian economic downturn further demonstrates, "localized instability" is becoming an anachronistic concept. The consequences of social unrest in one nation, whether resulting from a currency crisis or an environmental crisis, can quickly cross national boundaries. Several nations, including the United States, now recognize world population growth as a national security issue. As the U.S. Department of State Strategic Plan, issued in September 1997, explains, "Stabilizing population growth is vital to U.S. interests. . . . Not only will early stabilization of the world's population promote environmentally sustainable economic development in other countries, but it will benefit the United States by improving trade opportunities and mitigating future global crises."

One of the keys to helping countries quickly slow population growth, before it becomes unmanageable, is expanded international assistance for reproductive health and family planning. At the United Nations Conference on Population and Development held in Cairo in 1994, it was estimated that the annual cost of providing quality reproductive health services to all those in need in developing countries would amount to $17 billion in the year 2000. By 2015, the cost would climb to $22 billion.

Industrial countries agreed to provide one-third of the funds, with the developing countries providing the remaining two-thirds. While developing countries have largely honored their commitments, the industrial countries—and most conspicuously, the United States—have reneged on theirs. And in late 1998, the U.S. Congress—mired in the quicksand of anti-abortion politics—withdrew all funding for the U.N. Population Fund, the principal source of international family planning assistance. Thus was thrown aside the kind of assistance that helps both to slow population growth and to check the spread of the HIV virus.

In most nations, stabilizing population will require mobilization of domestic resources that may now be tied up in defense expenditures, crony capitalism or government corruption. But without outside assistance, many nations many still struggle to provide universal family planning. For this reason, delegates at Cairo agreed that the immense resources and power found in the First World are indispensable in this effort. And as wealth further consolidates in the North and the number living in absolute poverty increases in the South, the argument for assistance grows more and more compelling. Given the social consequences of one-third of the world heading into a demographic nightmare, failure to provide such assistance is unconscionable.

Lester Brown is president of the Worldwatch Institute and Brian Halweil is a staff researcher at the Institute.

The Misery Behind the Statistics

Women suffer most

Diana Brown

Today three jumbo jets crashed, killing everyone on board. You didn't hear about it? That's funny. Perhaps it was because nearly everyone killed was from the so-called third world. Or perhaps it was because they were all women. But perhaps the most likely explanation was that it wasn't really "news" because the same thing happened yesterday and the day before that and will go on happening tomorrow and the next day and the day after.

I am sure that by now you know that I am not writing about real jumbo jets, but an equivalent number of passengers. Every year, year in, year out, 600,000 women are dying, nearly all in the third world, from pregnancy-related causes, nearly all of which are preventable.[1] How many of us in the comfortable first world know? How many care? Some of us find it easier to worry about the impact on the global environment of explosive population growth than about the apparently hopeless difficulties of day-to-day life and death in distant countries of which we know little.

The problems are, however, related. Women are dying unnecessarily because they lack basic human rights and particularly because they lack full reproductive rights. These deficiencies fuel rapid population growth. There is plenty of evidence that many women in developing countries are having more children than they really want, but as Kalimi Mworia of the International Planned Parenthood Foundation (IPPF) in Nairobi has said, many third world women "do not own their own bodies."

Abuse and Inequality

Nowhere in the world do women enjoy full equality with men. A recent study by Agnes Wold and Christine Wennerås of peer review in the Swedish Medical Research Council[2] has shown that even in enlightened Scandinavia there is considerable bias against women in science. In a large number of less-developed countries, however, women and girls have to cope with gross inequalities.

Discrimination starts before birth.[3] In many countries sons are valued much more highly than daughters, and, in some, female fetuses are selectively aborted. Although female infanticide is much less prevalent than in the past, severe neglect of girl children can have an equivalent effect. Girls and women often have to work harder than boys and men and yet may be denied equal access to nutrition, health care, and education. In some countries young girls are sold into prostitution, and in quite a few they can be forced into early marriage. The adult woman may be unable to own land or inherit property. She may be denied access to credit and may have little hope of economic independence. Worldwide, girls and women are the victims of violent attacks and rapes. It is even possible for the victim of a rape to be jailed while her attacker goes free.

All of these abuses constitute a denial of human rights, and many are enshrined in law, despite countries' stated commitment to the Universal Declaration of Human Rights. Even where laws uphold equality or embody protective measures such as forbidding child marriage, they are not necessarily enforced. Laws often seem ineffective in combating strongly entrenched cultural practices, such as female genital mutilation or early marriage. (We also see from the example in Sweden quoted above that, even with full equality guaranteed by law, a male hierarchy is able to hold onto power by subtle means.) Nevertheless, legal equality is an important first step in improving the position of women. We in the developed world should be working energetically to achieve it. A 1992 UNICEF report referred to "the apartheid of gender" and pointed out that discrimination against women was an injustice on a far

From *Free Inquiry,* Spring 1999, pp. 25-27. © 1999 by *Free Inquiry.* Reprinted by permission.

greater scale than the apartheid system. Apartheid was rightly opposed by the international community on the ground that "a people's rights and opportunities—where they can live, what education and health care they will receive, what job they can do, what income they can earn, what legal standing they will have—should not depend on whether they were born black or white. Yet it seems that the world is prepared to accept, with none of the depth and breadth of opposition that has been seen during the apartheid years, that all of these things can depend on the accident of being born male or female."[4]

EMPOWERING WOMEN

It has been widely recognized that raising the status of women and giving them more control over their lives is an essential step on the road to population stabilization. If women are valued for themselves, son preference is reduced, with a consequent lowering of average family size. Educated women marry later and have smaller, better-spaced families who are more likely to be healthy and survive. This in turn leads to lower birthrates. Women with a measure of economic independence have more say in their reproductive lives and can (and do) choose to have smaller families.

Every year, year in, year out, 600,000 women are dying, nearly all in the third world, from pregnancy-related causes, nearly all of which are preventable.

The International Conference on Population and Development (ICPD) held in Cairo in 1994 reached agreement on the need for the empowerment of women and the improvement of their status. In particular, governments were urged to eliminate all forms of discrimination against female children and to work to eliminate preferences for sons. The achievements of Cairo were trammelled by the obstructive, antichoice behavior of the Vatican, which greatly weakened the international community's commitment to eliminating unsafe abortion, but it was notable for cooperative between the population lobby and feminists, groups who had previously been suspicious of one another, but who were now to some extent able to unite against a common enemy for the advancement of women.

FEMINIST SUSPICIONS

Even after Cairo, however, suspicions remained. Many feminists have viewed population advocates as fanatically wedded to "population control" and prepared to countenance any means to achieve this end. It is quite true that in the past some population programs have been coercive and insensitive to the reproductive needs of both men and women. A few still are. One problem is that, in countries where the power structure is overwhelmingly male, official programs can be run without a real understanding of the needs and problems of women. It is also possible to run population programs by focusing on the goal of eventual population stabilization and various intermediate targets without paying much attention to what people really want in the present.

Those concerned about population growth are also criticized for putting demographic goals first and "pursuing public policies that are likely to have the most direct impact on reducing birthrates even if they are not the most important in terms of improving the quality of people's lives."[5] The same critic also points out that family planning may be divorced from basic health care and funded at the latter's expense. Given the dramatic improvement that has resulted in quality of life wherever birthrates have been reduced, it is hard to see the validity of the first claim. According to UNICEF, "the responsible planning of births is one of the most effective and least expensive ways of improving the quality of life on earth," and "family planning could bring more benefits to more people at less cost than any other single technology now available to the human race."[6]

The second charge is clearly true in certain countries, but it is difficult to see how really poor countries can do otherwise. Given their very limited resources, they are never going to be able to provide all the services to their people that we would like to see. They are forced to prioritize. Faced with a rapidly growing population and therefore ever-increasing needs, it seems to make sense to give priority to slowing down population growth, provided that human rights are respected and that the measures taken do genuinely benefit the people who are affected by them.

THE NEED TO TALK NUMBERS

I have personally been attacked by certain feminists for daring to "talk numbers" in the context of population. There seems to be a misconception that, if one uses statistics in discussions about groups of people, then one is ceasing to think of them as people and must also be wedded to coercive methods of "population control." I disagree profoundly. A baby dies, and everyone who knows the family is sad. The world in general, however, knows nothing of that baby or its death. A mother dies as a result of an unsafe abortion, trying to terminate an unwanted pregnancy. This is a tragedy for her family, and particularly for her surviving children, who may even die as a result of their loss. The world remains ignorant. Statistics tell us that each year about 4 million newborn babies die. Each year there are about 20 million unsafe abortions.[7] These statistics help us to understand the scale of the problems and the human misery they embody. They make us realize that the problems need to be tackled urgently.

In the same way, the knowledge that a country's population is likely to double in only 25 years shows us that it is facing an uphill struggle to improve the lot of its people and that its standard of living may even deteriorate as a result of population pressure. This should galvanize us to action.

The real problem is not the population researchers statistics, but that the statistics are brushed aside. Except at international conferences, most developed countries have shown great insensitivity to the pain behind the figures and have been unwilling to live up to the funding commitments they made at Cairo, leaving the poorer countries to stagger along as best they can, parceling out their inadequate resources. Development aid is seen as a way of promoting the commerce of the donor country—only a week before I write, the British Minister for International Development was heavily criticized for saying that it was not part of her job to help British businesses achieve contracts overseas. Only a very few rich countries are meeting the U.N. target of 0.7% of gross national product going to overseas aid, with 4% of that money being devoted to population programs.

So much needs to be done. My hope is that population advocates and feminists can unite in the common cause of working for reproductive rights and empowerment of women. We may never agree in the details, but we should not fight one another. If we succeed, the prize will be a better quality of life for all humanity.

Notes

1. Data from World Health Organization. See also http://safemotherhood.org.
2. A. Wold and C. Wennerås, *Nature,* 387 (1997): 341–343.
3. For an accessible account of discrimination against girls, see *People and the Planet,* 7 (1998): 3. Their Web site is www.oneworld.org/patp/.
4. *The State of the World's Children,* UNICEF, 1992.
5. B. Hartmann, "Cairo Consensus Sparks New Hopes, Old Worries," *Forum for Applied Research and Public Policy,* Summer 1997.
6. *State of the World's Children,* UNICEF, 1992.
7. Data from World Health Organization.

Diana Brown represents the International Humanist and Ethical Union at the United Nations in Geneva and is a former chairman of Population Concern in London.

GRAINS OF HOPE

GENETICALLY ENGINEERED CROPS could revolutionize farming. Protesters fear they could also destroy the ecosystem. You decide

By J. MADELEINE NASH ZURICH

AT FIRST, THE GRAINS OF RICE THAT INGO Potrykus sifted through his fingers did not seem at all special, but that was because they were still encased in their dark, crinkly husks. Once those drab coverings were stripped away and the interiors polished to a glossy sheen, Potrykus and his colleagues would behold the seeds' golden secret. At their core, these grains were not pearly white, as ordinary rice is, but a very pale yellow—courtesy of beta-carotene, the nutrient that serves as a building block for vitamin A.

Potrykus was elated. For more than a decade he had dreamed of creating such a rice: a golden rice that would improve the lives of millions of the poorest people in the world. He'd visualized peasant farmers wading into paddies to set out the tender seedlings and winnowing the grain at harvest time in handwoven baskets. He'd pictured small children consuming the golden gruel their mothers would make, knowing that it would sharpen their eyesight and strengthen their resistance to infectious diseases.

And he saw his rice as the first modest start of a new green revolution, in which ancient food crops would acquire all manner of useful properties: bananas that wouldn't rot on the way to market; corn that could supply its own fertilizer; wheat that could thrive in drought-ridden soil.

But imagining a golden rice, Potrykus soon found, was one thing and bringing one into existence quite another. Year after year, he and his colleagues ran into one unexpected obstacle after another, beginning with the finicky growing habits of the rice they transplanted to a greenhouse near the foothills of the Swiss Alps. When success finally came, in the spring of 1999, Potrykus was 65 and about to retire as a full professor at the Swiss Federal Institute of Technology in Zurich. At that point, he tackled an even more formidable challenge.

Having created golden rice, Potrykus wanted to make sure it reached those for whom it was intended: malnourished children of the developing world. And that, he knew, was not likely to be easy. Why? Because in addition to a full complement of genes from Oryza sativa—the Latin name for the most commonly consumed species of rice—the golden grains also contained snippets of DNA borrowed from bacteria and daffodils. It was what some would call Frankenfood, a product of genetic engineering. As such, it was entangled in a web of hopes and fears and political baggage, not to mention a fistful of ironclad patents.

For about a year now—ever since Potrykus and his chief collaborator, Peter Beyer of the University of Freiburg in Germany, announced their achievement—their golden grain has illuminated an increasingly polarized public debate. At issue is the question of what genetically engineered crops represent. Are they, as their proponents argue, a technological leap forward that will bestow incalculable bene-

HOW TO MAKE GOLDEN RICE

A four-step process to feed the poor

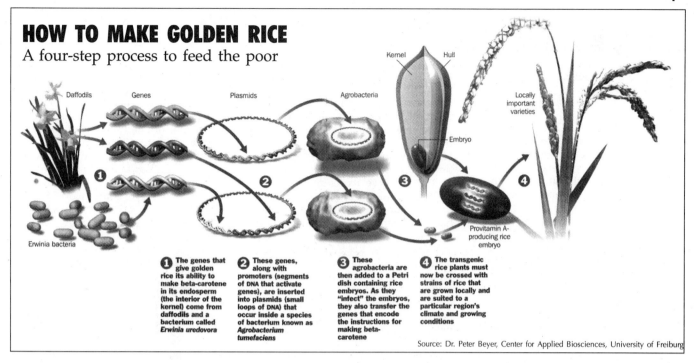

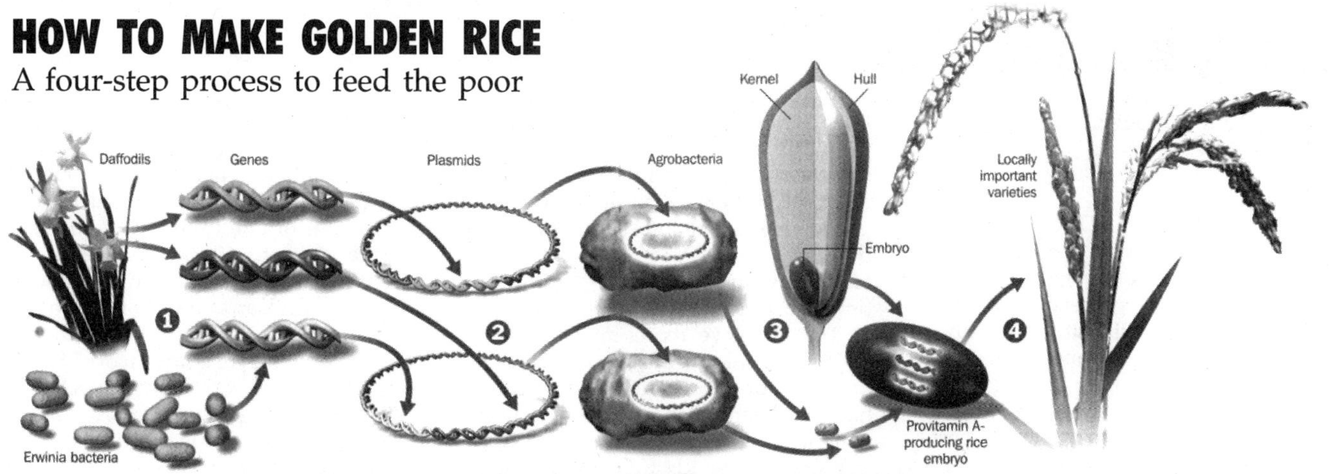

1 **The genes that give golden rice its ability to make beta-carotene in its endosperm (the interior of the kernel) come from daffodils and a bacterium called *Erwinia uredovora***

2 **These genes, along with promoters (segments of DNA that activate genes), are inserted into plasmids (small loops of DNA) that occur inside a species of bacterium known as *Agrobacterium tumefaciens***

3 **These agrobacteria are then added to a Petri dish containing rice embryos. As they "infect" the embryos, they also transfer the genes that encode the instructions for making beta-carotene**

4 **The transgenic rice plants must now be crossed with strains of rice that are grown locally and are suited to a particular region's climate and growing conditions**

Source: Dr. Peter Beyer, Center for Applied Biosciences, University of Freiburg

FROM THE TRANSGENIC GARDEN

COTTON

BEAUTIFUL BOLL: This plant has been given a bacterial gene to help it fight off worms that infest cotton crops

CORN

HEALTHY KERNEL: These corn seeds are protected by the same bacterial gene, one that ecologists fear could harm butterflies

PAPAYA

VIRAL RESISTANCE: Fruit carrying a gene from the ringspot virus are better able to withstand ringspot outbreaks

CANOLA

PROBLEM POLLEN: When transgenic seeds contaminated a non-transgenic shipment from Canada, European farmers cried foul

SOYBEANS

ROUNDUP READY: Will crops designed to take frequent spraying with Monsanto's top weed killer lead to Roundup-resistant weeds?

fits on the world and its people? Or do they represent a perilous step down a slippery slope that will lead to ecological and agricultural ruin? Is genetic engineering just a more efficient way to do the business of conventional crossbreeding? Or does the ability to mix the genes of any species—even plants and animals—give man more power than he should have?

The debate erupted the moment genetically engineered crops made their commercial debut in the mid-1990s, and it has escalated ever since. First to launch major protests against biotechnology were European environmentalists and consumer-advocacy groups. They were soon followed by their U.S. counterparts, who made a big splash at last fall's World Trade Organization meeting in Seattle and last week launched an offensive designed to target one company after another (see accompanying story). Over the coming months, charges that transgenic crops pose grave dangers will be raised in petitions, editorials, mass mailings and protest marches. As a result, golden rice, despite its humanitarian intent, will probably be subjected to the same kind of hostile scrutiny that has already led to curbs on the commercialization of these crops in Britain, Germany, Switzerland and Brazil.

The hostility is understandable. Most of the genetically engineered crops introduced so far represent minor variations on the same two themes: resistance to insect pests and to herbicides used to control the growth of weeds. And they are often marketed by large, multinational corporations that produce and sell the very agricultural chemicals farmers are spraying on their fields. So while many farmers have embraced such crops as Monsanto's Roundup Ready soybeans, with their genetically engineered resistance to Monsanto's Roundup-brand herbicide, that let them spray weed killer without harming crops, consumers have come to regard such things with mounting suspicion. Why resort to a strange new technology that might harm the biosphere, they ask, when the benefits of doing so seem small?

Indeed, the benefits have seemed small—until golden rice came along to suggest otherwise. Golden rice is clearly not the moral equivalent of Roundup Ready beans. Quite the contrary, it is an example—the first compelling example—of a geneti-

Taking It to Main Street

By MARGOT ROOSEVELT
SAN FRANCISCO

IT WAS THE SORT OF KITSCHY street theater you expect in a city like San Francisco. A gaggle of protesters in front of a grocery store, some dressed as monarch butterflies, others as Frankenstein's monster. Signs reading HELL NO, WE WON'T GROW IT! People in white biohazard jumpsuits pitching Campbell's soup and Kellogg's cornflakes into a mock toxic-waste bin. The crowd shouting, "Hey, hey, ho, ho—GMO has got to go!" And, at the podium, Jesse Cool, a popular restaurant owner, wondering what would happen if she served a tomato spliced with an oyster gene and a customer got sick. "I could get sued," she says.

But just as the California activists were revving up last week, similar rants and chants were reverberating in such unlikely places as Grand Forks, N.D., Augusta, Maine, and Miami—19 U.S. cities in all. This was no frolicking radical fringe but the carefully coordinated start of a nationwide campaign to force the premarket safety testing and labeling of those GMOs, or genetically modified organisms. Seven organizations— including such media-savvy veterans as the Sierra Club, Friends of the Earth and the Public Interest Research Groups—were launching the Genetically Engineered Food Alert, a million-dollar, multiyear organizing effort to pressure Congress, the Food and Drug Administration and individual companies, one at a time, starting with Campbell's soup.

The offensive represents the seeds of what could grow into a serious problem for U.S. agribusiness, which had been betting that science-friendly American consumers would remain immune to any "Frankenfood" backlash cross-pollinating from Europe or Japan. After all, this is (mostly) U.S. technology, and it has spread so quickly and so quietly that the proportion of U.S. farmland planted in genetically altered corn now stands at nearly 25%. Some 70% of processed food in American supermarkets, from soup to sandwich meat, contains ingredients derived from transgenic corn, soybeans and other plants. Yet all of a sudden, activists are "yelling fire in a movie theater," says Dan Eramian, spokesman for the Biotechnology Industry Organization (BIO).

How widespread is this protest movement? And how deep are its roots? We may soon find out, for it's emergence is a study in the warp-speed politics of the age of the Internet. This is a time when a Web designer named Craig Winters can start an organization called the Campaign to Label Genetically Engineered Food with a staff of one (himself), mount a website and sell 160,000 "Take Action Packets" in nine weeks. Want to know what the Chileans are doing about transgenic grain shipments? How South Korean labeling laws work? Just subscribe to one of the four biotech e-mail lists of the Institute for Agriculture and Trade Policy, based in Minneapolis, Minn.

Even so-called ecoterrorists who have uprooted scores of university test plots across the country in the past year use the Net to organize their lawbreaking protests. In an Internet posting from Santa Cruz last week, Earth First! beckons, "You're all invited to sunny California for a weekend of workshops, training and fun! We also have plenty of [genetically engineered] crops waiting for your night time gardening efforts." Says Carl Pope, the Sierra Club's executive director: "I've never seen an issue go so quickly."

(continued)

cally engineered crop that may benefit not just the farmers who grow it but also the consumers who eat it. In this case, the consumers include at least a million children who die every year because they are weakened by vitamin-A deficiency and an additional 350,000 who go blind.

No wonder the biotech industry sees golden rice as a powerful ally in its struggle to win public acceptance. No wonder its critics see it as a cynical ploy. And no wonder so many of those concerned about the twin evils of poverty and hunger look at golden rice and see reflected in it their own passionate conviction that genetically engineered crops can be made to serve the greater public good—that in fact such crops have a critical role to play in feeding a world that is about to add to its present population of 6 billion. As former President Jimmy Carter put it, "Responsible biotechnology is not the enemy; starvation is."

Indeed, by the year 2020, the demand for grain, both for human consumption and for animal feed, is projected to go up by nearly half, while the amount of arable land available to satisfy that demand will not only grow much more slowly but also, in some areas, will probably dwindle. Add to that the need to conserve overstressed water resources and reduce the use of polluting chemicals, and the enormity of the challenge becomes apparent. In order to meet it, believes Gordon Conway, the agricultural ecologist who heads the Rockefeller Foundation, 21st century farmers will have to draw on every arrow in their agricultural quiver, including genetic engineering. And contrary to public perception, he says, those who have the least to lose and the most to gain are not well-fed Americans and Europeans but the hollow-bellied citizens of the developing world.

GOING FOR THE GOLD

IT WAS IN THE LATE 1980S, AFTER HE BEcame a full professor of plant science at the Swiss Federal Institute of Technology, that Ingo Potrykus started to think about using genetic engineering to improve the nutritional qualities of rice. He knew that of some 3 billion people who depend on rice as their major staple, around 10% risk some degree of vitamin-A deficiency and the health problems that result. The reason, some alleged, was an overreliance

Taking It to Main Street *continued*

It started about two years ago, when the buzz from European anti-biotech protest groups began to ricochet throughout the Net, reaching the community groups that were springing up across the U.S. Many were galvanized by proposed FDA regulations that would have allowed food certified as "organic" to contain genetically modified ingredients—an effort shouted down by angry consumers. Meanwhile, Greenpeace began to target U.S. companies such as Gerber, which quickly renounced the use of transgenic ingredients, and Kellogg's, which has yet to do so. With so-called Frankenfoods making headlines, several other companies cut back on biotech: McDonald's forswore genetically engineered potatoes, and Frito-Lay decreed it would buy no more genetically modified corn.

But the issue that is now on the front burner dates back to 1992, when the FDA decided that biotech ingredients did not materially alter food and therefore did not require labeling. Nor, the agency declared, was premarket safety testing required, because biotech additives were presumed to be benign. Last March the Center for Food Safety and 53 other groups, including the Union of Concerned Scientists, filed a petition to force the FDA to change its policy.

Meanwhile, the biotech issue is gathering steam in Congress, where safety and labeling bills have been introduced by Democratic Representative Dennis Kucinich of Ohio and 55 co-sponsors in the House, and by Daniel Patrick Moynihan and Barbara Boxer in the Senate. Similar statewide bills are pending in Maine, Colorado and Oregon. Shareholder resolutions demanding safety testing and labeling have targeted a score of companies from life- science giants to supermarket chains.

Surveys indicate that between two-thirds and three-quarters of Americans want biotech food to be labeled. Then why not do it? Because companies fear such disclosure could spell disaster. "Our data show that 60% of consumers would consider a mandatory biotech label as a warning that it is unsafe," says Gene Grabowski, spokesman for the Grocery Manufacturers of America. "It is easier," BIO's Eramian points out, "to scare people about biotechnology than to educate them."

The labeling threat finally spurred a hitherto complacent industry into action. Last April, Monsanto, Novartis and five other biotech companies rolled out a $50 million television advertising campaign, with soft-focus fields and smiling children, pitching "solutions that could improve our world tomorrow."

But by then the opposition was morphing from inchoate splinter groups into something that looks like a mainstream coalition. In July 1999, some 40 environmentalists, consumer advocates and organic-food activists met in Bolinas, Calif., to map a national campaign. Rather than endorse a total ban on genetically modified foods that Greenpeace was pushing, says Wendy Wendlandt, political director of the state Public Interest Research Groups, "it was more practical to call for a moratorium until the stuff is safety tested and labeled, and companies are held responsible for any harmful effects."

In May the FDA announced that in the fall it would propose new rules for genetically engineered crops and products. Instead of safety testing, it would require only that companies publicly disclose their new biotech crops before they are planted. Labeling would be voluntary.

The critics' response came last week: a campaign to muster public opposition to the FDA's new rules and to target individual companies and their previous trademarks. The mock advertisements for "Campbull's Experimental Vegetable Soup," with the advisory, "Warning: This Product Is Untested," is only the first salvo. Some 18 other brand-name U.S. companies are on a tentative hit list, including General Mills, Coca-Cola and Kraft.

Will the companies succumb to the pressure, as they have in Europe? As of last week, Campbell claimed to be unfazed, with few customers registering concern, despite the spotlight. Even at the San Francisco rally, there was some ambivalence. "I may not eat Campbell's soup as much," offered Shanae Walls, 19, a student at Contra Costa College who was there with her Environmental Science and Thought class. But as the protesters tossed products from Pepperidge Farm—a Campbell subsidiary—into the toxic-waste bin, she had second thoughts. "I love those cookies," she said wistfully. "That might take some time."

on rice ushered in by the green revolution. Whatever its cause, the result was distressing: these people were so poor that they ate a few bowls of rice a day and almost nothing more.

The problem interested Potrykus for a number of reasons. For starters, he was attracted by the scientific challenge of transferring not just a single gene, as many had already done, but a group of genes that represented a key part of a biochemical pathway. He was also motivated by complex emotions, among them empathy. Potrykus knew more than most what it meant not to have enough to eat. As a child growing up in war-ravaged Germany, he and his brothers were often so desperately hungry that they ate what they could steal.

Around 1990, Potrykus hooked up with Gary Toenniessen, director of food security for the Rockefeller Foundation. Toenniessen had identified the lack of beta-carotene in polished rice grains as an appropriate target for gene scientists like Potrykus to tackle because it lay beyond the ability of traditional plant breeding to address. For while rice, like other green plants, contains light-trapping beta-carotene in its external tissues, no plant in the entire *Oryza* genus—as far as anyone knew—produced beta-carotene in its endosperm (the starchy interior part of the rice grain that is all most people eat).

It was at a Rockefeller-sponsored meeting that Potrykus met the University of Freiburg's Peter Beyer, an expert on the beta-carotene pathway in daffodils. By combining their expertise, the two scientists figured, they might be able to remedy this unfortunate oversight in nature. So in 1993, with some $100,000 in seed

THE GLOBAL FOOD FIGHT

1 BRUSSELS, 1998 France, Italy, Greece, Denmark and Luxembourg team up to block introduction of all new GM products in the European Union—including those approved by E.U. scientific advisory committees and even a few developed in these five countries. Several E.U. countries have also banned the importation and use of 18 GM crops and foods approved before the blockade went into effect. New safety rules could eventually break this logjam.

2 SEATTLE, NOVEMBER 1999 Taking to the streets to protest the spread of "Frankenfoods," among other issues, demonstrators trying to disrupt the World Trade Organization summit are tear-gassed and beaten by police.

3 MIDWESTERN U.S., 1999 A coalition of agricultural groups calls for a freeze on government approval of new GM seeds in light of dwindling markets in anti-GM European countries. Planting of GM corn drops from 25 million acres (10 million hectares) in 1999 to 19.9 million acres (8 million hectares) in 2000.

4 MONTREAL, JANUARY 2000 130 nations, including Mexico, Australia and Japan, sign the Cartagena Protocol on Biosafety, which requires an exporting country to obtain permission from an importing country before shipping GM seeds and organisms and to label such shipments with warnings that they "may contain" GM products.

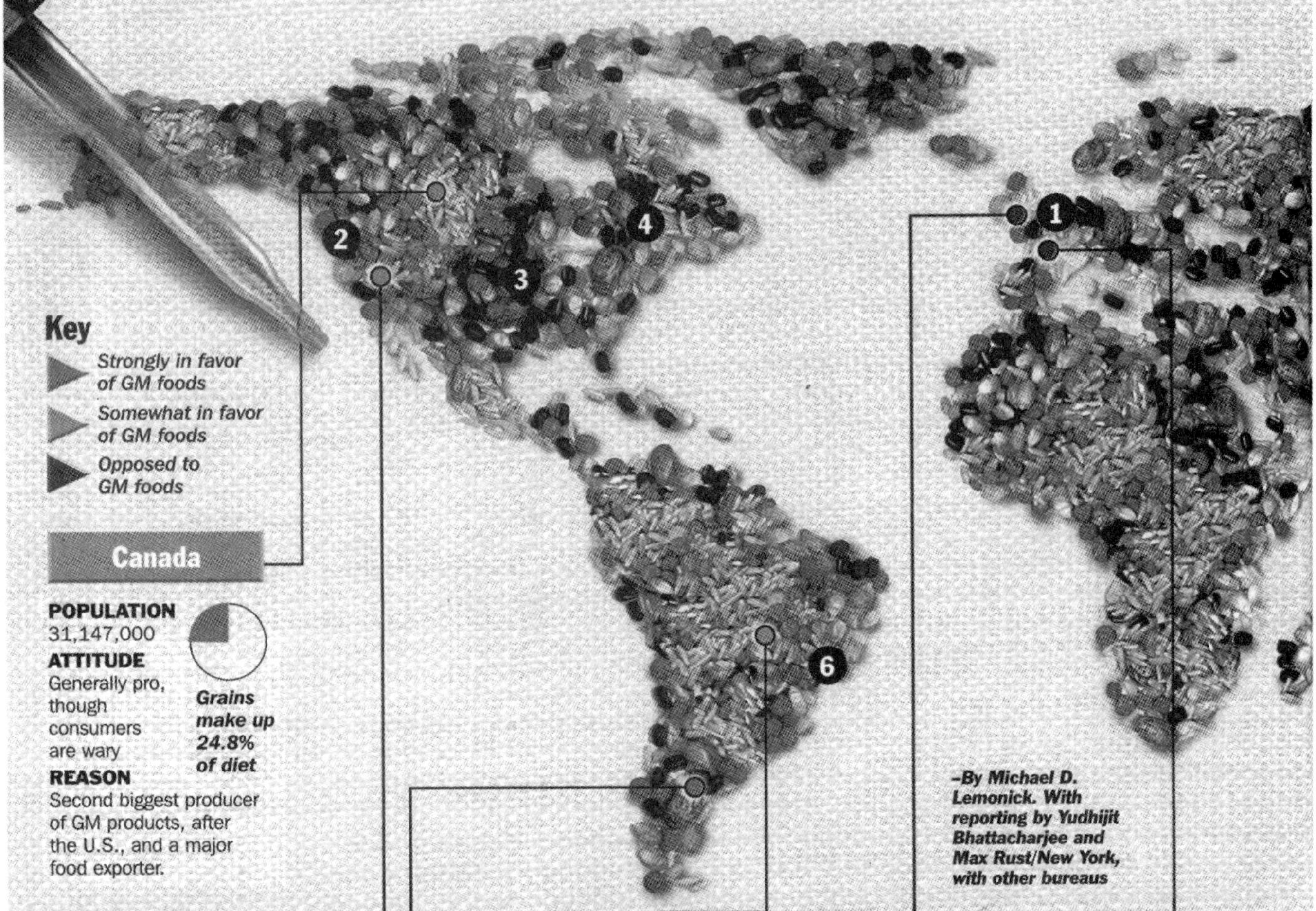

Canada

POPULATION 31,147,000

ATTITUDE Generally pro, though consumers are wary

Grains make up 24.8% of diet

REASON Second biggest producer of GM products, after the U.S., and a major food exporter.

–By Michael D. Lemonick. With reporting by Yudhijit Bhattacharjee and Max Rust/New York, with other bureaus

U.S.

POPULATION 278,357,000

ATTITUDE Cautiously pro

Grains make up 23.6% of diet

REASON As a major food exporter and home to giant agribiotech businesses, led by Monsanto, the country stands to reap huge profits from GM foods.

Argentina

POPULATION 37,031,000

ATTITUDE Pro

Grains make up 29.5% of diet

REASON Third largest producer of biotech crops in the world, after the U.S. and Canada.

Brazil

POPULATION 170,116,000

ATTITUDE Very cautiously pro

Grains make up 30.9% of diet

REASON The country is eager to participate in the potentially profitable biotech revolution but is worried about alienating anti-GM customers in Europe.

Britain

POPULATION 58,830,000

ATTITUDE Strongly anti

Grains make up 22.8% of diet

REASON "Mad cow" disease in beef and a report that GM potatoes caused immune-system damage in rats have alarmed most Brits. Markets ban GM foods, and experiments are tightly controlled.

France

POPULATION 59,079,000

ATTITUDE Strongly anti

Grains make up 24.3% of diet

REASON Like Britain, France has been stung by incidents with tainted food. Its attitude is also colored by hostility to U.S. imports and a desire to protect French farmers.

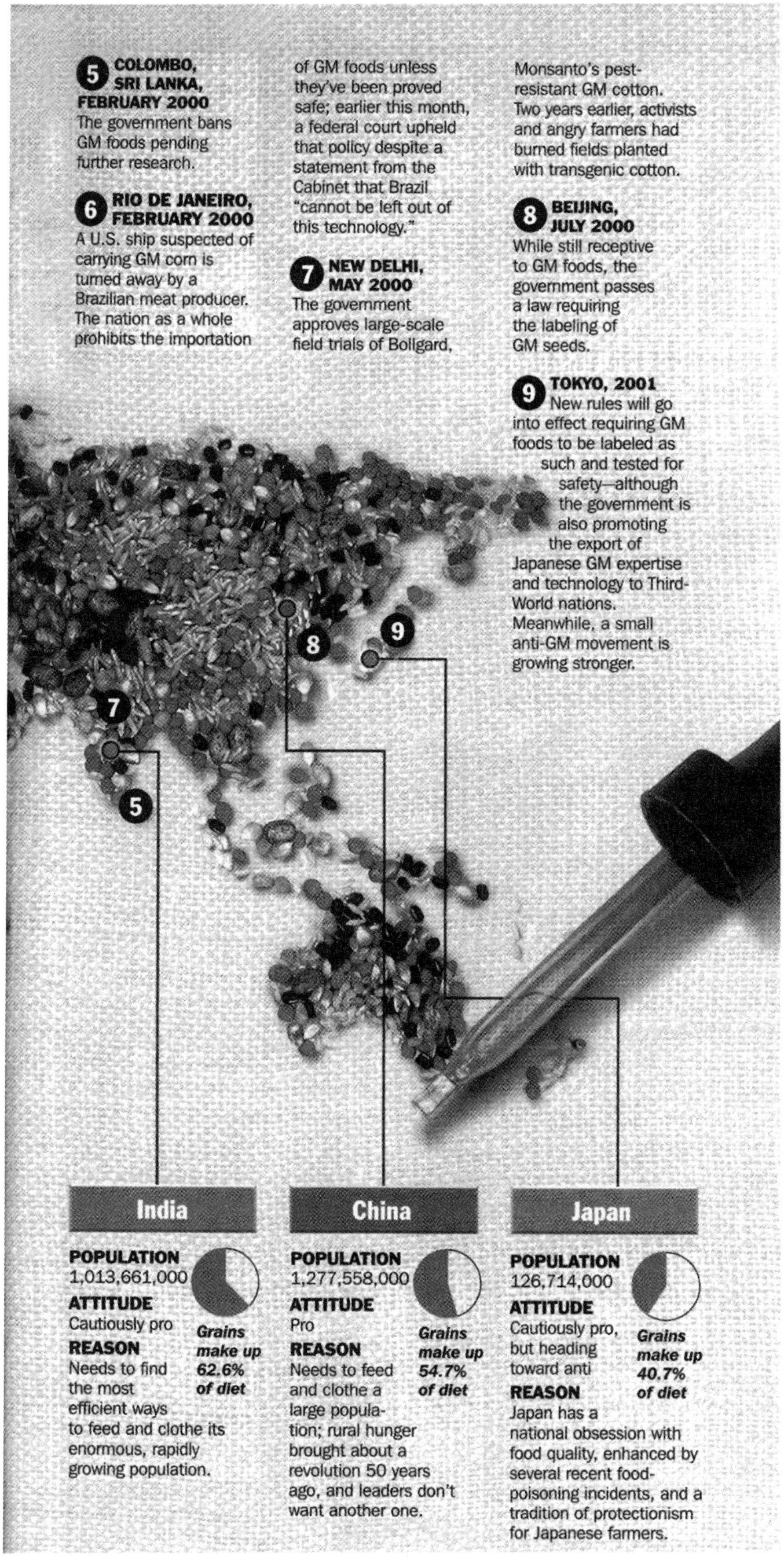

money from the Rockefeller Foundation, Potrykus and Beyer launched what turned into a seven-year, $2.6 million project, backed also by the Swiss government and the European Union. "I was in a privileged situation," reflects Potrykus, "because I was able to operate without industrial support. Only in that situation can you think of giving away your work free."

That indeed is what Potrykus announced he and Beyer planned to do. The two scientists soon discovered, however, that giving away golden rice was not going to be as easy as they thought. The genes they transferred and the bacteria they used to transfer those genes were all encumbered by patents and proprietary rights. Three months ago, the two scientists struck a deal with AstraZeneca, which is based in London and holds an exclusive license to one of the genes Potrykus and Beyer used to create golden rice. In exchange for commercial marketing rights in the U.S. and other affluent markets, AstraZeneca agreed to lend its financial muscle and legal expertise to the cause of putting the seeds into the hands of poor farmers at no charge.

No sooner had the deal been made than the critics of agricultural biotechnology erupted. "A rip-off of the public trust," grumbled the Rural Advancement Foundation International, an advocacy group based in Winnipeg, Canada. "Asian farmers get (unproved) genetically modified rice, and AstraZeneca gets the 'gold.' " Potrykus was dismayed by such negative reaction. "It would be irresponsible," he exclaimed, "not to say immoral, not to use biotechnology to try to solve this problem!" But such expressions of good intentions would not be enough to allay his opponents' fears.

WEIGHING THE PERILS

Beneath the hyperbolic talk of Frankenfoods and Superweeds, even proponents of agricultural biotechnology agree, lie a number of real concerns. To begin with, all foods, including the transgenic foods created through genetic engineering, are potential sources of allergens. That's because the transferred genes contain instructions for making proteins, and not all proteins are equal. Some—those in peanuts, for example—are well known for causing allergic reactions. To many, the possibility that golden rice might cause such a problem seems farfetched, but it nonetheless needs to be considered.

Then there is the problem of "genetic pollution," as opponents of biotechnology term it. Pollen grains from such wind-pollinated plants as corn and canola, for instance, are carried far and wide. To farmers, this mainly poses a nuisance. Transgenic canola grown in one field, for example, can very easily pollinate nontransgenic plants grown in the next. Indeed this is the reason behind the furor that recently erupted in Europe when it was discovered that canola seeds from Canada—unwittingly planted by farmers in England, France, Germany and Sweden—contained transgenic contaminants.

The continuing flap over Bt corn and cotton—now grown not only in the U.S. but also in Argentina and China—has provided more fodder for debate. Bt stands for a common soil bacteria, *Bacillus thuringiensis,* different strains of which produce toxins that target specific insects. By transferring to corn and cotton the bacterial gene responsible for making this toxin, Monsanto and other companies have produced crops that are resistant to the European corn borer and the cotton bollworm. An immediate concern, raised by a number of ecologists, is whether or not widespread planting of these crops will spur the development of resistance to Bt among crop pests. That would be unfortunate, they point out, because Bt is a safe and effective natural insecticide that is popular with organic farmers.

Even more worrisome are ecological concerns. In 1999 Cornell University entomologist John Losey performed a provocative, "seat-of-the-pants" laboratory experiment. He dusted Bt corn pollen on plants populated by monarch-butterfly caterpillars. Many of the caterpillars died. Could what happened in Losey's laboratory happen in cornfields across the Midwest? Were these lovely butterflies, already under pressure owing to human encroachment on their Mexican wintering grounds, about to face a new threat from high-tech farmers in the north?

The upshot: despite studies pro and con—and countless save-the-monarch protests acted out by children dressed in butterfly costumes—a conclusive answer to this question has yet to come. Losey himself is not yet convinced that Bt corn poses a grave danger to North America's monarch-butterfly population, but he does think the issue deserves attention. And others agree. "I'm not anti biotechnology per se," says biologist Rebecca Goldberg, a senior scientist with the Environmental Defense Fund, "but I would like to have a tougher regulatory regime. These crops should be subject to more careful screening before they are released."

Are there more potential pitfalls? There are. Among other things, there is the possibility that as transgenes in pollen drift, they will fertilize wild plants, and weeds will emerge that are hardier and even more difficult to control. No one knows how common the exchange of genes between domestic plants and their wild relatives really is, but Margaret Mellon, director of the Union of Concerned Scientists' agriculture and biotechnology program, is certainly not alone in thinking that it's high time we find out. Says she: "People should be responding to these concerns with experiments, not assurances."

And that is beginning to happen, although—contrary to expectations—the reports coming in are not necessarily that scary. For three years now, University of Arizona entomologist Bruce Tabashnik has been monitoring fields of Bt cotton that farmers have planted in his state. And in this instance at least, he says, "the environmental risks seem minimal, and the benefits seem great." First of all, cotton is self-pollinated rather than wind-pollinated, so that the spread of the Bt gene is of less concern. And because the Bt gene is so effective, he notes, Arizona farmers have reduced their use of chemical insecticides 75%. So far, the pink bollworm population has not rebounded, indicating that the feared resistance to Bt has not yet developed.

SQUEEZE ME: Scientists turned off the gene that makes tomatoes soft and squishy

ASSESSING THE PROMISE

ARE THE CRITICS OF AGRICULTURAL biotechnology right? Is biotech's promise nothing more than overblown corporate hype? The papaya growers in Hawaii's Puna district clamor to disagree. In 1992 a wildfire epidemic of papaya ringspot virus threatened to destroy the state's papaya industry; by 1994, nearly half the state's papaya acreage had been infected, their owners forced to seek outside employment. But then help arrived, in the form of a virus-resistant transgenic papaya developed by Cornell University plant pathologist Dennis Gonsalves.

In 1995 a team of scientists set up a field trial of two transgenic lines—UH SunUP and UH Rainbow—and by 1996, the verdict had been rendered. As everyone could see, the nontransgenic plants in the field trial were a stunted mess, and the transgenic plants were healthy. In 1998, after negotiations with four patent holders, the papaya growers switched en masse to the transgenic seeds and reclaimed their orchards. "Consumer acceptance has been great," reports Rusty Perry, who runs a papaya farm near Puna. "We've found that customers are more concerned with how the fruits look and taste than with whether they are transgenic or not."

Viral diseases, along with insect infestations, are a major cause of crop loss in Africa, observes Kenyan plant scientist Florence Wambugu. African sweet-potato fields, for example, yield only 2.4 tons per acre, vs. more than double that in the rest of the world. Soon Wambugu hopes to start raising those yields by introducing a transgenic sweet potato that is resistant to the feathery mottle virus. There really is no other option, explains Wambugu, who currently directs the International Service for the Acquisition of Agri-biotech Applications in Nairobi. "You can't control the virus in the field, and you can't breed in resistance through conventional means."

To Wambugu, the flap in the U.S. and Europe over genetically engineered crops seems almost ludicrous. In Africa, she notes, nearly half the fruit and vegetable harvest is lost because it rots on the way to market. "If we had a transgenic banana that ripened more slowly," she says, "we could have 40% more bananas than now." Wambugu also dreams of getting access to herbicide-resistant crops. Says she: "We could liberate so many people if our crops were resistant to herbicides that we could then spray on the surrounding weeds. Weeding enslaves Africans; it keeps children from school."

In Wambugu's view, there are more benefits to be derived from agricultural biotechnology in Africa than practically anywhere else on the planet—and this may be so. Among the genetic-engineering projects funded by the Rockefeller Foundation is one aimed at controlling striga, a weed that parasitizes the roots of African corn plants. At present there is little farmers can do about striga infestation, so tightly intertwined are the weed's roots with the roots of the corn plants it targets. But scientists have come to understand the source of the problem: corn roots exude chemicals that attract striga. So it may prove possible to identify the genes that are responsible and turn them off.

The widespread perception that agricultural biotechnology is intrinsically inimical to the environment perplexes the Rockefeller Foundation's Conway, who views genetic engineering as an important tool for achieving what he has termed a "doubly green revolution." If the technology can marshal a plant's natural defenses against weeds and viruses, if it can induce crops to flourish with minimal application of chemical fertilizers, if it can make dryland agriculture more productive without straining local water supplies, then what's wrong with it?

Of course, these particular breakthroughs have not happened yet. But as the genomes of major crops are ever more finely mapped, and as the tools for transferring genes become ever more precise, the possibility for tinkering with complex biochemical pathways can be expected to expand rapidly. As Potrykus sees it, there is no question that agricultural biotechnology can be harnessed for the good of humankind. The only question is whether there is the collective will to do so. And the answer may well emerge as the people of the world weigh the future of golden rice.

—With reporting by Simon Robinson/Nairobi

Unit 3

Unit Selections

Key Points to Consider

- How is the availability of natural resources affected by population growth?
- Do you think that the international community has adequately responded to problems of pollution and threats to our common natural heritage? Why or why not?
- What is the natural resource picture going to look like 30 years from now?
- How is society, in general, likely to respond to the conflicts between economic necessity and resource conservation?
- What is the likely future of energy supplies in both the industrial and the developing world?
- What transformations will societies that are heavy users of fossil fuels have to undergo in order to meet future energy needs?
- Can a sustainable economy be organized and what changes in behavior and values are necessary to accomplish this?

DUSHKIN ONLINE Links **www.dushkin.com/online/**

11. **Friends of the Earth**
    http://www.foe.co.uk/index.html
12. **National Geographic Society**
    http://www.nationalgeographic.com
13. **National Oceanic and Atmospheric Administration (NOAA)**
    http://www.noaa.gov
14. **Public Utilities Commission of Ohio (PUCO)**
    http://www.puc.state.oh.us/consumer/gcc/index.html
15. **SocioSite: Sociological Subject Areas**
    http://www.pscw.uva.nl/sociosite/TOPICS/
16. **United Nations Environment Programme (UNEP)**
    http://www.unep.ch

These sites are annotated on pages 4 and 5.

The Global Environment and Natural Resources Utilization

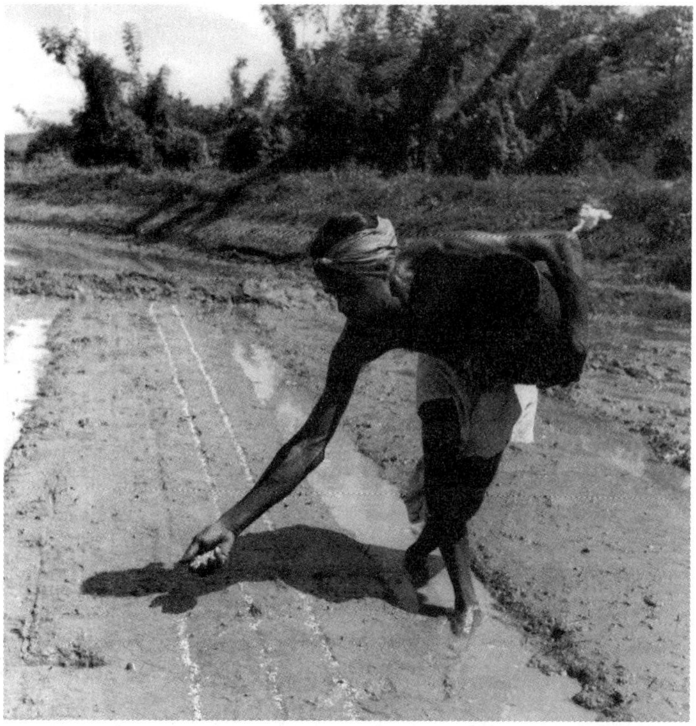

Beginning in the eighteenth century, the concept of the modern nation-state was initially conceived, and over many generations it evolved to the point where it is now difficult to imagine a world without national governments. These legal entities have been viewed as separate, self-contained units that independently pursue their "national interests." Scholars often described the world as a political community of independent units that interacted or "bounced off" each other (a concept that has been described as a billiard ball model).

This perspective of the international community as comprised of self-contained and self-directed units has undergone major rethinking in the past 30 years. The primarily reason for this is the international dimensions of the demands being placed on natural resources. The Middle East, for example, contains a majority of the world's oil reserves. The United States, Western Europe, and Japan are very dependent on this vital source of energy. This unbalanced supply and demand equation has created an unprecedented lack of self-sufficiency for the world's major economic powers.

The increased interdependence of countries is further illustrated by the fact that air and water pollution often do not respect political boundaries. One country's smoke is often another country's acid rain. The concept that independent political units control their own destiny, in short, makes less sense than it may have 100 years ago. In order to more fully understand why this is so, one must first look at how Earth's natural resources are being utilized and how this may be affecting the global environment.

The initial articles in the unit examine the broad dimensions of the uses and abuses of natural resources. The central theme in these articles is whether or not human activity is in fact bringing about fundamental changes in the functioning of Earth's self-regulating ecological systems. In many cases an unsustainable rate of usage is under way, and, as a consequence, an alarming decline in the quality of the natural resource base is taking place.

An important conclusion resulting from this analysis is that contemporary methods of resource utilization often create problems that transcend national boundaries. Global climate changes, for example, will affect everyone, and if these changes are to be successfully addressed, international collaboration will be required. The consequences of basic human activities such as growing and cooking food are profound when multiplied billions of times every day. A single country or even a few countries working together cannot have a significant impact on redressing these problems. Solutions will have to be conceived that are truly global in scope. Just as there are shortages of natural resources, there are also shortages of new ideas for solving many of these problems.

Unit 3 continues by examining specific natural resources. These case studies explore in greater detail new technologies, potential new economic incentives, and the impact that traditional power politics has on how natural resources are developed and for whose benefit.

The unit concludes with a discussion of the issues involved in moving from a perspective of the environment as simply an economic resource to be consumed to a perspective that has been defined as "sustainable development." This change is easily called for, but in fact it goes to the core of social values and basic economic activities. Developing sustainable practices, therefore, is a challenge of unprecedented magnitude.

Nature is not some object "out there" to be visited at a national park. It is the food we eat and the energy we consume. Human beings are joined in the most intimate of relationships with the natural world in order to survive from one day to the next. It is ironic how little time is spent thinking about this relationship. This lack of attention, however, is not likely to continue, for rapidly growing numbers of people and the increased use of energy-consuming technologies are placing unprecedented pressures on Earth's carrying capacity.

The Global Challenge

Circulating freely around the planet, the atmosphere and oceans are shared resources whose resiliency is being tested by ever-growing human demands.

MICHAEL H. GLANTZ

The atmosphere and the oceans are fluids that encircle the globe. Their movements can be described in physical and mathematical terms, or even by some popular adages: "what goes up, must come down" and "what goes around, comes around."

The atmosphere and oceans are two of Earth's truly global commons. In cycles that vary from days to centuries to millions of years, air and water circulate interactively around the globe irrespective of national boundaries and territorial claims.

With regard to the first adage, pollutants emitted into the atmosphere must come down somewhere on Earth's surface—unless, like the chlorofluorocarbons (CFCs), they can escape into the stratosphere until they are broken down by the Sun's rays. Depending on the form of the pollutant (gaseous or particulate), its size, or the height at which it has been ejected into the atmosphere, it can stay airborne for short or long periods. So, pollutants expelled into the air in one country and on one continent may make their way to other countries and continents. The same can be said of the various pollutants that are cast into the ocean. "What goes around, comes around" clearly applies to the global commons.

As human demands on the atmosphere and oceans escalate, the pressures on the commons are clearly increasing. Defining the boundaries between acceptable human impacts and crisis impacts is a demanding and rather subjective task.

The Atmosphere

The atmosphere is owned by no nation, but in a sense it belongs to all nations. Several types of human activity interact with geophysical processes to affect the atmosphere in ways that engender crisis situations. The most obvious example of local effects is urban air pollution resulting from automobile emissions, home heating and cooling, and industrial processes. The Denver "brown cloud" is a case in point, as is the extreme pollution in Mexico City. Such pollution can occur within one political jurisdiction or across state, provincial, or international borders. Air pollution is one of those problems to which almost everyone in the urban area contributes.

Acid rain is an example of pollution of a regional atmospheric commons. Industrial processes release pollutants, which can then interact with the atmosphere and be washed out by rainfall. Acid rain has caused the health of forest ecosystems to deteriorate in such locations as the northeastern part of North America, central Europe, and Scandinavia. The trajectories of airborne industrial pollutants moving from highly industrialized areas across these regions have been studied. The data tend to support the contention that while acid rain is a regional commons problem, it is also a problem of global interest.

A nation can put any chemical effluents it deems necessary for its well-being into its own airspace. But then the atmosphere's fluid motion can move those effluents across international borders. The purpose of the tall smokestack, for example, was to put effluents higher into the air, so they would be carried away and dispersed farther from their source. The tall stacks, in essence, turned local air pollution problems into regional ones. In many instances, they converted national pollution into an international problem.

Climate as a Global Commons

There is a difference between the atmosphere as a commons and the climate as a commons. Various societies have emitted a wide range of chemicals into the atmosphere, with little understanding of their potential effects on climate. For example, are industrial processes that produce large amounts of carbon dioxide

This article originally appeared in *The World & I*, April 1997, pp. 24-31. Reprinted by permission of *The World & I*, a publication of The Washington Times Corporation. © 1997.

(which contributes to atmospheric warming) or sulfur dioxide (which contributes to atmospheric cooling and acid rain) altering global climate? There seems to be a growing consensus among scientists that these alterations manifest themselves as regional changes in the frequencies, intensities, and even the location of extreme events such as droughts and floods.

Not all pollutants emitted in the air have an impact on the global climate system. But scientists have long known that some gases can affect global climate patterns by interacting with sunlight or the heat radiated from Earth's surface. Emission of such gases, especially CO_2, can result from human activities such as the burning of fossil fuels, tropical deforestation, and food production processes. The amount of CO_2 in the atmosphere has increased considerably since the mid 1700s and is likely to double the preindustrial level by the year 2050. Carbon dioxide is a highly effective greenhouse gas. Other greenhouse gases emitted to the atmosphere as a result of human activities include CFCs (used as refrigerants, foam-blowing agents, and cleansers for electronic components), nitrous oxide (used in fertilizers), and methane (emitted during rice production). Of these trace gases, the CFCs are produced by industrial processes alone; and others are produced by both industrial and natural processes.

The increase in greenhouse gases during the past two centuries has resulted primarily from industrial processes in which fossil fuels are burned. Thus, a large proportion of the greenhouse gases produced by human activity has resulted from economic development in the industrialized countries (a fact that developing countries are not reluctant to mention when discussing the global warming issue).

National leaders around the globe are concerned about the issue of climate change. Mandatory international limits on the emissions of greenhouse gases could substantially affect their own energy policies. Today, there are scientific and diplomatic efforts to better understand and deal with the prospects of global atmospheric warming and its possible impacts on society. Many countries have, for a variety of motives, agreed that there are reasons to limit greenhouse gas emissions worldwide. National representatives of the Conference of Parties meet each year to address this concern. In the meantime, few countries, if any, want to forgo economic development to avoid a global environmental problem that is still surrounded by scientific uncertainty.

The Oceans

The oceans represent another truly global commons. Most governments have accepted this as fact by supporting the Law of the Sea Treaty, which notes that the seas, which cover almost 70 percent of Earth's surface, are "the common heritage of mankind." In the early 1940s, Athelstan Spilhaus made a projection map that clearly shows that the world's oceans are really subcomponents of one global ocean.

There are at least three commons-related issues concerning the oceans: pollution, fisheries, and sea level. Problems and possible crises have been identified in each area.

The oceans are the ultimate sink for pollutants. Whether they come from the land or the atmosphere, they are likely to end up in the oceans. But no one really owns the oceans, and coastal countries supervise only bits and pieces of the planet's coastal waters. This becomes a truly global commons problem, as currents carry pollutants from the waters of one country into the waters of others. While there are many rules and regulations governing pollution of the oceans, enforcement is quite difficult. Outside a country's 200-mile exclusive economic zone are the high seas, which are under the jurisdiction of no single country.

In many parts of the world, fisheries represent a common property resource. The oceans provide many countries with protein for domestic food consumption or export. Obtaining the same amount of protein from the land would require that an enormous additional amount of the land's surface be put into agricultural production. Whether under the jurisdiction of one country, several countries, or no country at all, fish populations have often been exploited with incomplete understanding of the causes of variability in their numbers. As a result, most fish stocks that have been commercially sought after have collapsed under the combined pressures of natural variability in the physical environment, population dynamics, and fish catches. This is clearly a serious problem; many perceive it to be a crisis.

Bound Together by Air and Water

- "What goes up must come down" describes the fate of most pollutants ejected into the atmosphere. Taller smokestacks were used to assure that the pollutants did not come down "in my backyard."
- Fish stocks that naturally straddle the boundary between a country's protected zone and the open seas are a global resource requiring international protection measures.
- Sea level in all parts of the world would quickly rise some 8 meters (26 feet) if the vast West Antarctic ice sheet broke away and slid into the sea.
- Scientific controversy still surrounds the notion that human activities can produce enough greenhouse gases to warm the global atmosphere.

For example, an area in the Bering Sea known as the "Donut Hole" had, until recently, also been suffering from overexploitation of pollack stocks. In the midst of the Bering Sea, outside the coastal zones and jurisdictions of the United States and Russia, there is an open-access area that is subject to laws related to the high seas, a truly global commons. Fishermen from Japan and other countries were overexploiting the pollack in this area. But these stocks were part of the same population that also lived in the protected coastal waters of the United States and Russia. In other words, the pollack population was a straddling stock—it straddled the border between the controlled coastal waters and the high seas.

To protect pollack throughout the sea by limiting its exploitation, the two coastal states took responsibility for protecting the commons (namely, the Donut Hole) without having to nationalize it. They did so by threatening to close the Bering Sea to "outsiders," if the outsiders were unable to control their own exploitation of the commonly shared pollack stock. There are several other examples of the overexploitation of straddling stocks, such as the recent collapse of the cod fishery along the Georges Bank in the North Atlantic.

Another commons-related issue is the sea level rise that could result from global warming of the atmosphere. Whereas global warming, if it were to occur, could change rainfall and temperature patterns in yet-unknown ways both locally and regionally, sea level rise will occur everywhere, endangering low-lying coastal areas worldwide. Compounding the problem is the fact that the sea is also an attractor of human populations. For example, about 60 percent of the U.S. population lives within a hundred miles of the coast.

In many parts of the world, fisheries represent a common property resource.

This would truly be a global commons problem because *all* coastal areas and adjoining estuaries would suffer from the consequences of global warming. Concern about sea level rise is highest among the world's small island states, many of which (e.g., the Maldives) are at risk of becoming submerged even with a modest increase in sea level. In sum, there are no winners among coastal states if sea level rises.

Antarctica always appears on the list of global commons. Although it is outside the jurisdiction of any country, some people have questioned its classification as a global commons. It is a fixed piece of territory with no indigenous human population, aside from scientific visitors. It does have a clear link to the oceans as a global commons, however. One key concern about global warming is the possible disintegration of the West Antarctic ice sheet. Unlike Arctic sea ice, which sits in water, the West Antarctic ice sheet would cause sea level to rise an estimated eight meters if it broke away and fell into the Southern Ocean. Viewed from this perspective, the continent clearly belongs on the list of global commons. It is up to the global community to protect it from the adverse influences of human activities occurring elsewhere on the globe.

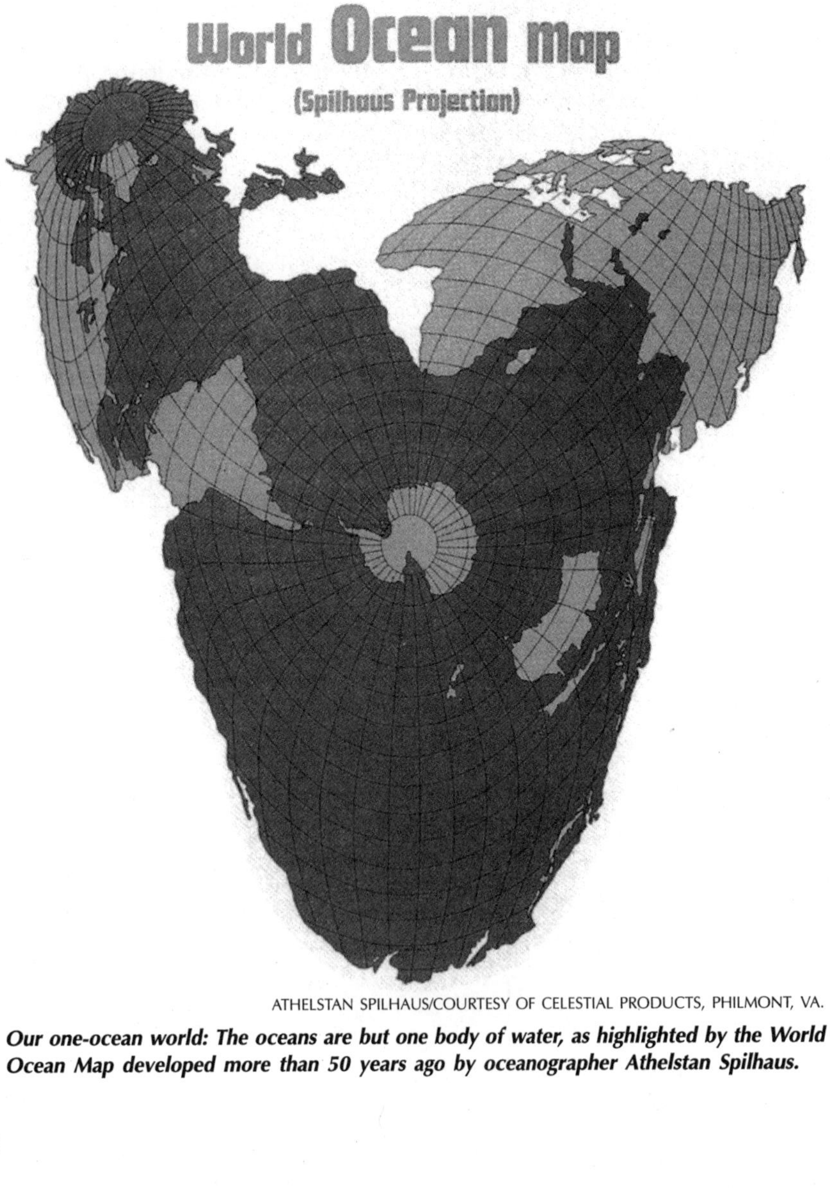

ATHELSTAN SPILHAUS/COURTESY OF CELESTIAL PRODUCTS, PHILMONT, VA.

Our one-ocean world: The oceans are but one body of water, as highlighted by the World Ocean Map developed more than 50 years ago by oceanographer Athelstan Spilhaus.

What's the Problem?

Are the changes in the atmosphere and oceans really problems? And if so, are they serious enough to be considered crises?

The consequences of the greenhouse effect are matters that scientists speculate about. But changes in the environment are taking place *now.* These changes are mostly incremental: low-grade, slow-onset, long-term, but gradually accumulating. They can be referred to as "creeping environmental problems." Daily changes in the environment are not noticed, and today's environment is not much different from yesterday's. In 5 or 10 years, however, those incremental changes can mount into a major environmental crisis [see "Creeping Environmental Problems," The World & I, June 1994, p. 218].

Just about every environmental change featuring human involvement is of the creeping kind. Examples include air pollution, acid rain, global warming, ozone depletion, tropical deforestation, water pollution, and nuclear waste accumulation. For many such changes, the threshold of irreversible damage is difficult to identify until it has been crossed. It seems that we can recognize the threshold only by the consequences that become manifest after we have crossed it. With regard to increasing amounts of atmospheric carbon dioxide, what is the critical threshold beyond which major changes in the global climate system might be expected? Although scientists regularly refer to a doubling of CO_2 from preindustrial levels, the truth of the matter is that a doubling really has little scientific significance except that it has been selected as some sort of marker or milestone.

In 5 or 10 years incremental changes can mount into a major environmental crisis.

Policymakers in industrialized and developing countries alike lack a good process for dealing with creeping environmental changes. As a result, they often delay action on such changes in favor of dealing with issues that seem more pressing. Creeping environmental problems tend to be put on the back burner; that is, they are ignored until they have emerged as full-blown crises. The ways that individuals and societies deal with slow-onset, incremental adverse changes in the environment are at the root of coping effectively with deterioration and destruction of local to global commons.

Societal concerns about human impacts on commonly owned or commonly exploited resources have been recorded for at least 2,500 years. Aristotle, for example, observed "that which is common to the greatest number has the least care bestowed upon it." How to manage a common property resource, whether it is a piece of land, a fish population, a body of water, the atmosphere, or outer space, will likely confound decisionmakers well into the future.

Michael H. Glantz is program director of the Environmental and Societal Impacts Group at the National Center for Atmospheric Research (NCAR) in Boulder, Colorado. NCAR is sponsored by the National Science Foundation.

CLIMATIC CHANGES THAT MAKE THE WORLD FLIP

Robert Matthews

Global warming's impact on the environment is not necessarily a drawn-out affair. Recent evidence shows that dramatic changes or 'climatic flips' could happen virtually overnight.

The once-green land of Ireland turned into a frozen wilderness. Harp seals swimming among ice-floes off the coast of France. Polar bears prowling the streets of Amsterdam. These are the images conjured up by the latest research into global warming.

Yes, you read that correctly: global warming—the rise in the world's average temperature caused by the trapping of the sun's heat by pollution in the atmosphere.

If you are baffled by that, then prepare to be shocked. For the same research is now suggesting that such dramatic changes in the climate of northern Europe could take place in as few as 10 years.

Again, this figure is not a misprint: no zero has gone missing. Scientists have recently uncovered compelling evidence that global warming can have a devastating impact on timescales far shorter than anyone believed possible. Not centuries, not even decades, but years, in what are being called "climatic flips". One leading expert has recently gone on record to warn that some north Atlantic countries could find themselves plunged into Arctic conditions over the space of just 10 years.

Risk of sudden upheaval

In geological terms, that is as fast as the blink of an eye. But even in human terms, such a rate of climatic change is incredibly—and quite probably intolerably—rapid. It is far from clear whether any economy or agricultural system could cope with such sudden upheaval.

By analysing icy sediments (ice-cores) extracted from deep beneath the earth's surface scientists can plot the course of climate change thousands of years ago.

Yet evidence is now mounting that such "climatic flips" not only can happen, but have happened in the past. It is evidence that adds new urgency to the global warming debate, which has lost much of its momentum in recent

Science correspondent of the London *Sunday Telegraph*

Reprinted with permission from the *Unesco Courier*, November 1999, pp. 10-13.

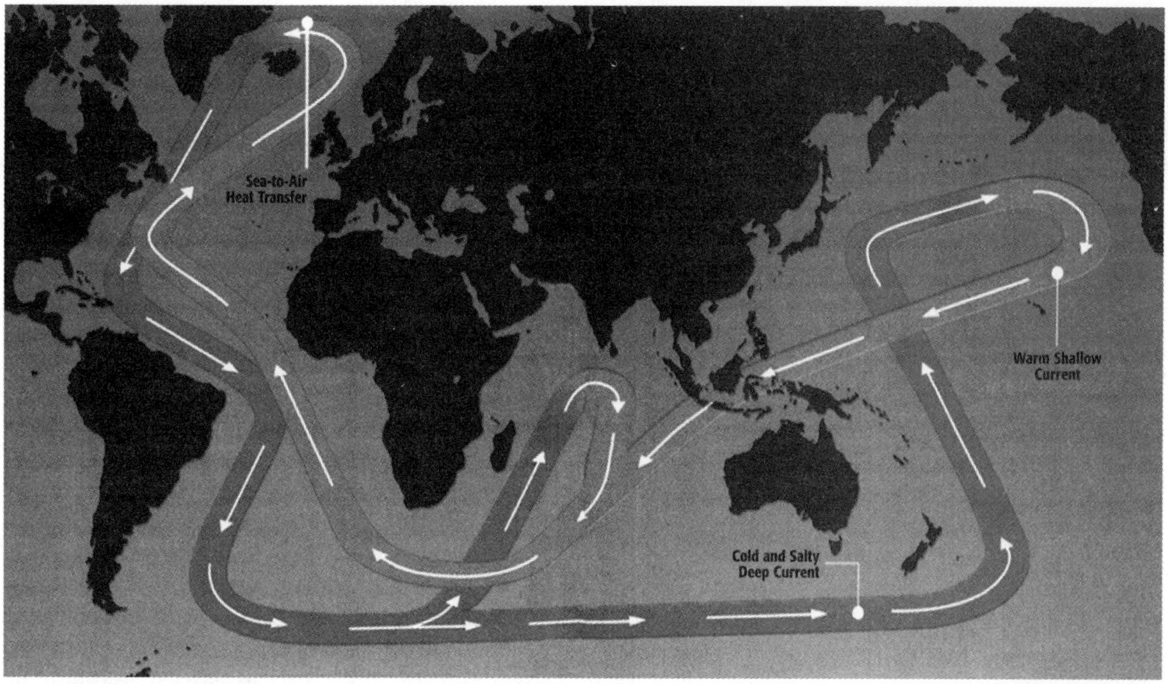

© WOCE, Southampton

Ocean currents continually transport heat around the globe like a liquid conveyor belt. Above, simplified chart of the circulation process.

years. It also highlights the frightening complexity of the task facing scientists trying to predict the earth's response to human activity.

Arguments about climatic change typically focus on how increasing levels of so-called greenhouse gases—principally carbon dioxide from burning fossil fuels—in the earth's atmosphere trap ever more of the sun's heat.

Huge efforts have been put into predicting the likely global temperature rise caused by the extra greenhouse gases, and current best estimates point to a rise of 1.5 degrees Celsius or so over the next century.

But while scientists warn that even so apparently small a rise in temperature could cause upheaval in everything from agricultural practices to the spread of disease, the *rate* of change hardly seems terrifying. Surely we can cope and have coped with events that change over several generations?

Such arguments are buttressed by another, apparently compelling, argument against rapid climate change. The earth's oceans have colossal thermal inertia, and would surely iron out any sudden upheaval: weight for weight, it takes ten times more energy to heat water than it does solid iron.

Small wonder, then, that scientists were unsurprised when they failed to find any signs of rapid climatic changes when they first studied ancient ocean sediments, the isotope levels of which retain a record of past temperatures.

The end of the Ice Age: a puzzling discovery

But this apparently comforting confluence of theory and data is now known to contain two huge loopholes. The first reared its head in the early 1980s, when a joint U.S.-European team of scientists working in Greenland made a puzzling discovery. They had extracted an ice-core from a site in the southern part of the country, and had measured isotope levels in the gas trapped at different depths in an attempt to gauge the temperature in the region over thousands of years.

Because the ice builds up relatively rapidly, the ice-core was expected to give the researchers the most fine-detailed picture yet of temperature changes in the region. Plotting out the corresponding temperatures, the researchers discovered something puzzling and disturbing.

As expected, the core showed the rise in temperature corresponding to the end of the last Ice Age around 11,000 years ago. But it also showed that the bulk of that warm-up had taken place in the space of just 40 years.

At the time, no one knew what to make of the result, which flew in the face of everything scientists then knew about climate change—or thought they knew. In the years that followed, however, further ice-cores were extracted, and they revealed an even more dramatic story: a 5- to 10-degree increase in temperature and doubling of precipitation over Greenland in the space of just 20 years.

Nothing in the earlier ocean sediment core data had prepared scientists for such a finding—nor could it. For this was the first loophole in the argument against sudden climatic flips: the absence of evidence from the original ocean sediment cores simply reflected the very broad-brush picture they gave of temperature change. They lacked the detail offered by ice-cores.

The history of science shows that finding evidence for some astonishing phenomenon is often only part of the story. To convince the scientific community at large, the evidence has to be backed up by a more comprehensive explanation.

Prompted by the Greenland findings, scientists have since tracked down locations where ocean sediment builds up fast enough to give a record of temperature comparable in detail to that from the ice-cores. And, sure enough, they reveal the same story of rapid climatic change in locations as far apart as California and India.

The history of science shows that finding evidence for some astonishing phenomenon is often only part of the story. To convince the scientific community at large, the evidence has to be backed up by a more comprehensive explanation. And for many years the standard explanation for why Ice Ages begin and end provided yet more reasons for thinking all climatic change must be slow and graceful.

That explanation rests on work by a Serbian scientist named Milutin Milankovitch, who in 1920 linked Ice Ages to changes in the shape of the earth's orbit. Caused by the push and pull of the other planets, these orbital changes altered the concentration of sunlight reaching the planet. Such changes would naturally take place very gradually, on time-scales of many thousands of years—a recipe for climatic change that is anything but abrupt.

A global heat transporter

Yet, once again, there is a loophole in this comforting argument—as Wallace Broecker of Columbia University, New York State, realized around the time climate experts were puzzling over the ice-core data.

This loophole centres on a very specific feature of the earth's oceans: their circulation patterns. Ocean currents transport heat around the globe like a vast conveyor belt. In the Atlantic, for example, warm water travels northwards from the Gulf of Mexico, passing its heat to the air by evaporation as it goes. This makes the current progressively cooler, saltier and denser until eventually, near Iceland, the water is so heavy that it sinks, and begins a long journey southward, along the ocean floor.

Broecker realized that this complex, subtle process—which he called "The Conveyor"—could be the Achilles heel of the earth's climate, allowing subtle changes to be turned into dramatic upheaval. For instead of having to alter the whole body of the oceans, just a small change in temperature might be enough to alter the behaviour of the Conveyor—and trigger radical and rapid climatic change over a large area.

For example, gradually melting ice from the Arctic could dilute the saltiness of the Conveyor to a critical density where it no longer sinks and begins its journey southward to pick up more heat. The Conveyor would, in effect, be switched off, isolating the north Atlantic from the warming waters of the tropics.The result would then be distinctly paradoxical, with a slight warming of the Arctic causing temperatures of north Atlantic countries to plunge.

Broecker's explanation is now widely believed to lie at the heart of rapid climate change in the past. Worryingly, however, global warming is predicted to have precisely the type of warming effect on the Arctic ice that threatens the existence of the Conveyor. Computer projections of the effect of pollution on global temperatures predict an inflow of cold, fresh water into the northern Atlantic—water that could dilute the Conveyor enough to switch it off.

The Achilles heel of the earth's climate

If that happened, says Broecker, winter temperatures in the north Atlantic region would fall by 10 or more degrees Celsius within 10 years, giving places like Dublin the climate of Spitsbergen, 400 km north of the Arctic Circle. "The consequences could be devastating," he says.

It is a scenario that gains credibility from ice-core data, according to climate expert Kendrick Taylor of the Desert Research Institute in Reno, Nevada. He says that many cores suggest that around 8,000 years ago there was a sudden plunge back to a "mini Ice Age" which lasted around 400 years. The most likely cause, says Taylor, was the release of melted ice-water from lakes in Canada into the Atlantic, which switched off the heat-transporting Conveyor.

"The change in freshwater flux to the oceans was large, but not that much different from what greenhouse-induced changes may produce in the future," he said in a recent paper in American Scientist. "It is ironic that greenhouse warming may lead to rapid cooling in eastern Northern America, Europe and Scandinavia."

So just how close is the Conveyor to switching off once again?The short answer is: no one knows. Computer models have still to identify the critical density of seawater at which the Conveyor will switch off, or the greenhouse gas concentrations needed to release the requisite amount of melt-water.

Cutting pollution buys time

What computer models have shown, says Taylor, is that reducing pollution emissions buys time—both by slowing the rate of global warming, and also by driving the climate more gently, which seems to increase its stability against rapid change.

But while scientists struggle to capture the full complexity of the climate on their supercomputers, evidence of other causes of dramatic climate change is beginning to emerge.

Last July, Professor Martin Claussen and his colleagues at the Potsdam Institute for Climate Science, Germany, reported evidence that today's Sahara desert was created in a sudden climatic "flip" that took place just 5,500 years ago, turning vast areas of lush grassland into an arid wilderness and devastating ancient civilizations.

Using a sophisticated computer model of the land, sea and atmosphere, the team has discovered just how subtle are some of the effects that can turn Milankovitch-style changes in the earth's orbit into major climate upheaval.

A MUDDY MYSTERY

The effects that scientists now believe can shape the earth's climate are astonishingly subtle, and one of the most bizarre centres on the connection between Ice Ages, earthquakes, and mud.

Last year a team from the Southampton Oceanography Centre in Britain announced in the journal *Nature* the discovery of a 450-billion-cubic-metre deposit on the sea-floor off the coast of Sardinia—the aftermath of a truly enormous slide of mud: enough to engulf the whole of France to a depth of a metre.

Carbon dating of the plankton above and below the mud bed suggest that the slide took place around 20,000 years ago—at the height of the last Ice Age. This was a time when so much water had been turned to ice that sea-levels were 120 metres lower than they are today—a fact that the team suspects is crucial to the cause of the colossal mudslide.

Formed out of thousands of years of river deposits, the mud would have been rich in organic matter—material that rots to produce huge amounts of methane gas. Normally this gas would have been locked into the mud by the huge pressure of sea-water lying over the submerged sediments. But as the Ice Age deepened and sea-levels fell, the mud deposits would find themselves exposed, and thus able to release their pent-up methane gas.

This gas is a very potent source of global warming, and the sudden release of huge amounts of it might have helped push the earth back out of the Ice Age.

Certainly the timing of the Sardinian mudslide—at the height of the last Ice Age—is intriguing, says team member professor Euan Nisbet of London's Royal Holloway College: "It is possible that a big slide could have released enough methane to act as a warming trigger."

It is an idea that has gained strength from a recent discovery by researchers at Duke University in North Carolina. In a paper also published in *Nature* last year, they argue that the sheer weight of ice pressing down on the earth's crust may have triggered huge earthquakes during the Ice Age.

Could these have triggered massive submarine mudslides, releasing methane that led to the end of Ice Age? As yet, no one knows. But it points to yet another astonishingly subtle link between the environment, climate—and us.

The Sahara's quick-change act

They found that over the last 9,000 years the gravitational pull of the planets has altered the tilt of the earth's axis by about half a degree, and changed the timing of earth's closest approach to the sun by around five months.

'The change in freshwater flux to the oceans was large, but not that much different from what greenhouse-induced changes may produce in the future. It is ironic that greenhouse warming may lead to rapid cooling in eastern Northern America, Europe and Scandinavia'

By themselves, such subtle changes should not cause major climatic effects. But when Claussen and his colleagues included the effect of vegetation in their computer model, they found that it caused rainfall levels to plummet over the Sahara region.

They traced the cause to "feedback" effects, in which a slight drop in vegetation level makes the earth's surface slightly better at reflecting sunlight, which causes rainfall levels to drop—prompting more vegetation loss, and so on.

According to Claussen, these feedback effects turned the vast, once-green Sahara into a brown wasteland within just 300 years. "It was the largest change in land cover during the last 6,000 years," he says. "It was very severe, ruining ancient civilizations."

The discovery is likely to force historians to rethink their explanations of events in the region. For according to Claussen, it contradicts the long-held belief that the collapse of agriculture in the region was caused by ancient farmers exhausting the soil: "Although humans lived in the Sahara and used the land to some extent, we think that ancient land use played only a negligibly small role."

The findings are also being seen as another warning of just how unstable even today's climate may be. "It is capable of changing very abruptly," says climate expert Andrew Goudie of Oxford University. "We've known that the extent of the Sahara has yo-yoed back and forwards for millions of years, and that about 8,000 years ago it was much wetter than today, with big rivers feeding into the Nile. But I hadn't realized just how rapid the change-over had been. It is salutary."

Temperature nose-dives

Also in July, a team of researchers from the universities of Illinois and Minnesota reported the discovery of another climatic "flip" in the northern hemisphere around 9,000 years ago, which temporarily plunged the region back into an Ice Age.

Using lake sediments from Minnesota, the team confirmed the existence of the cold snap around 8,200 years ago, as revealed by the ice core data. But they also found evidence for another dive in temperatures around 8,300 to 8,900 years ago. The team thinks this older cold snap was linked to the release of melted ice from lakes into the Atlantic—which may have switched off the Conveyor. But the researchers now think that the more recent flip most likely had another—and as yet unknown—origin.

What is clear is that until we know much more about the complexity of climate change, all bets about how much time we have to take action are definitely off. What evidence we do have increasingly points to the stark possibility that we may have far less time than we thought.

"I used to believe that change in climate happened slowly and would never affect me," admits Taylor. "Now I know that our climate could change significantly in my lifetime."

The Energy Question, Again

"Abundant, inexpensive, and reliable energy is taken for granted, and the citizens of rich countries seem to expect this to continue indefinitely. Reality is different: this veritable fairytale is threatened by many changes—some of which are already upon us, others that are discernible on the horizon."

VACLAV SMIL

The twentieth century was the first era dominated by fossil fuels and electricity, and their vastly expanded supply, lower cost, increasing flexibility of use, and ease of control have created the first high-energy civilization in history. This remarkable increase in power at our fingertips has transformed our world. Mechanization and chemization of agriculture have given us a plentiful and varied food supply: more than a fourfold increase in crop productivity during the twentieth century has been made possible by a roughly 150-fold increase of fossil fuels and electricity used directly and indirectly in global cropping.

Increased energy usage also undergirds longer life expectancies (in excess of 70 years throughout the affluent world), the result of better nutrition and medical advances whose dependence on energy inputs, ranging from food pasteurization to vaccine refrigeration, is little noticed. A reliable electricity supply has also created the first instantaneously interconnected global civilization. And inexpensive energy has allowed an unprecedented degree of personal mobility through mass ownership of cars and frequent air travel.

Although our societies are dependent on incessant flows of commercial energies, provision of these critical inputs is not commensurately valued by the supposedly rational markets. Some days the stockmarket value of corporations such as Microsoft or Oracle can reach levels higher than the entire capitalization of such giant energy-supply companies as PG&E or Consolidated Edison—yet the former enterprises cannot exist without the latter.

If the markets work this way, it is hardly surprising that our dependence on massive energy flows goes largely unnoticed. Abundant, inexpensive, and reliable energy is taken for granted, and the citizens of rich countries seem to expect this to continue indefinitely. Reality is different: this veritable fairytale is threatened by many changes—some of which are already upon us, others that are discernible on the horizon. Consequently, any appraisal of a civilization's outlook must include a closer examination of its changing energy affairs.

THE REVOLUTION IN ENERGY USE

At the beginning of the twentieth century, most people did not use fossil fuels, although in the United States average per capita primary consumption of coal and oil (and some hydroelectricity) already amounted to about 2.5 tons of oil equivalent (TOE). Yet much of this energy was wasted. After subtracting conversion losses—over 99 percent in early carbon-filament lightbulbs, 95 percent in steam locomotives, and about 80 percent in coal stoves—useful energy providing the desired services (light, locomotion, and heat) was less than 0.5 TOE.

At the century's end, the global consumption of primary commercial energies (coal, oil, natural gas, and hydro and nuclear electricity) has increased sixteenfold, with average annual per capita supply of commercial energy more than quadrupling to about 1.4 TOE. The flow of useful energy has increased dramatically because of higher efficiencies in traditional energy converters and new machines and devices introduced during the century. Today's best lighting is almost 20 percent efficient, while converters ranging from large electric motors to natural gas-fired furnaces have efficiencies in excess of 90 percent.

Consequently, affluent countries have experienced eight- to twelvefold increases in the per capita supply of useful energy during the twentieth century, and the gain has been twenty- or even thirtyfold in many low-income countries undergoing rapid modernization. This conservative calculation indicates that the world now has at its disposal about 25 times more useful commercial energy than it did in 1900, or more than eight times as much in per capita terms. And this energy now derives mostly from forms that are much more convenient to use than wood or coal, with hydrocarbons (crude oils and natural gases) supplying roughly two-thirds of the total. In rich countries coal now has just two markets: a small one for the production of metallurgical coke, and a large one for electricity generation.

The expanding use of electricity has been another key mark of twentieth-century progress. In 1900 less than 2 percent of the world's fossil-fuel output was converted to electricity; in 2000 the share surpassed 30 percent. Electricity is the preferred form of energy because of its high efficiency, instant and effortless access, perfect and easily adjustable flow, cleanliness, and silence at the point of use. In addition to revolutionizing industrial production and services, electricity has helped implement profound social changes by easing household chores through mass ownership of various appliances and by allowing instant global communication. And it has become an incredible bargain: after factoring in higher disposable incomes and improved conversion efficiencies, a unit of useful electrical service in the United States is as much as 600 times more affordable than it was a century ago.

Contrasts between energy flows that are now routinely controlled by millions of individuals, especially when compared to the experiences of their great-grandparents, provide more stunning illustrations of the expanded use of energy. In 1900 a fairly affluent American urban housewife could turn on inefficient, low-power bulbs whose power totaled less than 500 watts. Today's all-electric suburban house has scores of lights and appliances whose installed power capacity can exceed 30 kilowatts, a seventy- to eightyfold increase from 1900.

At the beginning of the twentieth century, a farmer holding the reins of two good horses and perched on a steel seat while plowing his field controlled a sustained delivery of no more than 2 horsepower. A hundred years later his grandson driving a large tractor while sitting in an upholstered, elevated, and air-conditioned cabin effortlessly controls more than 300 horsepower. Moreover, in 1900 an engineer operating a transcontinental locomotive controlled no more than about 1 megawatt, or roughly 1,340 horsepower, of steam power as the machine traveled at 60 miles an hour (100 km/h). Today a pilot of a Boeing 747 on the same route merely watches a computerized discharge of about 120 megawatts (more than 160,000 horsepower) as the jumbo jet cruises at 560 miles an hour (900 km/h) some 9 miles (11 km) above the ground.

Reasons for Concern

As the twenty-first century dawns, the last century's focus on achieving greater and more efficient use of energy will give way to heightened concern about global energy matters, especially in the next 10 to 20 years. First is the challenge of rising energy demand, particularly for hydrocarbons and electricity. The 1990s showed that consumption appears to be insatiable even in those rich nations that are already by far the largest users and importers of energy. Between 1989 and 1999, energy consumption rose about 15 percent in the United States, 17 percent in France, and 19 percent in Australia; despite a stagnating, even declining, economy, it expanded 24 percent in Japan. This trend has been driven almost completely by private consumption: industries and services have generally reduced energy use per dollar of their final products, but increased travel, larger homes equipped with more appliances, and higher consumer spending have pushed energy use to record levels.

Although nearly all these countries have low population growth, other realities—including mass immigration to both North America and Europe; profligate, debt-driven spending; and widespread emotional attachment to cars as extensions of personality—will promote higher demand for fuels and electricity. In most of the populous low-income countries whose potential energy demands amount to large multiples of current use, growth in energy consumption has recently been at least as high as, or higher than, that of the richer nations, although they remain far behind in relative consumption. Nothing indicates this better than international comparisons: North America's energy consumption mean is now about 8 TOE per capita, and the European average is approximately 4 TOE—but China's mean is 0.6, India's less than 0.3, and Bangladesh's not even 0.1 TOE. Long-term forecasts of energy use have been notoriously poor, but even conservative predictions see a 50 percent increase in the global primary energy consumption by 2020.

Satisfying the world's energy demand thus will be more challenging than in the past—and the task may become more difficult because of a widely anticipated decline in global crude oil production during the next 20 years, and because unequivocal indications of potentially serious global warming may become apparent. The first scenario would likely lead the Organization of Petroleum Exporting Countries (OPEC) to once again take control of the world oil market, a momentous change with implications ranging from much higher energy prices to the possibility of a dangerous escalation of geopolitical contests in the Middle East. Consequences of planetary climate change attributable largely to the generation of greenhouse gases from the combustion of fossil fuels can be foreseen only in qualitative terms: confident quantification of numerous impacts remains elusive.

Another concern is the absence of any commercially available and effective technical fixes to deal with these challenges: the dual task of securing expanded energy needs while reducing fossil-fuel dependence has no simple solution. Finally, there appears to be both an incomprehensible lack of urgency on the part of policymakers and the public in dealing with these realities and an institutional incapacity to make effective, no-regret decisions and to pursue long-range energy policies.

The affluent, high-energy nations and the low-income, low-energy modernizing countries thus appear to be at major, and very messy, energy crossroads: we obviously cannot proceed as we have for generations, but this retrospection does not point to any obvious, all-embracing solution. Unsure of what combination of new goals to follow, both governments and individuals prefer the delusions of an indefinite extension of the status quo to the pursuit of many effective, readily available measures that could help with the truly global task of ensuring adequate energy supply while minimizing its environmental impacts.

The coming oil crisis

Recent forecasts of an imminent decline of global oil extraction are just the latest additions to a long list of predictions of the end of the oil era. Previous forecasts proved wrong because the timing of this event depends not only on the little-known quantity of ultimately recoverable crude oil resources but also on the future rates of demand growth, which are determined by a complex interplay of energy substitutions, technical advances, government policies, and environmental considerations. For example, excessive concern about supply would be unnecessary if the gradual decline in production following the not-too distant peak of the global oil output would be more than compensated by cheap natural gas and a rapid diffusion of photovoltaics, which directly convert solar radiation to electricity. But natural gas may not be available for all desired substitutions, its prices are bound to increase, and photovoltaics are still far from being in the mainstream of commercial energy supply.

Unfortunately, several trends point to high probability of yet another oil crisis whose impact may be even greater than that of the oil crisis of 1973–1974 (OPEC's quintupling of prices from about $2 a barrel to just over $11 a barrel) and 1979–1980 (when the Iranian monarchy's 1979 collapse drove average prices up to $35 a barrel by 1981). OPEC's powers eventually were undercut by reduced energy consumption in rich countries and by the development of new, non-OPEC supplies. The cartel produced about 56 percent of all crude oil in 1973—but only 29 percent by 1985. Both these trends have changed. Global crude oil demand rose nearly 12 percent during the 1990s, and modernizing countries currently are putting a new strain on the export market. China, for decades self-sufficient in oil (and even a small oil exporter), became a net importer of petroleum and refined products in 1993; its imports in 2000 nearly doubled to 70 million tons, and conservative forecasts see purchases of 100 million tons by 2005 (only the United States and Japan would be larger oil importers).

Not surprisingly, OPEC's share of global crude oil output is back to over 40 percent, and increased extraction aimed at a temporary stabilization of rising prices, the absence of any major new non-OPEC supplies ready for immediate production, and the collapse of extraction in the countries of the former Soviet Union (by 2000 their 20 percent share of the world output had been halved) make it very likely that OPEC's share of the world oil market will once again

The United States now imports more than 20 percent of its total primary energy use, and almost 60 percent of all liquid fuels.

rise above 50 percent before 2010 (the cartel expects at least 46 percent by that time). Of even greater concern is the increasing share of OPEC exports that will be coming from its Middle Eastern member states, all Muslim and most either overtly anti-Western or only opportunistically friendly.[1] The stage thus is being set for a third round of sudden oil price increases and their unpredictable economic and geopolitical consequences. Recent increases in crude oil to almost $40 a barrel can be seen as a mere trial run of developments to come.

A no-regret strategy

It now appears increasingly unlikely that even an unlimited flow of cheap oil or inexpensive natural gas would allow the multiplication of future fossil-fuel use comparable to twentieth-century expansion. Although the complexities of global climate change preclude any confident quantitative forecasts, rising atmospheric levels of anthropogenic greenhouse gases may already be changing the earth's climate—and global warming conceivably could increase at an unprecedented rate during the twenty-first century, resulting in an unpredictable range of biospheric, economic, social, and political impacts.

These inherent uncertainties have made it easy to turn the debate about global climate change into pointless arguments about the actual extent and rate of future warming and about the magnitude of net losses (or even benefits) arising from that change. This is a counterproductive approach. Faced with such uncertainties, the only responsible way to act is as risk minimizers and to take bold steps to reduce greenhouse gas emissions: such a course makes perfect sense even if global warming eventually did not to occur, or if it proved to be a tolerable change. The no-regret strategy of reduced energy consumption in production and households, more efficient fossil-fuel use, the substitution of coal with natural gases, and the introduction of appropriate nonfossil-fuel conversions would cut greenhouse gas emissions and reduce photochemical smog, acid deposition, water pollution, and land degradation.

The high frequency and high levels of photochemical smog that now prevail in all the world's large cities—Atlanta or Athens, Bangkok or Beijing, Taipei or Toronto—have effects that have spilled to surrounding regions. High levels of ozone, the most aggressive oxidant in photochemical smog, have contributed to the worldwide epidemic of asthma and to higher respiratory mortality; ozone also has reduced crop yields, especially in the United States and China.

During the past two decades, emissions of acidifying sulfur and nitrogen oxides have been reduced (but far from eliminated) in North America and Europe, but they are increasing in Asia. Growing tanker shipments of crude oil, drilling for and refining hydrocarbons, coal mining, and thermal-electricity generation all result in water pollution. Surface extraction of coal, and infrastructures of fossil-fuel transportation and processing (tanker ports, oil storages, pipelines, refineries, power plants, high-voltage lines) also claim a great deal of land.

A no-regret strategy of reducing our fossil-fuel dependence would ease all these burdens. But despite the potentially immense and long-lasting consequences of global climate change and regardless of the undeniable benefits of reduced smog, acid deposition, and water and land degradation, inadequate progress has been made in this direction. The United States, the world's largest energy consumer, will not meet its Kyoto Treaty obligations requiring it to cut its carbon dioxide output to 7 percent below the 1990 level (this treaty requires the wealthy nations to cut their carbon dioxide emissions below their 1990 levels by 2007). And China, with its modernizing aspirations, refuses to sign any agreement limiting its expansion of fossil-fuel consumption. Two reasons explain this lack of commitment. First, there is no simple, single solution to this challenge of reducing emissions; and there has been an inexplicable absence of determination and commitment to pursue even those obviously effective steps that rely on well-known techniques, proper pricing (heavy subsidies have been common), and effective legislative measures.

Is there a fix?

None of the alternatives to fossil fuels that were extolled during the second half of the twentieth century as perfect solutions to our future energy needs has fulfilled its early promise. Most notably, between the mid-1950s and the early 1970s, many experts were convinced that by 2000 the world's energy use would be dominated by inexpensive nuclear electricity. The nuclear power industry, however, has undergone a dramatic devolution in all but one of the countries that pioneered its rise. Weaker post-1975 demand for electricity, runaway construction costs, safety concerns, and the unresolved problem of long-term disposal of radioactive wastes gradually ended the industry's growth. Public perception of intolerable risks was sealed by the core meltdown and the release of radioactivity during the 1986 disaster at the nuclear power plant in Chernobyl in the former Soviet Union. Although nuclear fission produced about 17 percent of global electricity by 2000 (22 percent in the United States, 70 percent in France), prospects for any major expansion outside China, and perhaps Japan, are very unlikely.

Nor have the "soft" energy sources—small-scale, decentralized conversions of solar radiation (mostly by using photovoltaic cells), biomass (into both liquid and gaseous fuels), and wind, ocean wave, and water flows—made the decisive difference promised by their advocates, who were opposed to nuclear power and fossil fuels. In the United States, these renewable, small-scale energy conversions (excluding large-scale hydro generation) supplied less than 4 percent of all primary energy use during the late 1990s. It is difficult to envisage a scenario where their share would go up four- or fivefold to 15–20 percent during the next two decades.

Prospects for major contributions by soft-energy sources in populous low-income countries are no brighter as rapid urbanization and industrialization of those nations require much-expanded large-scale supplies for the still-growing megacities of 10 to 20 million people, be they Beijing and Cairo, or Mexico City and New Delhi. And it remains highly uncertain how much and how fast large cities will be able to relieve their most pressing environmental problem—high levels of photochemical smog, which causes higher morbidities and mortalities and increases damage to crops and materials—through mass diffusion of low- or non-polluting vehicles.

This technical fix, too, has been tantalizingly close on the approximately ten-year—but always receding—horizon. At least one thing now appears clear: electric cars, promoted as the best solution just a few years ago, have fallen out of favor, and fuel-cell vehicles are now seen as the better option. Although various fuels are under consideration (gasoline, methanol, and hydrogen fuel cells), the initial operating costs of hydrogen-based transportation will be very high, and it is unclear how competitive these cars will be with the already available high-efficiency hybrid drives.

Not acting with foresight

Nearly 30 years ago, the Nixon administration came up with Project Independence, which aimed to make the United States self-sufficient in energy by the 1980s. Unrealistic as that plan was (the United States now imports more than 20 percent of its total primary energy use, and almost 60 percent of all liquid fuels), its framers at least tried to look well ahead. Higher energy prices were the main driving force, but legislative changes of the 1970s were not insignificant. These included better building codes reduced energy consumption in housing, and mandated limits of minimum car-fleet performance—corporate automotive fuel efficiency (CAFE) standards—that more than doubled the average United States rate from just 13.4 miles per gallon (MPG) in 1973 to 27.5 MPG in 1985.

These measures helped break OPEC's power, but the resulting slide in crude oil prices almost instantly stopped any serious effort to shape long-range American energy consumption. CAFE has remained at 27.5 MPG for the past

15 years—and that rate does not apply to sport utility vehicles (SUVS), which are classified as light trucks and commonly get less than 20 MPG. Why is SUV-obsessed America surprised when its falling oil output (down about 15 percent during the 1990s) and the rising gasoline demand (up about 7 percent since 1989) has, as it had to, bumped into OPEC's production ceiling and led to more than a 50 percent increase in gasoline prices in a matter of months?

Perhaps the most touching outcome of this situation was seeing President Bill Clinton beg "friendly" OPEC nations to boost their oil output, and hearing assorted members of Congress talk about the need for long-term energy policy—after the huge SUVS were allowed to gain more than half of the new car market. This absence of any rational policymaking is particularly regrettable in view of what could have been accomplished. Continuation of the 1973–1985 CAFE trend would have by now lifted the rate above 40 MPG—and this performance would still be far below the best technical capacity: the hybrid Honda Insight now delivers 61 MPG in the city and 70 MPG on the highway. Incremental progress to about 40 MPG would have been enough to halve United States crude oil imports and save at least $30 billion annually while greatly reducing photochemical smog and lowering carbon dioxide emissions.

Constructing catastrophic scenarios is easy, and, unfortunately, a combination of relatively rapid anthropogenic global warming, declining global crude oil production, rising rivalry over access to Middle Eastern hydrocarbons, the inability of new energy conversions to fill the growing oil gap, and the continuing refusal to pursue rational long-term solutions makes global warming an uncomfortably high probability. Fortunately, the outcome is still open. Will we act only when energy prices are soaring (as we did between 1973 and 1985), or when an acutely demonstrable environmental risk arises (as we did after the discovery of Antarctic ozone hole when we banned the use of chlorofluorocarbons)? Can only such drastic realities stimulate action—or will we adopt all those readily available, common-sense solutions as a matter of determined, long-range, no-regret energy policy? The fortunes of modern civilization will depend on this choice.

NOTE

1. OPEC states include Saudi Arabia, Kuwait, Iraq, Iran, Qatar, the United Arab Emirates, Libya, Algeria, Nigeria, Venezuela, and Indonesia.

VACLAV SMIL *is Distinguished Professor at the University of Manitoba and the author, most recently, of* Energies *(Cambridge, Mass.: MIT Press, 1997) and* Feeding the World *(Cambridge, Mass.: MIT Press, 2000).*

Invasive Species: Pathogens of Globalization

by Christopher Bright

World trade has become the primary driver of one of the most dangerous and least visible forms of environmental decline: Thousands of foreign, invasive species are hitch-hiking through the global trading network aboard ships, planes, and railroad cars, while hundreds of others are traveling as commodities. The impact of these bioinvasions can now be seen on every landmass, in nearly all coastal waters (which comprise the most biologically productive parts of the oceans), and probably in most major rivers and lakes. This "biological pollution" is degrading ecosystems, threatening public health, and costing billions of dollars annually. Confronting the problem may now be as critical an environmental challenge as reducing global carbon emissions.

Despite such dangers, policies aimed at stopping the spread of invasive "exotic" species have so far been largely ineffective. Not only do they run up against far more powerful policies and interests that in one way or another encourage invasion, but the national and international mechanisms needed to control the spread of non-native species are still relatively undeveloped. Unlike chemical pollution, for instance, bioinvasion is not yet a working category of environmental decline within the legal culture of most countries and international institutions.

In part, this conceptual blindness can be explained by the fact that even badly invaded landscapes can still look healthy. It is also a consequence of the ancient and widespread practice of introducing exotic species for some tangible benefit: A bigger fish makes for better fishing, a faster-growing tree means more wood. It can be difficult to think of these activities as a form of ecological corrosion—even if the fish or the tree ends up demolishing the original natural community.

The increasing integration of the world's economies is rapidly making a bad situation even worse. The continual expansion of world trade—in ways that are not shaped by any real understanding of their environmental effects—is causing a degree of ecological mixing that appears to have no evolutionary precedent. Under more or less natural conditions, the arrival of an entirely new organism was a rare event in most times and places. Today it can happen any time a ship comes into port or an airplane lands. The real problem, in other words, does not lie with the exotic species themselves, but with the economic system that is continually showering them over the Earth's surface. Bioinvasion has become a kind of globalization disease.

They Came, They Bred, They Conquered

Bioinvasion occurs when a species finds its way into an ecosystem where it did not evolve. Most of the time when this happens, conditions are not suitable for the new arrival, and it enjoys only a brief career. But in a small percentage of cases, the exotic finds everything it needs—and nothing capable of controlling it. At the very least, the invading organism is liable to suppress some native species by consuming resources that they would have used instead. At worst, the invader may rewrite some basic ecosystem "rules"—checks and balances that have developed between native species, usually over many millennia.

Although it is not always easy to discern the full extent of havoc that invasive species can wreak upon an ecosystem, the resulting financial damage is becoming increasingly difficult to ignore. Worldwide, the losses to agriculture might be anywhere from $55 billion to nearly $248 billion annually. Researchers at Cornell University recently concluded that bioinvasion might be costing the United States alone as much as $123 billion per year. In South and Central America, the growth of specialty export crops—upscale vegetables and fruits—has spurred the spread of whiteflies, which are capable of transmitting at least 60 plant viruses. The spread of these viruses has forced the abandonment of more than 1 million hectares of cropland in South America. In the wetlands of northern Nigeria, an exotic cattail is strangling rice paddies, ruining fish habitats, and slowly choking off the Hadejia-Nguru river system. In southern India, a tropical American shrub, the bush morning glory, is causing similar chaos throughout the basin of the Cauvery, one of the region's biggest rivers. In the late 1980s, the accidental release into the Black Sea of *Mnemiopsis leidyi*—a comb jelly native to the east coast of the Americas—provoked the collapse of the already highly stressed Black Sea fisheries, with estimated financial losses as high as $350 million.

Controlling such exotics in the field is difficult enough, but the bigger problem is preventing the machinery of the world trading system from releasing them in the first place. That task is becoming steadily more formidable as the trading system continues to grow. Since 1950, world trade has expanded sixfold in terms of value. More important in terms of potential invasions is the vast increase in the volume of goods traded. Look, for instance, at the ship, the primary mechanism of trade—80 percent of the world's goods travel by ship for at least part of their journey from manufacturer to consumer. From 1970 to 1996, the volume of seaborne trade nearly doubled.

Ships, of course, have always carried species from place to place. In the days of sail, shipworms bored into the wooden hulls, while barnacles and seaweeds attached themselves to the sides. A small menagerie of other creatures usually took up residence within these "fouling communities" Today, special paints and rapid crossing times have greatly reduced hull fouling, but each of the 28,700 ships in the world's major merchant fleets represents a honeycomb of potential habitats for all sorts of life, both terrestrial and aquatic.

Controlling invasive species is difficult enough, but the bigger problem is preventing the machinery of the world trading system from releasing them in the first place.

The most important of these habitats lies deep within a modern ship's plumbing, in the ballast tanks. The ballast tanks of a really big ship—say, a supertanker—may contain more than 200,000 cubic meters of water—equivalent to 2,000 Olympic-sized swimming pools. When those tanks are filled, any little creatures in the nearby water or sediment may suddenly become inadvertent passengers. A few days or weeks later, when the tanks are discharged at journey's end, they may become residents of a coastal community on the other side of the world. Every year, these artificial ballast currents move some 10 billion cubic meters of water from port to port. Every day, some 3,000 to 10,000 different species are thought to be riding the ballast currents. The result is a creeping homogenization of estuary and bay life. The same creatures come to dominate one coastline after another, eroding the biological diversity of the planet's coastal zones—and jeopardizing their ecological stability.

Some pathways of invasion extend far beyond ships. Another prime mechanism of trade is the container: the metal box that has revolutionized the transportation of just about every good not shipped in bulk. The container's effect on invasion ecology has been just as profound. For centuries, shipborne exotics were largely confined to port areas—but no longer. Containers move from ship to harbor crane to the flatbed of a truck or railroad car and then on to wherever a road or railroad leads. As a result, all sorts of stowaways that creep aboard containers often wind up far inland. Take the Asian tiger mosquito, for example, which can carry dengue fever, yellow fever, and encephalitis. The huge global trade in containers of used tires—which are, under the right conditions, an ideal mosquito habitat—has dispersed this species from Asia and the Indo-Pacific into Australia, Brazil, the eastern United States, Mozambique, New Zealand, Nigeria, and southern Europe. Even packing material within containers can be a conduit for exotic species. Untreated wood pallets, for example, are to forest pests what tires are to mosquitoes. One creature currently moving along this pathway is the Asian longhorn beetle, a wood-boring insect from China with a lethal appetite for deciduous trees. It has turned up at more than 30 locations around the United States and has also been detected in Great Britain. The only known way to eradicate it is to cut every tree suspected of harboring it, chip all the wood, and burn all the chips.

As other conduits for global trade expand, so does the potential for new invasions. Air cargo service, for example, is building a global network of virtual canals that have great potential for transporting tiny, short-lived creatures such as microbes and insects. In 1989, only three airports received more than 1 million tons of cargo; by 1996, there were 13 such airports. Virtually everywhere you look, the newly constructed infrastructure of the global economy is forming the groundwork for an ever-greater volume of biological pollution.

The Global Supermarket

Bioinvasion cannot simply be attributed to trade in general, since not all trade is "biologically dirty." The natural resource industries—especially agriculture, aquaculture, and forestry—are causing a disproportionate share of the problem. Certain trends within each of these industries are liable to exacerbate the invasion pressure. The migration of crop pests can be attributed, in part, to a global agricultural system that has become increasingly uniform and integrated. (In China, for example, there were about 10,000 varieties of wheat being grown at mid-century; by 1970 there were only about 1,000.) Any new pest—or any new form of an old pest—that emerges in one field may eventually wind up in another.

The key reason that South America has suffered so badly from white-flies, for instance, is because a pesticide-resistant biotype of that fly emerged in California in the 1980s and rapidly became one of the world's most virulent crop pests. The fly's career illustrates a common dynamic: A pest can enter the system, disperse throughout it, and then develop new strains that reinvade other parts of the system. The displacement of traditional developing-world crop varieties by commercial, homogenous varieties that require more pesticide, and the increasing development of pesticide resistance among all the major pest categories—insects, weeds, and fungi—are likely to boost this trend.

Similar problems pertain to aquaculture—the farming and exporting of fish, shellfish, and shrimp. Partly because of the progressive depletion of the world's most productive fishing grounds, aquaculture is a booming business. Farmed fish production exceeded 23 million tons by 1996, more than triple the volume just 12 years before. Developing countries in particular see aquaculture as a way of increasing protein supply.

But many aquaculture "crops" have proved very invasive. In much of the developing world, it is still common to release exotic fish directly into natural waterways. It is hardly surprising, then, that some of the most popular aquaculture fish have become true cosmopolitans. The Mozambique tilapia, for example, is now established in virtually every tropical and subtropical country. Many of these introductions—not just tilapia, but bass, carp, trout, and other types of fish—are implicated in the decline of native species. The constant flow of new introductions catalogued with such enthusiasm in the industry's publications are a virtual guarantee that tropical freshwater ecosystems are unraveling beneath the surface.

Aquaculture is also a spectacularly efficient conduit of disease. Perhaps the most virulent set of wildlife epidemics circling the Earth today involves shrimp production in the developing world. Unlike fish, shrimp are not a subsistence crop: They are an extremely lucrative export business that has led to the bulldozing of many tropical coasts to make way for shrimp ponds. One of the biggest current developments is an Indonesian operation that may eventually cover 200,000 hectares. A horde of shrimp pathogens—everything from viruses to protozoa—is chasing these operations, knocking out ponds, an occasionally ruining entire national shrimp industries: in Taiwan in 1987, in China in 1993, and in India in 1994. Shrimp farming has become, in effect, a form of "managed invasion." Since shrimp are important components of both marine and freshwater ecosystems worldwide, it is anybody's guess at this point what impact shrimpborne pathogens will ultimately have.

Managed invasion is an increasingly common procedure in another big biopolluting industry: forestry. Industrial roundwood production (basically, the cutting of logs for uses other than fuel) currently hovers at around 1.5 billion cubic meters annually, which is more than twice the level of the 1950s. An increasing amount of wood and wood pulp is coming out of tree plantations (not inherently a bad idea, given the rate at which the world is losing natural forests). In North America and Europe, plantation forestry generally uses native species, so the gradation from natural forest to plantation is not usually as stark as it is in developing countries, where exotics are the rule in industrial-plantation development.

For the most part, these developing-country plantations bear about as much resemblance to natural forests as corn fields do to undisturbed prairies. And like corn fields, they are maintained with heavy doses of pesticides and subjected to a level of disturbance—in particular, the use of heavy equipment to harvest the trees—that tends to degrade soil. Some plantation trees have launched careers as king-sized weeds. At least 19 species of exotic pine, for example, have invaded various regions in the Southern Hemisphere, where they have displaced native vegetation and, in some areas, apparently lowered the water tables by "drinking" more water than the native vegetation would consume. Even where the trees have not proved invasive, the exotic plantations themselves are displacing natural forest and traditional forest peoples. This type of tree plantation is almost entirely designed to feed wood to the industrialized world, where 77 percent of industrial roundwood is consumed. As with shrimp production, local ecological health is being sacrificed for foreign currency.

There is another, more poignant motive for the introduction of large numbers of exotic trees into the developing world. In many countries severely affected by forest loss, reforestation is recognized as an important social imperative. But the goal is often nothing more than increasing tree cover. Little distinction is made between plantation and forest or between foreign and native species. Surayya Khatoon, a botanist at the University of Karachi, observes that "awareness of the dangers associated with invasive species is almost nonexistent in Pakistan, where alien species are being planted on a large scale in so-called afforestation drives."

The industrial sources of biological pollution are very diverse, but they reflect a common mindset. Whether it is a tree plantation, a shrimp farm, or even a bit of landscaping in the back yard, the Earth has become a sort of "species supermarket"; if a species looks good for whatever it is that you have in mind, pull it off the shelf and take it home. The problem is that many of the traits you want the most—adaptability, rapid growth, and easy reproduction—also tend to make the organism a good candidate for invasion.

Launching a Counter-Attack

Since the processes of invasion are deeply embedded in the globalizing economy, any serious effort to root them out will run the risk of exhausting itself. Most industries and policymakers are striving to open borders, not erect new barriers to trade. Moreover, because bioinvasion is not yet an established policy category, jurisdiction over it is generally badly fragmented—or even absent—on both the national and international levels. Most countries have some relevant legislation—laws intended to discourage the movement of crop pests, for example—but very few have any overall legislative authority for dealing with the problem. (New Zealand is the noteworthy exception: Its Biosecurity Act of 1993 and its Hazardous Substances and New Organisms Act of 1996 do establish such an authority.) Although it is true that there are many treaties that bear on the problem in one way or another—23 at least count—there is not such thing as a bioinvasion treaty.

Even agreements that focus specifically on ecological problems have generally given bioinvasion short shrift. Agenda 21, for example—the blueprint for sustainable development that emerged from the 1992 Earth Summit in Rio de Janeiro—reflects little awareness of the dangers of exotic forestry and aquaculture. Among international agencies, only certain types of invasion seem to get much attention. There are treaties—such as the 1951 International Plant Protection Convention—that limit the movement of agricultural pests, but there is currently no clear international mechanism for dealing with ballast water releases. Obviously, in such a context, you need to pick your fights carefully.

They have to be important, winnable, and capable of yielding major opportunities elsewhere. The following three-point agenda offers some hope of slowing invasion over the near term.

Even international agreements that focus specifically on ecological problems have generally given bioinvasion short shrift.

The first item: Plug the ballast water pathway. As a technical problem, this objective is probably just on the horizon of feasibility, making it an excellent policy target. Strong national and international action could push technologies ahead rapidly. At present, the most effective technique is ballast water exchange, in which the tanks of a ship are pumped out and refilled in the open sea. (Coastal organisms, pumped into the tanks at the ship's last port of call, usually will not survive in the open ocean; organisms that enter the tanks in mid-ocean probably will not survive in the next port of call.) But it can take several days to exchange the water in all of a ship's ballast tanks, so the procedure may not be feasible for every leg of a journey, and the tanks never empty completely. In bad weather, the process can be too dangerous to perform at all. Consequently, other options will be necessary—filters or even toxins (that may not sound very appealing, but some common water treatment compounds may be environmentally sound). It might even be possible to build port-side ballast water treatment plants. Such a mixture of technologies already exists as the standard means of controlling chemical pollution.

This objective is drifting into the realm of legal possibility as well. As of July 1 this year, all ships entering U.S. waters must keep a record of their ballast water management. The United States has also issued voluntary guidelines on where those ships can release ballast water. These measures are a loose extension of the regulations that the United States and Canada have imposed on ship traffic in the Great Lakes, where foreign ballast water release is now explicitly forbidden. In California, the State Water Resources Control Board has declared San Francisco Bay "impaired" because it is so badly invaded—a move that may allow authorities to use regulations written for chemical pollution as a way of controlling ballast water. Australia now levies a small tax on all incoming ships to support ballast water research.

Internationally, the problem has acquired a high profile at the UN International Maritime Organization (IMO), which is studying the possibility of developing a ballast management protocol that would have the force of international law. No decision has been made on the legal mechanism for such an agreement, although the most likely possibility is an annex to MARPOL, the International Convention for the Prevention of Pollution from Ships.

Within the shipping industry, the responses to such proposals have been mixed. Although industry officials concede the problem in the abstract, the prospect of specific regulations has tended to provoke unfavorable comment. After an IMO meeting last year on ballast water management, a spokesperson for the International Chamber of Shipping argued that rigorous ballast exchange would cost the industry millions of dollars a year—and that internationally binding regulations should be avoided in favor of local regulation, wherever particular jurisdictions decide to address the problem. Earlier this year in California, a proposed bill that would have essentially prohibited foreign ballast water release in the state's ports provoked outcries from local port representatives, who argued that such regulations might encourage ship traffic to bypass California ports in favor of the Pacific Northwest or Mexico. Of course, any management strategy is bound to cost something, but the important question is: What impact will this additional cost have? It may not have much impact at all. In Canada, for example, the Vancouver Port Authority reported that its ballast water program has had no detectable effect on port revenues.

The second item on the agenda: Fix the World Trade Organization (WTO) Agreement on the Application of Sanitary and Phytosanitary Measures. This agreement, known as the SPS, was part of the diplomatic package that created the WTO in 1994. The SPS is supposed to promote a common set of procedures for evaluating risks of contamination in internationally traded commodities. The contaminants can be chemical (pesticide residues in food) or they can be living things (Asian longhorn beetles in raw wood).

One of the procedures required by the SPS is a risk assessment, which is supposed to be done before any trade-constricting barriers are imposed to prevent a contaminated good from entering a country. If you want to understand the fundamental flaw in this approach as it applies to bioinvasion, all you have to do is recall the famous observation by the eminent biologist E.O. Wilson: "We dwell on a largely unexplored planet." When it comes to the largest categories of living things—insects, fungi, bacteria, and so on—we have managed to name only a tiny fraction of them, let alone figure out what damage they can cause. Consider, for example, the rough, aggregate risk assessments done by the United States Department of Agriculture (USDA) for wood imported into the United States from Chile, Mexico, and New Zealand. The USDA found dozens of "moderate" and "high" risk pests and pathogens that have the potential for doing economic damage on the order of hundreds of millions of dollars at least—and ecological damage that is incalculable. But even with wide-open thoroughfares of invasion such as these, the SPS requirement in its current form is likely to make preemptive action vulnerable to trade complaints before the WTO.

Another SPS requirement intended to insure a consistent application of standards is that a country must not set up barriers against an organism that is already living within its borders unless it has an "official control program" for that species. This approach is unrealistic for both biological and financial reasons. Thousands of exotic species are likely to have invaded most of the world's countries and not even the wealthiest country could possibly afford to fight them all. Yet it certainly is possible to exacerbate a problem by introducing additional infestations of a pest, or by boosting the size of existing infestations, or even by increasing the genetic vigor of a pest population by adding more "breeding stock." The SPS does not like "inconsistencies"—if you are not controlling a pest, you have no right to object to more of it; if you try to block one pathway of invasion, you had better be trying to block all the equivalent pathways. Such an approach may be theoretically neat, but in the practical matter of dealing with exotics, it is a prescription for paralysis.

In the near term, however, any effort to repair the SPS is likely to be difficult. The support of the United States, a key member of the WTO, will be critical for such reforms. And although the United States has demonstrated a heightened awareness of the problem—as evidenced by President Bill Clinton's executive order to create an Invasive Species Council—it is not clear whether that commitment will be reflected in the administration's trade policy. During recent testimony before Congress, the U.S. Trade Representative's special trade negotiator for agricultural issues warned that the United States was becoming impatient with the "increasing use of SPS barriers as the 'trade barrier of choice.' " In the developing world, it is reasonable to assume that any country with a strong export sector in a natural resource industry would not welcome tougher regulations. Some developed countries, however, may be sympathetic to change. The European Union (EU) has sought very strict standards in its disputes with the United States over bans on beef from cattle fed with growth hormones and on genetically altered foods. It is possible that the EU might be willing to entertain a stricter SPS. The same might be true of Japan, which has attempted to secure stricter testing of U.S. fruit imports.

The third item: Build a global invasion database. Currently, the study of bioinvasion is an obscure and rather fractured enterprise. It can be difficult to locate critical information or relevant expertise. The full magnitude of the issue is still not registering on the public radar screen. A global database would consolidate existing information, presumably into some sort of central research institution with a major presence on the World Wide Web. One could "go" to such a place—either physically or through cyberspace—to learn about everything from the National Ballast Water Information Clearinghouse that the U.S. Coast Guard is setting up, to the database on invasive woody plants in the tropics that is being assembled at the University of Wales. The database would also stimulate the production of new media to encourage additional research and synthesis. It is a telling indication of how fragmented this field is that, after more than 40 years of formal study, it is just now getting its first comprehensive journal: *Biological Invasions.*

Better information should have a number of practical effects. The best way to control an invasion—when it cannot be prevented outright—is to go after the exotic as soon as it is detected. An emergency response capability will only work if officials know what to look for and what to do when they find it. But beyond such obvious applications, the database could help bring the big picture into focus. In the struggle with exotics, you can see the free-trade ideal colliding with some hard ecological realities. Put simply: It may never be safe to ship certain goods to certain places—raw wood from Siberia, for instance, to North America. The notion of real, permanent limits to economic activity will for many politicians (and probably some economists) come as a strange and unpalatable idea. But the global economy is badly in need of a large dose of ecological realism. Ecosystems are very diverse and very different from each other. They need to stay that way if they are going to continue to function.

Want to Know More?

Although the scientific literature on bioinvasion is enormous and growing rapidly, most of it is too technical to attract a readership outside the field. For a nontechnical, broad overview of the problem, readers should consult Robert Devine's ***Alien Invasion: America's Battle with Non-Native Animals and Plants*** (Washington: National Geographic Society, 1998) or Christopher Bright's ***Life Out of Bounds: Bioinvasion in a Borderless World*** (New York: W.W. Norton & Company, 1998).

If you have a long-term interest in bioinvasion, you will want to get acquainted with the book that founded the field: Charles Elton's ***The Ecology of Invasions by Animals and Plants*** (London: Methuen, 1958). A historical overview of bioinvasions can be found in Alfred Crosby's book ***Ecological Imperialism: The Biological Expansion of Europe, 900–1900*** (Cambridge: Cambridge University Press, 1986).

Many studies focus on invasion of particular regions. The focus can be very broad, as in P.S. Ramakrishnan, ed., ***Ecology of Biological Invasions in the Tropics,*** proceedings of an international workshop held at Nainital, India, (New Delhi: International Scientific Publications, 1989). Generally, however, the coverage is much narrower, as in Daniel Simberloff, Don Schmitz, and Tom Brown, eds., ***Strangers in Paradise: Impact and Management of Nonindigenous Species in Florida*** (Washington: Island Press, 1997). The other standard research tack has been to look at a particular type of invader. The most accessible results of this exercise are encyclopedic surveys such as Christopher Lever's ***Naturalized Mammals of the World*** (London: Longman, 1985) and his companion volumes on naturalized birds and fish. In the plant kingdom, the genre is represented by Leroy Holm, et al., ***World Weeds: Natural Histories and Distribution*** (New York: John Wiley and Sons, 1997).

There are many worthwhile documents available for anyone who is interested not just in the ecology of invasion, but also in its economic, social, and epidemiological implications. Just about every aspect of the problem is discussed in Odd Terje Sandlund, Peter Johan Schei, and Aslaug Viken, eds., ***Proceedings of the Norway/UN Conference on Alien Species*** (Trondheim: Directorate for Nature Management and Norwegian Institute for Nature Research, 1996). A groundbreaking study of invasion in the United States, with particular emphasis on economic effects, is ***Harmful Nonindigenous Species in the United States*** (Washington: Office of Technology Assessment, September 1993). An assessment of the ballast water problem is available from the National Research Council's Commission on Ships' Ballast Operations' ***Stemming the Tide: Controlling Introductions of Nonindigenous Species by Ships' Ballast Water*** (Washington: National Academy Press, 1996). Readers who are interested in exotic tree plantations as a form of "managed invasion" might look through Ricardo Carrere and Larry Lohmann's ***Pulping the South: Industrial Tree Plantations and the World Paper Economy*** (London: Zed Books, 1996) and the World Rainforest Movement's ***Tree Plantations: Impacts and Struggles*** (Montevideo: WRM, 1999). Unfortunately, there are no analogous studies of shrimp farms.

For links to relevant Web sites, as well as a comprehensive index of related FOREIGN POLICY articles, access **www.foreignpolicy.com.**

CHRISTOPHER BRIGHT *is a research associate at the Worldwatch Institute in Washington, DC, and author of* Life Out of Bounds: Bioinvasion in a Borderless World *(New York: W.W. Norton & Company, 1998).*

We *Can* Build a Sustainable Economy

The keys to securing the planet's future lie in stabilizing both human population and climate. The challenges are great, but several trends look promising.

By Lester R. Brown

The world economy is growing faster than ever, but the benefits of this rapid growth have not been evenly distributed. As population has doubled since mid-century and the global economy has nearly quintupled, the demand for natural resources has grown at a phenomenal rate.

Since 1950, the need for grain has nearly tripled. Consumption of seafood has increased more than four times. Water use has tripled. Demand for beef and mutton has tripled. Firewood demand has tripled, lumber demand has more than doubled, and paper demand has gone up sixfold. The burning of fossil fuels has increased nearly fourfold, and carbon emissions have risen accordingly.

These spiraling human demands for resources are beginning to outgrow the earth's natural systems. As this happens, the global economy is damaging the foundation on which it rests.

To build an environmentally sustainable global economy, there are many obstacles, but there are also several promising trends and factors in our favor. One is that we know what an environmentally sustainable economy would look like. In a sustainable economy:

- Human births and deaths are in balance.
- Soil erosion does not exceed the natural rate of new soil formation.
- Tree cutting does not exceed tree planting.
- The fish catch does not exceed the sustainable yield of fisheries.
- The number of cattle on a range does not exceed the range's carrying capacity.
- Water pumping does not exceed aquifer recharge.
- Carbon emissions and carbon fixation are in balance.
- The number of plant and animal species lost does not exceed the rate at which new species evolve.

We know how to build an economic system that will meet our needs without jeopardizing prospects for future generations. And with some trends already headed in the right direction, we have the cornerstones on which to build such an economy.

Stabilizing Population

With population, the challenge is to complete the demographic transition, to reestablish the balance between births and deaths that characterizes a sustainable society. Since populations are rarely ever #7 precisely stable, a stable population is defined here as one with a growth rate below 0.3%. Populations are effectively stable if they fluctuate narrowly around zero.

Thirty countries now have stable populations, including most of those in Europe plus Japan. They provide

From *The Futurist,* July/August 1996, pp. 8–12. © 1996 by The World Future Society, Bethesda, MD; http://www.wfs.org/wfs. Reprinted by permission.

the solid base for building a world population stabilization effort. Included in the 30 are all the larger industrialized countries of Europe—France, Germany, Italy, Russia, and the United Kingdom. Collectively, these 30 countries contain 819 million people or 14% of humanity. For this goal, one-seventh of humanity is already there.

The challenge is for the countries with the remaining 86% of the world's people to reach stability. The two large nations that could make the biggest difference in this effort are China and the United States. In both, population growth is now roughly 1% per year. If the global food situation becomes desperate, both could reach stability in a decade or two if they decided it were important to do so.

The world rate of population growth, which peaked around 2% in 1970, dropped below 1.6% in 1995. Although the rate is declining, the annual addition is still close to 90 million people per year. Unless populations can be stabilized with demand below the sustainable yield of local ecosystems, these systems will be destroyed. Slowing growth may delay the eventual collapse of ecosystems, but it will not save them.

The European Union, consisting of some 15 countries and containing 360 million people, provides a model for the rest of the world of an environmentally sustainable food/population balance. At the same time that the region has reached zero population growth, movement up the food chain has come to a halt as diets have become saturated with livestock products. The result is that Europe's grain consumption has been stable for close to two decades at just under 160 million tons—a level that is within the region's carrying capacity. Indeed, there is a potential for a small but sustainable export surplus of grain that can help countries where the demand for food has surpassed the carrying capacity of their croplands.

As other countries realize that continuing on their current population trajectory will prevent them from achieving a similar food/population balance, more and more may decide to do what China has done—launch an all-out campaign to stabilize population. Like China, other governments will have to carefully balance the reproductive rights of the current generation with the survival rights of the next generation.

Very few of the group of 30 countries with stable populations had stability as an explicit policy goal. In those that reached population stability first, such as Belgium, Germany, Sweden, and the United Kingdom, it came with rising living standards and expanding employment opportunities for women. In some of the countries where population has stabilized more recently, such as Russia and other former Soviet republics, the deep economic depression accompanying economic reform has substantially lowered birth rates, much as the Great Depression did in the United States. In addition, with the rising number of infants born with birth defects and deformities since Chernobyl, many women are simply afraid to bear children. The natural decrease of population (excluding migration) in Russia of 0.6% a year—leading to an annual population loss of 890,000—is the most rapid on record.

Not all countries are achieving population stability for the right reasons. This is true today and it may well be true in the future. As food deficits in densely populated countries expand, governments may find that there is not enough food available to import. Between fiscal year 1993 and 1996, food aid dropped from an all-time high of 15.2 million tons of grain to 7.6 million tons. This cut of exactly half in three years reflects primarily fiscal stringencies in donor countries, but also, to a lesser degree, higher grain prices in fiscal 1996. If governments fail to establish a humane balance between their people and food supplies, hunger and malnutrition may raise death rates, eventually slowing population growth.

Some developing countries are beginning to adopt social policies that will encourage smaller families. Iran, facing both land hunger and water scarcity, now limits public subsidies for housing, health care, and insurance to three children per family. In Peru, President Alberto Fujimori, who was elected overwhelmingly to his second five-year term in a predominantly Catholic country, said in his inaugural address in August 1995 that he wanted to provide better access to family-planning services for poor women. "It is only fair," he said, "to disseminate thoroughly the methods of family planning to everyone."

World Fertilizer and Grainland

(Per Person, 1950-94)

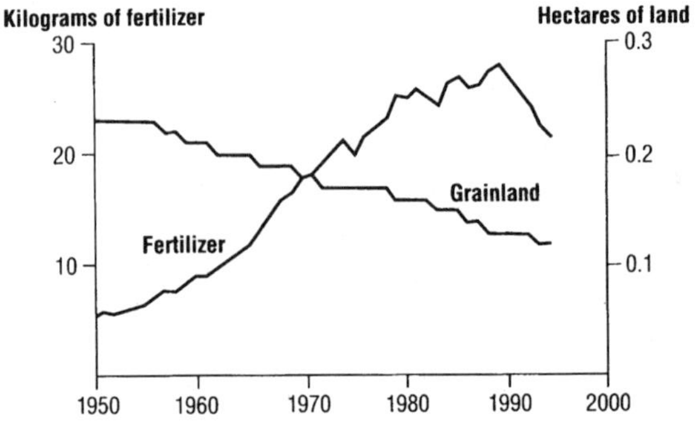

SOURCES: USDA, FAO, IFA

Stabilizing Climate

With climate, as with population, there is disagreement on the need to stabilize. Evidence that atmospheric carbon-dioxide levels are rising is clear-cut. So, too, is the greenhouse effect that these gases produce in the atmosphere. That is a matter of basic physics. What is debatable is the rate at which global temperatures will rise and what the precise local effects will be. Nonetheless, the consensus of the mainstream scientific community is that there is no alternative to reducing carbon emissions.

How would we phase out fossil fuels? There is now a highly successful "phase out" model in the case of chlorofluorocarbons (CFCs). After two British scientists discovered the "hole" in the ozone layer over Antarctica and published their findings in *Nature* in May 1985, the international community convened a conference in Montreal to draft an agreement designed to reduce CFC production sharply. Subsequent meetings in London in 1990 and Copenhagen in 1992 further advanced the goals set in Montreal. After peaking

World Wind Energy
(Generating Capacity, 1980-94)

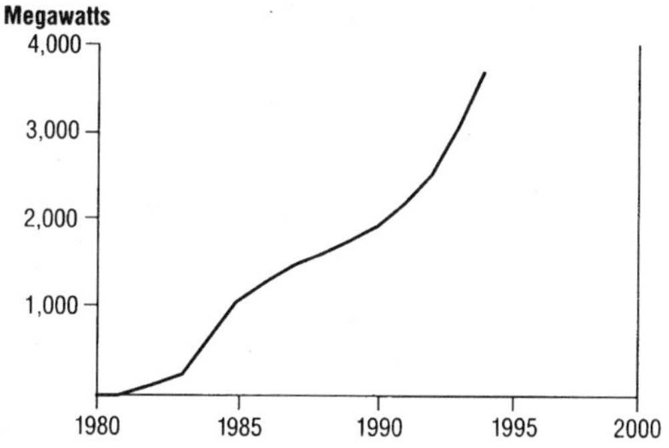

SOURCES: Gipe and Associates, BTM Consulting

in 1988 at 1.26 million tons, the manufacture of CFCs dropped to an estimated 295,000 tons in 1994—a decline of 77% in just six years.

As public understanding of the costs associated with global warming increases, and as evidence of the effects of higher temperatures accumulates, support for reducing dependence on fossil fuels is building. At the March 1995 U.N. Climate Convention in Berlin, environmental groups were joined in lobbying for a reduction in carbon emissions by a group of 36 island communities and insurance industry representatives.

The island nations are beginning to realize that rising sea levels would, at a minimum, reduce their land area and displace people. For some low-lying island countries, it could actually threaten their survival. And the insurance industry is beginning to realize that increasing storm intensity can threaten the survival of insurance companies as well. When Hurricane Andrew tore through Florida in 1992, it took down not only thousands of buildings, but also eight insurance firms.

In September 1995, the U.S. Department of Agriculture reported a sharp drop in the estimated world grain harvest because of crop-withering heat waves in the northern tier of industrial countries. Intense late-summer heat had damaged harvests in Canada and the United States, across Europe, and in Russia. If farmers begin to see that the productivity of their land is threatened by global warming, they, too, may begin to press for a shift to renewable sources of energy.

As with CFCs, there are alternatives to fossil fuels that do not alter climate. Several solar-based energy sources, including wind power, solar cells, and solar thermal power plants, are advancing rapidly in technological sophistication, resulting in steadily falling costs. The cost of photovoltaic cells has fallen precipitously over the last few decades. In some villages in developing countries where a central grid does not yet exist, it is now cheaper to install an array of photovoltaic cells than to build a centralized power plant plus the grid needed to deliver the power.

Wind power, using the new, highly efficient wind turbines to convert wind into electricity, is poised for explosive growth in the years ahead. In California, wind farms already supply enough electricity to meet the equivalent of San Francisco's residential needs.

The potential for wind energy is enormous, dwarfing that of hydropower, which provides a fifth of the world's electricity. In the United States, the harnessable wind potential in North Dakota, South Dakota, and Texas could easily meet national electricity needs. In Europe, wind power could theoretically satisfy all the continent's electricity needs. With scores of national governments planning to tap this vast resource, rapid growth in the years ahead appears inevitable.

A Bicycle Economy

Another trend to build on is the growing production of bicycles. Human mobility can be increased by investing in public transportation, bicycles, and automobiles. Of these, the first two are by far the most promising environmentally. Although China has announced plans to move toward an automobile-centered transportation system, and car production in India is expected to double by the end of the decade, there simply may not be enough land in these countries to support such a system and to meet the food needs of their expanding populations.

Against this backdrop, the creation of bicycle-friendly transportation systems, particularly in cities, shows great promise. Market forces alone have pushed bicycle production to an estimated 111 million in 1994, three times the level of automobile production. It is in the interest of societies everywhere to foster the use of bicycles and public transportation—to accelerate the growth in bicycle manufacturing while restricting that of automobiles. Not only will this help save cropland, but this technology can greatly increase human mobility without destabilizing climate. If food becomes increasingly scarce in the years ahead, as now seems likely, the land-saving, climate-stabilizing nature of bicycles will further tip the scales in their favor and away from automobiles.

The stabilization of population in some 30 countries, the stabilization of food/people balance in Europe, the reduction in CFC production, the dramatic growth in the world's wind power generating capacity, and the extraordinary growth in bicycle use are all trends for the world to build on. These cornerstones of an environmentally sustainable global economy provide glimpses of a sustainable future.

Regaining Control of Our Destiny

Avoiding catastrophe is going to take a far greater effort than is now being contemplated by the world's political leaders. We know what needs to be done, but politically we are unable to do it because of inertia and the investment of powerful interests in the status quo. Securing food supplies for the next generation depends on an all-out effort to stabilize population and climate, but we resist changing our reproductive behavior, and we refrain from converting our climate-destabilizing, fossil-fuel-based economy to a solar/hydrogen-based one.

As we move to the end of this century and beyond, food security may well come to dominate international affairs, national economic policy making, and—for much of humanity—personal concerns about survival. There is now evidence from enough countries that the old formula of substituting fertilizer for land is no longer working, so we need to search urgently for alternative formulas for humanly balancing our numbers with available food supplies.

Unfortunately, most national political leaders do not even seem to be aware of the fundamental shifts occurring in the world food economy, largely because the official projections by the World Bank and the U.N. Food and Agriculture Organization are essentially extrapolations of past trends.

If we are to understand the challenges facing us, the teams of economists responsible for world food supply-and-demand projections at these two organizations need to be replaced with an interdisciplinary team of analysts, including, for example, an agronomist, hydrologist, biologist, and meteorologist, along with an economist. Such a team could assess and incorporate into projections such things as the effect of soil erosion on land productivity, the effects of aquifer depletion on future irrigation water supplies, and the effect of increasingly intense heat waves on future harvests.

The World Bank team of economists argues that, because the past is the only guide we have to the future, simple extrapolations of past trends are the only reasonable way to make projections. But the past is also filled with a body of scientific literature on growth in finite environments, and it shows that biological growth trends typically conform to an S-shaped curve over time.

The risk of relying on these extrapolative projections is that they are essentially "no problem" projections. For example, the most recent World Bank projections, which use 1990 as a base and which were published in late 1993, are departing further and further from reality with each passing year. They show the world grain harvest climbing from 1.78 billion tons in 1990 to 1.97 billion tons in the year 2000. But instead of the projected gain of nearly 100 million tons since 1990, world grain production has not grown at all. Indeed, the 1995 harvest, at 1.69 billion tons, is 90 million tons below the 1990 harvest.

One of the most obvious needs today is for a set of country-by-country carrying-capacity assessments. Assessments using an interdisciplinary team can help provide information needed to face the new realities and formulate policies to respond to them.

Setting Priorities

The world today is faced with an enormous need for change in a period of time that is all too short. Human behavior and values, and the national priorities that reflect them, change in response to either new information or new experiences. The effort now needed to reverse the environmental degradation of the planet and ensure a sustainable future for the next generation will require mobilization on a scale comparable to World War II.

Regaining control of our destiny depends on stabilizing population as well as climate. These are both key to the achievement of a wide array of social goals ranging from the restoration of a rise in food consumption per person to protection of the diversity of plant and animal species. And neither will be easy. The first depends on a revolution in human reproductive behavior; the second, on a restructuring of the global energy system.

Serving as a catalyst for these gargantuan efforts is the knowledge that if we fail our future will spiral out of control as the acceleration of history overwhelms political institutions. It will almost guarantee a future of starvation, economic insecurity, and political instability. It will bring political conflict between societies and among ethnic and religious groups within societies. As these forces are unleashed, they will leave social disintegration in their wake.

Bicycles vs. Cars

(Worldwide Production, 1950-94)

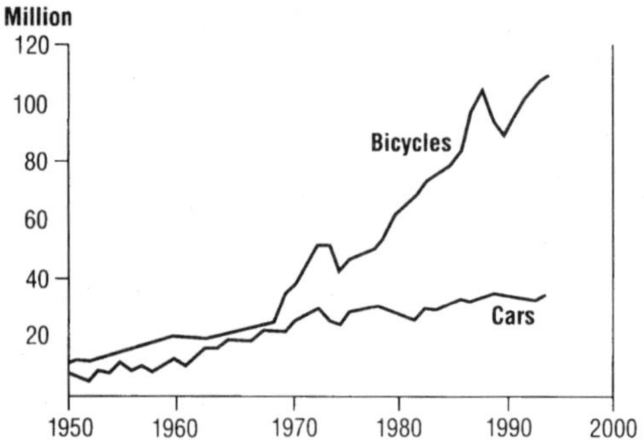

SOURCES: U.N., Interbike Directory

Offsetting the dimensions of this challenge, including the opposition to change that is coming from vested interests and the momentum of trends now headed in the wrong direction, are some valuable assets. These include a well-developed global communications network, a growing body of scientific knowledge, and the possibility of using fiscal policy—a potentially powerful instrument for change—to build an environmentally sustainable economy.

Policies for Progress

Satisfying the conditions of sustainability—whether it be reversing the deforestation of the planet, converting a throwaway economy into a reuse-recycle one, or stabilizing climate—will require new investment. Probably the single most useful instrument for converting an unsustainable world economy into one that is sustainable is fiscal policy. Here are a few proposals:

- **Eliminate subsidies for unsustainable activities.** At present, governments subsidize many of the very activities that threaten the sustainability of the economy. They support fishing fleets to the extent of some $54 billion a year, for example, even though existing fishing capacity already greatly exceeds the sustainable yield of oceanic fisheries. In Germany, coal production is subsidized even though the country's scientific community has been outspoken in its calls for reducing carbon emissions.
- **Institute a carbon tax.** With alternative sources of energy such as wind power, photovoltaics, and solar thermal power plants becoming competitive or nearly so, a carbon tax that would reflect the cost to society of burning fossil fuels—the costs, that is, of air pollution, acid rain, and global warming—could quickly tip the scales away from further investment in fossil fuel production to investment in wind and solar energy. Today's fossil-fuel-based energy economy can be replaced with a solar/hydrogen economy that can meet all the energy needs of a modern industrial society without causing disruptive temperature rises.
- **Replace income taxes with environmental taxes.** Income taxes discourage work and savings, which are both positive activities that should be encouraged. Taxing environmentally destructive activities instead would help steer the global economy in an environmentally sustainable direction. Among the activities to be taxed are the use of pesticides, the generation of toxic wastes, the use of virgin raw materials, the conversion of cropland to nonfarm uses, and carbon emissions.

The time may have come also to limit tax deductions for children to two per couple: It may not make sense to subsidize childbearing beyond replacement level when the most pressing need facing humanity is to stabilize population.

The challenge for humanity is a profound one. We have the information, the technology, and the knowledge of what needs to be done. The question is, Can we do it? Can a species that is capable of formulating a theory that explains the birth of the universe now implement a strategy to build an environmentally sustainable economic system?

About the Author

Lester R. Brown is president of the Worldwatch Institute, 1776 Massachusetts Avenue, N.W., Washington, D.C. 20036. Telephone 202/452-1999; fax 202/296-7365.

Unit 4

Unit Selections

Key Points to Consider

- Are those who argue that there is in fact a process of globalization overly optimistic? Why or why not?
- What are some of the impediments to a truly global political economy?
- How are the political economies of traditional societies different from those of the consumer-oriented societies?
- How are the nonindustrial countries dependent on the industrialized countries?
- What are some of the barriers that make it difficult for nonindustrial countries to develop?
- How are China, Malaysia, and other countries trying to alter their ways of doing business in order to meet the challenges of globalization? Are they likely to succeed?
- What is the nature of the debate surrounding the practices of international organizations like the IMF and WTO?

DUSHKIN ONLINE Links | www.dushkin.com/online/

17. **Belfer Center for Science and International Affairs (BCSIA)**
    http://ksgwww.harvard.edu/csia/
18. **Communications for a Sustainable Future**
    http://csf.colorado.edu
19. **U.S. Agency for International Development**
    http://www.info.usaid.gov
20. **Virtual Seminar in Global Political Economy/Global Cities & Social Movements**
    http://csf.colorado.edu/gpe/gpe95b/resources.html
21. **World Bank**
    http://www.worldbank.org

These sites are annotated on pages 4 and 5.

Political Economy

A defining characteristic of the twentieth century's social history was the contest between two dramatically opposing views about how economic systems should be organized. The focus of the debate was on what role government should play in the management of a country's economy. For some the dominant capitalist economic system appeared to be organized primarily for the benefit of the few. From their perspective, the masses were trapped in poverty, supplying cheap labor to further enrich the wealthy. These critics argued that the capitalist system could be changed only by gaining control of the political system and radically changing the ownership of the means of production. In striking contrast to this perspective, others argued that the best way to create wealth and eliminate poverty was the profit motive that encouraged entrepreneurs to innovate. An open and competitive marketplace that minimized government interference was the best system for making decisions about production, wages, and the distribution of goods and services.

The debate between socialism/communism on the one hand and capitalism on the other (with variations in between) has been characterized by both abstract theorizing and very pragmatic and often violent political conflict. The Russian and Chinese revolutions overthrew the old social order and created radical changes in the political and economic systems in these two important countries. The political structures that were created to support new systems of agricultural and industrial production (along with the centralized planning of virtually all aspects of economic activity) eliminated most private ownership of property. These two revolutions were, in short, unparalleled experiments in social engineering.

The collapse of the Soviet Union and the dramatic reforms that have taken place in China have recast the debate about how to best structure contemporary economic systems. Some believe that with the end of communism and the resulting participation of hundreds of millions of new consumers in the global market, an unprecedented era has been entered. Many have noted that this process of "globalization" is being accelerated by the revolution in communication and computer technologies. Proponents of this view argue that a new global economy is emerging that will ultimately eliminate national economic systems.

Others are less optimistic about the prospects of globalization. They argue that the creation of a single economic system where there are no boundaries to impede the flow of capital does not mean a closing of the gap between the world's rich and poor. Rather, they argue that giant corporations will have fewer legal constraints on their behavior, and this will lead to greater exploitation of workers and the accelerated destruction of the environment.

The use of the term "political economy" for the title of this unit is a recognition that economic and political systems are not separate. All economic systems have some type of marketplace where goods and services are bought and sold. Government (either national or international) regulates these transactions to some degree; that is, government sets the rules that regulate the marketplace.

One of the most important concepts in assessing the contemporary political economy is "development." For the purposes of this unit, the term "development" is defined as an improvement in the basic aspects of life: lower infant mortality rates, longer life expectancy, lower disease rates, higher rates of literacy, healthier diets, and improved sanitation. Judged by these standards, some countries are more "developed" than others. A fundamental question that a thoughtful reader must consider is whether globalization is resulting in increased development not only for a few people but for all of those participating in the global political economy.

The unit is organized into two sections. The first is a general discussion of the concept of globalization. How do various experts define the term, and what are their differing perspectives on it? For example, is the idea of a global economy merely wishful thinking by those who sit on top of the power hierarchy, self-deluded into believing that globalization is an inexorable force that will evolve in its own way, following its own rules? Or will there continue to be the traditional tensions of power politics, that is, between the rich and those who are either ascending or descending in power?

The second section focuses on case studies. These have been selected to help the reader draw his or her own conclusions about the validity of the globalization concept. What in fact is taking place in various countries and regions of the world? Can China and Russia play a self-determined role in the global economy? Does the contemporary system result in an age-old system of winners and losers, or can everyone positively benefit from its system of wealth creation and distribution?

The Complexities and Contradictions of Globalization

Globalization, we are told, is what every business should be pursuing, and what every nation should welcome. But what, exactly, is it? James Rosenau offers a nuanced understanding of a process that is much more real, and transforming, than the language of the marketplace expresses.

JAMES N. ROSENAU

The mall at Singapore's airport has a food court with 15 food outlets, all but one of which offering menus that cater to local tastes; the lone standout, McDonald's, is also the only one crowded with customers. In New York City, experts in *feng shui,* an ancient Chinese craft aimed at harmonizing the placement of man-made structures in nature, are sought after by real estate developers in order to attract a growing influx of Asian buyers who would not be interested in purchasing buildings unless their structures were properly harmonized.

Most people confronted with these examples would probably not be surprised by them. They might even view them as commonplace features of day-to-day life late in the twentieth century, instances in which local practices have spread to new and distant sites. In the first case the spread is from West to East and in the second it is from East to West, but both share a process in which practices spread and become established in profoundly different cultures. And what immediately comes to mind when contemplating this process? The answer can be summed up in one word: globalization, a label that is presently in vogue to account for peoples, activities, norms, ideas, goods, services, and currencies that are decreasingly confined to a particular geographic space and its local and established practices.

Indeed, some might contend that "globalization" is the latest buzzword to which observers resort when things seem different and they cannot otherwise readily account for them. That is why, it is reasoned, a great variety of activities are labeled as globalization, with the result that no widely accepted formulation of the concept has evolved. Different observers use it to describe different phenomena, and often there is little overlap among the various usages. Even worse, the elusiveness of the concept of globalization is seen as underlying the use of a variety of other, similar terms—world society, interdependence, centralizing tendencies, world system, globalism, universalism, internationalization, globality—that come into play when efforts are made to grasp why public affairs today seem significantly different from those of the past.

Such reasoning is misleading. The proliferation of diverse and loose definitions of globalization as well as the readiness to use a variety of seemingly comparable labels are not so much a reflection of evasive confusion as they are an early stage in a profound ontological shift, a restless search for new ways of understanding unfamiliar phenomena. The lack of precise formulations may suggest the presence of buzzwords for the inexplicable, but a more convincing interpretation is that such words are voiced in so many different contexts because

Reprinted with permission from *Current History* magazine, November 1997, pp. 360–364.

of a shared sense that the human condition is presently undergoing profound transformations in all of its aspects.

WHAT IS GLOBALIZATION?

Let us first make clear where globalization fits among the many buzzwords that indicate something new in world affairs that is moving important activities and concerns beyond the national seats of power that have long served as the foundations of economic, political, and social life. While all the buzzwords seem to cluster around the same dimension of the present human condition, useful distinctions can be drawn among them. Most notably, if it is presumed that the prime characteristic of this dimension is change—a transformation of practices and norms—then the term "globalization" seems appropriate to denote the "something" that is changing humankind's preoccupation with territoriality and the traditional arrangements of the state system. It is a term that directly implies change, and thus differentiates the phenomenon as a process rather than as a prevailing condition or a desirable end state.

Conceived as an underlying process, in other words, globalization is not the same as globalism, which points to aspirations for a state of affairs where values are shared by or pertinent to all the world's more than 5 billion people, their environment, and their role as citizens, consumers, or producers with an interest in collective action to solve common problems. And it can also be distinguished from universalism, which refers to those values that embrace all of humanity (such as the values that science or religion draws on), at any time or place. Nor is it coterminous with complex interdependence, which signifies structures that link people and communities in various parts of the world.

Although related to these other concepts, the idea of globalization developed here is narrower in scope. It refers neither to values nor to structures, but to sequences that unfold either in the mind or in behavior, to processes that evolve as people and organizations go about their daily tasks and seek to realize their particular goals. What distinguishes globalizing processes is that they are not hindered or prevented by territorial or jurisdictional barriers. As indicated by the two examples presented at the outset, such processes can readily spread in many directions across national boundaries, and are capable of reaching into any community anywhere in the world. They consist of all those forces that impel individuals, groups, and institutions to engage in similar forms of behavior or to participate in more encompassing and coherent processes, organizations, or systems.

Contrariwise, localization derives from all those pressures that lead individuals, groups, and institutions to narrow their horizons, participate in dissimilar forms of behavior, and withdraw to less encompassing processes, organizations, or systems. In other words, any technological, psychological, social, economic, or political developments that foster the expansion of interests and practices beyond established boundaries are both sources and expressions of the processes of globalization, just as any developments in these realms that limit or reduce interests are both sources and expressions of localizing processes.

Note that the processes of globalization are conceived as only capable of being worldwide in scale. In fact, the activities of no group, government, society, or company have never been planetary in magnitude, and few cascading sequences actually encircle and encompass the entire globe. Televised events such as civil wars and famines in Africa or protests against governments in Eastern Europe may sustain a spread that is worldwide in scope, but such a scope is not viewed as a prerequisite of globalizing dynamics. As long as it has the potential of an unlimited spread that can readily transgress national jurisdictions, any interaction sequence is considered to reflect the operation of globalization.

Obviously, the differences between globalizing and localizing forces give rise to contrary conceptions of territoriality. Globalization is rendering boundaries and identity with the land less salient while localization, being driven by pressures to narrow and withdraw, is highlighting borders and intensifying the deep attachments to land that can dominate emotion and reasoning.

In short, globalization is boundary-broadening and localization is boundary-heightening. The former allows people, goods, information, norms, practices, and institutions to move about oblivious to despite boundaries. The boundary-heightening processes of localization are designed to inhibit or prevent the movement of people, goods, information, norms, practices, and institutions. Efforts along this line, however, can be only partially successful. Community and state boundaries can be heightened to a considerable extent, but they cannot be rendered impervious. Authoritarian governments try to make them so, but their policies are bound to be undermined in a shrinking world with increasingly interdependent economies and communications technologies that are not easily monitored. Thus it is hardly surprising that some of the world's most durable tensions flow from the fact that no geographic borders can be made so airtight to prevent the infiltration of ideas and goods. Stated more emphatically, some globalizing dynamics are bound, at least in the long run, to prevail.

The boundary-expanding dynamics of globalization have become highly salient precisely because recent decades have witnessed a mushrooming of the facilities, interests, and markets through which a potential for worldwide spread can be realized. Likewise, the boundary-contracting dynamics of localization have also become increasingly significant, not least because some people and cultures feel threatened by the incursions of globalization. Their jobs, their icons, their belief systems, and their communities seem at risk as the boundaries that have sealed them off from the outside world in the past no longer assure protection. And there is, of course, a basis of truth in these fears. Globalization does intrude; its processes do shift jobs elsewhere; its norms do undermine traditional mores. Responses to these threats can vary considerably. At one extreme are adaptations that accept the boundary-broadening processes and make the best of them by integrating them into local customs and practices. At the other extreme are responses intended to ward off the globalizing processes by resort to ideological purities, closed borders, and economic isolation.

THE DYNAMICS OF FRAGMEGRATION

The core of world affairs today thus consists of tensions between the dynamics of globalization and localization. Moreover, the two sets of dynamics are causally linked, almost as if every increment of globalization gives rise to an increment of localization, and vice versa. To account for these tensions I have long used the term "fragmegration," an awkward and perhaps even grating label that has the virtue of capturing the pervasive interactions between the fragmenting forces of localization and the integrative forces of globalization.1 One can readily observe the unfolding of fragmegrative dynamics in the struggle of the European Union to cope with proposals for monetary unification or in the electoral campaigns and successes of Jean-Marie Le Pen in France, Patrick Buchanan in the United States, and Pauline Hanson in Australia—to mention only three examples.

It is important to keep in mind that fragmegration is not a single dynamic. Both globalization and localization are clusters of forces that, as they interact in different ways and through different channels, contribute to more encompassing processes in the case of globalization and to less encompassing processes in the case of localization. These various dynamics, moreover, operate in all realms of human activity, from the cultural and social to the economic and political.

In the political realm, globalizing dynamics underlie any developments that facilitate the expansion of authority, policies, and interests beyond existing socially constructed territorial boundaries, whereas the politics of localization involves any trends in which the scope of authority and policies undergoes contraction and reverts to concerns, issues, groups, and institutions that are less extensive than the prevailing socially constructed territorial boundaries. In the economic realm, globalization encompasses the expansion of production, trade, and investments beyond their prior locales, while localizing dynamics are at work when the activities of producers and consumers are constricted to narrower boundaries. In the social and cultural realms, globalization operates to extend ideas, norms, and practices beyond the settings in which they originated, while localization highlights or compresses the original settings and thereby inhibits the inroad of new ideas, norms, and practices.

It must be stressed that the dynamics unfolding in all these realms are long-term processes. They involve fundamental human needs and thus span all of human history. Globalizing dynamics derive from peoples' need to enlarge the scope of their self-created orders so as to increase the goods, services, and ideas available for their well-being. The agricultural revolution, followed by the industrial and postindustrial transformations, are among the major sources that have sustained globalization. Yet even as these forces have been operating, so have contrary tendencies toward contraction been continuously at work. Localizing dynamics derive from people's need for the psychic comforts of close-at-hand, reliable support—for

There is no inherent contradiction between localizing and globalizing tendencies.

the family and neighborhood, for local cultural practices, for a sense of "us" that is distinguished from "them." Put differently, globalizing dynamics have long fostered large-scale order, whereas localizing dynamics have long created pressure for small-scale order. Fragmegration, in short, has always been an integral part of the human condition.

GLOBALIZATION'S EVENTUAL PREDOMINANCE

Notwithstanding the complexities inherent in the emergent structures of world affairs, observers have not hesitated to anticipate what lies beyond fragmegration as global history unfolds. All agree that while the contest between globalizing and localizing dynamics is bound to be marked by fluctuating surges in both directions, the underlying tendency is for the former to prevail over the latter. Eventually, that is, the dynamics of globalization are expected to serve as the bases around which the course of events is organized.

Consensus along these lines breaks down, however, over whether the predominance of globalization is likely to have desirable or noxious consequences. Those who welcome globalizing processes stress the power of economic variables. In this view the globalization of national economies through the diffusion of technology and consumer products, the rapid transfer of financial resources, and the efforts of transnational companies to extend their market shares is seen as so forceful and durable as to withstand and eventually surmount any and all pressures toward fragmentation. This line acknowledges that the diffusion that sustains the processes of globalization is a centuries-old dynamic, but the difference is that the present era has achieved a level of economic development in which it is possible for innovations occurring in any sector of any country's economy to be instantaneously transferred to and adapted in any other country or sector. As a consequence,

> when this process of diffusion collides with cultural or political protectionism, it is culture and protectionism that wind up in the shop for repairs. Innovation accelerates. Productivity increases. Standards of living improve. There are setbacks, of course. The newspaper headlines are full of them. But we believe that the time required to override these setbacks has shortened dramatically in the developed world. Indeed, recent experience suggests that, in most cases, economic factors prevail in less than a generation. . . .
>
> Thus understood, globalization—the spread of economic innovations around the world and the political and cultural adjustments that accompany this diffusion—cannot be stopped. . . . As history teaches, the political organizations and ideologies that yield superior economic performance survive, flourish, and replace those that are less productive.[2]

While it is surely the case that robust economic incentives sustain and quicken the processes of globalization, this line of theorizing nevertheless suffers from not allowing for its own negation. The theory offers no alternative interpretations as to how the interaction of economic, political, and social dynamics will play out. One cannot demonstrate the falsity—if falsity it is—of the theory because any contrary evidence is seen merely as "setbacks," as expectable but temporary deviations from the predicted course. The day may come, of course, when event so perfectly conform to the predicted patterns of globalization that one is inclined to conclude that the theory has been affirmed. But in the absence of alternative scenarios, the theory offers little guidance as to how to interpret intervening events, especially those that highlight the tendencies toward fragmentation. Viewed in this way, it is less a theory and more an article of faith to which one can cling.

Other observers are much less sanguine about the future development of fragmegration. They highlight a litany of noxious consequences that they see as following from the eventual predominance of globalization: "its economism; its economic reductionism; its technological determinism; its political cynicism, defeatism, and immobilism; its de-socialization of the subject and resocialization of risk; its teleological subtext of inexorable global 'logic' driven exclusively by capital accumulation and the market; and its ritual exclusion of factors, causes, or goals other than capital accumulation and the market from the priority of values to be pursued by social action."3

Still another approach, allowing for either desirable or noxious outcomes, has been developed by Michael Zurn. He identifies a mismatch between the rapid extension of boundary-crossing activities and the scope of effective governance. Consequently, states are undergoing what is labeled "uneven denationalization," a primary process in which "the rise of international governance is still remarkable, but not accompanied by mechanisms for . . . democratic control; people, in addition, become alienated from the remote political process. . . . The democratic state in the Western world is confronted with a situation in which it is undermined by the process of globalization and overarched by the rise of international institutions."4

While readily acknowledging the difficulties of anticipating where the process of uneven denationalization is driving the world, Zurn is able to derive two scenarios that may unfold: "Whereas the pessimistic scenario points to instances of fragmentation and emphasizes the disruption caused by the transition, the optimistic scenario predicts, at least in the long run, the triumph of centralization." The latter scenario rests on the presumption that the increased interdependence of societies will propel them to develop ever more effective democratic controls over the very complex arrangements on which international institutions must be founded.

UNEVEN FRAGMEGRATION

My own approach to theorizing about the fragmegrative process builds on these other perspectives and a key presumption of my own—that there is no inherent contradiction between localizing and globalizing tendencies—to develop an overall hypothesis that anticipates fragmegrative outcomes and that allows for its own negation: the more pervasive globalizing tendencies become, the less resistant localizing reactions will be to further globalization. In other words, globalization and localization will coexist, but the former will continue to set the context for the latter. Since the degree of coexistence will vary from situation to situation (depending on the salience of the global economy and the extent to which ethnic and other noneconomic factors actively contribute to localization), I refer, borrowing from Zurn, to the processes depicted by the hypothesis as uneven fragmegration. The hypothesis allows for continuing pockets of antagonism between globalizing and localizing tendencies even as increasingly (but unevenly) the two accommodate each other. It does not deny the pessimistic scenario wherein fragmentation disrupts globalizing tendencies; rather it treats fragmentation as more and more confined to particular situations that may eventually be led by the opportunities and requirements of greater interdependence to conform to globalization.

For globalizing and localizing tendencies to accommodate each other, individuals have to come to appreciate that they can achieve psychic comfort in collectivities through multiple memberships and multiple loyalties, that they can advance both local and global values without either detracting from the other. The hypothesis of uneven fragmegration anticipates a growing appreciation along these lines because the contrary premise, that psychic comfort can only be realized by having a highest loyalty, is becoming increasingly antiquated. To be sure, people have long been accustomed to presuming that, in order to derive the psychic comfort they need through collective identities, they had to have a hierarchy of loyalties and that, consequently, they had to have a highest loyalty that could only be attached to a single collectivity. Such reasoning, however, is a legacy of the state system, of centuries of crises that made people feel they had to place nation-state loyalties above all others. It is a logic that long served to reinforce the predominance of the state as the "natural" unit of political organization and that probably reached new heights during the intense years of the cold war.

But if it is the case, as the foregoing analysis stresses, that conceptions of territoriality are in flux and that the failure of states to solve pressing problems has led to a decline in their capabilities and a loss of legitimacy, it follows that the notion that people must have a "highest loyalty" will also decline and give way to the development of multiple loyalties and an understanding that local, national, and transnational affiliations need not be mutually exclusive. For the reality is that human affairs are organized at all these levels for good reasons; people have needs that can only be filled by close-at-hand organizations and other needs that are best served by distant entities at the national or transnational level.

In addition, not only is an appreciation of the reality that allows for multiple loyalties and memberships likely to grow as the effectiveness of states and the salience of national loyalties diminish, but it also seems likely to widen as the benefits of the global economy expand and people become increasingly aware of the extent to which their well-being is dependent on events and trends elsewhere in the world. At the same time, the distant economic processes serving their needs are impersonal and hardly capable of advancing the need to share with others in a collective affiliation. This need was long served by the nation-state, but with fragmegrative dynamics having undermined the national level as a source of psychic comfort and with transnational entities seeming too distant to provide the psychic benefits of affiliation, the satisfactions to be gained through more close-at-hand affiliations are likely to seem ever more attractive.

THE STAKES

It seems clear that fragmegration has become an enduring feature of global life; it is also evident that globalization is not merely a buzzword, that it encompasses pervasive complexities and contradictions that have the potential both to enlarge and to degrade our humanity. In order to ensure that the enlargement is more prevalent than the degradation, it is important that people and their institutions become accustomed to the multiple dimensions and nuances as our world undergoes profound and enduring transformations. To deny the complexities and contradictions in order to cling to a singular conception of what globalization involves is to risk the many dangers that accompany oversimplification.

NOTES

1. For an extensive discussion of the dynamics of fragmegration, see James N. Rosenau, *Along the Domestic-Foreign Frontier: Exploring Governance in a Turbulent World* (Cambridge: Cambridge University Press, 1997), ch. 6.
2. William W. Lewis and Marvin Harris, "Why Globalization Must Prevail," *The McKinsey Quarterly,* no. 2 (1992), p. 115.
3. Barry K. Gills, "Editorial: 'Globalization' and the 'Politics of Resistance,' " *New Political Economy,* vol. 2 (March 1997), p. 12.
4. Michael Zurn, "What Has Changed in Europe? The Challenge of Globalization and Individualization," paper presented at a meeting on What Has Changed? Competing Perspectives on World Order (Copenhagen, May 14–16, 1993), p. 40.

JAMES N. ROSENAU *is University Professor of International Affairs at George Washington University. His latest book is* Along the Domestic-Foreign Frontier: Exploring Governance in a Turbulent World *(Cambridge: Cambridge University Press, 1997). This article draws on the author's "New Dimensions of Security: The Interaction of Globalizing and Localizing Dynamics,"* Security Dialogue, *September 1994, and "The Dynamics of Globalization: Toward an Operational Formulation,"* Security Dialogue, *September 1996).*

Dueling Globalizations:

A Debate Between Thomas L. Friedman and Ignacio Ramonet

DOSCAPITAL

by Thomas L. Friedman

If there can be a statute of limitations on crimes, then surely there must be a statute of limitations on foreign-policy clichés. With that in mind, I hereby declare the "post–Cold War world" over.

For the last ten years, we have talked about this "post–Cold War world." That is, we have defined the world by what it wasn't because we didn't know what it was. But a new international system has now clearly replaced the Cold War: globalization. That's right, globalization—the integration of markets, finance, and technologies in a way that is shrinking the world from a size medium to a size small and enabling each of us to reach around the world farther, faster, and cheaper than ever before. It's not just an economic trend, and it's not just some fad. Like all previous international systems, it is directly or indirectly shaping the domestic politics, economic policies, and foreign relations of virtually every country.

As an international system, the Cold War had its own structure of power: the balance between the United States and the USSR, including their respective allies. The Cold War had its own rules: In foreign affairs, neither superpower would encroach on the other's core sphere of influence, while in economics, underdeveloped countries would focus on nurturing their own national industries, developing countries on export-led growth, communist countries on autarky, and Western economies on regulated trade. The Cold War had its own dominant ideas: the clash between communism and capitalism, as well as détente, nonalignment, and perestroika. The Cold War had its own demographic trends: The movement of peoples from East to West was largely frozen by the Iron Curtain; the movement from South to North was a more steady flow. The Cold War had its own defining technologies: Nuclear weapons and the Second Industrial Revolution were dominant, but for many developing countries, the hammer and sickle were still relevant tools. Finally, the Cold War had its own defining anxiety: nuclear annihilation. When taken all together, this Cold War system didn't shape everything, but it shaped many things.

Today's globalization system has some very different attributes, rules, incentives, and characteristics, but it is equally influential. The Cold War system was characterized by one overarching feature: division. The world was chopped up, and both threats and opportunities tended to grow out of whom you

THOMAS L. FRIEDMAN *is a foreign affairs columnist for the* New York Times *and author of* The Lexus and the Olive Tree *(New York: Farrar, Straus, and Giroux, 1999).*

were divided from. Appropriately, that Cold War system was symbolized by a single image: the Wall. The globalization system also has one overarching characteristic: integration. Today, both the threats and opportunities facing a country increasingly grow from whom it is connected to. This system is also captured by a single symbol: the World Wide Web. So in the broadest sense, we have gone from a system built around walls to a system increasingly built around networks.

Once a country makes the leap into the system of globalization, its élite begin to internalize this perspective of integration and try to locate themselves within a global context. I was visiting Amman, Jordan, in the summer of 1998 when I met my friend, Rami Khouri, the country's leading political columnist, for coffee at the Hotel Inter-Continental. We sat down, and I asked him what was new. The first thing he said to me was "Jordan was just added to CNN's worldwide weather highlights." What Rami was saying was that it is important for Jordan to know that those institutions that think globally believe it is now worth knowing what the weather is like in Amman. It makes Jordanians feel more important and holds out the hope that they will profit by having more tourists or global investors visiting. The day after seeing Rami I happened to interview Jacob Frenkel, governor of the Bank of Israel and a University of Chicago-trained economist. He remarked to me: "Before, when we talked about macroeconomics, we started by looking at the local markets, local financial system, and the interrelationship between them, and then, as an afterthought, we looked at the international economy. There was a feeling that what we do is primarily our own business and then there are some outlets where we will sell abroad. Now, we reverse the perspective. Let's not ask what markets we should export to after having decided what to produce; rather, let's first study the global framework within which we operate and then decide what to produce. It changes your whole perspective."

Integration has been driven in large part by globalization's defining technologies: computerization, miniaturization, digitization, satellite communications, fiber optics, and the Internet. And that integration, in turn, has led to many other differences between the Cold War and globalization systems.

Unlike the Cold War system, globalization has its own dominant culture, which is why integration tends to be homogenizing. In previous eras, cultural homogenization happened on a regional scale—the Romanization of Western Europe and the Mediterranean world, the Islamization of Central Asia, the Middle East, North Africa, and Spain by the Arabs, or the Russification of Eastern and Central Europe, and parts of Eurasia, under the Soviets. Culturally speaking, globalization is largely the spread (for better and for worse) of Americanization—from Big Macs and iMacs to Mickey Mouse.

Whereas the defining measurement of the Cold War was weight, particularly the throw-weight of missiles, the defining measurement of the globalization system is speed—the speed of commerce, travel, communication, and innovation. The Cold War was about Einstein's mass-energy equation, $e=mc^2$. Globalization is about Moore's Law, which states that the performance power of microprocessors will double every 18 months. The defining document of the Cold War system was "the treaty." The defining document of the globalization system is "the deal." If the defining anxiety of the Cold War was fear of annihilation from an enemy you knew all too well in a world struggle that was fixed and stable, the defining anxiety in globalization is fear of rapid change from an enemy you cannot see, touch, or feel—a sense that your job, community, or workplace can be changed at any moment by anonymous economic and technological forces that are anything but stable.

If the defining economists of the Cold War system were Karl Marx and John Maynard Keynes, each of whom wanted to tame capitalism, the defining economists of the globalization system are Joseph Schumpeter and Intel chairman Andy Grove, who prefer to unleash capitalism. Schumpeter, a former Austrian minister of finance and Harvard University professor, expressed the view in his classic work *Capitalism, Socialism, and Democracy* (1942) that the essence of capitalism is the process of "creative destruction"—the perpetual cycle of destroying old and less efficient products or services and replacing them with new, more efficient ones. Grove took Schumpeter's insight that only the paranoid survive for the title of his book about life in Silicon Valley and made it in many ways the business model of globalization capitalism. Grove helped popularize the view that dramatic, industry-transforming innovations are taking place today faster and faster. Thanks to these technological breakthroughs, the speed at which your latest invention can

A Tale of Two Systems	Cold War	Globalization
"The Cold War had its own dominant ideas: the clash between communism and capitalism. . . . The driving idea behind globalization is free-market capatalism."	In 1961, dressed in military fatigues, Cuban president Fidel Castro made his famous declaration: "I shall be a Marxist-Leninist for the rest of my life." In February 1972, President Richard Nixon traveled to China to discuss a strategic alliance between the two countries against the USSR.	This January, Castro donned a business suit for a conference on globalization in Havana. Financier George Soros and conservative economist Milton Friedman were invited. In April 1999, Chinese premier Zhu Rongji came to Washington to discuss China's admission to the World Trade Organization.
"These countries that are most willing to let capitalism quickly destroy inefficient companies, so that money can be freed up and directed to more innovative ones, will thrive in the era of globalization. Those which rely on governments to protect them from such creative destruction will fall behind."	Many countries raised trade barriers and tried import substitution industrialization, nationalization, price controls, and interventionist policies. The International Monetary Fund (IMF) and the World Bank were always present but rarely heeded. **Result:** Hyperinflation, overwhelming external debt, corruption, and inefficient industries ruled the day. Only 8 percent of countries had liberal capital regimes in 1975 and foreign direct investment was at a low of $23 billion.	Economic development relies on private-sector ownership, transparency and accountability, as well as investments in human capital and social infrastructure. The IMF plays a critical role, but must be enmeshed in a web of other organizations that support social welfare and the environment while promoting economic growth. **Result:** Foreign direct investment increased five fold between 1990 and 1997, jumping into $644 billion, and the number of countries with liberal regimes tripled to 28 percent.
The balance between individuals and nation-states [has changed]. . . . So you have today not only a superpower, not only Supermarkets, but . . . Super-empowered individuals."	In 1956, there were 973 international nongovernmental organizations (NGOs) in the world. In 1972, the total volume of world trade was only a fraction larger than the gross national product of the USSR. In 1970, there were only 7,000 transnational corporations (TNCs) in the world.	In 1996, there were 5,472 international NGOs in the world. The estimated annual revenue of transnational organized crime as of 1997, $750 billion, is larger than the gross domestic product of Russia. By 1994 the number of TNCs grew to 37,000 parent companies with 200,000 affiliates worldwide—controlling 33 percent of the world's productive assets.

SOURCE: Quotes taken from *The Lexus and the Olive Tree,* by Thomas Friedman (New York: Farrar, Straus, and Giroux, 1999).

be made obsolete or turned into a commodity is now lightening quick. Therefore, only the paranoid will survive—only those who constantly look over their shoulders to see who is creating something new that could destroy them and then do what they must to stay one step ahead. There will be fewer and fewer walls to protect us.

If the Cold War were a sport, it would be sumo wrestling, says Johns Hopkins University professor Michael Mandelbaum. "It would be two big fat guys in a ring, with all sorts of posturing and rituals and stomping of feet, but actually very little contact until the end of the match, when there is a brief moment of shoving and the loser gets pushed out of the ring, but nobody gets killed." By contrast, if globalization were a sport, it would be the 100-meter dash, over and over and over. No matter how many times you win, you have to race again the next day. And if you lose by just one-hundredth of a second, it can be as if you lost by an hour.

Last, and most important, globalization has its own defining structure of power, which is much more complex than the Cold War structure. The Cold War system was built exclusively around nation-states, and it was balanced at the center by two superpowers. The globalization system, by contrast, is built around three balances, which overlap and affect one another.

The first is the traditional balance between nation-states. In the globalization system, this balance still matters. It can still explain a lot of the news you read on the front page of the paper, be it the containment of Iraq in the Middle East or the expansion of NATO against Russia in Central Europe.

The second critical balance is between nation-states and global markets. These global markets are made up of millions of investors moving money around the world with the click of a mouse. I call them the "Electronic herd." They gather in key global financial centers, such as Frankfurt, Hong Kong, London, and New York—the "supermarkets." The United States can destroy you by dropping bombs and the supermarkets can destroy you by downgrading your bonds. Who ousted President Suharto in Indonesia? It was not another superpower, it was the supermarkets.

The third balance in the globalization system—the one that is really the newest of all—is the balance between individuals and nation-states. Because globalization has brought down many of the walls that limited the movement and reach of people, and because it has simultaneously wired the world into networks, it gives more direct power to individuals than at any time in history. So we have today not only a superpower, not only supermarkets, but also super-empowered individuals. Some of these super-empowered individuals are quite angry, some of them quite constructive—but all are now able to act directly on the world stage without the traditional mediation of governments or even corporations.

Jody Williams won the Nobel Peace Prize in 1997 for her contribution to the International Campaign to Ban Landmines. She managed to build an international coalition in favor of a landmine ban without much government help and in the face of opposition from the major powers. What did she say was her secret weapon for organizing 1,000 different human rights and arms control groups on six continents? "E-mail."

By contrast, Ramzi Ahmed Yousef, the mastermind of the February 26, 1993, World Trade Center bombing in New York, is the quintessential "super-empowered angry man." Think about him for a minute. What was his program? What was his ideology? After all, he tried to blow up two of the tallest buildings in America. Did he want an Islamic state in Brooklyn? Did he want a Palestinian state in New Jersey? No. He just wanted to blow up two of the tallest buildings in America. He told the Federal District Court in Manhattan that his goal was to set off an explosion that would cause one World Trade Center tower to fall onto the other and kill 250,000 civilians. Yousef's message was that he had no message, other than to rip up the message coming from the all-powerful America to his society. Globalization (and Americanization) had gotten in his face and, at the same time, had empowered him as an individual to do something about it. A big part of the U.S. government's conspiracy case against Yousef (besides trying to blow up the World Trade Center in 1993, he planned to blow up a dozen American airliners in Asia in January 1995) relied on files found in the off-white Toshiba laptop computer that Philippine police say Yousef abandoned as he fled his Manila apartment in January 1995, shortly before his arrest. When investigators got hold of Yousef's laptop and broke into its files, they found flight schedules, projected detonation times, and sample identification documents bearing photographs of some of his coconspirators. I loved that—Ramzi Yousef kept all his plots on the C drive of his Toshiba laptop! One should have no illusions, though. The super-empowered angry men are out there, and they present the most immediate threat today to the United States and the stability of the new globalization system. It's not because Ramzi Yousef can ever be a superpower. It's because in today's world, so many people can be Ramzi Yousef.

So, we are no longer in some messy, incoherent "post–Cold War world." We are in a new international system, defined by globalization, with its own moving parts and characteristics. We are still a long way from fully understanding how this system is going to work. Indeed, if this were the Cold War, the year would be about 1946. That is, we understand as much about how this new system is going to work as we understood about how the Cold War would work in the year Churchill gave his "Iron Curtain" speech.

Nevertheless, it's time we recognize that there is a new system emerging, start trying to analyze events within it, and give it its own name. I will start the bidding. I propose that we call it "DOScapital."

A New Totalitarianism

by Ignacio Ramonet

We have known for at least ten years that globalization is the dominant phenomenon of this century. No one has been waiting around for Thomas Friedman to discover this fact. Since the end of the 1980s, dozens of authors have identified, described, and analyzed globalization inside and out. What is new in Friedman's work—and debatable—is the dichotomy he establishes between globalization and the Cold War: He presents them as opposing, interchangeable "systems." His constant repetition of this gross oversimplification reaches the height of annoyance.

Just because the Cold War and globalization are dominant phenomena in their times does not mean that they are both systems. A system is a set of practices and institutions that provides the world with a practical and theoretical framework. By this fight, the Cold War never constituted a system—Friedman makes a gross error by suggesting otherwise. The term "Cold War," coined by the media, is shorthand for a period of contemporary history (1946—89) characterized by the predominance of geopolitical and geostrategic concerns. However, it does not explain a vast number of unrelated events that also shaped that era: the expansion of multinational corporations, the development of air transportation, the worldwide extension of the United Nations, the decolonization of Africa, apartheid in South Africa, the advancement of environmentalism, or the development of computers and high-tech industries such as genetic engineering. And the list goes on.

Furthermore, tension between the West and the Soviet Union, contrary to Friedman's ideas, dates from before the Cold War. In fact, that very tension was formative in shaping the way democratic states understood Italian fascism in the 1920s, Japanese militarism in the 1930s, German rearmament after the rise of Adolf Hitler in 1933, and the Spanish Civil War between 1936 and 1939.

Friedman is right, however, to argue that globalization has a systemic bent. Step by step, this two-headed monster of technology and finance throws everything into confusion. Friedman, by contrast, tells a tale of globalization fit for Walt Disney. But the chaos that seems to delight our author so much is hardly good for the whole of humanity.

Friedman notes, and rightly so, that everything is now interdependent and that, at the same time, everything is in conflict. He also observes that globalization embodies (or infects) every trend and phenomenon at work in the world today—whether political, economic, social, cultural, or ecological. But he forgets to remark that there are groups from every nationality, religion, and ethnicity that vigorously oppose the idea of global unification and homogenization.

Furthermore, our author appears incapable of observing that globalization imposes the force of two powerful and contradictory dynamics on the world: fusion and fission. On the one hand, many states seek out alliances. They pursue fusion with others to build institutions, especially economic ones, that provide strength—or safety—in numbers. Like the European Union, groups of countries in Asia, Eastern Europe, North Africa, North America, and South America are signing free-trade agreements and reducing tariff barriers to stimulate commerce, as well as reinforcing political and security alliances.

But set against the backdrop of this integration, several multinational communities are falling victim to fission, cracking or imploding into fragments before the astounded eyes of their neighbors. When the three federal states of the Eastern bloc—Czechoslovakia, the USSR, and Yugoslavia—broke apart, they gave birth to some 22 independent states! A veritable sixth continent!

The political consequences have been ghastly. Almost everywhere, the fractures provoked by globalization have reopened old wounds. Borders are increasingly contested, and pockets of minorities give rise to dreams of annexation, secession, and ethnic cleansing. In the Balkans and the Caucasus, these tensions unleashed wars (in Abkhazia, Bosnia, Croatia, Kosovo, Moldova, Nagorno-Karabakh, Slovenia, and South Ossetia).

The social consequences have been no kinder. In the 1980s, accelerating globalization went hand in hand with the relentless ultraliberalism of British prime minister Margaret

Thatcher and U.S. president Ronald Reagan. Quickly, globalization became associated with increased inequality, hikes in unemployment, deindustrialization, and deteriorated public services and goods.

Now, accidents, uncertainty, and chaos have become the parameters by which we measure the intensity of globalization. If we sized up our globalizing world today, what would we find? Poverty, illiteracy, violence, and illness are on the rise. The richest fifth of the world's population owns 80 percent of the world's resources, while the poorest fifth owns barely .5 percent. Out of a global population of 5.9 billion, barely 500 million people live comfortably, while 4.5 billion remain in need. Even in the European Union, there are 16 million people unemployed and 50 million living in poverty. And the combined fortune of the 358 richest people in the world (billionaires, in dollars) equals more than the annual revenue of 45 percent of the poorest in the world, or 2.6 billion people. That, it seems, is the brave new world of globalization.

Beware of Dogma

Globalization has little to do with people or progress and everything to do with money. Dazzled by the glimmer of fast profits, the champions of globalization are incapable of taking stock of the future, anticipating the needs of humanity and the environment, planning for the expansion of cities, or slowly reducing inequalities and healing social fractures.

According to Friedman, all of these problems will be resolved by the "invisible hand of the market" and by macroeconomic growth—so goes the strange and insidious logic of what we in France call the *pensée unique.* The *pensée unique,* or "single thought," represents the interests of a group of economic forces—in particular, free-flowing international capital. The arrogance of the *pensée unique* has reached such an extreme that one can, without exaggerating, call it modern dogmatism. Like a cancer, this vicious doctrine imperceptibly surrounds any rebellious logic, then inhibits it, disturbs it, paralyzes it, and finally kills it. This doctrine, this *pensée unique,* is the only ideology authorized by the invisible and omnipresent opinion police.

The *pensée unique* was born in 1944, at the time of the Bretton Woods Agreement. The doctrine sprang from the world's large economic and monetary institutions—the Banque de France, Bundesbank, European Commission, International Monetary Fund, Organisation for Economic Cooperation and Development, World Bank, and World Trade Organization—which tap their deep coffers to enlist research centers, universities, and foundations around the planet to spread the good word.

Dazzled by the glimmer of fast profits, the champions of globalization are incapable of taking stock of the future.

Almost everywhere, university economics departments, journalists (such as Friedman), writers, and political leaders take up the principal commandments of these new tablets of law and, through the mass media, repeat them until they are blue in the face. Their dogma is echoed dutifully by the mouthpieces of economic information and notably by the "bibles" of investors and stockbrokers—the *Economist, Far Eastern Economic Review,* Reuters, and *Wall Street Journal,* for starters—which are often owned by large industrial or financial groups. And of course, in our media-mad society, repetition is as good as proof.

So what are we told to believe? The most basic principle is so strong that even a Marxist, caught offguard, would agree: The economic prevails over the political. Or as the writer Alain Minc put it, "Capitalism cannot collapse, it is the natural state of society. Democracy is not the natural state of society. The market, yes." Only an economy disencumbered of social speed bumps and other "inefficiencies" can steer clear of regression and crisis.

The remaining key commandments of the *pensée unique* build upon the first. For instance, the market's "invisible hand corrects the unevenness and malfunctions of capitalism" and, in particular, financial markets, whose "signals orient and determine the general movement of the economy." Competition and competitiveness "stimulate and develop businesses, bringing them permanent and beneficial modernization." Free trade without barriers is "a factor of the uninterrupted development of commerce and therefore of societies." Globalization of manufactured production and especially financial flows should be encouraged at all costs. The international division of labor "moderates labor demands and lowers labor costs." A strong currency is a must, as is deregulation and privatization at every turn. There is always "less of the state" and a constant bias toward the interests of capital to the detriment of the interests of labor, not to mention a callous indifference to ecological costs. The constant repetition of this catechism in the media by almost all political decision makers, Right and Left alike (think of British and German prime ministers Tony Blair and Gerhard Schroder's "Third Way" and "New Middle"), gives it such an intimidating power that it snuffs out every tentative free thought.

Magnates and Misfits

Globalization rests upon two pillars, or paradigms, which influence the way globalizers such as Friedman think. The first pillar is communication. It has tended to replace, little by little, a major driver of the last two centuries: progress. From schools to businesses, from families and law to government, there is now one command: Communicate.

The second pillar is the market. It replaces social cohesion, the idea that a democratic society must function like a clock. In a clock, no piece is unnecessary and all pieces are unified. From this eighteenth-century mechanical metaphor, we can derive a modern economic and financial version. From now on, everything must operate according to the criteria of the "master market." Which of our new values are most fundamental? Windfall profits, efficiency, and competitiveness.

In this market-driven, interconnected world, only the strongest survive. Life is a fight, a jungle. Economic and social Darwinism, with its constant calls for competition, natural selection, and adaptation, forces itself on everyone and everything. In this new social order, individuals are divided into "solvent" or "nonsolvent"—i.e., apt to integrate into the market or not. The market offers protection to the solvents only. In this new order, where human solidarity is no longer an imperative, the rest are misfits and outcasts.

Thanks to globalization, only activities possessing four principal attributes thrive—those that are planetary, permanent, immediate, and immaterial in nature. These four characteristics recall the four principal attributes of God Himself. And in truth, globalization is set up to be a kind of modern divine critic, requiring submission, faith, worship, and new rites. The market dictates the Truth, the Beautiful, the Good, and the Just. The "laws" of the market have become a new stone tablet to revere.

Friedman warns us that straying from these laws will bring us to ruin and decay. Thus, like other propagandists of the New Faith, Friedman attempts to convince us that there is one way, and one way alone—the ultraliberal way—to manage economic affairs and, as a consequence, political affairs. For Friedman, the political is in effect the economic, the economic is finance, and finances are markets. The Bolsheviks said, "All power to the Soviets!" Supporters of globalization, such as Friedman, demand, "All power to the market!" The assertion is so peremptory that globalization has become, with its dogma and high priests, a kind of new totalitarianism.

DOSCAPITAL 2.0

by Thomas L. Friedman

Ignacio Ramonet makes several points in his provocative and impassioned anti-globalization screed. Let me try to respond to what I see as the main ones.

Ramonet argues that the Cold War was not an international system. I simply disagree. To say that the ColdWar was not an international system because it could not explain everything that happened during the years 1946 to 1989—such as aerial transport or apartheid—is simply wrong. An international system doesn't explain everything that happens in a particular era. It is, though, a dominant set of ideas, power structures, economic patterns,

Diplomacy then: Soviet premier Nikita Khruschev and U.S. vice president Richard Nixon argue over the merits of capitalism in 1959's "Kitchen Debate" . . .

and rules that shape the domestic politics and international relations of more countries in more places than anything else.

Not only was the Cold War such an international system, but France had a very comfortable, unique, and, at times, constructive niche in that system, bridging the two superpower camps. Now that this old order is gone, it is obvious France is looking for a new, singular, and equally comfortable niche in today's system of globalization. Just as in the Cold War, France, like every other country, will have to define itself in relation to this new system. The obsession with globalization in the pages of *Le Monde diplomatique* is eloquent testimony to the fact that this search is alive and well in France.

Ramonet says that I "forget to remark that there are groups from every nationality, religion, ethnicity, etc., who vigorously oppose . . . globalization." In my book *The Lexus and the Olive Tree,* however, I have five separate chapters dealing with different aspects of that backlash. The penultimate chapter, in fact, lays out why I believe that globalization is not irreversible and identifies the five major threats to it: Globalization may be "just too hard" for too many people; it may be "just too connected" so that small numbers of people can disrupt the whole wired world today; it may be "just too intrusive" into people's lives; it may be 'lust too unfair to too many people"; and lastly, it may be "just too dehumanizing." My approach could hardly be called the Walt Disney version of globalization.

Frankly, I can and do make a much stronger case for the downsides of globalization than Ramonet does. I know that globalization is hardly all good, but unlike Ramonet I am not utterly blind to the new opportunities it creates for people—and I am not just talking about the wealthy few. Ask the high-tech workers in Bangalore, India, or Taiwan, or the Bordeaux region of France, or Finland, or coastal China, or Idaho what they think of the opportunities created by globalization. They are huge beneficiaries of the very market forces that Ramonet decries. Don't they count? What about all the human rights and environmental nongovernmental organizations that have been empowered by the Internet and globalization? Don't they count? Or do only French truck drivers count?

Ramonet says I am "incapable of observing that globalization imposes the force of two powerful contradictory dynamics on the world: fusion and fission." Say what? Why does he think I called my book *The Lexus and the Olive Tree?* It is all about the interaction between what is old and inbred—the quest for community, nation, family, tribe, identity, and one's own olive tree—and the economic pressures of globalization that these aspirations must interact with today, represented by the Lexus. These age-old passions are bumping up against, being squashed by, ripping through, or simply learning to live in balance with globalization.

What Ramonet can accuse me of is a belief that for the moment, the globalization system has been dominating the olive-tree impulses in most places. Many critics have pointed out that my observation that no two countries have ever fought a war against each other while they both had a McDonald's was totally disproved by the war in Kosovo. This is utter nonsense. Kosovo was only a temporary exception that in the end proved my rule. Why did airpower work to bring the Balkan war to a close after only 78 days? Because NATO bombed the Serbian tanks and troops out of Kosovo? No way. Airpower alone worked because NATO bombed the electricity stations, water system, bridges, and economic infrastructure in Belgrade—a modern European city, a majority of whose citizens wanted to be integrated with Europe and the globalization system. The war was won on the power grids of Belgrade, not in the trenches of Kosovo. One of the first things to be reopened in Belgrade was the McDonald's. It turns out in the end the Serbs wanted to wait in line for burgers, not for Kosovo.

. . . and now: Microsoft boss Bill Gates gives Russia's former first deputy premier Anatoly Chubais a crash course on the new economy in Moscow, 1997.

Ramonet falls into a trap that often ensnares French intellectuals, and others, who rail against globalization. They assume that the rest of the world hates it as much as they do, and so they are always surprised in the end when the so-called little people are ready to stick with it. My dear Mr. Ramonet, with all due respect to you and Franz Fanon, the fact is the wretched of the earth want to go to Disneyworld, not to the barricades. They want the Magic Kingdom, not *Les Misérables* Just ask them.

Finally, Ramonet says that I believe all the problems of globalization will be solved by the "invisible hand of the market." I have no idea where these quotation marks came from, let alone the thought. It certainly is not from anything I have written. The whole last chapter of my book lays out in broad strokes what I believe governments—the American government in particular—must do to "democratize" globalization, both economically and politically. Do I believe that market forces and the Electronic Herd are very powerful today and can, at times, rival governments? Absolutely. But do I believe that market forces will solve everything? Absolutely not. Ramonet, who clearly doesn't know a hedge fund from a hedge hog, demonizes markets to an absurd degree. He may think governments are powerless against such monsters, but I do not.

I appreciate the passion of Ramonet's argument, but he confuses my analysis for advocacy. My book is not a tract for or against globalization, and any careful reader will see that. It is a book of reporting about the world we now live in and the dominant international system that is shaping it—a system driven largely by forces of technology that I did not start and cannot stop. Ramonet treats globalization as a choice, and he implicitly wants us to choose something different. That is his politics. I view globalization as a reality, and I want us first to understand that reality and then, by understanding it, figure out how we can get the best out of it and cushion the worst. That is my politics.

Let me share a secret with Ramonet. I am actually rooting for France. I hope that it can preserve all that is good and unique in its culture and way of life from the brutalizing, homogenizing forces of globalization. There is certainly room for a different path between the United States and North Korea, and good luck to France in finding it. But the readers of *Le Monde diplomatique* will get a lot better idea of how to find that middle path by reading my book than by reading Ramonet's critique.

The wretched of the earth want to go to Disneyworld, not to the barricades. They want the Magic Kingdom, not Les Misérables. Just ask them.

Unfortunately, his readers will have to read *The Lexus and the Olive Tree* in a language other than French. The book is coming out in Arabic, Chinese, German, Japanese, and Spanish. There is only one major country where my American publisher could not find a local publisher to print it: France.

Let Them Eat Big Macs

by Ignacio Ramonet

It is truly touching when Thomas Friedman says, "The wretched of the earth want to go to Disneyworld, not to the barricades." Such a sentence deserves a place in posterity alongside Queen Marie-Antoinette's declaration in 1789, when she learned that the people of Paris were revolting and demanding bread: "Let them eat cake!"

My dear Mr. Friedman, do reread the 1999 *Human Development Report* from the United Nations Development Programme. It confirms that 1.3 billion people (or one-quarter of humanity) live on less than one dollar a day. Going to Disneyworld would probably not displease them, but I suspect they would prefer, first off, to eat well, to have a decent home and decent clothes, to be better educated, and to have a job. To obtain these basic needs, millions of people around the world (their numbers grow more numerous each day) are without a doubt ready to erect barricades and resort to violence.

I deplore this kind of solution as much as Friedman does. But if we are wise, it should never come to that. Rather, why not allocate a miniscule part of the world's wealth to the "wretched of the earth"? If we assigned just 1 percent of this wealth for 20 years to the development of the most unhappy of our human brothers, extreme misery might disappear, and with it, risks of endemic violence.

But globalization is deaf and blind to such considerations—and Friedman knows it. On the contrary, it worsens differences and divides and polarizes societies. In 1960, before globalization, the most fortunate 20 percent of the planet's population were 30 times richer than the poorest 20 percent. In 1997, at the height of globalization, the most fortunate were 74 times richer than the world's poorest! And this gap grows each day. Today, if you add up the gross national products of all the world's underdeveloped countries (with their 600 million inhabitants) they still will not equal the total wealth of the three richest people in the world. I am sure, my dear Mr. Friedman, that those 600 million people have only one thing on their minds: Disneyworld!

It is true that there is more to globalization than just the downsides, but how can we overlook the fact that during the last 15 years of globalization, per capita income has decreased in more than 80 countries, or in almost half the states of the world? Or that since the fall of communism, when the West supposedly arranged an economic miracle cure for the former Soviet Union—more or less, as Friedman would put it, new McDonald's restaurants—more than 150 million ex-Soviets (out of a population of approximately 290 million) have fallen into poverty?

If you would agree to come down out of the clouds, my dear Mr. Friedman, you could perhaps understand that globalization is a symptom of the end of a cycle. It is not only the end of the industrial era (with today's new technology), not only the end of the first capitalist revolution (with the financial revolution), but also the end of an intellectual cycle—the one driven by reason, as the philosophers of the eighteenth century defined it. Reason gave birth to modern politics and sparked the American and French Revolutions. But almost all that modern reason constructed—the state, society, industry, nationalism, socialism—has been profoundly changed. In terms of political philosophy, this transformation captures the enormous significance of globalization. Since ancient times, humanity has known two great organizing principles: the gods, and then reason. From here on out, the market succeeds them both.

Now the triumph of the market and the irresistible expansion of globalization cause me to fear an inevitable showdown between capitalism and democracy. Capitalism inexorably leads to the concentration of wealth and economic power in the hands of a small group. And this in turn leads to a fundamental question: How much redistribution will it take to make the domination of the rich minority acceptable to the majority of the world's population? The problem, my dear Mr. Friedman, is that the market is incapable of responding. All over the world, globalization is destroying the welfare state.

What can we do? How do we keep half of humanity from revolting and choosing violence? I know your response, dear Mr. Friedman: Give them all Big Macs and send them to Disneyworld!

Want to Know More?

An insightful overview of the social transformations that globalization has ushered in can be found in Malcolm Waters' ***Globalization*** (New York: Routledge, 1995). In ***Capitalism, Socialism, and Democracy*** (London: Harper, 1942), Joseph Schumpeter argues that only innovation can compensate for the destructive forces of the market. Benjamin Barber looks at culture clash in his book ***Jihad versus McWorld*** (New York: Times Books, 1995). William Greider argues for more managed globalization in *One* ***World Ready or Not: The Manic Logic of Global Capitalism*** (New York: Simon & Schuster, 1997). In his book, ***The Post-Corporate World: Life after Capitalism*** (San Francisco: Berrett-Koehler, 1999), David Korten stipulates that corporate capitalism could unravel the cohesion of society. Robert Reich considers how international labor markets will react to a shrinking world in ***The Work of Nations: Preparing Ourselves for the 21st Century*** (New York: Alfred A. Knopf, 1991). For a view on how information technology has changed the world economy, see Frances Cairncross' ***The Death of Distance*** (Cambridge: Harvard Business School Press, 1997). For a provocative advocate of Americanization, see David Rothkopf's **"In Praise of Cultural Imperialism"** (FOREIGN POLICY, Summer 1997). Refraining from taking sides, Dani Rodrik reexamines some of the faulty assumptions made on both sides of the globalization debate in ***"Sense and Nonsense in the Globalization Debate"*** (FOREIGN POLICY, Summer 1997). Ignacio Ramonet's wide-ranging commentary can be found in back issues of ***Le Monde diplomatique,*** archived online. Rigorous critiques of Thomas Friedman's new book, ***The Lexus and the Olive Tree*** (New York: Farrar Straus and Giroux, 1999) can be found in the ***New Yorker*** (May 10, 1999), ***Nation*** (June 14, 1999), ***Financial Times*** (May 15, 1999) and ***New Statesman*** (July 5,1999).

For links to relevant Web sites, as well as a comprehensive index of related FOREIGN POLICY articles, access **www.foreignpolicy.com.**

The Crisis of Globalization

James K. Galbraith

THE DOCTRINE known as the Washington Consensus was the Apostle's Creed of globalization. It was an expression of faith that markets are efficient, that states are unnecessary, that the poor and the rich have no conflicting interests, that things turn out for the best when left alone. It held that privatization and deregulation and open capital markets promote economic development, that governments should balance budgets and fight inflation and do almost nothing else.

This faith has now proved totally unfounded.

The truth is that people need to eat every day. Policies that guarantee that they can do so, and with steadily improving diets and housing and health and other material conditions of life over long time spans, are good policies. Policies that foster instability directly or indirectly, that prevent poor people from eating in the name of efficiency or liberalism or even in the name of freedom, are not good policies. And it is possible to distinguish policies that meet this minimum standard from policies that do not.

The push for competition, deregulation, privatization, and open capital markets has undermined economic prospects for many millions of the world's poorest people. It is therefore not merely a naive and misguided crusade. To the extent that it undermines the stable provision of daily bread, it is dangerous to the safety and stability of the world, including ourselves. The greatest single danger right now is in Russia, a catastrophic example of the failure of free market doctrine. But serious dangers have also emerged in Asia and Latin America and they are not going to go away soon.

There is, in short, a crisis of the Washington Consensus.

The crisis of the Washington Consensus is visible to everybody. But not everybody is willing to admit it. Indeed, as bad policies produced policy failures, those committed to the policies developed a defense mechanism. They saw every unwelcome case as an unfortunate exception. Mexico was an exception—there was a revolt in Chiapas, an assassination in Tijuana. Then Korea, Thailand, Indonesia became exceptions: corruption, crony capitalism on an unimaginably massive scale, was discovered, but *after* the crisis hit. And then there came the Russian exception. In Russia, we are told, Dostoyevskian criminality welled up from the corpse of Soviet communism to overcome the efficiencies and incentives of free markets.

But when the exceptions outnumber the examples, there must be trouble with the rules. Where are the success stories of liberalization, privatization, deregulation, sound money, and balanced budgets? Where are the emerging markets that have emerged, the developing countries that have developed, the transition economies that have truly completed a successful and happy transition? Look closely. Look hard. They do not exist.

In each of the supposed exceptions—Russia, Korea, Mexico, and also Brazil—state-directed development programs have been liberalized, privatized, deregulated. But then, capital inflows led to currency overvaluation, making imports cheap but exports uncompetitive. As early promises of "transformation" proved unrealistic, the investor mood soured. A flight to quality began, usually following moves to raise interest rates in the "quality" countries—notably the United States in 1994 and in early 1997. A very small move in U.S. interest rates in March 1997 precipitated the outflows of capital from Asia that led to the Thai crisis.

The Russian case is especially sad and dramatic. In 1917 the Bolshevik revolution promised a war-weary Russian people liberation and deliverance from oppression. It took them seventy years to forget the essential lesson of

Originally appeared in *Dissent* magazine, Summer 1999, pp. 12-16.

that experience, which is that there are no easy, sudden, miraculous transitions. In 1992, the advocates of shock therapy followed the Bolshevik path, against the good sense of much of the Russian political order, by Bolshevik means. This was the true meaning of Boris Yeltsin's 1993 military assault on the Russian Parliament, an act of violence that we in the West tolerated, to our shame, in the name of "economic reform."

Privatization and deregulation in Russia did not create efficient and competitive markets, but instead large and pernicious private monopolists, the oligarchs, and the mafiosi, with control over competing industrial empires and the news media. And these empires sponsored their own banks, which were not banks at all but rather simply speculative poo1s, serving none of the essential functions of commercial banks. Meanwhile, the state followed a rigid policy of limiting expenditures, so that even wages and pension obligations duly incurred were not paid—as if the United States government were to refuse to pay Social Security checks because of a budget deficit! The private sector literally ran out of money. The payments system ceased to function; tax collection became impossible because there was nothing to tax. The state financed itself through a pyramid scheme of short-term debts—the GKO market—which collapsed as pyramids must on August 17, 1998. This was the end of free-market radicalism in Russia—and still, the Washington Consensus holds that Russia must "stay the course" on "economic reform."

Throughout Asia in the 1990s, stable industrial growth gave way to go-go expansions based heavily on real-estate speculation and commercial office development. Many more office towers went up, in Bangkok, Djakarta, Hong Kong and Kuala Lumpur, than could reasonably be put to use, Once finished, these towers do not go away; they stay empty but available, and so remain a drug on the market, inhibiting new construction. Recovery from the crash of such bubbles is a slow process. It took five years or longer in the Texas of the mid-1980s.

As for Brazil, through the early fall of 1998 it was said that the International Monetary Fund (IMP) would restore confidence and keep the Brazilian *real* afloat. But the *real* has since been devalued and Brazil is heading for a deep recession. The problem here does not originate with Brazil, and cannot be resolved by any actions the Brazilians alone might take. It lies, rather, in the international capital markets. Investors with exposure in Asia, and with losses in Russia, must reduce their lending to other large borrowers, irrespective of conditions in those countries. It is this imperative that is Brazil's problem today.

ARE THERE alternatives? Yes. The grim history I've just outlined is not uniform. Over the past half-century, successful and prolonged periods of strong global development have always occurred in countries with strong governments, mixed economic structures and weakly developed capital markets. This was the case of Europe and Japan following World War II, of Korea and Taiwan in the eighties and nineties, of China after 1979. These cases, and not the free market liberal examples—such as, say, Argentina after the mid-1970s or Mexico after 1986 or the Philippines or Bolivia—are the success stories of global economic development in our time.

In Korea, for instance, the great period of economic development was, indeed, a time of repressive crony capitalism. After 1975, the Korean government took note of the fate of South Vietnam, drew its own conclusions about the depth of American commitment and embarked on a program of heavy and chemical industrialization that emphasized dual-use technologies: the first major product of Hyundai Heavy Industries, for example, was a knock-off of the M-60 tank.

The Korean industrialization policy was not, in any static sense, efficient. No market would have chosen this course of action. The major players in the Korean economy—the state, the banks, the conglomerates known as *chaebols*—were yoked together in pursuit of their goals. Workers and their wage demands were repressed. And the initial search for markets was by no means entirely successful. There wasn't a big demand for those tanks, and so Hyundai decided to try building passenger cars instead.

Yet, when one adds up the balance sheet of the Korean model, can anyone seriously argue that the country would be richer today if it had done nothing in 1975? That it would be more middle class or more democratic?

It is true that Korea experienced the first harsh blows of the Asian financial crisis. But why? By 1997, the industrial policy was a thing of the distant past. Korean banks had become deregulated in 1992. What they did was to diversify—supporting vast expansion and industrial diversification schemes of the *chaebol* (Samsung's adventure into motor cars, for example) and lending to such places as Indonesia, where the Koreans evidently bought paper recommended to them by their American counterparts. The crash of Indonesia spread to Korea by these financial channels. It was not a crisis of crony capitalism, but of crony banking—deregulated and globalized.

One can multiply cases, but let us look at just one other, that of China.

China is a country with a fifty-year tradition of one-party government. For thirty of those years, it was a case study in regimentation, ideology, and economic failure. At one point, there occurred an entirely avoidable, catastrophic famine during which twenty or thirty million people perished. In the first years of the Great Proletarian Cultural Revolution, village rations amounted to less than a pound of rice per day.

Beginning in 1979, however, China embarked on reforms that changed the face of the country. These began with the most massive agricultural reform in human history, reforms that effectively ended food poverty in China in five years. After that, policies that welcomed long-term direct investment, that fostered township and village enterprises, joint ventures, and private enterprises, put into place a vast and continuing improvement in human living standards. Over twenty years, average living standards quadrupled; indeed growth has been so rapid that many people can perceive the improvement in their standard of living from month to month.

China's case demonstrates the potential effectiveness of sustained development policies—of policies that emphasize the priority of steady improvement over long periods of time. Unlike Russia, China made the mistake of the Great Leap Forward only once. And it never liberalized its capital markets or its capital account, for fear that such actions would prove a fatal lure, unleashing a cycle of boom and bust that a poor nation cannot tolerate for long.

China is no democracy. It is not politically free. But one must also acknowledge that the Chinese government has delivered on the essential economic demands of the Chinese people, namely food and housing, and that an alternative regime that did not deliver on these needs would not have been able to deliver internal peace, democracy, or human rights either.

So, what can the United States do now? To begin with, we can recognize that globalized finance makes the Federal Reserve the central banker to much of the developing world. Interest rate cuts last fall had an important stabilizing effect on global markets. But this effect is temporary; and the Fed's powers are limited. After a cut, another one is eventually required; and the cut from one to one-half percent lacks the force of the reduction from six percent to four. There is a strong case for lower interest rates, but we must also remember that the long term arrives when such short-term policies run out of steam.

Then there is fiscal policy. If it is a good idea for Japan to run a deficit to fight the global recession, why is it wise for the United States to be running a surplus that vastly offsets the deficit in Japan? It isn't. The United States should expand its own economy using all the tools available for this purpose.

Then there is the matter of what we preach to the world and the policies we support. If it is a good idea for the government of the United States to grow in line with our economy, then it is also a good idea for the governments of other countries to grow as their economies do. Global development policy should be geared toward strengthening that capacity, not crippling it.

Every functional private economy has, and needs, a core of state, regional, and municipal enterprises and distribution channels to assure food and basic necessities to low-income populations. Such systems stabilize the market institutions, which work better for people with higher incomes. They help prevent criminal monopolization of critical distribution networks by setting up an accountable alternative. International assistance should seek to strengthen these public networks where they exist and to build them where they do not. Efforts to do just this in Russia today, under the present government, should be supported and not opposed.

There is an obvious conflict between pro-growth policies and "investor confidence." Investors like to be repaid in the short run. But given that conflict, it is a fool's bargain to place investor confidence above the pursuit of development. Strong national governments have a sovereign right to regulate capital flows and banks operating on their soil—as much right as any nation has to control the flow of people across its national frontiers and to regulate their activities at home. A Tobin

Tax on foreign exchange should be enacted here, not only to slow speculation in the United States, but also to signal our acceptance of this principle for other countries, for whom different mechanisms of capital control may be more suitable in different cases.

Beyond this, a major reconstruction of world financial practices, aimed at restoring stability and strengthening the regulatory and planning capacities of national governments, is in order. The IMF needs new leadership, not tied to recent dogmas. But the IMF is also too small, and too thinly spread, to be useful in helping countries with the design and implementation of effective national development schemes. Regional financial institutions, as suggested for Asia by Japanese Deputy Finance Minister Eisuke Sakakibara, are therefore also needed, and U.S. opposition to them should be dropped.

MOST OF ALL, we must give up illusions. The neoliberal experiment is a failure. And it is a failure not because of unforeseeable events, but because it was and is systematically and fundamentally flawed. We need many changes from this naive and doomed vision of an ungoverned world order. We need large changes, and the need is great while time, I believe, is short. We must bring the Reagan era to a final end. We must return to development policies for the people whose needs matter most in the large scheme of things, namely the millions of hard-working people in poor countries who need to eat every day.

JAMES K. GALBRAITH is the author of *Created Unequal: The Crisis in American Pay*. He is working on a new book on global inequality.

Globalization and American Power

Kenneth N. Waltz

ASSOCIATING interdependence with democracy, peace and prosperity is nothing new. Before World War I, the close interdependence of states was thought of as heralding an era of peace among nations, and democracy and prosperity within them. In his widely read book, *The Great Illusion,* Norman Angell summed up the texts of generations of classical and neoclassical economists and drew from them the dramatic conclusion that wars would no longer be fought because they would not pay. World War I instead produced the great disillusion, which reduced political optimism to a level that remained low almost until the end of the Cold War—"almost", because beginning in the 1970s a new optimism, strikingly similar to the old, began to resurface. Interdependence was again associated with peace, and increasingly with democracy, which began to spread wonderfully to Latin America, to Asia and, with the Soviet Union's collapse, to Eastern Europe. In 1989 Francis Fukuyama foresaw in these pages a time when all states would be liberal democracies, and more recently Michael Doyle projected that this would happen sometime between 2050 and 2100.[1]

Robert Keohane and Joseph Nye, in their 1977 book *Power and Interdependence,* strengthened the notion that interdependence promotes peace by arguing that simple interdependence had become complex interdependence, binding the economic and hence the political interests of states ever more tightly together. Now we hear from many sides that interdependence has reached yet another height, transcending states and establishing a *Borderless World,* the title and theme of Kenichi Ohmae's 1990 book. People, firms and markets matter more; states matter less. Each tightening of the economic screw raises the benefits of economic exchange and makes war among the more advanced states increasingly costly. The simple and plausible propositions are that as the benefits of peace rise, so do the costs of war; when states perceive wars to be immensely costly, they will be disinclined to fight them. Still, war is not abolished, because even the strongest economic forces cannot conquer fear or eliminate concern for national honor. Generally, however, economic interests dominate and markets begin to supplant politics at home and abroad. That economics depresses politics and limits its significance is taken to be a happy thought.

The State of the State

GLOBALIZATION is the fad of the 1990s, and globalization is made in America. Thomas Friedman's *The Lexus and the Olive Tree* (1999) is perhaps the most exultant celebration of the American way, of market capitalism and liberal democracy. Free markets, transparency and flexibility are the watchwords. The "electronic herd" moves vast amounts of capital in and out of countries according to their political and economic merits. Capital moves almost instantaneously into countries with stable governments, progressive economies, open accounting and honest dealing, and out of countries lacking those qualities. States can defy the "herd", but they will pay a price, usually a steep one, as did Thailand, Malaysia, Indonesia and South Korea in the late 1990s. Some countries may defy the herd inadvertently (the countries just mentioned); others out of ideological conviction (Cuba and North Korea); some because they can afford to (oil-rich countries); others because history has simply passed them by (many African countries).

Countries wishing to attract capital and to gain the benefits of today's and tomorrow's technology must don the "golden straitjacket", a package of policies including balanced budgets, economic deregulation, openness to investment and trade, and a stable currency. The herd decides which countries to reward and which to punish, and nothing can be done about its decisions. The herd has no telephone number. When it decides to withdraw capital from a country, there is no one to complain to or petition for relief. Decisions of the herd are not made; they happen, and they happen because many individual investors make simultaneous decisions on similar grounds to invest or to withdraw their funds. Globalization is a process shaped by markets, not by governments.

Globalization means homogenization. Prices, products, wages, wealth, rates of interest and profit tend to converge the world over. Like any powerful movement for change, globalization encounters resistance—in America from religious fundamentalists, labor unions and their allies; abroad from anti-Americanists; everywhere from cultural traditionalists. The "end of the Cold War and the collapse of communism have discredited all models other than liberal democracy." The statement is by democratic theorist Larry Diamond, and Friedman repeats it with approval. There is but one best way, and America has found it. As Friedman puts it, "It's a post-industrial world, and America today is good at everything that is post-industrial." The herd does not care about forms of government as such, but it values and rewards "stability, predictability, transparency, and the ability to transfer and protect its private property." The message to all governments is clear: conform or suffer.

There is much in what Friedman says, and he says it very well. But how much? And, specifically, what is the effect of closer interdependence on the conduct of the internal and external affairs of nations?

First, we should ask how far globalization has proceeded. In fact, much of the world has been left out of the process: most of Africa and Latin America, Russia, all of the Middle East (except Israel), and large parts of Asia. Moreover, for many countries the degree of participation in the global economy varies by region. Northern Italy, for example, is in; southern Italy is out. Globalization is not truly global, but is mainly limited to northern latitudes. Linda Weiss points out that, as of 1991, 81 percent of the world stock of foreign direct investment was located in high-wage northern countries: the United States, followed by the United Kingdom, Germany and Canada. She adds that the concentration of investment in these countries has increased by 12 percent since 1967.[2] Obviously, the world is not one.

Second, we should compare the interdependence of nations today with interdependence earlier. The rapid growth of international trade and investment from the mid-1850s into the 1910s preceded a prolonged period of war, internal revolution and national insularity. During the years of post-World War II recovery, protectionist policies lingered as the United States opened its borders to trade while taking a relaxed attitude toward countries that protected their markets. One might say that from 1914 into the 1960s an interdependence deficit developed, which helps to explain the steady growth of interdependence thereafter. Among the richest twenty-four industrial economies (the OECD countries), exports grew at about twice the rate of GDP after 1960. In 1960 exports accounted for 9.5 percent of their national GDPs; in 1900 that figure was 20.5 percent.[3] Finding that the level of interdependence in 1999 approximately equals that of 1910 is hardly surprising. What is true of trade also holds for capital flows, again as a percentage of GDP.

Third, money markets may be the only economic sector that has become truly global. Finance capital moves freely across the frontiers of OECD countries and quite freely elsewhere. Still, with the movement of financial assets as with commodities, the present remains like the past. Despite today's ease of communication, financial markets in 1900 were at least as integrated as they are now.

Yet many globalizers underestimate the extent to which the new resembles the old. In any competitive system the winners are imitated by the losers. In political as in economic development, latecomers imitate the practices and adopt the institutions of the countries that have shown the way. Occasionally, someone finds a way to outflank, to invent a new way or to ingeniously modify an old way to gain an advantage; and then the process of imitation begins anew. That competitors begin to look like one another if the competition is close and continuous is a familiar story. But the apostles of globalization argue that the process has now sped up immensely. In the old political era, the strong vanquished the weak; in the new economic era, says Friedman, quoting Klaus Schwab, "the fast eat the slow." No longer is it "do what the strong party says or risk physical punishment", but "do what the electronic herd requires or remain impoverished." In a competitive system, a few do exceptionally well, some get along, and many bring up the rear.

If states must conform to the ways of the more successful among them or pay a stiff price for not doing so, we then have to ask what becomes of the state itself. The message of globalizers is that economic and technological forces impose on states a near uniformity of political and economic forms and functions. A glance at just the past seventy-five years, however, reveals that a variety of political and economic systems have produced impressive results and have been admired in their day for doing so.

In the 1930s and again in the 1950s, the Soviet Union's economic growth rates were among the world's highest, so impressive in the 1950s that America feared being overtaken and passed by. In the 1970s, West European welfare states with managed and directed economies were highly regarded. In the late 1970s through the 1980s, the Japanese brand of neomercantilism was thought to be the wave of the future, and Western Europe and the United States worried about being able to keep up. Imitate or perish was the counsel of some; pry the Japanese economy open and make it compete on our grounds was the message of others. America did not do much of either, yet in the 1990s its economy, too, has flourished.

Yet it is odd—and intellectually reckless—to conclude from a decade's experience that the one best model has at last appeared. True globalization, if it were realized, would mean a near uniformity of conditions across countries. But even in the 1990s, one finds little evidence of this. The advanced countries of the world have enjoyed or suffered distinct fates. Major West European countries were plagued by high and persistent unemployment; many Northeast and Southeast Asian countries experienced economic stagnation or collapse, while China continued to do quite well; and we know about the United States.

Globalizers, to be sure, do not claim that globalization is complete, only that the process is irreversible. Some evidence supports the conclusion, some does not. Looking at the big picture, one notices that nations whose economies have faltered or failed have been more fully controlled, directed and supported by the state than has the American economy. Soviet-style economies failed miserably, in China only the free-market sector flourishes, the once much-favored Swedish model has proved wanting, and the economies of the European Union suffer from high unemployment and low growth. One can easily add more examples. From these it is tempting to leap to the conclusion that America has indeed found, or stumbled onto, the one best way.

Obviously, Thomas Friedman thinks so. Tip O'Neill, when he was a congressman from Massachusetts, declared that all politics are local. Wrong, Friedman now says, all politics have become global. "The electronic herd", he writes, "turns the whole world into a parliamentary system, in which every government lives under the fear of a no-confidence vote from the herd."

BUT IT IS hard to believe that economic processes direct or determine a nation's policies, that spontaneous individual decisions about where to place resources reward or punish a national economy so strongly that a government either does what pleases the "herd" or its economy fails to prosper or even risks collapse. We all recall recent cases, some of them mentioned above, that seem to support Friedman's thesis. Mentioning them both makes a point and raises doubts.

For one thing, even if all politics has become global, economies remain local to a surprising extent. Countries with large economies continue to do most of their business at home. Sectors of the American economy that are scarcely involved in international trade—such as government, construction, nonprofit organizations, utilities, and wholesale and retail trade—employ 82 percent of Americans.[4] As Paul Krugman observes, "The United States is still almost 90 percent an economy that produces goods and services for its own use." For the world's three largest economies—the United States, Japan, and the European Union taken as a unit—exports account for 12 percent or less of GDP.[5] The world, then, is less interdependent than is usually supposed. Moreover, developed countries, oil imports aside, do the bulk of their external business with one another, which means that their dependence on imported commodities that they could not easily produce themselves is further reduced.

Reinforcing the parochial pattern of productivity, the famous footloose corporations also turn out to be firmly anchored in their home bases. A study of the world's one hundred largest corporations concludes that not one of them could be called truly "global" or "footloose." Another study found exactly one multinational corporation that seemed to be leaving its home base: Britain's chemical company, ICI. On all the important counts—location of assets, site of research and development, ownership, management—the importance of a corporation's home base is marked. And the technological prowess of corporations corresponds closely to that of the countries in which they are located.

Again, within advanced countries at similar levels of development that are closely interrelated, one would expect uniformities of form and function to be most fully displayed. Indeed, GDP per work hour among seven of the most prosperous countries nearly came into alignment between the 1950s and the 1980s.[6] Yet, while countries at a high level of development do tend to converge in productivity, that is something of a tautology. Stephen Woolcock, looking at forms of corporate governance within the European Union, finds a "spectrum of approaches" and expects it to persist for the foreseeable future.[7] Since the 1950s, for example, the economies of Germany and France have grown more closely together as each became the principal trading partner of the other. But a study of the two countries concludes that France has copied German policies yet has been unwilling or unable to copy German institutions.[8]

THE MOST telling refutation of the belief that state power has sharply declined is to be found in the state's capacity for transformation. Because technological innovation is rapid, and because economic conditions at home and abroad change often, states that adapt easily to such changes enjoy considerable advantages. International politics remains inter-national. National systems display a great deal of resilience. Those that adapt well grow and prosper; others just manage to get along. In this spirit, Ezra Taft Benson, when he was President Eisenhower's secretary of agriculture, gave this kindly advice to America's small farmers: "Get big or get out."

Success in competitive systems requires the units of the system to adopt ways they would often prefer to avoid. The United States looked to be heavy-footed in the 1980s when Japan's economy was booming. It seemed that the Ministry of International Trade and Industry was manned by geniuses who guided Japan's economy effortlessly to its impressive accomplishments. Now it is the United States that appears light-footed. Students of American government point out that one of the advantages of a federal system is that the separate states can act as laboratories for socioeconomic experimentation. When some states succeed, others imitate them. The same thought applies to nations.

States adapt, but they also protect themselves. Different nations, with distinct institutions and traditions, protect themselves in different ways. Japan fosters industries, defends them, and manages its trade. The United States uses its political, economic and military leverage to manipulate international events to promote its interests. Thus, as David E. Spiro elaborately shows, international markets and institutions did not recycle petrodollars after 1974; the United States did. Despite many statements to the contrary, the United States worked effectively through different administrations and under different cabinet secretaries to undermine markets and thwart international institutions. Its leverage enabled it to manipulate the oil crisis to serve its own interests.[9]

Many of the interdependence boosters of the 1970s expected the state to wither and fade away. Charles Kindleberger, for example, wrote in 1969 that "the nation-state is just about through as an economic unit." Globalizers of the 1990s believe that this time it really is happening. The state has lost its "monopoly over internal sovereignty", Wolfgang H. Reinecke writes, and as "an externally sovereign actor" it "will become a thing of the past."[10] But even as this is being asserted it is striking that, internally, the range of governmental functions and the extent of state control over societies and economies has seldom been fuller than it is now. After World War II, West European governments spent about 25 percent of their nations' products; now the figure is about 50 percent. In many parts of the world the concern has been not over the diminished internal powers of the state but over their increase. And although state control has lessened somewhat recently, does anyone really believe that economically advanced states have returned to a 1930s level—let alone to a nineteenth-century level—of governmental regulation?

States perform essential political, social and economic functions, and no other organization rivals them in these respects. They foster the institutions that make internal peace and prosperity possible. In the state of nature, as Kant put it, there is "no mine and thine." States turn possession into property and thus make saving, production and prosperity possible. The sovereign state with fixed borders has proved to be the best organization for keeping peace internally and fostering the conditions for economic well-being.

We do not have to wonder what happens to society and the economy when a state begins to fade away, for we have all too many examples. A few obvious ones are China in the 1920s and 1930s and again during the Cultural Revolution, many African states since their independence, and currently post-Soviet Russia. The less competent a state, the more likely it is to dissolve into component parts or be unable to adapt to transnational developments. Challenges at home and abroad test the mettle of states. In modern times, enough states have always passed the test to keep the international system functioning as a system of states. The challenges vary but states endure. They have proved to be hardy survivors.

The State in International Politics

ECONOMIC globalization would mean that the world economy, or at least the globalized portion of it, would be not merely interdependent but integrated. The difference between an interdependent and an integrated world is a qualitative one and not a mere matter of proportionately more trade and greater and more rapid flows of capital. With integration, the world would look like one big state. Economic markets and interests, however, cannot perform the functions of government. Integration requires or presumes a government to protect, direct and control.

Interdependence, in contrast, is "the mere mutualism" of states, as Emile Durkheim put it. Interdependence is not only looser than is usually thought but is also politically less consequential. Interdependence did not produce the world-shaking events of 1989–91. A *political* event, the failure of one of the world's two great powers, did that. Had the configuration of international politics not fundamentally changed, neither the unification of Germany nor the war against Saddam Hussein would have been possible. The most important events in international politics are explained by differences in the capabilities of states, not by economic forces operating across states or transcending them. Interdependence theorists, and globalizers even more so, argue that the international economic interests of states work against their going to war. True, they do; yet if one asks whether economic interests or nuclear weapons inhibit war more strongly, the answer obviously is nuclear weapons.

Europe's great powers prior to World War I were tightly bound together economically. They nevertheless fought a long and bloody war. The United States and the Soviet Union were not even loosely connected economically. They nevertheless sustained an uneasy peace for four and a half decades. The most important causes of peace, as of war, are found in international-political conditions, including the weaponry available to states. Events following the Cold War dramatically demonstrate the political weakness of economic forces. The integration (not just the interdependence) of the parts of the Soviet Union and Yugoslavia, with all of their entangling economic interests, did not prevent their disintegration. Governments and people sacrifice welfare and even security in pursuit of national, ethnic and religious ends.

National *politics,* not international markets, account for many international *economic* developments. Many students of politics and economics believe that economic blocs are becoming more common. But economic interests and market forces do not create blocs; governments do. Without governmental decisions the Coal and Steel Community, the European Economic Community, and the European Union would not have emerged. American governments forged NAFTA, and it was Japan that fashioned an East and Southeast Asian producing and trading area. Governments intervene much more in international economic matters today than they did in the earlier era of interdependence. Before World War I, foreign ministry officials were famed for their lack of knowledge of, or interest in, economic affairs. Because governments have become much more active in economic affairs at home and abroad, interdependence has become less of an autonomous force in international politics.

The many commentators who exaggerate the closeness of interdependence, and even more so the extent of globalization, think of individual states rather than of the international political system as a whole. Many small states import and export large shares of their gross national products. But states with large GNPS do not. When most of the great powers were smaller, they depended heavily on one another both economically and militarily. Great Britain and Germany before World War I were each other's second-best customers for both exports and imports, and their trade accounted for a huge proportion of their GNPS—52 and 38 percent, respectively. After World War II, the world's two great powers were barely dependent on others, while a number of other states depended heavily on them. The terms of political, economic and military competition are set by the larger units of the international political system. Through centuries of multipolarity, with five or so great powers of comparable size competing with one another, the international system was highly interdependent. Under bipolarity and unipolarity the degree of interdependence has declined markedly.

States are differentiated from one another not by function but primarily by capability. For two reasons inequalities across states have greater political impact than inequalities across income groups within states. First, the inequalities of states are larger and have been growing more rapidly. Rich countries have become richer while poor countries have remained poor. Second, in a system without central governance, the influence of the units of greater capability is disproportionately large because there are no effective laws and institutions to direct and constrain them. They are able to work the system to their advantage, as the petrodollar example cited above shows.

In the international system as it exists today, the United States is truly blessed. Precisely because the United States depends relatively little on others, it has a wide range of policy choices and the ability both to bring pressure on others and to assist them. The "herd" with its capital may flee from countries when it collectively decides that they are politically and economically unworthy, but some countries abroad, like some firms at home, are so important that they cannot be allowed to fail. National governments and international agencies then come to the rescue. The United States is the country that most often has the ability and the will to step in. The agency that most often acts is the IMF, and most countries think of the imf as the enforcement arm of the U.S. Treasury. Thomas Friedman believes that when the "herd" makes its decisions, there is no appeal, but often there is one, and it is for a bailout organized by the United States.

The international economy, like national economies, operates within a set of rules and institutions that have to be made and sustained. Britain to a large extent provided this service prior to World War I; no one did between the wars, and the United States has done so since.

The Unhidden Fist

IF, ECONOMICALLY, the United States is the world's most important country, militarily it is the decisive one. Thomas Friedman puts the point simply: the world is sustained by "the presence of American power and America's willingness to use that power against those who would threaten the system of globalization. . . . The hidden hand of the market will never work without a hidden fist." But the fist is in full view.

On its military forces, the United States outspends the next seven biggest spenders combined. When force is required to keep or to restore the peace, either the United States leads the way or the peace is not kept. The Cold War militarized international politics. Relations between the United States and the Soviet Union, and among some other countries as well, came to be defined largely in a single dimension: the military one.

Oddly, the end of the Cold War has elevated the importance of the military component in American foreign policy. Thus, William J. Perry and Ashton B. Carter, former secretary and assistant secretary of defense, have recently offered the concept of "preventive defense" as a guide to American policy. Preventive defense is conducted by American defense officials engaging in "security and military dialogue with regional states"; it calls for "a more robust defense to defense program."[11] Indeed, in many of the successor states of the Soviet Union, and in some other parts of the world as well, our defense personnel carry out what American policy there is.

The United States continues to spend, too, at a Cold War pace. In real terms, America's 1995 military budget approximately equaled the 1980 budget, and in 1980 the Cold War was at its height. The fact that most other countries have reduced their budgets more than the United States has heightened its military dominance. Some say that the world is not really unipolar because the United States often needs, or at least seeks, the help of others. The truth, however, remains: the stronger have many more ways of coping with adversities than the weak have, and the latter depend on the former much more than the other way around. The United States is the only country that can organize and lead a military coalition, as it did in Iraq and in the Balkans. Some states have little choice but to participate, partly because of the pressure the strong can bring to bear on the weak and partly because of the needs of the latter. West European countries and Japan are more dependent on Middle Eastern oil than is the United States, and Western Europe is more affected by what happens in Eastern Europe than is the United States.

As expected, the beneficiaries resent their benefactor, which leads to talk of righting the imbalance of power. Yet when the imbalance between one and the rest is great, catching up is difficult. French leaders especially bemoan the absence of multipolarity and call for greater European strength, but one cannot usefully will the end without willing the means. The uneven distribution of capabilities continues to be the key to understanding international politics.

America continues to garrison much of the world and to look for ways of keeping troops in foreign countries rather than withdrawing them, as one might have expected it to do at the Cold War's end.[12] The 1992 draft of the Pentagon's Defense Planning Guidance advocated "discouraging the advanced industrialized nations from . . . even aspiring to a larger global or regional role." The United States may at times seek help from others, but not too much help, lest it lose its leading position in one part of the world or another. The document, when it was leaked, provoked criticism. In response, emphasis was placed on its being only a draft, but its tenets continue to guide American policy.

Discontent in the Caboose

IN A SYSTEM of balanced states, the domination by one or some of them has in the past been prevented by the reaction of others acting as counterweights. The states of Europe held each other in balance through the first three hundred years of the modern state system. In the following fifty years, the United States and the Soviet Union checked each other, each protecting its sphere and attempting to manage affairs within it. Since the end of the Cold War, the United States has been alone in the world; no state or combination of states provides an effective counterweight.

What are the implications for international politics? The more interdependent the system, the more a surrogate for government is needed. Some Americans believe that the United States provides this service and that, because of its moderation, other states will continue to appreciate, or at least to accept, its managerial role. Benign hegemony is, however, something of a contradiction in terms. "One reads about the world's desire for American leadership only in the United States", a British diplomat has remarked. "Everywhere else one reads about American arrogance and unilateralism."

American leaders seem to believe that America's preeminent position will last indefinitely. The United States would then remain the dominant power without rivals rising to challenge it, a position without precedent in modern history. When Americans speak of preserving the balance in East Asia through our military presence, the Chinese understandably take this to mean that we intend to maintain the strategic hegemony we now enjoy in the *absence* of a balance of power. When China makes steady though modest efforts to improve the quality of its inferior forces, we see a future threat to our and others' interests. Whatever worries the United States has in East Asia and whatever threats it feels, Japan experiences them earlier, feels them more severely, and reacts to them. China then worries as Japan improves its airlift and sealift capabilities and as the United States bolsters its forces in Korea. The actions and reactions of China, Japan and Korea, with or without American participation, are creating a new balance of power in East Asia, which is becoming part of the new balance of power in the world.

In the Cold War, the United States won a decisive victory. Victory in war, however, often breeds lasting enmities. Magnanimity in victory is rare. Winners of wars, facing few impediments to the exercise of their wills, often act in ways that create future enemies. Thus Germany, by taking Alsace and most of Lorraine from France in 1871, earned its lasting enmity; and the Allies' harsh treatment of Germany after World War I produced a similar effect. In contrast, Bismarck persuaded the Kaiser not to march his armies along the road to Vienna after the great victory at Königgratz in 1866. In the Treaty of Prague, Prussia took no Austrian territory. Thus Austria, having become Austria-Hungary, was available as an alliance partner for Germany in 1879.

Rather than learning from history, the United States repeats past errors by expanding NATO eastward and extending its influence over what used to be the province of the vanquished. This alienates Russia and nudges it toward China instead of drawing it toward Europe and America. Despite much talk about the "globalization" of international politics, American political leaders to a dismaying extent think of East *or* West rather than of their interaction.

McGeorge Bundy once described the United States as "the locomotive at the head of mankind, and the rest of the world the caboose." America's pulling power is at a peak that cannot be sustained, for two main reasons. First, America is a country of 276 million people in a world of 6 billion, representing less than 5 percent of the world's total population. The country's physical capabilities and political will cannot sustain present international burdens indefinitely. Second, other countries may not enjoy being placed at the back of the train. Both friends and foes will react as countries always have to the threatened or real predominance of one among them: they will work to right the balance. The present condition of international politics is unnatural. Both the predominance of America and, one may hope, the militarization of international affairs will diminish with time.

Many globalizers believe that the world is increasingly ruled by markets. Looking at the state of states leads one to a different conclusion. The main difference between international politics now and earlier is not found in the increased interdependence of states but in their growing inequality. With the end of bipolarity, the distribution of capabilities among states has become extremely lopsided. Rather than elevating economic forces and depressing political ones, the inequalities of international politics enhance the political role of one country. Politics as usual prevails over economics.

Notes

1. Doyle, *Ways of War and Peace: Realism, Liberalism, and Socialism* (New York: W. W. Norton, 1997), pp. 480–1.
2. Weiss, *The Myth of the Powerless State: Governing the Economy in a Global Era* (Cambridge, UK: Polity Press, 1998), p. 186.
3. Robert Wade, "Globalization and its Limits: Reports of the Death of the National Economy are Grossly Exaggerated", in *National Diversity and Global Capitalism,* ed. Suzanne Berger and Ronald Dore (Ithaca, NY: Cornell University Press, 1996), p. 62. Cf. Weiss, *Myth,* Table 6-1.
4. Robert Z. Lawrence, "Workers and Economists II: Resist the Binge", *Foreign Affairs* (March/April 1994).
5. Weiss, *Myth,* p. 176.
6. Robert Boyer, "The Convergence Hypothesis Revisited: Globalization but Still the Century of Nations", in *National Diversity,* p. 37.
7. Woolcock, "Competition among Forms of Corporate Governance in the European Community: The Case of Britain", in *National Diversity,* p. 196.
8. Andrea Boltho, "Has France Converged on Germany?", *National Diversity,* chap. 3.
9. Spiro, *The Hidden Hand of American Hegemony: Petrodollar Recycling and International Markets* (Ithaca, NY: Cornell University Press, 1999), especially chap. 6.
10. Reinecke, "Global Public Policy", *Foreign Affairs* (November/December 1997), p. 137.
11. Perry and Carter, *Preventive Defense: A New Security Strategy for America* (Washington, DC: Brookings Institution Press, 1999), pp. 9, 11.
12. Hans Binnendijk, for example, has urged Americans to develop a case for leaving American troops in South Korea even if the North should no longer be a threat. See *Strategic Assessment 1996: Instruments of U.S. Power* (Washington, DC: National Defense University Press, 1996), p. 2.

Kenneth N. Waltz, former Ford Professor of Political Science at the University of California, Berkeley, is a research asssociate of the Institute of War and Peace Studies and adjunct professor at Columbia University. An earlier version of this essay was published in the December issue of *PS: Political Science & Politics.*

Reality Check

The WTO and Globalization After Seattle

PETER D. SUTHERLAND

The Seattle Ministerial Conference *of the World Trade Organization (WTO) demonstrated with disturbing force the huge confusions that haunt the public mind and much of global politics about the nature of trade and the process now known as globalization. The notion that globalization is an international conspiracy on the part of industrial-country governments and large firms to marginalize the poorest* nations, to exploit low wages and social costs wherever they may be found, to diminish cultures in the interests of an Anglo-Saxon model of lifestyle and language, and even to undermine human rights and cut away democratic processes that stand in the way of ever more open markets is, of course, utter nonsense. Yet the Seattle demonstrations vividly exhibited the worrying tendency to equate these concerns and others to the existence and potential development of the World Trade Organization, the institutional and legal face of the world trade system.

This outpouring of misconceived, ill-understood propaganda against a system that has brought vast gains to most nations over the past few decades is extraordinarily dangerous. It is a threat to the prospects of a better life for many millions, perhaps billions, of people at the start of the new millennium. If left unquestioned and unchallenged in the interests of political correctness or political advantage, this sentiment could set the cause of economic and social development back 20 years. This threat is made all the more serious by the difficult new challenges facing governments today. Still, Seattle showed more clearly some of the institutional difficulties of managing effective decision-making processes, with over 100 countries truly interested and involved in managing the geopolitical realities of the 21st century.

The Biggest Straw Man

In order to understand the dangers implied by attacks on the WTO, one must first distinguish between "globalization" and the World Trade Organization. Neither as a body of international law nor as a governmental institution can the WTO be regarded as synonymous with globalization. The WTO, like its predecessor the General Agreement on Tariffs and Trade (GATT), is a collection of rules and undertakings voluntarily entered into and implemented by governments on the basis of consensus among those governments to provide a predictable, stable, and secure environment in which all types of firms can trade and invest. A small transfer of national sovereignty (insofar as any purely intergovernmental structure can affect sovereignty) in the interest of internationally enforceable disciplines brings economic gains for all and prevents economic muscle from being the sole arbiter of commercial advantage. It is easy to argue that in a period when business is as likely to be conducted at the global level as at the national, the WTO recovers a degree of sovereignty for governments that otherwise find themselves no longer able to influence significant aspects of their economic future.

Of course, open and secure markets have encouraged global trade and investment. They have provided jobs, consumer choice, and rising personal wealth in large parts of the world, including many developing countries. Governments everywhere want to see their firms able to trade, and they actively seek inward investment by foreign firms. But that is not the whole story of globalization. The WTO has had only a marginal effect on other significant elements, most of which relate to the mobility of people, information, culture, technology and capital. Air transport, telecommunications, the media, and now the internet are four of the most crucial drivers of globalization. While they are not without their dangers or inadequacies, few would seriously argue that they have not brought widespread benefits. These innovations represent the positive face of the global economy.

Are the more troublesome aspects of globalization really a reflection of the trading system, or do they represent quite different policy failures, including poor education and training, misplaced and inefficient government intervention in industry, corruption in both the public and private sectors, poor governance, crime, lack of transparency in regulatory systems, inadequate or inappropriate social security and pensions systems, and so on? Admittedly, the trading system has not always provided the right results; for instance, it ought to be able to deliver more for the least-developed countries, even if it cannot solve all their problems. However, equating the WTO with the difficulties of the global economy risks damaging a system which has given much and still has more to offer. Such thinking also neglects the

From the *Harvard International Review,* Winter/Spring 2000, pp. 20-24. © 2000 by Harvard International Review.

importance of the WTO's fundamental role in simply facilitating trade and investment. The tendency to turn to the trade rules to resolve every challenge facing mankind—the environment, human rights, and labor standards—is almost as dangerous as the desire to dismantle the system in order to halt a process of globalization that is beyond the realm of any institution.

Fruits of the Uruguay Round

The first thing governments need to do in the current atmosphere of sometimes dubiously motivated protest and fear is to stop apologizing for the WTO and start defending it. The GATT helped create three decades of remarkably healthy economic growth. It succeeded in a low-profile manner because, in the 1950s and 1960s, high customs duties could be brought down steadily without attracting much political controversy. By the time the Uruguay Round was launched in 1986, the world was left with the hard cases of international trade. Negotiators finally had to face up to protectionism in the most sensitive industries of the developed countries, particularly in textiles, clothing, footwear, agriculture, steel, and automobiles. They also came to realize that the next stages of reducing protection and opening markets, and thus reestablishing the kind of trade growth spurred by the GATT, would mean moving some of the focus of negotiation from conditions at the border (such as tariffs and quota restrictions) to the heart of domestic regulation and sectoral support.

Immense political effort was required at the highest levels of government, but the Uruguay Round succeeded and established the WTO in the process. The advances made on all fronts cannot be underestimated. Policies in agriculture underwent a revolution: all market-access restrictions were translated into transparent tariffs, and the process of winding back the most distorting features of domestic support and export subsidies was initiated. A higher level of practical liberalization for farm goods might have been preferred, but the fundamental policy changes are irreversible and provide the basis to go further next time. Similarly, in textiles and clothing all the countries maintaining heavy quantitative controls on imports are committed to phasing them out. It will take nearly ten years, but the agreement at Uruguay marked a fundamental change of heart and direction.

A "human face" for the trading system is appropriate if it does not serve to undermine the foundations of the system and the huge gains it has provided humanity over the past 50 years.

Many other trade rules were amended, clarified, or added to the system. The practice of "negotiating" so-called "voluntary export restraints" affecting automobiles, steel, cutlery, and many other products for which consumers were forced to pay far more than was reasonable was outlawed. Some of the most damaging features of anti-dumping practices were cut back. Modern rules on technical barriers to trade and health and-safety regulation were also put in place.

An agreement requiring intellectual property rights to be available and enforceable in all WTO countries was concluded for the first time, despite doubts and difficulties in some industrial and developing countries. There were two final jewels in the crown. First, an agreement on trade in services brought GATT-like disciplines and concessions in sectors as diverse as banking, telecommunications, professional services, travel, tourism, and the audio-visual industry. Financial services and telecommunications were the subject of additional valuable packages of concessions in the past three years, and the new negotiations, beginning this year, will take the process of progressive liberalization in the services sector much further. Second, the entire body of WTO disciplines and concessions was made enforceable through a tough dispute-settlement procedure that has now been used in nearly 200 cases.

It has become almost an article of faith that while all of these developments were good for the industrialized countries and some of the more advanced developing countries, many poorer countries lost out. Some critics suggest that these countries did not benefit from the results of the round, and that they were, in fact, further marginalized and impoverished. According to these critics, such marginalization is not surprising because developing countries had little or no voice in the negotiations that culminated in agreement at the end of 1993.

Such a position is an insult to the abilities of the many developing-country trade negotiators who participated fully in the Uruguay Round. Although I took responsibility at a comparatively late stage, I can attest to the effectiveness and strength of purpose of these officials and ministers from poorer nations. They had considerable influence on the original development of the Uruguay Round agenda; worked assiduously through the eight-year process of examination and elucidation of issues, and negotiation of texts; and were in the foreground during the tough final months of bargaining. Certainly the United States, the European Union, and Japan were more influential, and many of the Uruguay Round texts pay particular attention to their interests. But the developing countries succeeded for the first time in any trade round in welding an influence on the final outcome quite disproportionate to their share of world trade. The WTO is very much their institution and the rules of world trade are as much their rules as those of the industrial countries.

CUSTODIAN OF TRADE RULES

Created in 1995 at the end of the Uruguay Round trade negotiations, the World Trade Organization (WTO) became the sole, permanent international institution overseeing the rules of global trade.The WTO administers and enforces the multilateral agreements and national market access commitments reached at the end of the Uruguay Round. These include the amended General Agreement on Tariffs and Trade (GATT), the legal framework that the WTO succeeded. The WTO currently has more than 135 member-states, with nearly 30 others negotiating for accession.

The organization's highest decision-making body is the Ministerial Conference, which meets at least once every two years, most recently in Seattle. The organization's regular work is conducted by the General Council, which is composed of Geneva-based diplomats or trade officials from capitals. The General Council constitutes the Dispute Settlement Body, which has already handled some 200 trade disputes, and convenes on a regular basis as the Trade Policy Review Body to examine the individual trade policies of WTO members.

Three councils that are responsible for the principal international trade policy sectors covered by the Uruguay Round agreements report to the General Council: the Councils for Trade in Goods, Trade in Services, and Trade-Related Aspects of Intellectual Property. Each Council has a number of subsidiary committees. For example, the Council for Trade in Goods has 11 committees, including those on anti-dumping measures, subsidies, and agriculture. Temporary working groups are established to handle specific questions such as the accession of new members.

New trade agreements are normally negotiated within separate structures. At various stages informal contact is necessary between trade ministers and even heads of state to secure politically difficult decisions. Traditionally, the Director-General has brought delegations together on an informal basis to clarify positions and to seek out solutions where there is a negotiating impasse. In the case of so-called "Green Room" meetings, this has entailed assembling selective groups of the most directly interested members. All agreements made in the Green Room environment must be taken back to the general membership for consideration. With very few exceptions, all decisions in the WTO are made by consensus. **–HIR**

Myths and Realities

So, if it is untrue that developing countries were ignored in the establishment of the WTO, is it at least true that they saw few practical benefits in terms of trade and investment? Again, the answer is no. A few measures demonstrating the long-term trends rather than the short-term aberrations bolster the point. Are developing countries benefiting from more open industrial-country markets? The answer is yes; despite the fall in trade during 1997 because of the drop in commodity prices and the Asian financial crisis, the share of developing countries and the transition economies in the imports of developed countries increased to 25 percent in 1998 from 22.8 percent in 1994. Has the developing countries' share in world trade grown? Again, yes. Despite the setbacks of 1997–1998, the latest WTO figures show that the share of developing countries in world exports of manufactures in 1998 was one percent higher than in 1994, and 6.4 percent higher than in 1990. The same overall growth trend can be observed for merchandise exports generally as well as agricultural products.

What about investment? Have developing countries seen an inward flow of productive investment, as they should if they offer more open markets with stable trade regimes based upon WTO disciplines? As with trade, the picture is mixed, with considerable variations in performance. However, figures from the UN Conference on Trade and Development show that overall inward foreign direct investment (FDI) flows to the developing world rose steadily and consistently from an average of US$35 billion a year in the period 1987–92 to US$166 billion in 1998. Taken as a percentage of gross fixed capital formation, FDI inflows to developing countries rose from an average of 3.9 percent in the period 1987–92 to 10.3 percent in 1998.

There is nothing fundamentally wrong with the system that calls for a wholesale rethinking on behalf of the developing countries. It is accepted that some developing countries have had difficulty in implementing some Uruguay Round commitments. Political and conceptual difficulties have hampered the implementation of certain intellectual property commitments in countries like India. In some of the poorest economies, the absence of solid institutional and technological infrastructure has made the implementation of agreements such as those on customs valuation and health and safety standards difficult. But patience and the right kind of technical assistance can resolve such problems over time. They are not evidence of a systemic failure in the WTO.

Indeed, many developing countries are successfully integrating themselves into the global economy through their commitment to WTO obligations. The failure of the Seattle meeting effectively blocked the continuation of that process or, at the very least, reduced opportunities for further progress. Essentially all that remains is the potential for negotiations on trade in services and agriculture that were mandated in the Uruguay Round agreements. This is not a small agenda, and any successful conclusion in the near future remains in question.

What has been lost or suspended is a larger and, in some respects more urgent, agenda. Developing countries have clearly been denied much that they rightly expected in the implementation of Uruguay Round commitments. They had reasonable demands that industrial countries implement in better faith the agreement to phase out textiles and clothing quotas. The agricultural agreement should have brought them more commercial advantage than has been the case. Anti-dumping legislation has continued to operate too stringently to the disadvantage of poorer countries. On the other hand, these countries have sometimes had difficulties in meeting their own obligations. That is hardly surprising since they have been required to go much further, much faster than was ever expected of industrial countries. In most cases, additional time needed for implementation of commitments should willingly be provided along with generous technical assistance efforts and the necessary funding for institutional capacity-building.

The least developed countries have been denied the duty-free treatment in market access that has long been promised and discussed in the context of a new round. The entire world has lost the commercial opportunities that would have sprung from global tariff and non-tariff-barrier negotiations covering industrial products. It is estimated that a 50-percent reduction in industrial tariffs would raise some US$270 billion in global income per year, and that developing countries could benefit from as much as 95 percent of the gains from liberalizing trade in manufactures.

Before the Next Round

Perhaps those opportunities will re-emerge, but the immediate priority is not to rush to launch a new round. Governments need to learn the lessons of the Seattle meeting and prepare the ground for the multilateral trading system to move forward on the basis of willing consensus among governments. I would propose four major areas as needing profound reconsideration.

First, coherence in trade policy-making is needed. Until now, this has tended to mean cooperation between the secretariats of the WTO and other major international institutions like the World Bank and the International Monetary Fund. Coherence should now take on a different meaning. It should ensure that the stances of WTO member governments in trade negotiations reflect a domestic consensus. Government departments must coordinate effectively among themselves so that, for instance, environmental, public health, or development concerns are factored into trade-policy decision-making early on. Governments must listen to and work with many different constituencies in an open and transparent manner. Only then can the WTO be clear of the foolish charge that it is some form of government-business conspiracy.

Second, negotiations and decision-making within the WTO itself need to become more coherent and effective. This may require a high level management structure in Geneva, perhaps based upon a restricted constituency-based management or advisory board. Senior policy makers should come to Geneva regularly to set the body's business in the fullest context, including financial development, environmental concerns, and other considerations. Moreover, both the preparatory process and the Seattle ministerial meeting demonstrated that while full transparency is vital—and the institution will have to steel itself to become yet more open—efficient and effective decision-making is necessary if continued paralysis is to be avoided. Of course, negotiating positions may often be so far apart that compromise is simply not possible. Recent history suggests, however, that the techniques of negotiating in a multilateral environment are either inoperable or have been forgotten.

Third, careful consideration must now be given to the speed and intensity with which a new round or any other effort to extend the trading system is pursued. There can be little doubt that the Seattle meeting was both premature and over-burdened with proposals that were poorly thought-out, unnecessary, or premature. Is there really an urgent need to launch a broad-based new trade round in the immediate future? If one believes that neither agriculture nor services negotiations can progress outside such a round, then perhaps the answer is a qualified "yes." But, if the reality is such that an early start would be unlikely to move forward with any conviction, then perhaps governments should take a deep breath and await a more propitious time. Nothing would damage the WTO's image further than another failed attempt to initiate a round.

Fourth, regardless of a new round, governments must now live up to their responsibilities and start energetically defending the principles on which the WTO is based. A "human face" for the trading system is appropriate if it does not serve to undermine the foundations of the system and the huge gains it has provided humanity over the past 50 years. It is perfectly possible to understand and respond to the concerns of those who doubt the value of the system without holding it hostage to local politics. The critics must understand that however justified their causes, the world would not be a better place without the WTO and without continued efforts to make it still more effective for all its members.

This is a turning point for the global trading system. How governments respond to the challenges raised by the Seattle Ministerial Conference could have an overwhelming influence on the contribution that the institution can have on the creation of a better society in the future. Globalization remains a fact and an opportunity. The WTO is one of the most effective instruments at our disposal for translating the opportunity into the reality of improved welfare for billions of citizens. There is no question that it could be a better instrument. But it is the best that we have at our disposal and are likely to have in the future. Governments must learn to use it wisely, change it carefully, and support it convincingly.

PETER D. SUTHERLAND was Director-General of the General Agreement on Tariffs and Trade and World Trade Organization and is Co-Chairman of BP Amoco and Chairman at Goldman Sachs International.

Where Have All the Farmers Gone?

The globalization of industry and trade is bringing more and more uniformity to the management of the world's land, and a spreading threat to the diversity of crops, ecosystems, and cultures. As Big Ag takes over, farmers who have a stake in their land—and who often are the most knowledgeable stewards of the land—are being forced into servitude or driven out.

by Brian Halweil

Since 1992, the U.S. Army Corps of Engineers has been developing plans to expand the network of locks and dams along the Mississippi River. The Mississippi is the primary conduit for shipping American soybeans into global commerce—about 35,000 tons a day. The Corps' plan would mean hauling in up to 1.2 million metric tons of concrete to lengthen ten of the locks from 180 meters to 360 meters each, as well as to bolster several major wing dams which narrow the river to keep the soybean barges moving and the sediment from settling. This construction would supplement the existing dredges which are already sucking 85 million cubic meters of sand and mud from the river's bank and bottom each year. Several different levels of "upgrade" for the river have been considered, but the most ambitious of them would purportedly reduce the cost of shipping soybeans by 4 to 8 cents per bushel. Some independent analysts think this is a pipe dream.

Around the same time the Mississippi plan was announced, the five governments of South America's La Plata Basin—Bolivia, Brazil, Paraguay, Argentina, and Uruguay—announced plans to dredge 13 million cubic meters of sand, mud, and rock from 233 sites along the Paraguay-Paraná River. That would be enough to fill a convoy of dump trucks 10,000 miles long. Here, the plan is to straighten natural river meanders in at least seven places, build dozens of locks, and construct a major port in the heart of the Pantanal—the world's largest wetland. The Paraguay-Paraná flows through the center of Brazil's burgeoning soybean heartland—second only to the United States in production and exports. According to statements from the Brazilian State of Mato Grasso, this "Hidrovía" (water highway) will give a further boost to the region's soybean export capacity.

Lobbyists for both these projects argue that expanding the barge capacity of these rivers is necessary in order to improve competitiveness, grab world market share, and rescue farmers (either U.S. or Brazilian, depending on whom the lobbyists are addressing) from their worst financial crisis since the Great Depression. Chris Brescia, president of the Midwest River Coalition 2000, an alliance of commodity shippers that forms the primary lobbying force for the Mississippi plan, says, "The sooner we provide the waterway infrastructure, the sooner our family farmers will benefit." Some of his fellow lobbyists have even argued that these projects are essential to feeding the world (since the barges can then more easily speed the soybeans to the world's hungry masses) and to saving the environment (since the hungry masses will not have to clear rainforest to scratch out their own subsistence).

Probably very few people have had an opportunity to hear both pitches and compare them. But anyone who has may find something amiss with the argument that U.S. farmers will become more competitive versus their Brazilian counterparts, at the same time that Brazilian farmers will, for the same reasons, become more competitive with

From *World Watch,* September/October 2000, pp. 12-28. © 2000 by the Worldwatch Institute. Reprinted by permission.

their U.S. counterparts. A more likely outcome is that farmers of these two nations will be pitted against each other in a costly race to maximize production, resulting in short-cut practices that essentially strip-mine their soil and throw long-term investments in the land to the wind. Farmers in Iowa will have stronger incentives to plow up land along stream banks, triggering faster erosion of topsoil. Their brethren in Brazil will find themselves needing to cut deeper into the savanna, also accelerating erosion. That will increase the flow of soybeans, all right—both north and south. But it will also further depress prices, so that even as the farmers are shipping more, they're getting less income per ton shipped. And in any case, increasing volume can't help the farmers survive in the long run, because sooner or later they will be swallowed by larger, corporate, farms that can make up for the smaller per-ton margins by producing even larger volumes.

So, how can the supporters of these river projects, who profess to be acting in the farmer's best interests, not notice the illogic of this form of competition? One explanation is that from the advocates' (as opposed to the farmers') standpoint, this competition isn't illogical at all—because the lobbyists aren't really representing farmers. They're working for the commodity processing, shipping, and trading firms who want the price of soybeans to fall, because these are the firms that buy the crops from the farmers. In fact, it is the same three agribusiness conglomerates—Archer Daniels Midland (ADM), Cargill, and Bunge—that are the top soybean processors and traders along both rivers.

Welcome to the global economy. The more brutally the U.S. and Brazilian farmers can batter each-other's prices (and standards of living) down, the greater the margin of profit these three giants gain. Meanwhile, another handful of companies controls the markets for genetically modified seeds, fertilizers, and herbicides used by the farmers—charging oligopolistically high prices both north and south of the equator.

In assessing what this proposed digging-up and reconfiguring of two of the world's great river basins really means, keep in mind that these projects will not be the activities of private businesses operating inside their own private property. These are proposed public works, to be undertaken at huge public expense. The motive is neither the plight of the family farmer nor any moral obligation to feed the world, but the opportunity to exploit poorly informed public sentiments about farmers' plights or hungry masses as a means of usurping public policies to benefit private interests. What gets thoroughly Big Muddied, in this usurping process, is that in addition to subjecting farmers to a gladiator-like attrition, these projects will likely bring a cascade of damaging economic, social, and ecological impacts to the very river basins being so expensively remodeled.

What's likely to happen if the lock and dam system along the Mississippi is expanded as proposed? The most obvious effect will be increased barge traffic, which will accelerate a less obvious cascade of events that has been underway for some time, according to Mike Davis of the Minnesota Department of Natural Resources. Much of the Mississippi River ecosystem involves aquatic rooted plants, like bullrush, arrowhead, and wild celery. Increased barge traffic will kick up more sediment, obscuring sunlight and reducing the depth to which plants can survive. Already, since the 1970s, the number of aquatic plant species found in some of the river has been cut from 23 to about half that, with just a handful thriving under the cloudier conditions. "Areas of the river have reached an ecological turning point," warns Davis. "This decline in plant diversity has triggered a drop in the invertebrate communities that live on these plants, as well as a drop in the fish, mollusk, and bird communities that depend on the diversity of insects and plants." On May 18, 2000, the U.S. Fish and Wildlife Service released a study saying that the Corps of Engineers project would threaten the 300 species of migratory birds and 12 species of fish in the Mississippi watershed, and could ultimately push some into extinction. "The least tern, the pallid sturgeon, and other species that evolved with the ebbs and flows, sandbars and depths, of the river are progressively eliminated or forced away as the diversity of the river's natural habitats is removed to maximize the barge habitat," says Davis.

The outlook for the Hidrovía project is similar. Mark Robbins, an ornithologist at the Natural History Museum at the University of Kansas, calls it "a key step in creating a Florida Everglades-like scenario of destruction in the Pantanal, and an American Great Plains-like scenario in the Cerrado in southern Brazil." The Paraguay-Paraná feeds the Pantanal wetlands, one of the most diverse habitats on the planet, with its populations of woodstorks, snailkites, limpkins, jabirus, and more than 650 other species of birds, as well as more than 400 species of fish and hundreds of other less-studied plants, mussels, and marshland organisms. As the river is dredged and the banks are built up to funnel the surrounding wetlands water into the navigation path, bird nesting habitat and fish spawning grounds will be eliminated, damaging the indigenous and other traditional societies that depend on these resources. Increased barge traffic will suppress river species here just as it will on the Mississippi. Meanwhile, herbicide-intensive soybean monocultures—on farms so enormous that they dwarf even the biggest operations in the U.S. Midwest—are rapidly replacing diverse grasslands in the fragile Cerrado. The heavy plowing and periodic absence of ground cover associated with such farming erodes 100 million tons of soil per year. Robbins notes that "compared to the Mississippi, this southern river system and surrounding grassland is several orders of magnitude more diverse and has suffered considerably less, so there is much more at stake."

Supporters of such massive disruption argue that it is justified because it is the most "efficient" way to do business. The perceived efficiency of such farming might be compared to the perceived efficiency of an energy system based on coal. Burning coal looks very efficient if you ignore its long-term impact on air quality and climate stability. Similarly, large farms look more efficient than small farms if you don't count some of their largest costs—the loss of the genetic diversity that underpins agriculture, the pollution caused by agro-chemicals, and the dislocation of rural cultures. The simultaneous demise of small, independent farmers and rise of multinational food giants is troubling not just for those who empathize with dislocated farmers, but for anyone who eats.

An Endangered Species

Nowadays most of us in the industrialized countries don't farm, so we may no longer really understand that way of life. I was born in the apple orchard and dairy country of Dutchess County, New York, but since age five have spent most of my life in New York City—while most of the farms back in Dutchess County have given way to spreading subdivisions. It's also hard for those of us who get our food from supermarket shelves or drive-thru windows to know how dependent we are on the viability of rural communities.

Whether in the industrial world, where farm communities are growing older and emptier, or in developing nations where population growth is pushing the number of farmers continually higher and each generation is inheriting smaller family plots, it is becoming harder and harder to make a living as a farmer. A combination of falling incomes, rising debt, and worsening rural poverty is forcing more people to either abandon farming as their primary activity or to leave the countryside altogether—a bewildering juncture, considering that farmers produce perhaps the only good that the human race cannot do without.

Since 1950, the number of people employed in agriculture has plummeted in all industrial nations, in some regions by more than 80 percent. Look at the numbers, and you might think farmers are being singled out by some kind of virus:

- In Japan, more than half of all farmers are over 65 years old; in the United States, farmers over 65 outnumber those under 35 by three to one. (Upon retirement or death, many will pass the farm on to children who live in the city and have no interest in farming themselves.)
- In New Zealand, officials estimate that up to 6,000 dairy farms will disappear during the next 10 to 15 years—dropping the total number by nearly 40 percent.
- In Poland, 1.8 million farms could disappear as the country is absorbed into the European Union—dropping the total number by 90 percent.
- In Sweden, the number of farms going out of business in the next decade is expected to reach about 50 percent.
- In the Philippines, Oxfam estimates that over the next few years the number of farm households in the corn producing region of Mindanao could fall by some 500,000—a 50 percent loss.
- In the United States, where the vast majority of people were farmers at the time of the American Revolution, fewer people are now full-time farmers (less than 1 percent of the population) than are full-time prisoners.
- In the U.S. states of Nebraska and Iowa, between a fifth and a third of farmers are expected to be out of business within two years.

Of course, the declining numbers of farmers in industrial nations does not imply a decline in the importance of the farming sector. The world still has to eat (and 80 million more mouths to feed each year than the year before), so smaller numbers of farmers mean larger farms and greater concentration of ownership. Despite a precipitous plunge in the number of people employed in farming in North America, Europe, and East Asia, half the world's people still make their living from the land. In sub-Saharan Africa and South Asia, more than 70 percent do. In these regions, agriculture accounts, on average, for half of total economic activity.

Some might argue that the decline of farmers is harmless, even a blessing, particularly for less developed nations that have not yet experienced the modernization that moves peasants out of backwater rural areas into the more advanced economies of the cities. For most of the past two centuries, the shift toward fewer farmers has generally been assumed to be a kind of progress. The substitution of high-powered diesel tractors for slow-moving women and men with hoes, or of large mechanized industrial farms for clusters of small "old fashioned" farms, is typically seen as the way to a more abundant and affordable food supply. Our urban-centered society has even come to view rural life, especially in the form of small family-owned businesses, as backwards or boring, fit only for people who wear overalls and go to bed early—far from the sophistication and dynamism of the city.

Urban life does offer a wide array of opportunities, attractions, and hopes—some of them falsely created by urban-oriented commercial media—that many farm families decide to pursue willingly. But city life often turns out to be a disappointment, as displaced farmers find themselves lodged in crowded slums, where unemployment and ill-health are the norm and where they are worse off than they were back home. Much evidence suggests that farmers aren't so much being lured to the city as they are being driven off their farms by a variety of structural changes in the way the global food chain operates. Bob Long, a rancher in McPherson County, Nebraska, stated in a recent *New York Times* article that passing the farm onto his son would be nothing less than "child abuse."

As long as cities are under the pressure of population growth (a situation expected to continue at least for the next three or four decades), there will always be pressure for a large share of humanity to subsist in the countryside. Even in highly urbanized North America and Europe, roughly 25 percent of the population—275 million people—still reside in rural areas. Meanwhile, for the 3 billion Africans, Asians, and Latin Americans who remain in the countryside—and who will be there for the foreseeable future—the marginalization of farmers has set up a vicious cycle of low educational achievement, rising infant mortality, and deepening mental distress.

Hired Hands on Their Own Land

In the 18th and 19th centuries, farmers weren't so trapped. Most weren't wealthy, but they generally enjoyed stable incomes and strong community ties. Diversified farms yielded a range of raw and processed goods that the farmer could typically sell in a local market. Production costs tended to be much lower than now, as many of the needed inputs were home-grown: the farmer planted seed that he or she had saved from the previous year, the farm's cows or pigs provided fertilizer, and the diversity of crops—usually a large range of grains, tubers, vegetables, herbs, flowers, and fruits for home use as well as for sale—effectively functioned as pest control.

Things have changed, especially in the past half-century, according to Iowa State agricultural economist Mike Duffy. "The end of World War II was a watershed period," he says. "The widespread introduction of chemical fertilizers and synthetic pesticides, produced as part of the war effort, set in motion dramatic changes in how we farm—and a dramatic decline in the number of farmers." In the post-war period, along with increasing mechanization, there was an increasing tendency to "outsource" pieces of the work that the farmers had previously done themselves—from producing their own fertilizer to cleaning and packaging their harvest. That outsourcing, which may have seemed like a welcome convenience at the time, eventually boomeranged: at first it enabled the farmer to increase output, and thus profits, but when all the other farmers were doing it too, crop prices began to fall.

Before long, the processing and packaging businesses were adding more "value" to the purchased product than the farmer, and it was those businesses that became the dominant players in the food industry. Instead of farmers outsourcing to contractors, it became a matter of large food processors buying raw materials from farmers, on the processors' terms. Today, most of the money is in the work the farmer no longer does—or even controls. In the United States, the share of the consumer's food dollar that trickles

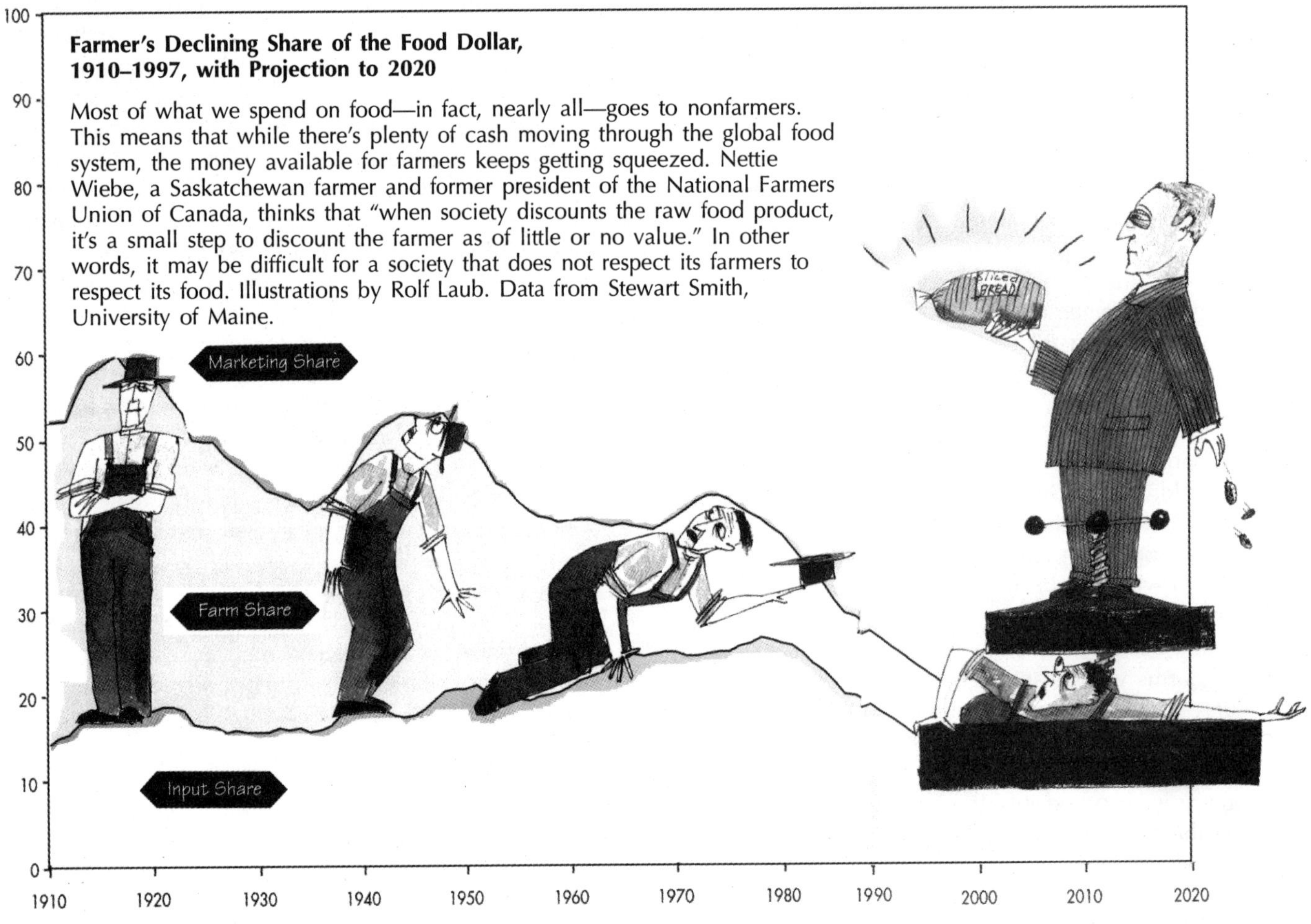

Farmer's Declining Share of the Food Dollar, 1910–1997, with Projection to 2020

Most of what we spend on food—in fact, nearly all—goes to nonfarmers. This means that while there's plenty of cash moving through the global food system, the money available for farmers keeps getting squeezed. Nettie Wiebe, a Saskatchewan farmer and former president of the National Farmers Union of Canada, thinks that "when society discounts the raw food product, it's a small step to discount the farmer as of little or no value." In other words, it may be difficult for a society that does not respect its farmers to respect its food. Illustrations by Rolf Laub. Data from Stewart Smith, University of Maine.

ConAgra: *Vertical Integration, Horizontal Concentration, Global Omnipresence*

Three conglomerates (ConAgra/DuPont, Cargill/Monsanto, and Novartis/ADM) dominate virtually every link in the North American (and increasingly, the global) food chain. Here's a simplified diagram of one conglomerate.

KEY: ↓ Vertical integration of production links, from seed to supermarket ↔ Concentration within a link

INPUTS Distribution of farm chemicals, machinery, fertilizer, and seed ↓	↔ 3 companies dominate North American farm machinery sector 6 companies control 63% of global pesticide market 4 companies control 69% of North American seed corn market 3 companies control 71% of Canadian nitrogen fertilizer capacity **ConAgra** distributes all of these inputs, and is in a joint venture with DuPont to distribute DuPont's transgenic high-oil corn seed.
FARMS ↓	↔ The farm sector is rapidly consolidating in the industrial world, as farms "get big or get out." Many go under contract with **ConAgra** and other conglomerates; others just go under. In the past 50 years, the number of farmers has declined by 86% in Germany, 85% in France, 85% in Japan, 64% in the U.S., 59% in South Korea, and 59% in the U.K.
GRAIN COLLECTION ↓	↔ A proposed merger of Cargill and Continental Grain will control half of the global grain trade; **ConAgra** has about one-quarter.
GRAIN MILLING ↓	↔ **ConAgra** and 3 other companies account for 62% of the North American market.
PRODUCTION OF BEEF, PORK, TURKEY, CHICKEN, AND SEAFOOD ↓	↔ **ConAgra** ranks 3rd in cattle feeding and 5th in broiler production. ↔ **ConAgra** Poultry, Tyson Foods, Perdue, and 3 other companies control 60% of U.S. chicken production
PROCESSING OF BEEF, PORK, TURKEY, CHICKEN, AND SEAFOOD ↓	↔ IBP, **ConAgra,** Cargill, and Farmland control 80% of U.S. beef packing ↔ Smithfield, **ConAgra**, and 3 other companies control 75% of U.S. pork packing
SUPERMARKETS	↔ **ConAgra** divisions own Wesson oil, Butterball turkeys, Swift Premium meats, Peter Pan peanut butter, Healthy Choice diet foods, Hunt's tomato sauce, and about 75 other major brands.

back to the farmer has plunged from nearly 40 cents in 1910 to just above 7 cents in 1997, while the shares going to input (machinery, agrochemicals, and seeds) and marketing (processing, shipping, brokerage, advertising, and retailing) firms have continued to expand. (See graph "Farmer's Declining Share of the Food Dollar") The typical U.S. wheat farmer, for instance, gets just 6 cents of the dollar spent on a loaf of bread—so when you buy that loaf, you're paying about as much for the wrapper as for the wheat.

Ironically, then, as U.S. farms became more mechanized and more "productive," a self-destructive feedback loop was set in motion: over-supply and declining crop prices cut into farmers' profits, fueling a demand for more technology aimed at making up for shrinking margins by increasing volume still more. Output increased dramatically, but expenses (for tractors, combines, fertilizer, and seed) also ballooned—while the commodity prices stagnated or declined. Even as they were looking more and more modernized, the farmers were becoming less and less the masters of their own domain.

On the typical Iowa farm, the farmer's profit margin has dropped from 35 percent in 1950 to 9 percent today. In order to generate the same income, this farm would need to be roughly four times as large today as in 1950—or the farmer would need to get a night job. And that's precisely what we've seen in most industrialized nations: fewer farmers on bigger tracts of land producing a greater share of the total food supply. The farmer with declining margins buys out his neighbor and expands or risks being cannibalized himself.

There is an alternative to this huge scaling up, which is to buck the trend and bring some of the input-supplying and post-harvest processing—and the related profits—back onto the farm. But more self-sufficient farming would be highly unpopular with the industries that now make lucrative profits from inputs and processing. And since these industries have much more political clout than the farmers do, there is little support for rescuing farmers from their increasingly servile condition—and the idea has been largely forgotten. Farmers continue to get the message that the only way to succeed is to get big.

The traditional explanation for this constant pressure to "get big or get out" has been that it improves the efficiency of the food system—bigger farms replace smaller farms, because the bigger farms operate at lower costs. In some respects, this is quite true. Scaling up may allow a farmer to spread a tractor's cost over greater acreage, for example. Greater size also means greater leverage in purchasing inputs or negotiating loan rates—increasingly important as satellite-guided combines and other equipment make farming more and more capital-intensive. But these economies of scale typically level off. Data for a wide range of crops produced in the United States show that the lowest production costs are generally achieved on farms that are much smaller than the typical farm now is. But large farms can tolerate lower margins, so while they may not *produce* at lower cost, they can afford to *sell* their crops at lower cost, if forced to do so—as indeed they are by the food processors who buy from them. In short, to the extent that a giant farm has a financial benefit over a small one, it's a benefit that goes only to the processor—not to the farmer, the farm community, or the environment.

This shift of the food dollar away from farmers is compounded by intense concentration in every link of the food chain—from seeds and herbicides to farm finance and retailing. In Canada, for example, just three companies control over 70 percent of fertilizer sales, five banks provide the vast majority of agricultural credit, two companies control over 70 percent of beef packing, and five companies dominate food retailing. The merger of Philip Morris and Nabisco will create an empire that collects nearly 10 cents of every dollar a U.S. consumer spends on food, according to a company spokesperson. Such high concentration can be deadly for the bottom line, allowing agribusiness firms to extract higher prices for the products farmers buy from them, while offering lower prices for the crop they buy from the farmers.

An even more worrisome form of concentration, according to Bill Heffernan, a rural sociologist at the University of Missouri, is the emergence of several clusters of firms that—through mergers, takeovers, and alliances with other links in the food chain—now possess "a seamless and fully vertically integrated control of the food system from gene to supermarket shelf." (See diagram "ConAgra") Consider the recent partnership between Monsanto and Cargill, which controls seeds, fertilizers, pesticides, farm finance, grain collection, grain processing, livestock feed processing, livestock production, and slaughtering, as well as some well-known processed food brands. From the standpoint of a company like Cargill, such alliances yield tremendous control over costs and can therefore be extremely profitable.

But suppose you're the farmer. Want to buy seed to grow corn? If Cargill is the only buyer of corn in a hundred mile radius, and Cargill is only buying a particular Monsanto corn variety for its mills or elevators or feedlots, then if you don't plant Monsanto's seed you won't have a market for your corn. Need a loan to buy the seed? Go to Cargill-owned Bank of Ellsworth, but be sure to let them know which seed you'll be buying. Also mention that you'll be buying Cargill's Saskferco brand fertilizer. OK, but once the corn is grown, you don't like the idea of having to sell to Cargill at the prices it dictates? Well, maybe you'll feed the corn to your pigs, then, and sell them to the highest bidder. No problem—Cargill's Excel Corporation buys pigs, too. OK, you're moving to the city, and renouncing the farm life! No more home-made grits for breakfast, you're buying corn flakes. Well, good news: Cargill Foods supplies corn flour to the top cereal makers. You'll notice, though, that all the big brands of corn flakes seem to have pretty much the same hefty price per ounce. After all, they're all made by the agricultural oligopoly.

As these vertical food conglomerates consolidate, Heffernan warns, "there is little room left in the global food system for independent farmers"—the farmers being increasingly left with "take it or leave it" contracts from the remaining conglomerates. In the last two decades, for example, the share of American agricultural output produced under contract has more than tripled, from 10 percent to 35 percent—and this doesn't include the contracts that farmers must sign to plant genetically engineered seed. Such centralized control of the food system, in which farmers are in effect reduced to hired hands on their own land, reminds Heffernan of the Soviet-style state farms, but with the Big Brother role now being played by agribusiness executives. It is also reminiscent of the "company store" which once dominated small American mining or factory towns, except that if you move out of town now, the store is still with you. The company store has gone global.

With the conglomerates who own the food dollar also owning the political clout, it's no surprise that agricultural policies—including subsidies, tax breaks, and environmental legislation at both the national and international levels—do not generally favor the farms. For example, the conglomerates command growing influence over both private and public agricultural research priorities, which might explain why the U.S. Department of Agriculture (USDA), an agency ostensibly beholden to farmers, would help to develop the seed-sterilizing Terminator technology—a biotechnology that offers farmers only greater dependence on seed companies. In some cases the influence is indirect, as manifested in government funding decisions, while in others it is more blatant. When Novartis provided $25 million to fund a research partnership with the plant biology department of the University of California at Berkeley, one of the conditions was that Novartis has the first right of refusal for any patentable inventions. Under those circumstances, of course, the UC officials—mindful of where their funding comes from—have strong incentives to give more attention to technologies like the Terminator seed, which shifts profit away from the farmer, than to technologies that directly benefit the farmer or the public at large.

Even policies that are touted to be in the best interest of farmers, like liberalized trade in agricultural products, are increasingly shaped by non-farmers. Food traders, processors, and distributors, for example, were some of the principal architects of recent revisions to the General Agreement on Trade and Tariffs (GATT)—the World Trade Organization's predecessor—that paved the way for greater trade flows in agricultural commodities. Before these revisions, many countries had mechanisms for assuring that their farmers wouldn't be driven out of their own domestic markets by predatory global traders. The traders, however, were able to do away with those protections.

The ability of agribusiness to slide around the planet, buying at the lowest possible price and selling at the highest, has tended to tighten the squeeze already put in place by economic marginalization, throwing every farmer on the planet into direct competition with every other farmer. A recent UN Food and Agriculture Organization assessment of the experience of 16 developing nations in implementing the latest phase of the GATT concluded that "a common reported concern was with a general trend towards the concentration of farms," a process that tends to further marginalize small producers and exacerbate rural poverty and unemployment. The sad irony, according to Thomas Reardon, of Michigan State University, is that while small farmers in all reaches of the world are increasingly affected by cheap, heavily subsidized imports of foods from outside of their traditional rural markets, they are nonetheless often excluded from opportunities to participate in food exports themselves. To keep down transaction costs and to keep processing standardized, exporters and other downstream players prefer to buy from a few large producers, as opposed to many small producers.

As the global food system becomes increasingly dominated by a handful of vertically integrated, international corporations, the servitude of the farmer points to a broader society-wide servitude that OPEC-like food cartels could impose, through their control over food prices and food quality. Agricultural economists have already noted that the widening gap between retail food prices and farm prices in the 1990s was due almost exclusively to exploitation of market power, and not to extra services provided by processors and retailers. It's questionable whether we should pay as much for a bread wrapper as we do for the nutrients it contains. But beyond this, there's a more fundamental question. Farmers are professionals, with extensive knowledge of their local soils, weather, native plants, sources of fertilizer or mulch, native pollinators, ecology, and community. If we are to have a world where the land is no longer managed by such professionals, but is instead managed by distant corporate bureaucracies interested in extracting maximum output at minimum cost, what kind of food will we have, and at what price?

Agrarian Services

No question, large industrial farms can produce lots of food. Indeed, they're designed to maximize quantity. But when the farmer becomes little more than the lowest-cost producer of raw materials, more than his own welfare will suffer. Though the farm sector has lost power and profit, it is still the one link in the agrifood chain accounting for the largest share of agriculture's public goods—including half the world's jobs, many of its most vital communities, and many of its most diverse landscapes. And in providing many of these goods, small farms clearly have the advantage.

Local economic and social stability: Over half a century ago, William Goldschmidt, an anthropologist working at the USDA, tried to assess how farm structure and size affect the health of rural communities. In California's San Joaquin Valley, a region then considered to be at the cutting edge of agricultural industrialization, he identified two small towns that were alike in all basic economic and geographic dimensions, including value of agricultural production, except in farm size. Comparing the two, he found an inverse correlation between the sizes of the farms and the well-being of the communities they were a part of.

The small-farm community, Dinuba, supported about 20 percent more people, and at a considerably higher level of living—including lower poverty rates, lower levels of economic and social class distinctions, and a lower crime rate—than the large-farm community of Arvin. The majority of Dinuba's residents were independent entrepreneurs, whereas fewer than 20 percent of Arvin's residents were—most of the others being agricultural laborers. Dinuba had twice as many business establishments as Arvin, and did 61 percent more retail business. It had more schools, parks, newspapers, civic organizations, and churches, as well as better physical infrastructure—paved streets, sidewalks, garbage disposal, sewage disposal and other public services. Dinuba also had more institutions for democratic decision making, and a much broader participation by its citizens. Political scientists have long recognized that a broad base of independent entrepreneurs and property owners is one of the keys to a healthy democracy.

The distinctions between Dinuba and Arvin suggest that industrial agriculture may be limited in what it can do for a community. Fewer (and less meaningful) jobs, less local spending, and a hemorrhagic flow of profits to absentee landowners and distant suppliers means that industrial farms can actually be a net drain on the local economy. That hypothesis has been corroborated by Dick Levins, an agricultural economist at the University of Minnesota. Levins studied the economic receipts from Swift County, Iowa, a typical Midwestern corn and soybean community, and found that although total farm sales are near an all-time high, farm income there has been dismally low—and that many of those who were once the financial stalwarts of the community are now deeply in debt. "Most of the U.S. Corn Belt, like Swift County, is a colony, owned and operated by people who don't live there and for the benefit of those who don't live there," says Levin. In fact, most of the land in Swift County is rented, much of it from absentee landlords.

This new calculus of farming may be eliminating the traditional role of small farms in anchoring rural economies—the kind of tradition, for example, that we saw in the emphasis given to the support of small farms by Japan, South Korea, and Taiwan following World War II. That emphasis, which brought radical land reforms and targeted investment in rural areas, is widely cited as having been a major stimulus to the dramatic economic boom those countries enjoyed.

Not surprisingly, when the economic prospects of small farms decline, the social fabric of rural communities begins to tear. In the United States, farming families are more than twice as likely as others to live in poverty. They have less education and lower rates of medical protection, along with higher rates of infant mortality, alcoholism, child abuse, spousal abuse, and mental stress. Across Europe, a similar pattern is evident. And in sub-Saharan Africa, sociologist Deborah Bryceson of the Netherlands-based African Studies Centre has studied the dislocation of small farmers and found that "as de-agrarianization proceeds, signs of social dysfunction associated with urban areas [including petty crime and breakdowns of family ties] are surfacing in villages."

People without meaningful work often become frustrated, but farmers may be a special case. "More so than other occupations, farming represents a way of life and defines who you are," says Mike Rosemann, a psychologist who runs a farmer counseling network in Iowa. "Losing the family farm, or the prospect of losing the family farm, can generate tremendous guilt and anxiety, as if one has failed to protect the heritage that his ancestors worked to hold onto." One measure of the despair has been a worldwide surge in the number of farmers committing suicide. In 1998, over 300 cotton farmers in Andhra Pradesh, India, took their lives by swallowing pesticides that they had gone into debt to purchase but that had nonetheless failed to save their crops. In Britain, farm workers are two-and-a-half times more likely to commit suicide than the rest of the population. In the United States, official statistics say farmers are now five times as likely to commit suicide as to die from farm accidents, which have been traditionally the most frequent cause of unnatural death for them. The true number may be even higher, as suicide hotlines report that they often receive calls from farmers who want to know which sorts of accidents (Falling into the blades of a combine? Getting shot while hunting?) are least likely to be investigated by insurance companies that don't pay claims for suicides.

Whether from despair or from anger, farmers seem increasingly ready to rise up, sometimes violently, against government, wealthy landholders, or agribusiness giants. In recent years we've witnessed the Zapatista revolution in Chiapas, the seizing of white-owned farms by landless blacks in Zimbabwe, and the attacks of European farmers on warehouses storing genetically engineered seed. In the book *Harvest of Rage,* journalist Joel Dyer links the 1995 Oklahoma City bombing that killed nearly 200 people—as well as the rise of radical right and antigovernment militias in the U.S. heartland—to a spreading despair and anger stemming from the ongoing farm crisis. Thomas Homer-Dixon, director of the Project on Environment, Population, and Security at the University of Toronto, regards farmer dislocation, and the resulting rural unemployment and poverty, as one of the major security threats for the coming decades. Such dislocation is responsible for roughly half of the growth of urban populations across the Third World, and such growth often occurs in volatile shantytowns that are already straining to meet the basic needs of their residents. "What was an extremely traumatic transition for Europe and North America from a rural society to an urban one is now proceeding at two to three times that

In the Developing World, an Even Deeper Farm Crisis

"One would have to multiply the threats facing family farmers in the United States or Europe five, ten, or twenty times to get a sense of the handicaps of peasant farmers in less developed nations," says Deborah Bryceson, a senior research fellow at the African Studies Centre in the Netherlands. Those handicaps include insufficient access to credit and financing, lack of roads and other infrastructure in rural areas, insecure land tenure, and land shortages where population is dense.

Three forces stand out as particularly challenging to these peasant farmers:

Structural adjustment requirements, imposed on indebted nations by international lending institutions, have led to privatization of "public commodity procurement boards" that were responsible for providing public protections for rural economies. "The newly privatized entities are under no obligation to service marginal rural areas," says Rafael Mariano, chairman of a Filipino farmers' union. Under the new rules, state protections against such practices as dumping of cheap imported goods (with which local farmers can't compete) were abandoned at the same time that state provision of health care, education, and other social services was being reduced.

Trade liberalization policies associated with structural adjustment have reduced the ability of nations to protect their agricultural economies even if they want to. For example, the World Trade Organization's Agreement on Agriculture will forbid domestic price support mechanisms and tariffs on imported goods—some of the primary means by which a country can shield its own farmers from overproduction and foreign competition.

The growing emphasis on agricultural grades and standards—the standardizing of crops and products so they can be processed and marketed more "efficiently"—has tended to favor large producers, and to marginalize smaller ones. Food manufacturers and supermarkets have emerged as the dominant entities in the global agri-food chain, and with their focus on brand consistency, ingredient uniformity, and high volume, smaller producers often are unable to deliver—or aren't even invited to bid.

Despite these daunting conditions, many peasant farmers tend to hold on long after it has become clear that they can't compete. One reason, says Peter Rosset of the Institute for Food and Development Policy, is that "even when it gets really bad, they will cling to agriculture because of the fact that it at least offers some degree of food security—that you can feed yourself." But with the pressures now mounting, particularly as export crop production swallows more land, even that fallback is lost.

speed in developing nations," says Homer-Dixon. And, these nations have considerably less industrialization to absorb the labor. Such an accelerated transition poses enormous adjustment challenges for India and China, where perhaps a billion and a half people still make their living from the land.

Ecological stability: In the Andean highlands, a single farm may include as many as 30 to 40 distinct varieties of potato (along with numerous other native plants), each having slightly different optimal soil, water, light, and temperature regimes, which the farmer—given enough time—can manage. (In comparison, in the United States, just four closely related varieties account for about 99 percent of all the potatoes produced.) But, according to Karl Zimmerer, a University of Wisconsin sociologist, declining farm incomes in the Andes force more and more growers into migrant labor forces for part of the year, with serious effects on farm ecology. As time becomes constrained, the farmer manages the system more homogenously—cutting back on the number of traditional varieties (a small home garden of favorite culinary varieties may be the last refuge of diversity), and scaling up production of a few commercial varieties. Much of the traditional crop diversity is lost.

Complex farm systems require a highly sophisticated and intimate knowledge of the land—something small-scale, full-time farmers are more able to provide. Two or three different crops that have different root depths, for example, can often be planted on the same piece of land, or crops requiring different drainage can be planted in close proximity on a tract that has variegated topography. But these kinds of cultivation can't be done with heavy tractors moving at high speed. Highly site-specific and management-intensive cultivation demands ingenuity and awareness of local ecology, and can't be achieved by heavy equipment and heavy applications of agrochemicals. That isn't to say that being small is always sufficient to ensure ecologically sound food production, because economic adversity can drive small farms, as well as big ones, to compromise sustainable food production by transmogrifying the craft of land stewardship into the crude labor of commodity production. But a large-scale, highly mechanized farm is simply not equipped to preserve landscape complexity. Instead, its normal modus is to use blunt management tools, like crops that have been genetically engineered to churn out insecticides, which obviate the need to scout the field to see if spraying is necessary at all.

In the U.S. Midwest, as farm size has increased, cropping systems have gotten more simplified. Since 1972, the number of counties with more than 55 percent of their acreage planted in corn and soybeans has nearly tripled, from 97 to 267. As farms scaled up, the great simplicity of managing the corn-soybean rotation—an 800 acre farm, for instance, may require no more than a couple of weeks planting in the spring and a few weeks harvesting in the fall—became its big selling point. The various arms of the agricultural economy in the region, from extension services to grain elevators to seed suppliers, began to solidify around this corn-soybean rotation, reinforcing the farmers' movement away from other crops. Fewer and fewer farmers kept livestock, as beef and hog production became "economical" only in other parts of the country where it was becoming more concentrated. Giving up livestock meant eliminating clover, pasture mixtures, and a key source of fertilizer in the Midwest, while creating tremendous manure concentrations in other places.

But the corn and soybean rotation—one monoculture followed by another—is extremely inefficient or "leaky" in its use of applied fertilizer, since low levels of biodiversity tend to leave a range of vacant niches in the field, including different root depths and different nutrient preferences. Moreover, the Midwest's shift to monoculture has subjected the country to a double hit of nitrogen pollution, since not only does the removal and concentration of livestock tend to dump inordinate amounts of feces in the places (such as Utah and North Carolina) where the livestock operations are now located, but the monocultures that remain in the Midwest have much poorer nitrogen retention than they would if their cropping were more complex. (The addition of just a winter rye crop to the corn-soy rotation has been shown to reduce nitrogen runoff by nearly 50 percent.) And maybe this disaster-in-the-making should really be regarded as a triple hit, because in addition to contaminating Midwestern water supplies, the runoff ends up in the Gulf of Mexico, where the nitrogen feeds massive algae blooms. When the algae die, they are decomposed by bacteria, whose respiration depletes the water's oxygen—suffocating fish, shellfish, and all other life that doesn't escape. This process periodically leaves 20,000 square kilometers of water off the coast of Louisiana biologically dead. Thus the act of simplifying the ecology of a field in Iowa can contribute to severe pollution in Utah, North Carolina, Louisiana, *and* Iowa.

The world's agricultural biodiversity—the ultimate insurance policy against climate variations, pest outbreaks, and other unforeseen threats to food security—depends largely on the millions of small farmers who use this diversity in their local growing environments. But the marginalization of farmers who have developed or inherited complex farming systems over generations means more than just the loss of specific crop varieties and the knowledge of how they best grow. "We forever lose the best available knowledge and experience of place, including what to do with marginal lands not suited for industrial production," says Steve Gleissman, an agroecologist at the University of California at Santa Cruz. The 12 million hogs produced by Smithfield Foods Inc., the largest hog producer and processor in the world and a pioneer in vertical integration, are nearly genetically identical and raised under identical conditions—regardless of whether they are in a Smithfield feedlot in Virginia or Mexico.

As farmers become increasingly integrated into the agribusiness food chain, they have fewer and fewer controls over the totality of the production process—shifting more and more to the role of "technology applicators," as opposed to managers making informed and independent decisions. Recent USDA surveys of contract poultry farmers in the United States found that in seeking outside advice on their operations, these farmers now turn first to bankers and then to the corporations that hold their contracts. If the contracting corporation is also the same company that is selling the farm its seed and fertilizer, as is often the case, there's a strong likelihood that the company's procedures will be followed. That corporation, as a global enterprise with no compelling local ties, is also less likely to be concerned about the pollution and resource degradation created by those procedures, at least compared with a farmer who is rooted in that community. Grower contracts generally disavow any environmental liability.

And then there is the ecological fallout unique to large-scale, industrial agriculture. Colossal confined animal feeding operations (CAFOs)—those "other places" where livestock are concentrated when they are no longer present on Midwestern soy/corn farms—constitute perhaps the most egregious example of agriculture that has, like a garbage barge in a goldfish pond, overwhelmed the scale at which an ecosystem can cope. CAFOs are increasingly the norm in livestock production, because, like crop monocultures, they allow the production of huge populations of animals which can be slaughtered and marketed at rock-bottom costs. But the disconnection between the livestock and the land used to produce their feed means that such CAFOs generate gargantuan amounts of waste, which the surrounding soil cannot possibly absorb. (One farm in Utah will raise over five million hogs in a year, producing as much waste each day as the city of Los Angeles.) The waste is generally stored in large lagoons, which are prone to leak and even spill over during heavy storms. From North Carolina to South Korea, the overwhelming stench of these lagoons—a combination of hydrogen sulfide, ammonia, and methane gas that smells like rotten eggs—renders miles of surrounding land uninhabitable.

A different form of ecological disruption results from the conditions under which these animals are raised. Because massive numbers of closely confined livestock are highly susceptible to infection, and because a steady diet of antibiotics can modestly boost animal growth, overuse of antibiotics has become the norm in industrial animal production. In recent months, both the Centers for Disease Control and Prevention in the United States and the World Health Organization have identified such industrial feeding operations as principal causes of the growing antibiotic resistance in food-borne bacteria like *salmonella* and *campylobacter.* And as decisionmaking in the food chain grows ever more concentrated—confined behind fewer corporate doors—there may be other food safety issues that you won't even hear about, particularly in the burgeoning field of genetically modified organisms (GMOs). In reaction to growing public concern over GMOs, a coalition that ingenuously calls itself the "Alliance for Better Foods"—actually made up of large food retailers, food processors, biotech companies and corporate-financed farm organizations—has launched a $50 million public "educational" campaign, in addition to giving over $676,000 to U.S. lawmakers and political parties in 1999, to head off the mandatory labeling of such foods.

Perhaps most surprising, to people who have only casually followed the debate about small-farm values versus factory-farm "efficiency," is the fact that a wide body of evidence shows that small farms are actually more productive than large ones—by as much as 200 to 1,000 percent greater output per unit of area. How does this jive with the often-mentioned productivity advantages of large-scale mechanized operations? The answer is simply that those big-farm advantages are always calculated on the basis of how much *of one crop* the land will yield per acre. The greater productivity of a smaller, more complex farm, however, is calculated on the basis of how much food *overall* is produced per acre. The smaller farm can grow several crops utilizing different root depths, plant heights, or nutrients, on the same piece of land simultaneously. It is this "polyculture" that offers the small farm's productivity advantage.

To illustrate the difference between these two kinds of measurement, consider a large Midwestern corn farm. That farm may produce more corn per acre than a small farm in which the corn is grown as part of a polyculture that also includes beans, squash, potato, and "weeds" that serve as fodder. But in overall output, the polycrop—under close supervision by a knowledgeable farmer—produces much more food overall, whether you measure in weight, volume, bushels, calories, or dollars.

The inverse relationship between farm size and output can be attributed to the more efficient use of land, water, and other agricultural resources that small operations afford, including the efficiencies of intercropping various plants in the same field, planting multiple times during the year, targeting irrigation, and integrating crops and livestock. So in terms of converting inputs into outputs, society would be better off with small-scale farmers. And as population continues to grow in many nations, and the agricultural resources per person continue to shrink, a small farm structure for agriculture may be central to meeting future food needs.

Rebuilding Foodsheds

Look at the range of pressures squeezing farmers, and it's not hard to understand the growing desperation. The situation has become explosive, and if stabilizing the erosion of farm culture and ecology is now critical not just to farmers but to everyone who eats, there's still a very challenging question as to what strategy can work. The agribusiness giants are deeply entrenched now, and scattered protests could have as little effect on them as a mosquito bite on a tractor. The prospects for farmers gaining political strength on their own seem dim, as their numbers—at least in the industrial countries—continue to shrink.

A much greater hope for change may lie in a joining of forces between farmers and the much larger numbers of other segments of society that now see the dangers, to their own particular interests, of continued restructuring of the countryside. There are a couple of prominent models for such coalitions, in the constituencies that have joined forces to fight the Mississippi River Barge Capacity and Hidrovía Barge Capacity projects being pushed forward in the name of global soybean productivity.

The American group has brought together at least the following riverbedfellows:

- National environmental groups, including the Sierra Club and National Audubon Society, which are alarmed at the prospect of a public commons being damaged for the profit of a small commercial interest group;
- Farmers and farmer advocacy organizations, concerned about the inordinate power being wielded by the agribusiness oligopoly;
- Taxpayer groups outraged at the prospect of a corporate welfare payout that will drain more than $1 billion from public coffers;
- Hunters and fishermen worried about the loss of habitat;
- Biologists, ecologists, and birders concerned about the numerous threatened species of birds, fish, amphibians, and plants;
- Local-empowerment groups concerned about the impacts of economic globalization on communities;
- Agricultural economists concerned that the project will further entrench farmers in a dependence on the export of low-cost, bulk commodities, thereby missing valuable opportunities to keep money in the community through local milling, canning, baking, and processing.

A parallel coalition of environmental groups and farmer advocates has formed in the Southern hemisphere to resist the Hidrovía expansion. There too, the river campaign is part of a larger campaign to challenge the hegemony of industrial agriculture. For example, a coalition has formed around the Landless Workers Movement, a grassroots organization in Brazil that helps landless laborers to organize occupations of idle land belonging to wealthy landlords. This coalition includes 57 farm advocacy organizations based in 23 nations. It has also brought together environmental groups in Latin America concerned about the related ventures of logging and cattle ranching favored by large landlords; the mayors of rural towns who appreciate the boost that farmers can give to local economies; and organizations working on social welfare in Brazil's cities, who see land occupation as an alternative to shantytowns.

The Mississippi and Hidrovía projects, huge as they are, still constitute only two of the hundreds of agro-industrial developments being challenged around the world. But the coalitions that have formed around them represent the kind of focused response that seems most likely to slow the juggernaut, in part because the solutions these coalitions propose are not vague or quixotic expressions of

Past and Future: Connecting the Dots

Given the direction and speed of prevailing trends, how far can the decline in farmers go? The lead editorial in the September 13, 1999 issue of *Feedstuffs,* an agribusiness trade journal, notes that "Based on the best estimates of analysts, economists and other sources interviewed for this publication, American agriculture must now quickly consolidate all farmers and livestock producers into about 50 production systems . . . each with its own brands," in order to maintain competitiveness. Ostensibly, other nations will have to do the same in order to keep up.

To put that in perspective, consider that in traditional agricul ture, each farm is an independent production system. In this map of Ireland's farms circa 1930, each dot represents 100 farms, so the country as a whole had many thousands of independent production systems. But if the *Feedstuffs* prognosis were to come to pass, this map would be reduced to a single dot. And even an identically keyed map of the much larger United States would show the country's agriculture reduced to just one dot.

idealism, but are site-specific and practical. In the case of the alliance forming around the Mississippi River project, the coalition's work has included questioning the assumptions of the Corps of Engineers analysis, lobbying for stronger antitrust examination of agribusiness monopolies, and calling for modification of existing U.S. farm subsidies, which go disproportionately to large farmers. Environmental groups are working to re-establish a balance between use of the Mississippi as a barge mover and as an intact watershed. Sympathetic agricultural extensionists are promoting alternatives to the standard corn-soybean rotation, including certified organic crop production, which can simultaneously bring down input costs and garner a premium for the final product, and reduce nitrogen pollution.

The United States and Brazil may have made costly mistakes in giving agribusiness such power to reshape the rivers and land to its own use. But the strategy of interlinked coalitions may be mobilizing in time to save much of the world's agricultural health before it is too late. Dave Brubaker, head of the Spira/GRACE Project on Industrial Animal Production at the Johns Hopkins University School of Public Health, sees these diverse coalitions as "the beginning of a revolution in the way we look at the food system, tying in food production with social welfare, human health, and the environment." Brubaker's project brings together public health officials focused on antibiotic overuse and water contamination resulting from hog waste; farmers and local communities who oppose the spread of new factory farms or want to close down existing ones; and a phalanx of natural allies with related campaigns, including animal rights activists, labor unions, religious groups, consumer rights activists, and environmental groups.

"As the circle of interested parties is drawn wider, the alliance ultimately shortens the distance between farmer and consumer," observes Mark Ritchie, president of the Institute for Agriculture and Trade Policy, a research and advocacy group often at the center of these partnerships. This closer proximity may prove critical to the ultimate sustainability of our food supply, since socially and ecologically sound buying habits are not just the passive *result* of changes in the way food is produced, but can actually be the most powerful *drivers of* these changes. The explosion of farmers' markets, community-supported agriculture, and other direct buying arrangements between farmers and consumers points to the growing numbers of nonfarmers who have already shifted their role in the food chain from that of choosing from the tens of thousands of food brands offered by a few dozen companies to bypassing such brands altogether. And, since many of the additives and processing steps that take up the bulk of the food dollar are simply the inevitable consequence of the ever-increasing time commercial food now spends in global transit and storage, this shortening of distance between grower and consumer will not only benefit the culture and ecology of farm communities. It will also give us access to much fresher, more flavorful, and more nutritious food. Luckily, as any food marketer can tell you, these characteristics aren't a hard sell.

Brian Halweil is a staff researcher at the Worldwatch Institute.

"China is not scrambling to dismantle socialism; it is scrambling to regulate a market system that it has—for better or worse, intentionally or inadvertently—adopted thoroughly."

Beyond the Transition: China's Economy at Century's End

EDWARD S. STEINFELD

In the early months of 1999, the negotiations over China's entry into the World Trade Organization were dramatically transformed. For 13 years Chinese negotiators had steadfastly attempted to gain China's admittance to the WTO on terms that would have permitted China to protect its vast state-owned industrial sector and seal off its most lucrative markets from foreign competition. For 13 years the developed member economies of the WTO—especially the United States—had fought equally hard to ensure the opposite: that China would gain entry on only the strictest of free market terms.

For both parties, the negotiations were a concrete expression of longer-term visions of China's internal development and external relations. For Americans, WTO accession had become a vehicle to force China to relinquish its special status as an economy neither wholly planned, wholly marketized, nor wholly subject to international norms of competition. For Chinese, accession had become a way to formalize in the global arena China's unique blend of socialism and capitalism, a blend that generated vast exports while preserving the domestic institutions of state socialism—state banks, state firms, and extensive state monopolies in key manufacturing and service sectors.

In early 1999 all this changed. Just months before Prime Minister Zhu Rongji's scheduled April visit to the United States, Chinese representatives to the WTO accession talks suddenly offered extraordinary concessions on nearly every issue previously contested. China pledged to throw open to foreign competition its agricultural and industrial markets. Tariffs on most goods would fall by nearly three-fifths, matching levels maintained by most developed trading nations, and tariffs on information-technology products imported from abroad would be eliminated entirely. Foreign firms operating in China would, after a three-year phase-in period, be granted full trading and distribution rights. Key service sectors such as banking and insurance—long protected by the Chinese government, and long sought after by Western business concerns—would be thrown open to foreign competitors within three to five years. Even in the sensitive area of telecommunications, foreigners would be granted unprecedented access to fixed-line and wireless operations in the largest Chinese markets.

The concessions embodied something entirely new: an emerging belief among Chinese leaders that modernization required not protection, but the exposure of Chinese firms to foreign competition and foreign markets. Yet far more certain were the short-term economic costs that WTO accession would

EDWARD S. STEINFELD *is an assistant professor at MIT's Sloan School of Management and author of* Forging Reform in China *(New York: Cambridge University Press, 1998).*

surely impose. By the late 1990s, approximately half of China's 75,000 state-owned industrial enterprises were officially operating in the red. Perhaps even more troubling, many nominally profitable firms were in real terms incurring huge losses and facing insolvency. With the elimination of government subsidies and the introduction of foreign competition mandated by WTO membership, many of these state firms, would be driven out of business. Millions of Chinese urban workers would be threatened with unemployment in a nation that has only the barest of social safety nets. While fully integrating China into the global economy might make sense over the long term, the short-term costs—whether measured economically, socially, or even politically—would be monumental.

That Chinese leaders were willing to absorb such costs underscores the depth of the policy reversals they were undertaking. Encouraging precisely this kind of change has been the aim of America's Asia policy for well over a decade, and across several administrations. It is especially unfortunate—indeed, incomprehensible—that the Clinton administration failed to close a deal on China's WTO accession during Zhu Rongji's April visit. Long-term American interests were clearly permitted to be sidetracked by short-term political wrangling in Washington.

The Unplanned Market

Given the downward slide in Sino-American relations since the NATO air campaign against Yugoslavia this spring, the bombing of the Chinese embassy in Belgrade during that campaign, and the publication of the Cox committee report on Chinese espionage in the United States, the time frame for China's entry into the WTO is uncertain at best. Still, the concessions offered by Zhu in April—and repeated in July—signal a fundamental turning point in the logic of Chinese reform policy. Since the last 1970s, Chinese policymakers had attempted to tweak the socialist system by gradually introducing market forces. The basic idea was to preserve the economy's socialist core—state firms and state banks—by introducing change along the margins. These incremental measures over time saw markets established, state planning effectively eliminated, prices liberalized, and non-state-owned industry allowed to prosper, but the underlying logic remained constant. Reforms would be introduced, but always as part of an overriding effort to preserve the traditional core of the economy.

The concessions of 1999 represented a thorough reversal of course. Instead of reform serving to sustain the core, the core itself would be destroyed to save reform, along with the growth, prosperity, and stability that reform has brought China. In the new view, instead of using market forces to save state socialism, state socialism itself would have to be sacrificed to preserve the market economy.

What explains this shift? Why would policy-makers change course so substantially and at such apparent risk? Why take a 20-year strategy of gradualism, incrementalism, and partial market reform—one that had brought unprecedented growth—and replace it with something far more radical and potentially destabilizing?

The answer relates to a fundamental realization by China's leaders, namely Prime Minister Zhu Rongji and his advisers. In contrast to many observers, Zhu's group has come to understand that the Chinese economy today is not simply transitioning from plan to market. Nor is the policy challenge simply to dismantle the old machinery of state intervention so that free market forces can somehow spontaneously prevail. Rather, the Chinese system today after two decades of incremental reform already is a market economy, albeit one desperately lacking the governance mechanisms that make modern market economies function smoothly. Many aspects of the Chinese market have the feel of "Dodge City" capitalism. Free market forces are reigning, but in ways that now threaten sustained economic growth.

Free market forces are reigning, but in ways that now threaten sustained economic growth.

China today is not wrestling with the same problems it faced two decades ago at the dawn of reform. The challenge then was to dismantle the command plan, create markets, free up prices, and empower individual economic producers. The appropriate comparisons were with nations like the Soviet Union, Yugoslavia, Hungary, or any others that had attempted—or were attempting—to reform socialism.

Through two decades of policy experimentation China did dismantle the plan, did create markets, did free up prices, and did empower producers. In so doing, the country managed to shift itself from the institutional problems of socialism to the institutional problems of capitalism. The nation, in effect, was pulled from one pole of the economic spectrum all the way over to the other. China today has complex, market-oriented firms, but they operate in a setting utterly devoid of appropriate mechanisms of corporate governance. The nation also has a vast and varied banking system, but it operates in an environment of desperately distorted rules and regulations.

China is not scrambling to dismantle socialism; it is scrambling to regulate a market system that it has—for better or worse, intentionally or inadvertently—adopted thoroughly. In this sense, the appropriate comparisons are with South Korea, Thailand, Indonesia, and even Japan—all nations that achieved phenomenal success through markets but have slammed into trouble when underlying institutions of market governance have failed to keep pace with growth.

Indeed, the urgency of changes pursued by Chinese policymakers stems directly from lessons drawn from the East Asian financial crisis. Before the crisis, "sustaining the core" in China did not imply the absence of a market environment; it did suggest efforts within a market context to protect state firms—and by extension, state employees—from competition and the threat of bankruptcy. Protecting state firms, in turn, implied subsidization through the state-owned banking system. Funds pumped in by individual depositors simply were pumped out to firm-level borrowers who—although they may have been utterly unsustainable in commercial terms—happened to have been favored by the government.

As Chinese leaders came to understand in 1998 and 1999, a similar phenomenon led to trouble in market economies across Asia. Whether in South Korea, Japan, Thailand, or Indonesia, large firms throughout the late 1980s and 1990s—despite plummeting commercial prospects—were showered with loans from banks that were often themselves agents of the state. As levels of nonperforming loans accumulated and patterns of capital misallocation deepened, the risks of long-term economic decline—and short-term panic—intensified. Since 1997 the costs have been obvious even to the most casual observers of East Asia.

What is so interesting is not that these events have overtaken the Asian "dragons," the rapidly developing market economies of the region; after all, boom-bust cycles and financial panic have been the bane, and perennial ailment, of capitalist systems throughout history. The real curiosity is that these phenomena, which are so closely related to developed market systems, are occurring in China. Hence, Chinese policymakers are moving rapidly, and radically, to undertake what was unthinkable just five years ago: the dismantlement of the Chinese economy's traditional state-owned core.

Growth On The "Institutional Cheap"

At the dawn of reform in 1978, the Chinese economy embodied the basic logic of socialist command economies worldwide. China's political economy in the late 1970s had been shaped by leadership decisions 25 years earlier to pursue forced-draft industrialization. Responding to both ideological and national security imperatives, policymakers in the 1950s were determined to lift China from its agricultural past and build heavy industry as rapidly as possible. Unfortunately, neither China's natural factor endowments nor its societal institutions favored heavy industrial growth. Capital was scarce, and therefore relatively expensive. Furthermore, China lacked the financial institutions to transfer capital, via the market, from those who had it—individual savers—to those who could use it—industrial enterprises.

Policymakers circumvented the problem by deliberately intervening and distorting prices. The costs of capital, basic industrial inputs, energy, and wages were drastically suppressed below market-clearing levels. The suppression of prices also committed the government to direct involvement in allocation, for only through allocation plans could the state ensure that factors that had been artificially priced low ended up in key heavy industrial sectors. Similarly, the government was forced to step in and mircromanage individual enterprises. This occurred because managers—operating under conditions of distorted prices, allocation by plan, and annual output targets—faced systemic incentives to overconsume and underproduce.

Simply to govern enterprises in such an environment, the state was pushed in two related directions. First, it would directly control the hiring and firing of managerial personnel in the firm. Second, it would constrain managers through compulsory production plans and output targets. By economic necessity, the industrial firm became little more than an extension of the state, the production arm of a vast industrial bureaucracy. The pattern was then reinforced by political necessity, since the industrial employer served as the main vehicle for state coercive power and the prime arena in which the state interacted with citizen.

The system, despite its faults, achieved some success, especially in basic industrial growth. During the first five year plan (1953–1957), national income expanded at an average annual rate of 8.9 percent while industrial output surged annually by 18.7 percent. The results were especially dramatic in heavy industrial sectors. From 1952 through the mid-1960s, the gross value of industrial output in the machinery sector expanded annually by more than 25 percent.

Besides fostering growth, the command system allowed China to channel investment capital, collect taxes, and govern enterprises on the "institutional cheap." By distorting prices accordingly, the government could ensure that virtually all savings in the economy went to the state sector. Government-set prices guaranteed that state-owned enterprises earned substantial profits, which were remitted almost in their entirety to the government budget. Central planners then decided to whom these savings would flow back down as investment, and the banks simply disbursed funds accordingly. Instead of requiring a complex fiscal apparatus to collect revenue from society at large, the state could simply remove the profits accumulating in state-owned enterprises and reallocate them through the investment plan. Similarly, little need in any market sense existed for banks or other financial intermediaries, since the price mechanism itself—when supplemented by government allocation—channeled financial resources to industrial end-users. Finally, in the area of enterprise governance, the state could exert substantial authority over a wide array of economic producers simply by controlling the flow of investment and material inputs. The control may have been faulty, and always subject to the manipulation of producers, but ultimately the government determined which assets flowed to which producers.

Unfortunately for China, growth on the institutional cheap came at tremendous long-term cost. Between the 1950s and the 1970s, the amount of gross investment required to achieve a given increase in output rose by more than 80 percent. Because of inherent inefficiencies, the system eventually achieved less bang for its investment buck. In the fifth five year plan (1976–1980), the investment cost of producing a kilowatt hour of electricity had tripled since the third five year plan (1966–1970), while the investment cost of producing a ton of steel had nearly doubled. Meanwhile, by the mid- to late 1970s, levels of inventories and unfinished construction were soaring. Between 1976 and 1978, inventories in the state-owned sector exceeded 95 percent of national income.

Enter The Market

The Chinese economy by the late 1970s was thus in deep trouble, and aspects of the command system bore a significant share of the blame. Clearly, the immediate answer involved economic liberalization: the phase-out of state price controls, the opening up of product markets, the exposure of industrial sectors to competition, and the extension of autonomy to economic producers. Whether rapidly or gradually, barriers to marketization and entrepreneurship had to be pushed aside and something entirely new allowed to come forth. Indeed, this removal of market impediments is precisely what occurred during the first decade and a half of reform.

Policymakers through the 1980s and 1990s introduced a broad array of market-enhancing measures. Whether China should have moved more quickly than it did is a matter of debate, but the key point is that it did indeed move. Economic transactions were encouraged to flow horizontally between producers and consumers rather than vertically between producers and the state. Prices for nearly all goods—from industrial inputs to finished consumer products—were liberalized, and product markets were allowed to thrive. An entire export-oriented, non-state-owned industrial sector was permitted to emerge in China's rural areas, often with the eager support and under the careful tutelage of local government. Partly as a result of this development, savings in the economy shifted from the state sector to the household sector, and banks started to play a real role in financial intermediation. The monobank system of the prereform era was allowed to give way to the diversified set of banking institutions generally found in middle-income market economies. Today, in addition to a central bank, China has three state policy banks, four wholly state-owned commercial banks, and eleven joint-stock commercial banks, most with extensive national or regional branch networks.

At the individual enterprise level, managers even in the state sector were granted unprecedented freedom to run their operations, deciding everything from product mix to long-term investment strategies. Whether from the micro or macro perspective, one would be hard pressed to characterize this system as anything but marketized.

Still the state—despite its encouragement of markets—persisted in defending key players in the traditional system. The old system of planning may have been aggressively dismantled, and the old incentives and behaviors forced into retreat, but the players themselves were protected. Throughout the reform era, state-owned enterprises were rarely if ever put out of business. A particular kind of market system resulted, one that shared most of the attributes of developing capitalist economies, but one also set up to devote extensive resources to the sustenance of a vast number of commercially nonviable firms.

On the positive side, this particular system achieved impressive and sustained macro-level growth. Since 1978, China's GDP has expanded at an average annual rate of 9.5 percent, with particularly noteworthy gains in the non-state-owned portion of the economy. At the start of reform, almost 80 percent of total annual industrial output (by value) was produced by traditional state firms. By 1997, in a substantially larger overall economy, that figure had declined to approximately 25 percent. New industrial entrants have steadily chiseled away at the state's monopoly over production.

On the more negative side, however, is the particular pattern of credit expansion and financial intermediation that has emerged through the 1980s and 1990s. As noted earlier, the elimination of state-controlled prices and the opening of many industrial sectors to new nonstate entrants led to a dramatic shift in the locus of national economic savings. In the prereform economy, almost all savings occurred in the state sector, mostly in the form of financial surpluses accumulating in state-owned manufacturing enterprises. Today, savings accumulate in the household sector: households deposit their funds in banks, and the banking system channels those funds as investment into industrial firms. It is not entirely surprising, therefore, that the reform era has been marked by a massive expansion of credit. In 1978 total lending by Chinese financial institutions stood at just over 50 percent of GDP; that figure grew to over 100 percent by 1997.

The Costs Of Growth

While nothing is intrinsically wrong with an expansion of credit, the real question is to whom credit is directed and how it is employed. It is used to achieve real returns and an expansion of assets, or is it simply frittered away in value-destroying activities? Unfortunately for China, the latter outcome has systematically dominated the former. As long as the Chinese government remained adamantly committed to supporting the state-owned enterprises, most domestic credit was directed toward state industry. In other words, traditional borrowers—many of whom are today insolvent—have been eating up the vast bulk of available investment capital in the Chinese system. Chinese banks continue to channel the bulk of their funds toward the least productive portion of the industrial economy, the state-owned sector. By the mid-1990s, state-owned enterprises accounted for under 35 percent of industrial output value, but were consuming almost 75 percent of national industrial investment.

The central role state banks play in financial intermediation in China stems directly from the government's commitment to sustaining state firms. By severely restricting the growth of alternative channels of intermediation—whether private commercial banks, stock markets, or corporate bond markets—the government ensured that state-owned banks would become the primary repositories for savings accumulating in the economy. Moreover, the government could then use its control over state banks to channel those savings to favored borrowers, namely state firms. The more that industrial firms were showered with capital, the softer their budget constraints became, and the fewer the incentives for productive, asset-expanding behavior. Declining performance simply increased the need for bailout loans. As pressure on the banking system expanded, the government was forced to tighten control to ensure a sufficient flow of capital both into the banks and onward to favored borrowers. A vicious circle developed, one at least generally comparable to the situation in Japan or South Korea.

As in South Korea or Japan, this pattern in China recently has led to a rapid escalation of indebtedness in the modern industrial sector. The liabilities of industrial state-owned enterprises in China soared from approximately 11 percent of total assets in 1978 to almost 80 percent of assets by 1994, and the Chinese state sector as a whole by 1995 was exhibiting debt-to-equity ratios of over 500 percent. That liabilities were rising so quickly suggests not only that firms were borrowing, but also that the borrowed funds tended to be devoted to nonproductive investment. A significant portion of loans funded the operating expenses of loss-making firms, many of which—because of poorly enforced accounting standards—remained only nominally profitable. Funds were also being devoted to capacity expansion, even in the absence of tangible demand for industrial outputs.

In the midst of such extensive borrowing by the state sector, nonperforming loans in the Chinese banking system have skyrocketed. By the mid-1990s, government estimates placed the level of nonperforming loans in the state banking system at approximately 20 percent of all assets. Such levels imply that the Chinese banking system today is technically insolvent. Of course, whether insolvency constitutes as much of a problem in state-owned systems as it does in private ones is debatable, and given China's high levels of household savings, the banking system remains liquid for now.

Nevertheless, China today clearly is wrestling with a significant and potentially unsustainable problem of capital misallocation. The bulk of national investment is directed toward the least productive portion of the economy, often with little or no return. It is difficult to imagine that this will not adversely affect overall growth over the long term. Indeed, it is precisely this concern that accounts for the centrality of state-owned enterprise and banking reform on the current policy agenda. The question is not so much whether the current pattern of capital allocation will adversely affect growth, but to what extent and what to do about it.

What Pacific Century?

For years the futurists declared that Asia would rule the world economy in the 21st century. That isn't likely to happen. What's getting in the way? Asian values.

Louis Kraar

Judging from the confident forecasts by a chorus of experts, the Pacific Century should be dawning about now. Nearly 30 years ago, futurist Herman Kahn argued that by the year 2000, Japan was sure to become the world's No. 1 nation. His influential book *The Emerging Japanese Superstate* depicted the triumph of a new brand of capitalism, under which wise government bureaucrats set the course while diligent workers who respected authority labored to create national wealth. More recently, trend forecaster John Naisbitt roamed the lecture circuit trumpeting that "Asia will become the dominant region of the world—economically, politically, and culturally." Many Asian leaders, of course, echoed that idea.

Well, it hasn't happened. Economic stagnation for most of the past decade has made Japan—still Asia's biggest economy by far—look more like a supermess lately. And the Asian financial crisis in mid-1997 has hampered the rest of East Asia.

And yet the predictions keep coming, this time about China. Says Fred Hu in a new Goldman Sachs report: "It is likely that within the first two to three decades of the next millennium, China will overtake the U.S. as the largest economy." He also predicts that by then Chinese consumers will have a purchasing power "larger than all of Europe's."

Even if China does grow that large, it is unlikely to dominate the world economy in the next century. And the same holds true for the rest of East Asia too. Why? Fundamentally, the old Asian success formula has failed miserably as a model for Asia as well as for the rest of us. The government bureaucrats and autocrats who claimed to have all the answers for spurring economic growth stumbled over their own inherent weaknesses—rampant corruption, collusion with favored companies, and cronyism that funneled questionable loans to friends and family of government leaders. Says Kishore Mahbubani, Singapore's cerebral ambassador to the United Nations: "The key lesson that all East Asian economic managers have learned [from the financial crisis] is that they are accountable not only to domestic actors but to the international financial markets and their key players."

That doesn't mean, though, that we should count Asia out. Over the next century it will continue to play a huge and crucial role. The region's remarkable progress over the past three decades is genuine. Never before in history have nations climbed from poverty to prosperity in one generation—as South Korea did—an accomplishment that indeed seemed like a miracle. The Asian financial crisis, a mere blip in the span of a century, has forced the region to start reforming its worst weaknesses—from shaky banking systems to corrupt business practices. Most crisis-afflicted economies, such as Thailand and Korea, are already growing again. Moreover, the fundamental strengths that originally ignited much excitement about Asia's prospects are alive and well. They include high savings rates, robust investment in education, relatively young populations, and ambitious entrepreneurs.

Over much of the next century East Asian economies almost certainly will continue expanding faster than mature Western economies. The region will serve as both a major production base and a voracious market. Asia today is the world's dominant producer (and a significant consumer) of steel, ships, semiconductors, and notebook computers. Judging from the speed at which Asia is plugging into the digital world, it will stay at the forefront in applying new technologies for communications and electronic commerce. Taiwan, for instance, is a supplier and designer of sophisticated components for computers and mobile phones. Hong Kong and Singapore are hurrying to become hubs for cyber-commerce.

So Asia may someday be able to lay claim to a Pacific Century. Trouble is, to get there it must first change some of its vaunted "Asian values." These include a respect for authority and a willingness to sacrifice individualism for the good of the society. It turns out, however, that these supposedly special values—which some government leaders still claim to be potent economic drivers—are glaring weaknesses. In fact, they get in the way of economic development.

It is true that Asian values served the region well for years. Says Ungsuh Kenneth Park, a thoughtful Korean economist: "East Asian societies achieved rapid growth with strong governments, meek people, and wide cooperation for achieving national goals. This is the sine qua non for every society, anywhere in the history of mankind, at an early stage of economic and social mobilization." But the world is changing, and Asia must change with it. Park continues, "Once basic needs are met, people everywhere demand greater participation in the decisions that shape their lives."

The "Asian values" argument has often served as a convenient justification for authoritarian regimes. "It is altogether shameful to cite Asian values as an excuse for autocratic practices and denial of basic rights and civil liberties," Malaysia's former Deputy Premier Anwar Ibrahim, a reform-minded Muslim intellectual, has said repeatedly. He should know, having been removed from office last year, jailed, beaten by the police, and convicted of dubious corruption charges. His real crime apparently was challenging Malaysia's Prime Minister Mahathir Mohamad, who claims that Asian values are superior to the "moral degeneration" of the West. Mahathir is on the wrong side of history, though.

In the next century Asia will travel slowly and fitfully down the long road toward democracy and the rule of law. Its educated and ever-increasing middle class will no longer bow to the will of strong-man regimes. This assertive spirit is clearly visible in Thailand, Taiwan, Indonesia, and South Korea, which over the past decade have replaced dictatorial regimes with various forms of representative government. The sharp pains caused by the Asian economic crisis last year, for example, prompted Indonesians to dump President Suharto, who made all the big decisions for three decades and enriched his friends and family but allowed no audible dissent. Indonesians are struggling to build a more open society, in which officials are accountable to the public.

Even China, where the Communist Party has maintained a monopoly on power for 50 years, will need to rely on the consent of the governed in the 21st century. Chinese leaders argue that stability is what counts. But a society going through the traumatic changes of rapid development, which produce many losers as well as winners among its citizens, especially needs honest administration and an independent legal system. Without the rule of law, foreign investors as well as Chinese citizens are subject to the shifting whims of officials. Lee Kuan Yew, who built modern Singapore and is no champion of Western-style democracy, foresees China's going "from a centralized to a more participatory system of governance" within the next 50 years. Lee also warns that China must clean up its "most pernicious problem," corruption embedded in its administrative culture, or face a dangerous political powder keg.

Japan will suffer for decades to come from a tribal reluctance to disturb its own social harmony by freely allowing failing corporations to restructure. Americans and Europeans, who once eagerly studied Japanese management techniques in the '80s, have belatedly discovered the dark side of the system. Even the most troubled Japanese companies are pressured to continue employing surplus workers and retaining inefficient suppliers, while collusion between government and business often hides the true financial state of banks and corporations. Allowing bureaucrats to set industrial priorities has left Japan surprisingly uncompetitive in such growth fields as financial services and computer software.

A new challenge for the Japanese lies just ahead. By the year 2025, Japan will become the world's leading geriatric nation, with nearly 26% of its people age 65 or older. Karel Van Wolferen, a Japan expert who once viewed the country as almost omnipotent, now hopes that Japan somehow will succeed in "reinventing" itself. Perhaps as a retirement community?

So the new century, it seems, will belong not to Asia, America, or any other single geographic entity but to an increasingly interdependent world economy. Welcome to the Global Century, in which innovative Asians will flourish, but not dominate.

Unit 5

Unit Selections

Key Points to Consider

- Are violent conflicts and warfare increasing or decreasing today? Explain your response.
- What changes have taken place in recent years in the types of conflicts and who participates?
- How is military doctrine changing to reflect new political realities?
- How is the national security policy of the United States likely to change? What about Russia and China?
- What institutional structures can be developed to reduce the danger of nuclear war?

DUSHKIN ONLINE Links

www.dushkin.com/online/

22. **DefenseLINK**
http://www.defenselink.mil
23. **Federation of American Scientists (FAS)**
http://www.fas.org
24. **ISN International Relations and Security Network**
http://www.isn.ethz.ch
25. **The NATO Integrated Data Service (NIDS)**
http://www.nato.int/structur/nids/nids.htm

These sites are annotated on pages 4 and 5.

Conflict

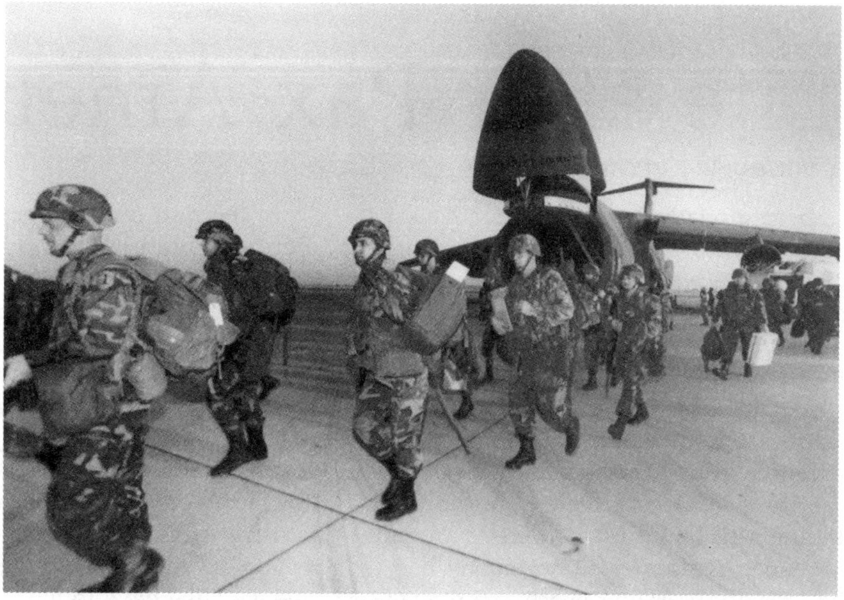

Do you lock your door at night? Do you secure your personal property to avoid theft? These are basic questions that have to do with your sense of personal safety and security. Most individuals take steps to protect what they have, including their lives. The same is true for groups of people, including countries.

In the international arena, governments frequently pursue their national interest by entering into mutually agreeable "deals" with other governments. Social scientists call these types of arrangements "exchanges" (i.e., each side gives up something it values in order to gain something it values even more). In simple terms, it functions like this: "I have the oil that you need. I will sell it to you if in turn you will sell me the agricultural products that I lack." Whether on the governmental level or the personal level ("If you help me with my homework, then I will drive you home this weekend"), this is the process used by most individuals and groups to "secure" and protect what is of value. The exchange process, however, can break down. When threats and punishments replace mutual exchanges, conflict ensues. Neither side benefits and there are costs to both. Further, each may use threats and hope that the other will capitulate, but if efforts at intimidation and coercion fail, the conflict may escalate into violent confrontation.

With the end of the cold war, issues of national security have changed. In the early 1990s agreements between the former Soviet Union and the United States, for example, led to the elimination of support for participants in low-intensity conflicts in Central America, Africa, and Southeast Asia. Fighting the cold war by proxy is now a thing of the past. In addition, cold war military alliances have either collapsed or have been significantly redefined. Despite these historic changes, there still is no shortage of conflicts in the world today.

The unit begins with a discussion of broad security issues in the post–cold war era. A general focus is provided in these initial articles on the United States and Europe. This discussion is followed by a more focused analysis of the types of conflicts that are redefining contemporary security issues.

The unit concludes by examining perhaps the most important of all global issues—the avoidance of nuclear war. Many experts initially predicted that the collapse of the Soviet Union would decrease the threat of nuclear war. However, many now believe that the threat has increased as control of nuclear weapons has become less centralized and the command structure less reliable. In addition, the proliferation of nuclear weapons into South Asia is a new security issue. What these changing circumstances mean for strategic weapons policy in the United States is also a topic of considerable debate. With this changing political context as the backdrop, the prospects for arms control and increased international cooperation are reviewed.

Like all the other global issues described in this anthology, international conflict is a dynamic problem. It is important to understand that conflicts are not random events, but follow patterns and trends. Forty-five years of cold war established discernable patterns of international conflict as the superpowers contained each other with vast expenditures of money and technological know-how. The consequence of this stalemate was often a shift to the developing world for conflict by superpower proxy.

The changing circumstances of the post–cold war era generate a series of important new policy questions: Will there be more nuclear proliferation? Is there an increased danger of so-called "rogue" states destabilizing the international arena? Will there be an new emphasis on low-intensity conflicts related to the interdiction of drugs or will some other unforeseen issue determine the world's hot spots? Will the United States and its European allies lose interest in security issues that do not directly involve their economic interests and simply look the other way as age-old ethnic conflicts become brutally violent? Can the international community develop viable institutions to mediate and resolve disputes before they become violent? The answers to these and related questions will determine the patterns of conflict in the post–cold war era.

Life after Pax Americana

Charles A. Kupchan

This decade has been a relatively easy one for American strategists. America's preponderant economic and military might has produced a unipolar international structure, which has in turn provided a ready foundation for global stability. Hierarchy and order have devolved naturally from power asymmetries, making less urgent the mapping of a new international landscape and the formulation of a new grand strategy. The Bush and Clinton administrations do deserve considerable credit for presiding over the end of the Cold War and responding sensibly to isolated crises around the globe. But America's uncontested hegemony has spared them the task of preserving peace and managing competition and balancing among multiple poles of power—a challenge that has consistently bedeviled statesmen throughout history.

The coming decade will be a far less tractable one for the architects of U.S. foreign policy. Although the United States will remain atop the international hierarchy for the near term, a global landscape in which power and influence are more equally distributed looms ahead. With this more equal distribution of power will come a more traditional geopolitics and the return of the competitive balancing that has been held in abeyance by America's preponderance. Economic globalization, nuclear weapons, new information technologies, and the spread of democracy may well tame geopolitics and dampen the rivalries likely to accompany a more diffuse distribution of power. But history provides sobering lessons in this respect. Time and again, postwar lulls in international competition and pronouncements about the obsolescence of war have given way to the return of power balancing and eventually to great-power conflict.

The foreign policy team that takes office in 2001 will therefore face the onerous task of piecing together a grand strategy for managing the return to multipolarity. The challenge will be as demanding politically as it is intellectually. Recognizing that new power centers are emerging and adjusting to their rise will meet political resistance after 50 years of American primacy. Politicians and strategists alike will have to engage in long-term planning and pursue policies that respond to underlying trends rather than immediate challenges. But American elites must rise to the occasion. The coming decade represents a unique window of opportunity; the United States should plan for the future while it still enjoys preponderance, and not wait until the diffusion of power has already made international politics more competitive and unpredictable.

In the next section I explain how and why a transition to a multipolar world is likely to come about in the near term. The United States will not be eclipsed by a rising challenger, as is usually the case during transitions in international hierarchy. Instead, a shrinking American willingness to be the global protector of last resort will be the primary engine of a changing global landscape. The key challenge, I then argue, will not be in preparing for battle with the next contender for hegemony but in weaning Europe and East Asia of their excessive dependence on the current hegemon, the United States. Europeans and East Asians alike have found it both comfortable and cheap to rely on American power and diplomacy to provide their security. Americans have gone along with the deal for decades because of the importance of containing the Soviet Union and the profitability of being at the center of global politics.

But now that communist regimes are a dying breed and the Cold War is receding into the past, America's protective umbrella will slowly retract. If this retrenchment in the scope of America's engagement abroad is not to result in the return of destructive power balancing to Europe and East Asia, the United States and its main regional partners must start now to prepare for life after Pax Americana.

Benign Power

Most analysts of international politics trace change in the distribution of power to two sources: the secular diffusion over time and space of productive capabilities and material resources; and balancing against concentrations of power motivated by the search for security and prestige. Today's great powers will become tomorrow's has-beens as nodes of innovation and efficiency move from the core to the periphery of the international system. In addition, reigning hegemons threaten rising secondary states and thereby provoke the formation of countervailing coalitions. Taken together, these dynamics drive the cyclical pattern of the rise and fall of great powers.[1]

In contrast to this historical pattern, neither the diffusion of power nor balancing against the United States will be important factors driving the coming transition in the international system. It will be decades before any single state can match the United States in terms of either economic or military capability. Current power asymmetries are extreme by histori-

 From the *World Policy Journal,* Vol. XVI, No. 3, Fall 1999, pp. 20-27.

cal standards. The United States spends more on defense than all other great powers combined and more on defense research and development than the rest of the world combined. Its gross economic output dwarfs that of most other countries and its expenditure on R&D points to a growing qualitative edge in a global economy increasingly dominated by high-technology sectors.[2] Nor is balancing against American power likely to provoke a countervailing coalition. The United States is separated from both Europe and Asia by large expanses of water, making American power less threatening. Furthermore, it is hard to imagine that the United States would engage in behavior sufficiently aggressive to provoke opposing alliances. Even in the wake of NATO's air campaign against Yugoslavia, U.S. forces are for the most part welcomed by local powers in Europe and East Asia. Despite sporadic comments from French, Russian, and Chinese officials about America's overbearing behavior, the United States is generally viewed as a benign power, not as a predatory hegemon.[3]

The Rise of Europe

The waning of unipolarity is therefore likely to stem from two novel sources: regional amalgamation in Europe and shrinking internationalism in the United States. Europe is in the midst of a long-term process of political and economic integration that is gradually eliminating the importance of borders and centralizing authority and resources. To be sure, the European Union is not yet an amalgamated polity with a single center of authority. Nor does Europe have a military capability commensurate with its economic resources.

But trend lines do indicate that Europe is heading in the direction of becoming a new pole of power. Now that its single market is accompanied by a single currency, Europe has a collective weight on matters of trade and finance rivaling that of the United States. The aggregate wealth of the European Union's 15 members is already roughly equal to America's, and the coming entry of the new democracies of Central Europe will tilt the balance in the EU's favor.

Europe has also recently embarked on efforts to forge a common defense policy and to acquire the military wherewithal to operate independently of U.S. forces. The European Union has appointed a high representative to oversee security policy, is establishing a policy planning unit, and is starting to lay the political groundwork for revamping its forces. It will be decades, if ever, before the EU becomes a unitary state, especially in light of its impending enlargement to the east, but as its resources grow and its decision-making becomes more centralized, power and influence will become more equally distributed between the two sides of the Atlantic.

American Reluctance

The rise of Europe and its leveling effect on the global distribution of power will occur gradually. Of more immediate impact will be a diminishing appetite for robust internationalism in the United States. Today's unipolar landscape is a function not just of America's preponderant resources but also of its willingness to use them to underwrite international order. Accordingly, should the will of the body politic to bear the costs and risks of international leadership decline, so too would America's position of global primacy.

On the face of it, the appetite of the American polity for internationalism has diminished little, if at all, since the collapse of the Soviet Union. Both the Bush and Clinton administrations have pursued ambitious and activist foreign policies. The United States has taken the lead in building an open international economy and promoting financial stability, and it has repeatedly deployed its forces to trouble spots around the globe. But American internationalism is now at a high-water mark and, for three compelling reasons, it will begin to dissipate in the years ahead.

First, the internationalism of the 1990s has been sustained by a period of unprecedented economic growth in the United States. A booming stock market, an expanding economy, and substantial budget surpluses have created a political atmosphere conducive to trade liberalization, expenditure on the military, and repeated engagement in solving problems in less fortunate parts of the globe.

Yet, even under these auspicious conditions, the internationalist agenda has shown signs of faltering. Congress, for example, has mustered only a fickle enthusiasm for free trade, approving NAFTA in 1993 and the Uruguay Round in 1994, but then denying President Clinton fast-track negotiating authority in 1997. Congress has also been skeptical of America's interventions in Bosnia and Kosovo, tolerating them, but little more. When the stock market sputters and growth stalls (and this is a matter of when, not if), these inward-looking currents will grow much stronger. The little support for free trade that still exists will dwindle. And such stinginess is likely to spread into the security realm, intensifying the domestic debate over burden sharing and calls within Congress for America's regional partners to shoulder increased defense responsibilities.

Second, although the United States has pursued a very activist defense policy during the 1990s, it has done so on the cheap. Clinton has repeatedly authorized the use of force in the Balkans and in the Middle East. But he has relied almost exclusively on air power, successfully avoiding the casualties likely to accompany the introduction of ground troops in combat. In Somalia, the one case in which U.S. ground troops suffered significant losses, Clinton ordered the withdrawal of U.S. forces from the operation. In NATO's campaign against Yugoslavia, week after week of bombing only intensified the humanitarian crisis and increased the likelihood of a southward spread of the conflict. Nevertheless, the United States blocked the use of ground forces and insisted that aircraft bomb from 15,000 feet to avoid being shot down.

Congress revolted despite these operational constraints minimizing the risks to U.S. personnel. A month into the campaign, the House of Representatives voted 249 to 180 to refuse funding for sending U.S. ground troops to Yugoslavia without congressional permission. Even a resolution that merely endorsed the bombing campaign failed to win approval (the vote was 213 to 213). In short, the American polity appears to have near zero tolerance for casualties. The illusion that internationalism can be maintained with no or minimal loss of life will likely come back to haunt the United States in the years ahead, limiting its ability to use force in the appropriate manner when necessary.

Third, generational change is likely to take a toll on the character and scope of U.S. engagement abroad. The younger Americans already rising to positions of influence in the public and private sectors have not lived through the formative experiences—the Second World War and the rebuilding of Europe—that serve as historical anchors of internationalism. Individuals schooled in the 1990s and now entering the work force will not even have first-hand experience of the Cold War. These Americans will not necessarily be isolationist, but they will certainly be less interested in and knowledgeable about foreign affairs than their older colleagues—a pattern already becoming apparent in the Congress. In the absence of a manifest threat to American national security, making the case for engagement and sacrifice abroad thus promises to grow increasingly difficult with time. Trend lines clearly point to a turning inward, to a nation tiring of carrying the burdens of global leadership.

Bad News and Good News

The bad news is that the global stability that unipolarity has engendered will be jeopardized as power becomes more equally distributed in the international system. The good news is that this structural change will occur through different mechanisms than in the past, and therefore *may* be easier to manage peacefully.

The rising challenger is Europe, not a unitary state with hegemonic ambitions. Europe's aspirations will be moderated by the self-checking mechanisms inherent in the EU and by cultural and linguistic barriers to centralization. In addition, the United States is likely to react to a more independent Europe by stepping back and making room for an EU that appears ready to be more self-reliant and more muscular. Unlike reigning hegemons in the past, the United States will not fight to the finish to maintain its primacy and prevent its eclipse by a rising challenger. On the contrary, the United States will cede leadership willingly as its economy slows and it grows weary of being the security guarantor of last resort.

The prospect is thus not one of clashing titans, but of no titans at all. Regions long accustomed to relying on American resources and leadership to preserve the peace may well be left to fend for themselves. These are the main reasons that the challenge for American grand strategy as the next century opens will be to wean Europe and East Asia of their dependence on the United States and put in place arrangements that will prevent the return of competitive balancing and regional rivalries in the wake of an American retrenchment.

Europe on Its Own

It is fortunate that the near-term challenge to U.S. primacy will come from Europe. After decades of close cooperation, Europe and North America enjoy unprecedented levels of trust and reciprocity. European states have gone along with U.S. leadership not just because they have not had the power and influence to do otherwise; despite cavils, they also welcome the particular brand of international order sustained by the United States. A more equal distribution of power across the Atlantic will no doubt engender increased competition between a collective Europe and the United States. But such conflict is likely to be restricted to economic matters and muted by the mutual benefits reaped from high levels of trade and investment. Furthermore, the underlying coincidence of values between North America and Europe means that even when interests diverge, geopolitical rivalry is not likely to follow. Efforts to preserve an Atlantic consensus may well lead to a lowest common denominator and produce inaction (as has occurred repeatedly in the Balkans). But it is hard to imagine the United States and Europe engaging in militarized conflict.

In this sense, the key concern for the coming decade is not the emergence of balancing between Europe and the United States, but the reemergence of balancing and rivalries *within* a Europe no longer under American protection. The European Union is well on its way to erecting a regional order that can withstand the retraction of American power. Through a steady process of pooling sovereignty, Europe has nurtured a supranational character and identity that make integration irreversible. Nevertheless, guaranteeing a self-sustaining and coherent European polity requires that Europe and the United States together pursue three initiatives.

A Window of Opportunity

To begin, Europe must follow through with the initial steps it has taken to create a military establishment capable of carrying out major missions without the assistance of U.S. forces. The United States should be far more forthcoming in welcoming this initiative, and stop worrying that an independent European military would undercut the transatlantic security link by fueling calls in Congress for the withdrawal of U.S. troops. NATO will be in much better shape five years hence if Europe is carrying a fair load than if Congress continues to see a Europe free-riding on American soldiers. Far from expediting a U.S. departure from the continent, a serious European military will only increase the chances that a mature and balanced transatlantic partnership emerges and that America maintains a presence in Europe.

Europe now has a window of opportunity to make serious progress on the defense front. A number of factors afford this opening: British willingness to take the lead on forging a collective defense policy; recognition within the EU of Europe's excessive dependence on U.S. capability (made clear by the campaign against Yugoslavia); and the appointment of a new European Commission, with Romani Prodi as its president and Javier Solana as its high representative for security policy.

The top priorities for EU members include moving to all-volunteer forces so that defense expenditures can go toward buying capability and force-projection assets, not paying poorly trained conscripts. Europe's defense industry must be consolidated to improve economies of scale, and more funding should go toward research and development and improving the technological sophistication of weapons and intelligence systems. Europe must also make tough decisions about an appropriate division of labor among its member states if it is to build a balanced and capable force structure.

Promoting a stable peace in southeastern Europe is the second key piece of unfinished business for Europe and the United States. The task of halting ethnic conflict in the Balkans repeatedly paralyzed both NATO and the EU throughout the decade. The European enterprise would have been set back grievously had NATO failed to act in Bosnia and Kosovo. Now that the fighting has stopped, the international community must take advantage of the opportunity to construct a lasting peace. That goal ultimately means drawing the Balkans into the European Union. Rapprochement between Greece and Turkey and resolution of the Cyprus problem are no less important if Europe is to avoid being engulfed in persistent crises in its southeast. In its quest to help ensure that Europe does not again fall prey to national rivalries, the United States should make southeastern Europe a top regional priority.

Embracing Russia in a wider Europe is the third step needed to prevent the return of rivalries and shifting balances of power to the continent. Russia in the years ahead will gradually reassume its position as one of Europe's great powers. If Russia is included in the European enterprise, its resources and influence will likely be directed toward furthering continent-wide integration. If it is excluded from the European project, Russia will likely seek a coalition to balance against Europe. Indeed, the enlargement of NATO has already increased the likelihood of such balancing by raising the prospect that Russia's entire western flank will abut the Atlantic Alliance.

Instead of using NATO to protect against a threat that no longer exists, its members should use the organization as a vehicle for anchoring Russia in Europe.[4] The EU is the more appropriate vehicle for this task, but its enlargement is lagging way behind NATO's because of the institutional changes and financial costs entailed in adding new members. Furthermore, the integration of Russia into the Atlantic community, in part because of European resistance on cultural grounds, will require considerable American influence and leadership—assets that NATO provides. While it is still Europe's chief peacemaker and protector, the United States needs to ensure that Russia is included in Europe's historic process of pacification and integration.

East Asia Estranged

Preparing East Asia to rely less on American power is far more complicated and dangerous than the parallel task in Europe. The key difference is that European states took advantage of America's protective umbrella to pursue reconciliation, rapprochement, and an ambitious agenda of regional cooperation and integration. Europeans have accordingly succeeded in fashioning a regional order that is likely to withstand the retraction of American power. In contrast, states in East Asia have hidden behind America's presence, pursuing neither reconciliation nor regional integration. East Asia's major powers remain estranged.

The United States therefore faces a severe trade-off in East Asia between the balancing provoked by its predominant role in the region and the intraregional balancing that would ensue in the wake of an American retrenchment. America's sizable military presence in East Asia keeps the peace and checks regional rivalries. But it also alienates China and holds in place a polarized political landscape.

As China's economy and military capability grow, its efforts to balance against the United States could become more pronounced. Were the United States to back off from its role as regional arbiter and protector, relations with China would improve, but at the expense of regional stability. Japan and Korea would no doubt increase their own military capabilities, risking a regionwide arms race and spiraling tensions.

If the United States is to escape the horns of this dilemma, it must help repair the region's main cleavage and facilitate rapprochement between East Asia's two major powers: Japan and China. Just as reconciliation between France and Germany was the critical ingredient in building a stable zone of peace in Europe, Sino-Japanese rapprochement is the sine qua non of a self-sustaining regional order in East Asia.

Primary responsibility for improving Sino-Japanese ties lies with Japan. With an economy and political system much more developed than China's, Japan has far more latitude in exploring openings in the relationship. Japan can also take a major step forward by finally acknowledging and formally apologizing for its behavior during the Second World War. The United States can further this process by welcoming and helping to facilitate overtures between Tokyo and Beijing.

Washington should also help dislodge the inertia that pervades politics in Tokyo by making it clear to the Japanese that they cannot indefinitely rely on American guarantees to ensure their security. Japan therefore needs to take advantage of America's protective umbrella while it lasts, pursuing the policies of reconciliation and integration essential to constructing a regional security order resting on cooperation rather than deterrence.

If overtures from Tokyo succeed in reducing tensions between China and Japan, the United States would be able to play a less prominent role in the region, making possible an improvement in its own relations with China. As it buys time for Sino-Japanese rapprochement to get underway, Washington should avoid the rhetoric and policies that might induce China to intensify its efforts to balance against Japan and the United States. Talk of an impending Chinese military threat is both counterproductive and misguided; the Chinese military is nowhere near world-class.[5] The United States should also avoid provocative moves, such as deploying antimissile defenses in the Western Pacific theater or supporting a Taiwanese policy of moving toward formal independence. China can do its part to strengthen its relationship with the United States by containing saber-rattling over Taiwan, halting the export of weapons to rogue states, and avoiding actions and rhetoric that could inflame territorial disputes in the region.

A Global Directorate

If my analysis is correct, the most dangerous consequence of a return to multipolarity is not balancing between North America, Europe, and East Asia, but the reemergence of national rivalries and competitive balancing within Europe and East Asia as American retrenchment proceeds. It is for this reason that American grand strategy should focus on facilitating regional integration in Europe and East Asia as a means of preparing both areas to assume far more responsibility for managing their own affairs.

The ultimate vision that should guide U.S. grand strategy is the construction of a concert-like directorate of the major powers in North America, Europe, and East Asia. These major powers would together manage developments and regulate relations both within and among their respective regions.

Mustering the political will and the foresight to pursue this vision will be a formidable task. The United States will need to begin ceding influence and autonomy to regions that have grown all too comfortable with American primacy. Neither American statesmen, long accustomed to calling the shots, nor statesmen in Europe and East Asia, long accustomed to passing the buck, will find the transition an easy one.

But it is far wiser and safer to get ahead of the curve and shape structural change by design, than to find unipolarity giving way to a chaotic multipolarity by default. It will take a decade, if not two, for a new international system to evolve. But the decisions taken by the first American administration of the twenty-first century will play a critical role in determining whether multipolarity reemerges peacefully or brings with it the competitive jockeying that in the past has so frequently led to great-power war.

Notes

1. See Robert Gilpin, *War and Change in World Politics* (Cambridge: Cambridge University Press, 1981); Paul M. Kennedy, *The Rise and Fall of the Great Powers* (New York: Random House, 1987); and Christopher Layne, "The Unipolar Illusion: Why New Great Powers Will Rise," *International Security,* vol. 17 (spring 1993).
2. William C. Wohlforth, "The Stability of a Unipolar World," *International Security,* vol. 24 (summer 1999).
3. On the concept of benign power, see Charles Kupchan, "After Pax Americana: Benign Power, Regional Integration, and the Sources of a Stable Multipolarity," *International Security,* vol. 23 (fall 1998).
4. See Charles Kupchan, "Rethinking Europe," *The National Interest,* no. 56 (summer 1999).
5. See Bates Gill and Michael O'Hanlon, "China's Hollow Military," *The National Interest,* no. 56 (summer 1999); and Gerald Segal, "Does China Matter?" *Foreign Affairs,* vol. 78 (September/October 1999).

Charles A. Kupchan is associate professor of international affairs at Georgetown University and a senior fellow at the Council on Foreign Relations. He is the author, among other works, of The Vulnerability of Empire.

An Anachronistic Policy

The Strategic Obsolescence of the "Rogue Doctrine"

MICHAEL T. KLARE

It has been ten years since General Colin Powell, then Chairman of the Joint Chiefs of Staff, manufactured the "Rogue Doctrine" as the basic template for US military strategy in the post-Cold War era. With the Soviet Union in irreversible decline and no other superpower adversary in sight, Powell elected to focus US strategy on the threat allegedly posed by hostile Third World powers—the so-called "rogue states." Although intended largely as an interim measure—a means of maintaining defense spending at near-Cold War levels until a more credible threat appeared on the horizon—the anti-rogue strategy has become the defining paradigm for American security policy. But while immensely popular on Capitol Hill, the Rogue Doctrine has become increasingly irrelevant to the security environment in which American forces operate.

Under current US military policy, the Department of Defense is required to maintain sufficient strength to simultaneously fight and defeat two Iraq-like regional adversaries. These adversaries—generally assumed to include Iraq, Iran, Libya, and North Korea—are said to be dangerous because of their potent military capabilities, history of antagonism toward the West, and their pursuit of weapons of mass destruction (WMD). Although not linked by treaty or formal alliance, these states are said to pose a threat because of their common disregard for the accepted norms of international society.

The Rogue Doctrine is presently the main guiding principle for the structure, orientation, and disposition of US military forces. Other tasks are, of course, assigned to the armed forces on a regular basis, as demonstrated most recently by the air war against Serbia. But these other missions, including multilateral peacekeeping operations, are considered "add-ons" to the primary mission of fighting the rogues; they do not govern the basic organization of the Armed Services. Just as US forces were once trained and equipped for the overriding task of resisting a Warsaw Pact invasion of Western Europe—the "Fulda Gap mentality"—they are now trained and equipped to repeat Operation Desert Storm again and again.

The Rogue Doctrine also significantly influences US foreign policy. For instance, much effort has been put into isolating Iran from the international community, despite the fact that most of the United States' allies do not share Washington's views on the necessity of doing so. The United States also expends great political capital in trying to maintain economic sanctions on Iraq—even though a growing number of states have concluded that the sanctions have outlived their usefulness.

Unfortunately, the Rogue Doctrine has been subjected to very little critical analysis. Few in Congress have questioned the rationale behind the "two war" policy that now governs US strategy, or its US$275 billion per year cost (soon to rise to US$300 billion). The mass media has not behaved any better; references to the "rogue state threat" are common, but are rarely accompanied by any analysis of political and military developments in the states involved or of the changing nature of the security environment. If we are to adopt a realistic approach to future perils, therefore, it is essential to look more critically at the dominant US security paradigm.

The Rise of the Rogue Doctrine

The origins of the Rogue Doctrine can be traced to the final weeks of 1989, when General Colin Powell commenced a search for a new, post-Soviet military doctrine. Recognizing that the threat of a US-Soviet clash had lost all plausibility in the wake of the Berlin Wall's collapse, Powell sought to construct a new threat scenario that would justify the preservation of America's super-

From the *Harvard International Review*, Summer 2000, pp. 46-51. © 2000 by Harvard International Review.

power capabilities in a world with no Soviet-like opponent. Working closely with General Lee Butler, then Director of the Strategic Plans and Policy Directorate (J-5) of the Joint Staff, Powell conceived of a strategy in which regional threats, not the monolithic threat of the Soviet Union, would govern US military planning in the years to come.

In constructing this strategy, Powell was fully aware that identifying a credible successor to the USSR was essential if the Pentagon was to avert a major military downsizing at the hands of Congress. Within days of the Wall's collapse, many members of Congress and other prominent figures began talking of a substantial "peace dividend" that would be made possible through a sizable reduction in US military spending. Fearful that precipitous congressional action would also deprive the Department of Defense of any sense of strategic coherence, Powell sought to establish a new strategic paradigm that could be used to argue against deep cuts in military spending and at the same time imbue the armed forces with a new sense of purpose.

Powell did not waste any time starting this project. Just one week after the Berlin Wall's collapse, on November 15, 1989, he presented his initial ideas to then President George Bush. According to an official record of this meeting (which concerned the Pentagon's five-year planning document for Fiscal Years 1990–1994), Powell argued, "The drastically different strategic environment projected for 1994 called for a major restructuring of US security policy, strategy, force structure, and capabilities. With a diminished Soviet threat and sharply reduced resources, the focus of strategic planning should shift from global war with the Soviet Union to regional and contingency responses to non-Soviet threats."

To address this threat, Powell contended that the United States would require sufficient military strength to fight and win two regional conflicts simultaneously This need, in turn, established the requirement for a "Base Force" of 1.6 million active-duty personnel (down by about one-fourth from the 1989 level of 2.1 million), with a standing complement of 12 active Army divisions, 16 active Air Force tactical fighter wings, and 450 warships.

In advancing the Base Force concept, Powell did not use the term "rogue state," or any comparable expression. Nevertheless, the basic outlines of the Pentagon's current, anti-rogue posture were already present in his November briefing to the President. In the weeks that followed, senior Pentagon officials began speaking more frequently of the threat posed by well-armed, antagonistic Third World powers. In April 1990, for instance, Army Chief of Staff General Carl E. Vuono discussed this threat in *Sea Power* magazine and contends, "The proliferation of military power in what is often called the 'Third World' presents a troubling picture. Many Third World nations now possess mounting arsenals of tanks, heavy artillery, ballistic missiles, and chemical weapons . . . The United States cannot ignore the expanding military power of these countries, and the Army must retain the capability to defeat potential threats wherever they occur. This could mean confronting a well-equipped army in the Third World." Aside from its prophetic character—at this time the Iraqi invasion of Kuwait and the onset of Operation Desert Shield was but five months away—this article is striking because of its vivid portrayal of what would later be termed the rogue-state threat.

General Powell and his aides continued to marshal support for the new strategy throughout the spring of 1990, and, on June 26, they presented the fully developed Base Force concept to President Bush and Secretary of Defense Richard Cheney. After much discussion, Bush gave his formal approval to Powell's plan and instructed his staff to prepare a speech outlining its general parameters. A scheduled appearance by the President at the Aspen Institute in Colorado on August 2, 1990 was then selected as a suitable occasion to deliver this address.

In his speech at the Aspen Institute, Bush reiterated many of the themes first articulated by Generals Powell and Vuono. "In a world less driven by an immediate threat to Europe and the danger of global

All in the nuclear family. Going nuclear has not made Pakistan a rogue state in US eyes. Former Prime Minister Nawaz Sharif visits US Secretary of Defense William Cohen at the Pentagon in December 1998.

Photo courtesy US Department of Defense

war," he declared, "the size of our forces will increasingly be shaped by the needs of regional conflict." In line with this new posture, "America must possess forces able to respond to threats in whatever corner of the globe they may occur."

Bush's speech at the Aspen Institute in August was given more attention than might otherwise have been the case because a few hours earlier, on the night of August 1, Iraqi troops began pouring into Kuwait. Bush made reference to the Kuwait situation in his comments, leading many commentators to view the speech as a spontaneous response to the Iraqi invasion. Certainly the president's harsh attacks on Saddam Hussein, along with the announcement of Operation Desert Shield on August 7, led most people to telescope all of these events together. But from a historical point of view it is essential to remember that the "regional strategy" announced by Bush on August 2 was a response *not* to the Iraqi invasion of Kuwait but rather to the collapse of the Berlin Wall in November 1989 and the growing enfeeblement of the Soviet Union.

The Doctrine's Golden Age

The period from August 1990 to February 1998 constitutes what might be called the "golden age" of the Rogue Doctrine. When Iraqi forces rolled into Kuwait, Congress discontinued its discussion of the "peace dividend" and abandoned all plans for a significant reduction in military strength. Although some in Congress bemoaned the early decision to rely on force instead of economic sanctions to drive Iraq out of Kuwait, most Americans supported Operation Desert Storm once US forces were committed to battle. Furthermore, as news of the elaborate Iraqi preparations for nuclear, chemical, and biological warfare became widely known, the "rogue state" concept took hold in the think tanks and the media, driving out all competing strategic paradigms.

The 1991 Gulf conflict also legitimized the view, first articulated by Generals Powell and Vuono, that America's most likely future adversaries would be well-armed regional powers like Iraq. On March 19, 1991, less than three weeks after the fighting in the Gulf had ended, Cheney told Congress that "the Gulf War presaged very much the type of conflict we are most likely to confront again in this new era—major regional contingencies against foes well-armed with advanced conventional and unconventional munitions." Other senior officials quickly agreed, giving the rogue doctrine an almost canonical status.

The potency of the rogue-state model became especially evident in 1993, when President Clinton entered the White House. During the 1992 campaign, Clinton had promised to adopt a new foreign and military policy in response to the dramatic changes of at the end of the Cold War era. Seeking to make good on this promise, Clinton's first Secretary of Defense, Les Aspin, ordered a "bottom-up review" (BUR) of US military policy. But while Aspin implied that the BUR would produce a dramatic transformation of US strategy, the final product looked a great deal like the Base Force concept originally developed by Colin Powell in 1989. As in the Powell plan, the BUR called for maintenance of sufficient forces to fight and win two major regional conflicts (MRCs) at more or less the same time. The only discernible difference between the two plans is that Aspin spoke of fighting two MRCs "nearly simultaneously," not all at once as in the Powell plan.

In presenting the Bottom-Up-Review to the public, Aspin and Powell articulated the Rogue Doctrine in its mature form. Development of the new strategy, Aspin declared, was driven by a need to contain "rogue leaders set on regional domination through military aggression while simultaneously pursuing nuclear, biological, and chemical weapons capabilities." In meeting these threats, the Pentagon's principal objective would be "to project power into regions important to our interests and to defeat potentially hostile regional powers, such as North Korea and Iraq."

Opposition to rogue states also became a defining theme in the foreign policy of the Clinton administration. This opposition was communicated in a variety of ways. Continuous pressure was brought to bear on Iraq through non-stop air patrols and periodic missile attacks. Libya was subjected to UN-imposed economic sanctions in 1992, when Libyan strongman Colonel Muammar Qaddafi refused to extradite two government officials accused of complicity in the 1988 Lockerbie airline bombing. North Korea was threatened with similar sanctions in 1994, when it refused access to its nuclear sites by inspectors from the International Atomic Energy Agency in accordance with the Nuclear Non-Proliferation Treaty. And Iran was subjected to a unilateral US ban on trade and investment in 1995 in response to its alleged proliferation activities.

The popularity of the Rogue Doctrine was demonstrated again in 1997, when the Department of Defense conducted yet another review of American military posture. This study, known as the Quadrennial Defense Review (QDR), was expected to move beyond the BUR in addressing the emerging challenges of the post-Cold War era. As in 1993, however, the Department of Defense chose to embrace the status quo: a two-war posture aimed at defeating hostile Third World states.

Challenges to the Rogue Doctrine

Today, the Rogue Doctrine appears thoroughly entrenched in US military thinking. None of the presidential candidates has expressed any disagreement with the Doctrine's basic premises, and no one in Congress or in the major think tanks has proposed an alternative vision. In all likelihood, then, this policy will continue to govern US strategic planning when a new administration takes office in 2001.

The Rogue Doctrine remains popular in Washington because it points to a clearly identifiable set of enemies—no easy feat in this time of ambiguous threats and shifting loyalties—and because it can be used to justify the preservation of the existing military establishment, which no one in authority would like to alter. In addition, special interests, including the military think tanks and organizations, the manufacturers of high-tech weaponry, and so on, share a common interest in maintaining the status quo. So entrenched has this strategy become that none of its proponents feel the need to subject it to any sort of systematic reassessment based on a considered analysis of the existing world security environment; instead, the Doctrine is treated as unshakable wisdom, sufficient onto itself.

The fact that senior American officials have endorsed this Doctrine in such a dogmatic fashion should set off alarm bells all over the country. History suggests that the unquestioning embrace of a given strategy year after year can spell disaster when objective conditions no longer coincide with the strategy's basic assumptions. And in this case, there are many signs that the Rogue Doctrine is seriously out of touch with existing world conditions. In particular, I see five significant problems with the Doctrine:

Lack of support from America's allies. Although President Bush was able to organize a truly extraordinary coalition to fight Saddam Hussein in 1990–91, his successors have not been able to preserve that alliance or to employ it against other hostile states. In fact, no US ally has yet accepted the proposition that there is an identifiable category of "rogue" states, and few appear willing to join the United States in efforts to punish the regimes in question. Iraq remains under UN economic sanctions, but many countries seek to lift the sanctions and end Baghdad's total isolation from the world community. North Korea continues to be viewed as a pariah state by many, but the government of Kim Dae Jung in South Korea has made clear its desire to effect a rapprochement with the North. And no states have agreed to copy the stringent economic sanctions imposed on Iran by Washington. The lack of allied backing for the Rogue Doctrine became especially evident in February 1998, when President Clinton sought to mobilize international support for military action against Iraq in response to its failure to open certain weapons sites to UN inspection. While the British government did agree to provide some military forces for joint action against Baghdad, most US allies provided only token support or none at all. Particularly striking was the lack of support from long-term American allies in the Gulf, including Saudi Arabia. When Washington initiated the bombing of Iraq in December of 1998, the lack of international support for such action stood in sharp contrast to the situation in 1990–91.

Insufficiently menacing rogues. To be successful over the long run, the Rogue Doctrine requires that the "rogues" act like the outlaws they are said to be. But none of the nominal rogues has engaged in unambiguously aggressive behavior since 1991, and most seem determined to establish good—or at least businesslike—relations with the Western world. Saddam Hussein has continued to defy the world community with respect to weapons inspections, but he has not precipitated a replay of the 1990 invasion of Kuwait, or anything remotely like it. North Korea has also refrained from overtly aggressive moves, and in 1994 agreed to dismantle its nuclear weapons program. Libya has rebuilt its ties with other African nations and has turned over the two suspects in the Lockerbie case for a trial in the Netherlands. Iran has gone even further, offering lucrative oil-and gas-development concessions to prominent Western firms.

Also significant is the fact that the military capabilities possessed by the rogues have not grown appreciably since 1990, and in some cases have deteriorated. Bear in mind that both the BUR and the QDR assume that America's future regional adversaries will resemble the Iraq of 1990—that is, a force of nearly one million soldiers equipped with thousands of tanks, artillery pieces, and armored personnel carriers. At present, however, the Iraqi military is only one-third of its pre-Desert Storm strength, and none of the other rogue states is significantly better off. Only North Korea comes close to prewar Iraq in actual numbers, but its military hardware is thought to be markedly inferior to that possessed by South Korea. As a result, it is very difficult to portray the rogues in the same menacing tones used to describe Iraq in 1990.

Political ferment in Iran. American rhetoric has always portrayed Iran, like the other rogues, as an authoritarian state dominated by anti-American tyrants. "While their political systems vary," presidential security advisor Anthony Lake wrote of such states in 1994, "their leaders share a common antipathy toward popular participation that might undermine the existing regimes." But while this image might convincingly be used to describe Iran in the 1980s, when the Ayatollah Khomeini exercised paramount power, it is less persuasive today, given the growing pluralism in the Iranian political system. While it is clear that conservative clergy still exercise enormous power in Tehran, their dominance has been challenged through popular elections, mass demonstrations, and an increasingly vociferous press.

By far the most striking development in this regard was the election of Mohammad Khatami—an outspoken advocate of reform—as President of Iran. Although it is clear that Khatami faces a strong challenge from conservative clerics in the Iranian parliament, he has significantly diminished the anti-American tenor of Iranian public discourse and has sought new openings to the West. Khatami has also traveled to Saudi Arabia and improved relations with Iran's other neighbors in the Persian Gulf area. All this has made it harder to characterize Iran as an unrepentant "rogue" that must be isolated from the world community.

The Indian and Pakistani nuclear tests. Perhaps the greatest blow to the Rogue Doctrine occurred on May 11, 1998, when the Indian government detonated the first of five nuclear devices and declared itself a nuclear power. This event, coupled with the Pakistani nuclear tests a few weeks later, shattered the claim that the threat of proliferation was essentially interchangeable with the rogue state threat. (In 1996, for instance, Secretary of Defense William Perry declared that the illicit demand for nuclear and missile technology comes primarily from a group of nations some call the Rogues Gallery.) Since then, it has become increasingly apparent that India and Pakistan have progressed much further down the road of proliferation than any of the nominal rogues.

It is true, of course, that the rogues continue to pose a threat of proliferation. But Iraq's WMD capabilities were severely damaged by Operation Desert Storm and the subsequent activities of UNSCOM, and North Korea agreed to abandon its nuclear weapons program under the Agreed Framework of 1994. Iran is suspected of pursuing a nuclear weapons program, but its main nuclear facilities are subject to periodic International Atomic Energy Agency (IAEA) inspection; progress—if any—is thought to be slow. By contrast, it is clear that India and Pakistan have jumped far ahead in the development of both nuclear weapons and ballistic missiles. It is also evident that other friendly states, including South Korea and Taiwan, have acquired ballistic missiles or are seeking to build them. To be successful, therefore, America's nonproliferation efforts will have to shift their focus from the rogues to these other, supposedly friendly states.

The emergence of other types of security threats. Finally, it is abundantly clear that the world security environment harbors a wide variety of threats to global stability, many of which lie far beyond the terrain of the rogue state threat. These include, but are not limited to, the proliferation of ethnic and internal conflict, "state collapse" in areas of social and political upheaval, growing competition over scarce resources, and severe environmental degradation. All of these dangers have begun to place significant burdens on the attention of US policymakers, and all have required the deployment of significant American resources, including, in some cases, military resources. Yet none of these problems is explained by the rogue-state paradigm, nor can they be successfully addressed by using the responses developed to combat the rogues.

Of course, it can be argued the forces developed to defeat the rogue states in full-scale combat can also be used to perform other missions, including peacekeeping operations and humanitarian intervention of the sort conducted in Kosovo. To some degree this is true. But the strategy and tactics of peacekeeping and other unconventional missions are not the same as those employed in major regional conflicts. In many cases, American troops have been found to be ill trained and ill equipped for the sort of missions they have been obliged to perform. As new threats emerge, moreover, this problem is likely to prove even more common.

All of these developments have significantly diminished the Rogue Doctrine's utility in providing guidance for US security policy. It is still necessary to pay close attention to the military behavior of the rogues, just as it is necessary to monitor the behavior of other regional powers. But a continued reliance on the rogue-state model as the paramount source of military guidance will leave US leaders and US forces increasingly ill-prepared for the wider range of challenges the United States is sure to face in the years ahead.

If the United States is to face successfully the security threats of the 21st century, it must conduct the sort of "bottom-up" review that was promised twice in the 1990s yet was never really performed. The security environment has changed substantially from that of 1990, yet we cling to the same strategic paradigm adopted in that year by General Colin Powell. A comprehensive review of those changes would indicate that the rogue-state threat has been accorded disproportionate attention in comparison to other security threats. The time has come to abandon the Rogue Doctrine in favor of a more realistic and prudent policy.

MICHAEL T. KLARE is Professor of Peace and World Security Studies at Hampshire College and author of *Rogue States and Nuclear Outlaws: America's Search for a New Foreign Policy.*

EUROPE at Century's End

The Challenge Ahead

BY RICHARD N. HAASS

The year 1999 marks the end of the first decade of the post–Cold War world. For Europe, a region central to the Cold War—where it both began and ended—1999 is also proving to be a year of historic import, the most important on the continent since 1989, when the wall came down and Europe's division came to an abrupt and for the most part unanticipated end.

This claim can be justified by pointing to many events and trends, including the fitful progress toward reconciliation in Northern Ireland and Germany's emergence as a more "normal" country, one able to use military force beyond its borders as part of a nondefensive NATO action. Still, four developments in 1999 stand out: European Monetary Union and the launch of the euro; the entry of Poland, Hungary, and the Czech Republic into NATO and the articulation of a new strategic concept for the Alliance

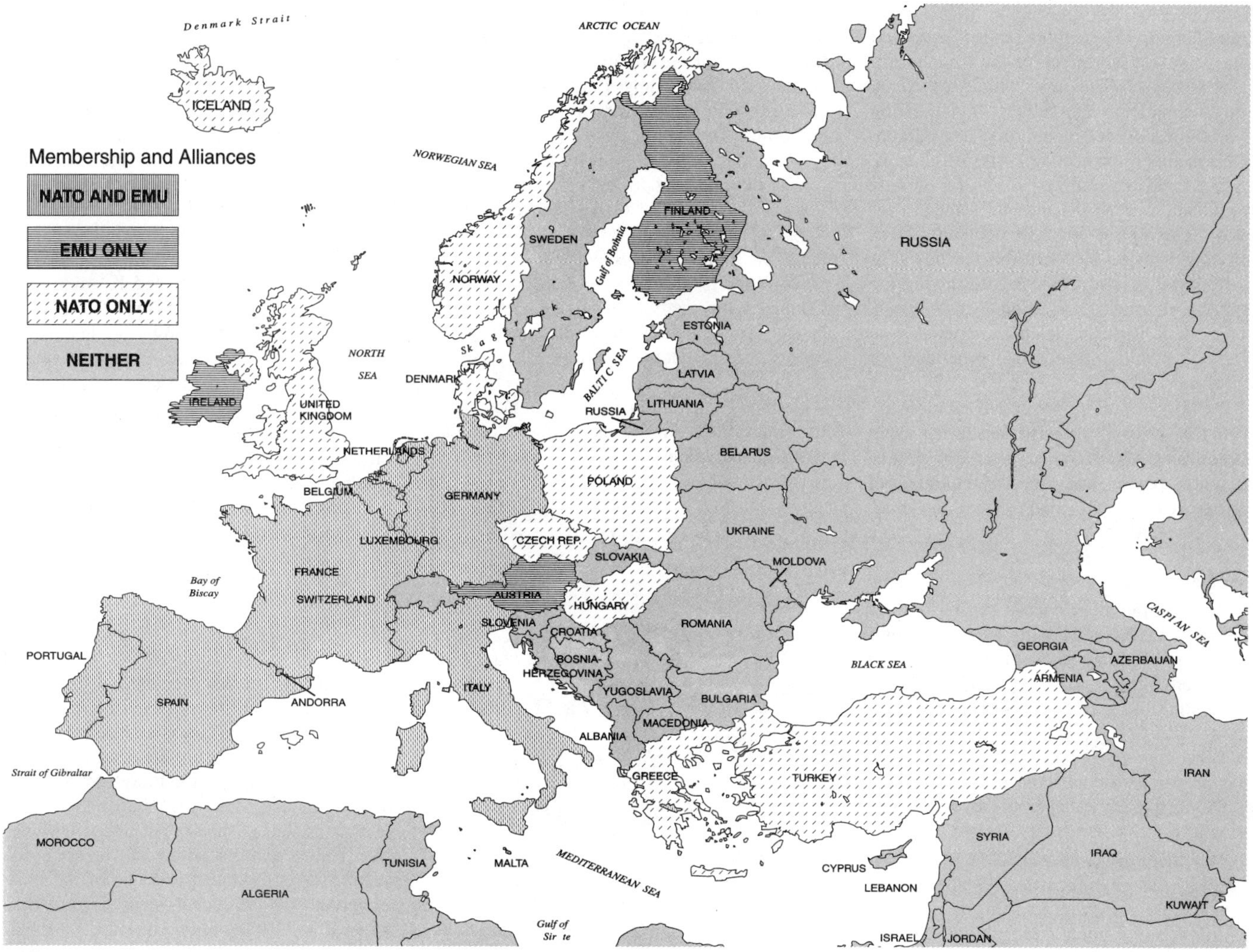

GLENN PIERCE

as it passed the half-century mark; the continuing deterioration of conditions within Russia and in U.S.-Russian relations; and the Kosovo conflict, the largest military clash on the continent since the Second World War.

Bearish on Russia

Russia is in many ways the most vexing, significant, and unexpected problem to cloud Europe's horizon. Russian weakness is proving a more complex challenge to Europe and the United States than did Soviet strength. The stakes are great, not so much in the economic sphere, where the actual or potential global impact is limited given Russia's small and increasingly barter-driven economy, but rather strategically, given Russia's ability to influence events in Europe through its political and military power and its nuclear arsenal.

But Russia's economic situation has grave strategic implications. An economically weak Russia is much more likely to pose a strategic threat, be it through arms sales to problem countries, authorized (or unauthorized) provision of technology to the unconventional weapons programs of so-called rogue states, a greater reliance on nuclear weapons to offset a growing inferiority in conventional arms, and, most worrisome, a loss of control over its own nuclear arsenal.

There is no single answer to the challenge posed by a weak Russia. It is, however, possible to rule out some alleged answers that are clearly misguided, including neglect. Russia needs help from the outside, but only on a conditional basis. Conditionality is necessary if economic assistance is to gain the required political support within donor societies and if funds are to do anything more than enrich corrupt individuals within Russia. Among the other lessons of the past few years is that market economic reform cannot occur (much less be sustained) in a vacuum if it is to be something other than crony capitalism; basic infrastructure improvements—property rights, securities regulation, generally accepted accounting practices, bankruptcy proceedings, and so on—are essential.

All this will take time, though, something that does not square with the urgent challenges posed by Russia's enormous but unsafe nuclear arsenal. Bruce Blair and Clifford Gaddy suggest a range of measures, from the relatively modest—a U.S.-Russian accord to reduce the alert status of their weapons to lessen the chance of crisis instability, a cut in the number of deployed strategic nuclear systems to well below START

> The United States cannot have it both ways, urging that Europe do more, but do America's bidding and no more.

II levels—to the ambitious, including a grand bargain in which the United States and Europe would buy much of the Russian nuclear stockpile. The latter would be costly but so would the alternatives—modernizing U.S. nuclear forces or building large defensive systems to protect against a Russian attack. Moreover, trading bombs for dollars would improve American and European security and bolster Russia's economy. Such thinking may be too "outside the box" for many but it is hard to see where staying the course—and seeing conditions within Russia or in U.S.-Russian relations continue to worsen—would serve any American or European interest.

Working out a constructive relationship with Russia over the past decade has been complicated by differences over how best to promote peace and security throughout Europe. Until 1999, much of the disagreement centered on Western plans to enlarge NATO by offering membership to former members of the Warsaw Pact, among others.

These differences caused strains but not a breach in relations with Russia, as evidenced by Russian willingness to sign an agreement—the so-called Founding Act—that institutionalized NATO-Russian consultations. Russia's participation in the Bosnia peacekeeping effort was another sign that it was prepared to contribute to European security despite its unhappiness over NATO's growth.

Whether such a restrained "agreement to disagree" can continue if NATO enlargement proceeds is less clear. Bringing Russia into NATO at some point is an option, but one that would require the emergence of a very different Russia—and result in the emergence of a very different NATO. But regardless of whether Russia ever formally joins NATO, James Goodby is correct when he argues that European security will benefit directly and dramatically from a Russia that is democratic, prosperous, and stable—and not alienated from the United States and the countries of Western Europe. Avoiding such alienation, Goodby suggests, will require sensitivity and compromise on both sides: the West will have to keep Russian concerns in mind as it uses force in Europe and proceeds with NATO enlargement; Russia for its part must work with the United States and Europe in combating the proliferation of weapons of mass destruction, terrorism, and threats to innocent peoples from their governments. The only thing that is certain is that making Europe "whole and free"—not to mention peaceful and prosperous—promises to be a long-term, difficult proposition. For the immediate future, James Goldgeier puts forward the logical and, to many, persuasive argument that it makes no sense to stop NATO enlargement now. To do so would only redraw the line dividing Europe and deny the advantages of NATO membership to other deserving states. But further enlargement is hardly problem free. Beyond its economic costs and the risk that it would further complicate Alliance decisionmaking is the risk that adding Baltic states to the Alliance could trigger a crisis with Russia—and within Russia.

Alas, one need not wait for a decision on NATO enlargement to set off a crisis with Russia; the war in Kosovo has done that. Russians are unhappy and angry over the attacks on their fellow Slavs. That these attacks were carried out without UN Security Council authorization and by an enlarged NATO from which they are thus far excluded makes matters that much worse. The Russian reaction is both deep and wide, reflecting widespread frustration in that country over its reduced circumstances at home and its reduced status abroad.

The Russian reaction to the NATO attacks on Yugoslavia is both deep and wide, reflecting widespread frustration in that country over its reduced circumstances at home and its reduced status abroad.

The war in Kosovo is also a crisis for NATO. For the 40 years of the Cold War, NATO unity was forged around a common threat; under Article 5 of the NATO treaty, Alliance members pledged to defend one another against external attack. With the demise of the Soviet Union and the end of the Cold War, many analysts and politicians believe that NATO must evolve or risk fading away. They argue that NATO remains valuable—especially in keeping the United States involved in Europe's security, given the limits on what Europeans are able and willing to do in the defense realm, the potential primacy of a unified Germany and uncertainty over how Russia will evolve—but that a continued focus on defending against a nonexistent threat is not enough.

The principal alternative mission for NATO, as set forth by Ivo Daalder, is to broaden its mandate from combating external threats to countries within the treaty area to promoting peace and security throughout all of Europe. The change could come about in two ways: through continued enlargement and through taking on the sorts of challenges that developed in Bosnia and Kosovo.

When leaders of NATO's 19 member states convened in Washington last April, they agreed to such a new strategic concept. That they did so amidst the war in Kosovo, however, highlighted the gap between rhetoric and reality. It is one thing to talk about meeting challenges to European peace, quite another to do it. The risk for NATO is that the experience of Kosovo will jeopardize the Alliance's cohesion just at a time it is seeking to define a new purpose.

Economic Europe

Few if any observers predicted at the outset of 1999 that NATO would be the European or transatlantic institution that would most come under strain during the year. The European Union (EU) was the more obvious candidate. Indeed, the year began with the launch of the 11-member European Monetary Union and its common currency, the euro. This is the latest and one of the most important of the many steps Europe has taken toward integration over the past half century—and, as Robert Solomon points out, the first time since the fall of the Roman Empire that much ofWestern Europe has had a single currency

Creation of the euro effectively brings about a single European financial market, which should facilitate economic activity and, with it, growth. Still, the euro is not without its skeptics. Many question whether member governments can and will maintain the necessary fiscal discipline if they are faced with high unemployment or recession. The euro and EMU are the products of a continent that is increasingly controlled collectively in the economic sphere—while governments and politicians are still mostly elected in national and local contexts. Whether this tension can be managed remains to be seen.

On the American side of the Atlantic, there are those who doubt whether the euro is good for the United States. Some fear it will make Europe more of a closed market or weaken the role and value of the dollar. Others predict it will lead to greater European political and military unity—and greater independence from the United States. Elizabeth Pond takes a relatively sanguine view of these possibilities—but points out that the euro is likely to promote economic reform within Europe and make Europe more like America, benefiting some American investors and exporters but posing severe hardships for others who lose out to new competitors. As the U.S.-European skirmish over bananas indicates, trade frictions and protectionist pressures are never less than dormant and can surface with a vengeance, bearing adverse consequences for transatlantic political and economic relations.

In trade as in other matters, it is obvious that the United States and Europe, though drawn together in many ways, do not always or automatically see eye to eye. One specific disagreement involves Turkey a country the EU has kept at arm's length for a host of reasons, including dissatisfaction with Turkey's handling of its Kurdish problem and human rights more generally, tensions between Turkey and EU member Greece, and concern that Turkish entry into the EU could have adverse consequences for agricultural policy and labor markets. The United States has for the most part taken a more sympathetic approach to Turkey, a country viewed as vital not only for its contributions to European security but also for its links to the greater Middle East. As Heinz Kramer explains, bridging these transatlantic differences will require new flexibility in European thinking—and internal reform in Turkey itself, something that its domestic politics threaten to make more not less difficult.

The Way Ahead

The challenges facing Europe in 1999 and beyond are enormous. Indeed, the agenda could hardly be more crowded or daunting: Kosovo and the broader problem of bringing stability to the former Yugoslavia; ensuring the success of EMU; enlarging and deepening both the EU and NATO; and promoting Russian democracy, economic revival, and integration with the rest of the continent.

Many of these challenges are as much transatlantic as European in nature and will require close collaboration between the United States and Europe—whether as individual states, within NATO, within the EU, or within some other forum. Consultations using all these frameworks will remain essential—and would be more useful if Europe begins to speak with one voice on matters of security. Also useful would be a transatlantic commitment to open trade, to meet the norms and adhere to the decisions of the World Trade Organization; trade can be a source of prosperity or discord but not both.

But consultation and even compromise will not be sufficient. For the transatlantic tie to work and for Europe to prosper, Europeans must be prepared to assume a greater share of the burden of action, especially in the military domain. They must be ready not just to spend somewhat more on their military capacity, but to spend it on forces that are relevant for the post–Cold War world rather than its predecessor. Europeans will need, too, to resist the temptation to oppose American leadership simply out of resentment.

At the same time, the United States will have to accept that a greater European willingness and capacity to share the burdens of European and global security will translate into enhanced European influence, especially if Europe is prepared to act politically and militarily under EU rather than NATO auspices. The United States cannot have it both ways, urging that Europe do more, but do America's bidding and no more. In addition, the United States will need to curb its enthusiasm for economic sanctions in general and for secondary sanctions—those imposed on countries (often European) who do not support U.S. sanctions against such countries as Iran Libya, or Cuba—in particular.

But whatever the specific changes and compromises, it is critical that the two sides get it right. Europe and the United States remain essential to one another. It is not simply a matter of economics, although transatlantic trade and investment count for a lot. Nor is it simply a shared interest in Europe's stability, although this too obviously matters a great deal to both Europeans and Americans. Rather, it is that both Americans and Europeans have a major stake in what sort of a world emerges in the aftermath of the Cold War. Their ability to help bring about a world to their liking—one that promotes their common interests and values alike—depends on their ability to agree on a set of common priorities and work together on their behalf. Transatlantic cooperation proved central to the successful outcome of the Cold War; continued partnership is likely to prove no less central to the course of 1999 and the years that follow.

Richard N. Haass, vice president and director of the Brookings Foreign Policy Studies program, is the author of The Reluctant Sheriff: The United States after the Cold War *(Brookings, 1997) and editor of* Transatlantic Tensions: The United States, Europe, and Problem States *(Brookings, 1999).*

The research on Europe and Russia was made possible by the German Marshall Fund of the United States, the Carnegie Corporation of New York, the John M. Olin Foundation, and the John D. and Catharine T. MacArthur Foundation.

ETHNIC CONFLICT

Ethnic conflict seems to have supplanted nuclear war as the most pressing issue on the minds of policymakers. But if yesterday's high priests of mutually assured destruction were guilty of hyper-rationality, today's prophets of anarchy suffer from a collective hysteria triggered by simplistic notions of ethnicity. Debates about intervention in Rwanda or stability in Bosnia demand a more sober perspective.

—by Yahya Sadowski

The Number of Ethnic Conflicts Rose Dramatically at the End of the Cold War

Nope. The idea that the number of ethnic conflicts has recently exploded, ushering us into a violent new era of ethnic "pandaemonium," is one of those optical illusions that round-the-clock and round-the-world television coverage has helped to create. Ethnic conflicts have consistently formed the vast majority of wars ever since the epoch of decolonization began to sweep the developing countries after 1945. Although the number of ethnic conflicts has continued to grow since the Cold War ended, it has done so at a slow and steady rate, remaining consistent with the overall trend of the last 50 years.

In 1990 and 1991, however, several new and highly visible ethnic conflicts erupted as a result of the dissolution of the Soviet Union and Yugoslavia. The clashes between the armies of Croatia, Serbia, and Slovenia, and the agonizing battle that pitted Bosnia's Croats, Muslims, and Serbs against each other, occurred on Europe's fringes, within easy reach of television cameras. The wars in Azerbaijan, Chechnya, Georgia, and Tajikistan, while more distant, were still impressive in the way that they humbled the remnants of the former Soviet colossus. Many observers mistook these wars for the start of a new trend. Some were so impressed that they began to reclassify conflicts in Angola, Nicaragua, Peru, and Somalia—once seen as ideological or power struggles—as primarily ethnic conflicts.

The state-formation wars that accompanied the "Leninist extinction" now appear to have been a one-time event—a flash flood rather than a global deluge. Many of these battles have already been brought under control. Indeed, the most striking trend in warfare during the 1990s has been its decline: The Stockholm International Peace Research Institute documented just 27 major armed conflicts (only one of which, India and Pakistan's slow-motion struggle over Kashmir, was an interstate war) in 1996, down from 33 such struggles in 1989. Once the Cold War ended, a long list of seemingly perennial struggles came to a halt: the Lebanese civil war, the Moro insurrection in the Philippines, regional clashes in Chad, the Eritrean secession and related battles in Ethiopia, the Sahrawi independence struggle, fratricide in South Africa, and the guerrilla wars in El Salvador and Nicaragua.

The majority of the wars that survive today are ethnic conflicts—but they are mostly persistent battles that have been simmering for decades. They include the (now possibly defunct) IRA insurgency in the United Kingdom; the struggle for Kurdish autonomy in Iran, Iraq, and Turkey; the Israeli-Palestinian tragedy; the Sri Lankan civil war; and long-standing regional insurrections in Burma, India, and Indonesia.

Most Ethnic Conflicts Are Rooted in Ancient Tribal or Religious Rivalries

No way. The claim that ethnic conflicts have deep roots has long been a standard argument for not getting involved. According to political journalist Elizabeth Drew's famous account, President Bill Clinton in 1993 had intended to intervene in Bosnia until he read Robert Kaplan's book *Balkan Ghosts,* which, as Drew said, conveyed the notion that "these people had been killing each other in tribal and religious wars for centuries." But the reality is that most ethnic conflicts are expressions of "modern hate" and largely products of the twentieth century.

The case of Rwanda is typical. When Europeans first stumbled across it, most of the country was already united under a central monarchy whose inhabitants spoke the same language, shared the same cuisine and culture, and practiced the same religion. They were, however, divided into several castes. The largest group, the Hutus, were farmers. The ruling aristocracy, who collected tribute from all other groups, was recruited from the Tutsis, the caste of cattle herders. All groups supplied troops for their common king, and intermarriage was not unusual. Social mobility among castes was quite possible: A rich Hutu who purchased enough cattle could climb into the ranks of the Tutsi; an impoverished Tutsi could fall into the ranks of the Hutu. Anthropologists considered all castes to be members of a single "tribe," the Banyarwanda.

Then came the Belgians. Upon occupying the country after World War I, they transformed the system. Like many colonial powers, the Belgians chose to rule through a local élite—the Tutsis were eager to collaborate in exchange for Belgian guarantees of their local power and for privileged access to modern education. Districts that had been under Hutu leadership were brought under Tutsi rule. Until 1929, about one-third of the chiefs in Rwanda had been Hutu, but then the Belgians decided to "streamline" the provincial administration by eliminating all non-Tutsi chiefs. In 1933, the Belgians issued mandatory identity cards to all Rwandans, eliminating fluid movement between castes and permanently fixing the identity of each individual, and his or her children, as either Hutu or Tutsi. As the colonial administration penetrated and grew more powerful, Belgian backing allowed the Tutsis to increase their exploitation of the Hutus to levels that would have been impossible in earlier times.

Ethnic Africa

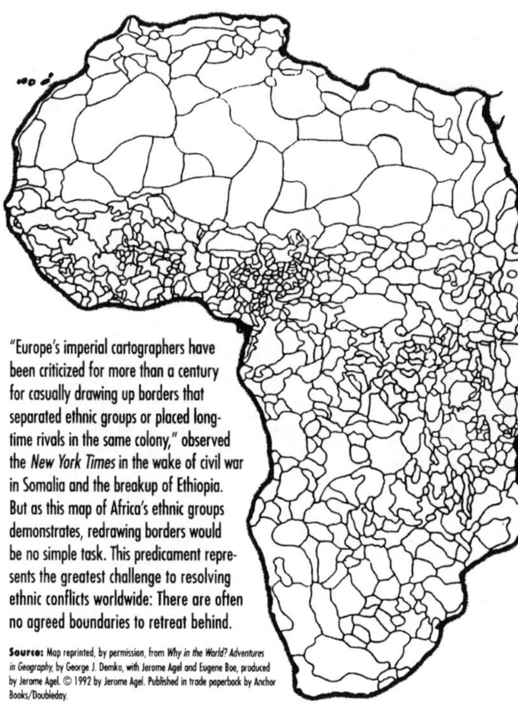

"Europe's imperial cartographers have been criticized for more than a century for casually drawing up borders that separated ethnic groups or placed long-time rivals in the same colony," observed the *New York Times* in the wake of civil war in Somalia and the breakup of Ethiopia. But as this map of Africa's ethnic groups demonstrates, redrawing borders would be no simple task. This predicament represents the greatest challenge to resolving ethnic conflicts worldwide: There are often no agreed boundaries to retreat behind.

Source: Map reprinted, by permission, from *Why in the World? Adventures in Geography,* by George J. Demko, with Jerome Agel and Eugene Boe, produced by Jerome Agel. © 1992 by Jerome Agel. Published in trade paperback by Anchor Books/Doubleday.

In the 1950s, the Belgians came under pressure from the United Nations to grant Rwanda independence. In preparation, Brussels began to accord the majority Hutus—the Tutsis constituted only 14 percent of the population—a share of political power and greater access to education. Although this policy alarmed the Tutsis, it did not come close to satisfying the Hutus: Both groups began to organize to defend their interests, and their confrontations became increasingly militant. Centrist groups that included both Hutus and Tutsis were gradually squeezed out by extremists on both sides. The era of modern communal violence began with the 1959 attack on a Hutu leader by Tutsi extremists; Hutus retaliated, and several hundred people were killed. This set in motion a cycle of violence that culminated in December 1963, when Hutus massacred 10,000 Tutsis and drove another 130,000–150,000 from the country. These tragedies laid the seeds for the genocide of 1994.

The late emergence of ethnic violence, such as in Rwanda, is the norm, not an exception. In Ceylon, riots that pitted Tamils against Sinhalese did not erupt until 1956. In Bosnia,

Major Genocides since World War II

COUNTRY	DATES	VICTIMS	NUMBER OF DEATHS (IN THOUSANDS)
USSR	1943–47	Repatriated nationals and ethnic minorities	500–1,100
China	1950–51	Landlords	800–3,000
Sudan	1955–72	Southern nationalists	100–500
Indonesia	1965–66	Communists and ethnic Chinese	80–1,000
China	1966–75	Cultural revolution victims	400–850
Uganda	1971–79	Opponents of Idi Amin	100–500
Pakistan	1971	Bengali nationalists	1,250–3,000
Cambodia	1975–79	Urbanites	800–3,000
Afghanistan	1978–89	Opponents of the regime	1,000
Sudan	1983–98	Southern nationalists	100–1,500
Iraq	1984–91	Kurds	100–282
Bosnia	1991–95	Bosnian Muslims and Croats	25–200
Burundi	1993–98	Hutu, Tutsi	150+
Rwanda	1994	Tutsi	500–1,000

Sources: Barbara Harff, "Victims of the State: Genocides, Politicides and Group Repression since 1945," *International Review of Victimology.* 1 (1989): 23–41; Conflict Resolution Program, *1995–1996 State of World Conflict Report* (Atlanta: Carter Center, 1997); *Los Angeles Times;* and the *Encyclopaedia Britannica.*

Serbs and Croats coexisted with one another, and both claimed Muslims as members of their communities, until World War II—and peaceful relations resumed even after the bloodshed of that conflict. Turks and Kurds shared a common identity as Ottomans and wore the same uniforms during World War I; in fact, the first Kurdish revolt against Turkish rule was not recorded until 1925. Muslims and Jews in Palestine had no special history of intercommunal hatred (certainly nothing resembling European anti-Semitism) until the riots of 1921, when nascent Arab nationalism began to conflict with the burgeoning Zionist movement. Although Hindu-Muslim clashes had a long history in India, they were highly localized; it was only after 1880 that the contention between these two groups began to gel into large-scale, organized movements. Of course, the agitators in all these conflicts tend to dream up fancy historic pedigrees for their disputes. Bosnian Serbs imagine that they are fighting to avenge their defeat by the Ottoman Turks in 1389; Hutus declare that Tutsis have "always" treated them as subhumans; and IRA bombers attack their victims in the name of a nationalist tradition they claim has burned since the Dark Ages. But these mythologies of hatred are themselves largely recent inventions.

Ethnic Conflict Was Powerful Enough to Rip Apart the USSR

Yeah, right. The idea that the Soviet Union was destroyed by an explosion of ethnic atavism has been put forth by a number of influential thinkers, most notably Senator Daniel Patrick Moynihan. But this theory is not only historically inaccurate, it has misleading policy implications. The collapse of states is more often the cause of ethnic conflicts rather than the result.

Prior to 1991, ethnic consciousness within the Soviet Union had only developed into mass nationalism in three regions: the Baltic states, Transcaucasia, and Russia itself. Russian nationalism posed no threat to Soviet rule: It had been so successfully grafted onto communism during World War II that even today Leninists and Russian ultranationalists tend to flock to the same parties. In Transcaucasia, the Armenians and Georgians had developed potent national identities but were much more interested in pursuing local feuds (especially with Muslims) than in dismantling the Soviet Union. Only in the Baltic states, which had remained sovereign and independent until 1940, was powerful nationalist sentiment channeled directly against Moscow.

When the August 1991 coup paralyzed the Communist Party, the last threads holding the Soviet state together dissolved. Only then did rapid efforts to spread nationalism to other regions appear. In Belarus, Ukraine, and across Central Asia, the *nomenklatura,* searching for new instruments to legitimate their rule, began to embrace—and sometimes invent—nationalist mythologies. It was amidst this wave of post-Soviet nationalism that new or rekin-

Tribal Wisdom

"For centuries, [Yugoslavia] marked a tense and often violent fault line between empires and religions. The end of the Cold War and the dissolution of that country . . . surfaced all those ancient tensions again. . . ."

—U.S. president Bill Clinton, addressing the U.S. Naval Academy in 1994

"We are confronted by contradictory phenomena in which both the factors of integration and cooperation and the tendencies of division and dispersal are both apparent. The technological and communications revolution is offset by the eruption of nationalist conflicts and ethnic hatreds."

—Egyptian foreign minister Amr Moussa, before the UN General Assembly in 1996

"In this Europe of ours, where no one would have thought a struggle between ethnic groups possible, tragically this has come about. It may serve to open people's eyes to the unspeakable possibilities in the future, even in unexpected places. Today we are threatened by the danger . . . of racial, religious, and tribal hatred."

—Italian president Oscar Luigi Scalfaro in 1997

"Yet even as the waves of globalization unfurl so powerfully across our planet, so does a deep and vigorous countertide. . . . What some have called a 'new tribalism' is shaping the world as profoundly on one level as the 'new globalism' is shaping it on another."

—His Highness the Aga Khan, at the Commonwealth Press Union Conference in Cape Town in 1996

" . . . all over the world, we see a kind of reversion to tribalism. . . . We see it in Russia, in Yugoslavia, in Canada, in the United States. . . . What is it about, all this globalization of communication that is making people return to more—to smaller units of identity?"

—Neil Postman, chair of the department of culture and communication at New York University, in 1995

dled ethnic conflicts broke out in Chechnya, Moldova, Ukraine, and elsewhere. Yet even amid the chaos of state collapse, ethnonationalist movements remained weaker and less violent than many had expected. Despite the predictions of numerous pundits, revivalist Islamic movements only took root in a couple of places (Chechnya and Tajikistan). Relations between indigenous Turkic peoples and Russian immigrants across most of Central Asia remained civil.

Ethnic Conflicts Are More Savage and Genocidal Than Conventional Wars

Wrong. Although this assumption is inaccurate, the truth is not much more comforting. There appears to be no consistent difference between ethnic and nonethnic wars in terms of their lethality. In fact, the percentage of civilians in the share of total casualties is rising for all types of warfare. During World War I, civilian casualties constituted about 15 percent of all deaths. That number skyrocketed to 65 percent during World War II, which, by popularizing the use of strategic bombing, blockade-induced famine, and guerrilla warfare, constituted a real, albeit underappreciated, watershed in the history of human slaughter. Ever since, the number of civilian dead has constituted two-thirds or more of the total fatalities in most wars. Indeed, according to UNICEF, the share of civilian casualties has continued to grow since 1945— rising to almost 90 percent by the end of the 1980s and to more than 90 percent during this decade.

Furthermore, ethnic wars are less likely to be associated with genocide than "conventional" wars. The worst genocides of modern times have not been targeted along primarily ethnic lines. Rather, the genocides within Afghanistan, Cambodia, China, the Soviet Union, and even, to a great extent, Indonesia and Uganda, have focused on liquidating political dissidents: To employ the emerging vocabulary, they were politicides rather than ethnicides. Indeed, the largest genocides of this century were clearly ideologically driven politicides: the mass killings committed by the Maoist regime in China from 1949 to 1976, by the Leninist/Stalinist regime in the Soviet Union between 1917 and 1959, and by the Pol Pot regime in Cambodia between 1975 and 1979.

Finally, some pundits have claimed that ethnic conflicts are more likely to be savage because they are often fought by irregular, or guerrilla, troops. In fact, (a) ethnic wars are usually fought by regular armies, and (b) regular armies are quite capable of vicious massacres. Contrary to the stereotypes played out on television, the worst killing in Bosnia did not occur where combatants were members of irregular militias, reeling drunk on *slivovitz*. The core of the Serb separatist forces consisted of highly disciplined troops that were seconded from the Yugoslav army and led by a spit-and-polish officer corps. It was precisely these units that made the massacres at Srebrenica possible: It required real organizational skill to take between 6,000 and 10,000 Bosnian troops prisoner, disarm and transport them to central locations, and systematically murder them and distribute their bodies among a network of carefully concealed mass graves. Similarly, the wave of ethnic cleansing that followed the seizure of northern and eastern Bosnia by the Serbs in 1991 was not the spontaneous work of crazed irregulars. Transporting the male Bosnian population to concentration camps at Omarska and elsewhere required the talents of men who knew how to coordinate military attacks, read railroad schedules, guard and (under-) supply large prison populations, and organize bus transport for expelling women and children.

Globalization Makes Ethnic Conflict More Likely

Think again. The claim that globalization—the spread of consumer values, democratic institutions, and capitalist enterprise —aggravates ethnic and cultural violence is at the core of Samuel Huntington's "clash of civilizations" hypothesis, Robert Kaplan's vision of "the coming anarchy," and Benjamin Barber's warning that we face a future of "Jihad vs. McWorld." Although these suggestions deserve further study, the early indications are that globalization plays no real role in spreading ethnic conflict and may actually inhibit it.

Despite the fears of cultural critics that the broad appeal of "Baywatch" heralds a collapse of worldwide values, there is not much concrete evidence linking the outbreak of ethnic wars to the global spread of crude materialism via film, television, radio, and boombox. Denmark has just as many television sets as the former Yugoslavia but has not erupted into ethnic carnage or even mass immigrant bashing. Meanwhile, Burundi, sitting on the distant outskirts of the global village with only one television set for every 4,860 people, has witnessed some of the worst violence in this decade.

The spread of democratic values seems a slightly more plausible candidate as a trigger for ethnic violence: The recent progress of democracy in Albania, Armenia, Croatia, Georgia, Moldova, Russia, Serbia, and South Africa has been attended by ethnic feuding in each country. But this is an inconsistent trend. Some of the most savage internal conflicts of the post-Cold War period have occurred in societies that were growing less free, such as Egypt, India (which faced major secessionist challenges by Kashmiris, Sikhs, Tamils, etc.), Iran, and Peru. For that matter, many of the worst recent ethnic conflicts occurred in countries where the regime type was unstable and vacillated back and forth between more and less free forms, as in Azerbaijan, Bosnia, Lebanon, Liberia, Nigeria, and Tajikistan. Conversely, in numerous cases, such as the so-called third wave of democratization that swept Latin America and East Asia during the 1980s, political liberalization seems to have actually reduced most forms of political violence.

Investigating the impact of economic globalization leads to three surprises. First, the countries affected most by globalization—that is, those that have shown the greatest increase in international trade and benefited most significantly from foreign direct investment—are not the newly industrializing economies of East Asia and Latin America but the old industrial societies of Europe and North America. Second, ethnic conflicts are found, in some form or another, in every type of society: They are not concentrated among poor states, nor are they unusually common among countries experiencing economic globalization. Thus, the bad news is that ethnic conflicts do not disappear when societies "modernize."

The good news, however, lies in the third surprise: Ethnic conflicts are likely to be much less lethal in societies that are developed, economically open, and receptive to globalization. Ethnic battles in industrial and industrializing societies tend either to be argued civilly or at least limited to the political violence of marginal groups, such as the provisional IRA in the United Kingdom, Mohawk secessionists in Canada, or the Ku Klux Klan in the United States. The most gruesome ethnic wars are found in poorer societies—Afghanistan and Sudan, for example—where economic frustration reinforces political rage. It seems, therefore, that if economic globalization contributes to a country's prosperity, then it also dampens the level of ethnic violence there.

Fanaticism Makes Ethnic Conflicts Harder to Terminate

Not really. Vojislav Seselj, the commander of one of the most murderous Serb paramitary groups in Bosnia, once warned that if U.S. forces were used there, "the war [would] be total.... We would have tens of thousands of volunteers, and we would score a glorious victory. The Americans would have to send thousands of body bags. It would be a new Vietnam." Of course, several years later, after Serb forces had been handily defeated by a combination of Croat ground forces and NATO airpower, the president of the Serb separatists, Radovan Karadzic, admitted their leadership had thought all along that "if the West put in 10,000 men to cut off our supply corridors, we Serbs would be finished." Militarily, ethnic conflicts are not intrinsically different from any other type of combat. They can take on the form of guerrilla wars or conventional battles; they can be fought by determined and disciplined cadres or by poorly motivated slobs. How much military force will be required to end the fighting varies widely from one ethnic conflict to the next.

However, achieving a military victory and building a durable peace are two very different matters. Sealing the peace in ethnic conflicts may prove harder for political—not military—reasons. Ethnic conflicts are fought among neighbors, among people who live intermingled with one other, forced to share the same resources and institutions. When two states end a war, they may need only to agree to stop shooting and respect a mutual border. But in ethnic conflicts there are often no established borders to retreat behind. Sometimes, ethnic disputes can be resolved by drawing new borders—creating new states (such as Bangladesh and "rump" Pakistan) that allow the quarreling groups to live apart. Other times, they can be terminated by convincing the combatants that they must share power peaceably and learn to coexist. This is the objective of the Dayton accord on Bosnia.

In either case, ending ethnic warfare often requires the expensive and delicate construction of new political institutions. Not only may this be more difficult than terminating a "normal" interstate war, it may also take much longer. Building truly effective states takes time. For this reason, ethnic wars whose participants are already organized into states or protostates (which was true of the combatants in Croatia and Bosnia) are probably easier to bring to a conclusion than battles in regions—Afghanistan, for example, not to speak of Somalia where real states have yet to congeal.

Want to Know More?

The classic introduction to the study of ethnic conflict is still Donald Horowitz, ***Ethnic Groups in Conflict*** (Berkeley: University of California Press, 1985). The Stockholm International Peace Research Institute (SIPRI) inventories changing patterns of warfare in the ***SIPRI Yearbook*** (Oxford: Oxford University Press, annual). For a specialist's tally of particular ethnic conflicts, see Ted Robert Gurr, ***Minorities at Risk: A Global View of Ethnopolitical Conflicts*** (Washington: U.S. Institute of Peace, 1993). An absorbing overview of the evolving relations between Tutsi and Hutu is Gérard Prunier, ***The Rwanda Crisis: History of a Genocide*** (New York: Columbia University Press, 1995). The Human Rights Watch report, ***Slaughter among Neighbors: The Political Origins of Communal Violence*** (New Haven: Yale University Press, 1995), provides a broader survey of modern hate. An excellent account of the diversity of forms that ethnicity and nationalism have taken in territories of the former Soviet Union is Ronald Grigor Suny's ***The Revenge of the Past: Nationalism, Revolution and the Collapse of the Soviet Union*** (Stanford: Stanford University Press, 1993). Neal Ascherson reflects upon issues of nationality and ethnicity in his book ***Black Sea*** (New York: Hill & Wang, 1995), which chronicles the expansive history of a region that has been a nexus of several Asian and European cultures. David Rohde's chilling ***Endgame: The Betrayal and Fall of Srebrenica*** (New York: Farrar Straus & Giroux, 1997) documents the careful organizational planning underlying the genocide in Bosnia. A recent work that dissects the question of whether, or how, the United States should intervene in ethnic conflicts is David Callahan's ***Unwinnable Wars: American Power and Ethnic Conflict*** (New York: Hill & Wang, 1998).

For links to relevant Web sites, as well as a comprehensive index of related articles, access **www.foreignpolicy.com**.

The Nuclear Agenda

Arms Control and Missile Defense Are Back in the News

by James M. Lindsay

The nuclear debate is back. After fading from the public eye in the 1990s, arms control and missile defense are once again at the forefront of the American national security agenda. Not surprisingly, the debate has broken down along well-worn lines. Arms control advocates argue that the United States should seek to limit and eliminate nuclear weapons, and they dismiss the idea of missile defense as a dangerous and costly folly. Missile defense advocates in turn question the value of arms control and argue that the United States should move aggressively to defend itself against missile attack. **Which side is right?** Neither and both. And therein lie the political and diplomatic challenges facing the next administration.

From *Brookings Review*, Fall 2000, pp. 8-11. © 2000 by the Brookings Review. Reprinted by permission.

Multilateral Arms Control

The first major issue on the nuclear agenda is the future of multilateral arms control, which the Senate threw into doubt with its rejection of the Comprehensive Test Ban Treaty last year. Substantive opposition to the treaty focused on the test ban's verifiability and on the need for tests to ensure the safety and reliability of the U.S. nuclear deterrent. But the treaty's rejection ultimately had more to do with the bitter partisanship that now characterizes executive-legislative relations than with policy. In a less divisive political environment, a compromise probably could have been achieved.

The consequences of the Senate vote are all too often exaggerated. As the opponents correctly point out, the test ban treaty was never going to be a cure-all. No paper pledge can end nuclear proliferation by itself, and the countries most likely to acquire nuclear weapons are the ones least likely to abide by the treaty's strictures. At the same time, the established nuclear powers continue to abide by the informal test ban that has been in place since the early 1990s. None looks poised to resume testing.

But on the whole the test ban's defeat does represent a missed opportunity to advance U.S. interests. Making the informal test ban binding would have raised the diplomatic costs to any country wishing to resume testing and (ironically enough) locked in U.S. nuclear superiority. The treaty also would have made it easier for the United States to detect clandestine nuclear explosions. It would create a worldwide monitoring system, including sensors in countries such as Russia, China, and Iran that are closed to U.S. intelligence. And nuclear tests have only limited value in checking the safety and reliability of the U.S. nuclear arsenal. The U.S. weapons laboratories estimate that less than 1 percent of the defects found in the weapons stockpile have been uncovered through testing.

The Senate vote has also damaged U.S. diplomacy on nuclear proliferation. This is most evident in the foundering effort to strengthen the inspection provisions of the Non-Proliferation Treaty (NPT). In 1997, the signatories to the NPT agreed to develop more intrusive inspections in exchange for a written pledge by the established nuclear powers to negotiate and ratify a test ban treaty. With the United States unwilling to live up to its end of the bargain, many other countries are unwilling to live up to theirs. Today, more than 120 countries have still not reached agreement with the International Atomic Energy Agency on the specifics of the new inspection regime. The administration's decision to join Russia, China, Britain, and France at the NPT review conference earlier this year in renewing their joint commitment to the complete elimination of nuclear weapons did little to restore momentum to the push for tougher inspections.

The arrival of a new administration creates an opportunity to depoliticize the test ban treaty and to reconsider it on the merits. Some Senate opponents have expressed regret that the vote took place—62 senators had publicly called for postponing it—and have suggested they might reassess their opposition if their substantive concerns are addressed. The Clinton administration took a step in this direction by asking former Chairman of the Joint Chiefs of Staff Gen. John Shalikashvili to lead a bipartisan dialogue with the Senate on ways to make the treaty acceptable. The challenge is that with the Senate now formally on record against the treaty, addressing its concerns may require more than high-level briefings and cosmetic amendments. But if the price of Senate approval means rewriting core elements of the treaty, the whole enterprise is probably doomed. There are no signs that the other major powers are willing to reopen the treaty, and Russia, China, and other countries would undoubtedly exploit any American decision to do so for their own diplomatic advantage.

The START Talks and Deep Cuts

The second major issue on the nuclear agenda is reducing the size of the U.S. and Russian offensive nuclear arsenals. During the 1990s, both countries agreed to cut their forces sharply. The 1991 Strategic Arms Reduction Treaty (START I) required each side to reduce its stock of strategic offensive nuclear weapons by more than a third, down to 6,000 warheads apiece. The START II Treaty, signed during George Bush's last month in office, required both countries to cut their arsenals further, to between 3,000 and 3,500 warheads. And in March 1997, Presidents Bill Clinton and Boris Yeltsin agreed at the Helsinki summit to commit their governments to negotiate another reduction, to 2,000 to 2,500 weapons each.

The relatively quick presidential agreement, however, was not matched by similar legislative dispatch. The Senate and the Duma easily approved START I, but START II became embroiled in a power struggle between Yeltsin and the Duma's communist-led opposition. In 1997, when it was clear that the Duma would not approve the treaty in time to implement all its terms by the deadline of 2003, Moscow and Washington agreed to extend the treaty's completion date to 2007. Russian irritation over NATO expansion and the Kosovo War further delayed action on START II. After seven years of squabbling, the Duma finally approved the treaty and the extension protocol last March. Even then the Duma conditioned its approval on the willingness of the United States to ratify two amendments to the 1972 Anti-Ballistic Missile Treaty and to continue to abide by that treaty's provisions. The Senate, which has approved START II, has yet to take up either the agreement extending its implementation or the two ABM amendments.

Although action on START II remains to be completed, talks on START III have begun. Moscow now proposes reducing each side's force to between 1,000 and 1,500 warheads. The proposal reflects Russia's interests. By most estimates, budgetary pressures will force it to cut its arsenal to 1,000 warheads or less by the end of the decade.

The Clinton administration has stuck by the original Helsinki numbers, pointing out that top American military officers insist that the United States needs at least 2,000 warheads to maintain its nuclear deterrent. Other opponents of going down to 1,000 warheads argue that deep cuts would force the military to abandon the land-based leg of the nuclear triad, thereby making it theoretically easier for an aggressor to wipe out the U.S. deterrent in a first strike. And some opponents argue that it amounts to trading something for nothing because Moscow will go down to 1,000 warheads no matter what the United States does.

None of these arguments against deep cuts is compelling, and the United States should seek over the long term to reduce its nuclear arsenal to below a thousand warheads. The Pentagon's estimate of what it needs for a robust nuclear deterrent itself depends on presidential planning guidance, guidance that still reflects Cold War thinking. No one seriously contends that Russia is planning a deliberate first strike, and whatever residual threat Russia poses will fall as its arsenal shrinks. Nor is it plausible to argue that the United States can deter the rest of the world with 2,500 warheads but not 1,000 or 1,500. As for the triad, it could be maintained with as few as 1,500 warheads, and its eventual disappearance should not be a cause for alarm but a source of relief that the United States no longer faces a Soviet-style threat.

In embracing the Russian call for deep cuts, the United States would not be doing Moscow a favor but advancing its own interests. The Defense Department expects to save $1.5 billion a year by going down to 2,500 warheads. It would save hundreds of millions of dollars more by going down to 1,000. These are not huge sums by Pentagon standards, but they will help the services meet their growing procurement needs in the years to come. A firm commitment to deep cuts would also enable the United States to counter critics who charge that it has abandoned the cause of arms control and regain the moral high ground in the effort to halt the spread of nuclear weapons. And most important, deep cuts would improve American security by reducing the number of missiles aimed at the United States.

As important as reducing the size of Russia's arsenal is reducing the chances of accidental launch.

But numbers of warheads tell only part of the story. As important as reducing the size of Russia's arsenal is reducing the chances of accidental launch. Russia continues to maintain its nuclear forces on high alert even as its early warning system falls into increasing disrepair—a combination that invites disaster. Both countries recognize the problem, and in June they agreed to set up a shared early warning center in Moscow. Much more can be done, however, particularly in the area of reducing alert levels. The United States and Russia should take steps such as separating warheads from launchers, which would slow down the rate at which a crisis could develop.

The question remains, of course, how best to achieve the goals of slashing offensive weapons and reducing the chances of accidental launch. The Clinton administration relied on the traditional approach of negotiating formal arms control treaties. While such agreements provide clarity about each side's obligations, they are time consuming to negotiate. Governor Bush has proposed reducing the U.S. arsenal unilaterally—though he has not said to what number—and inviting the Russians to follow suit. The main question here is whether Congress would tolerate unilateral reductions, especially if it believes Moscow is dragging its feet in response. Congress barred Clinton from unilaterally reducing the U.S. nuclear arsenal to START II levels until the Duma approved the treaty.

National Missile Defense

The third issue on the nuclear agenda and the one with potentially the most far-reaching consequences is national missile defense. President Clinton has pushed development of a ground-based defense that uses "hit-to-kill" technology to destroy warheads in space, though he has left the decision whether to deploy it to his successor. Unlike the more ambitious Strategic Defense Initiative, the Clinton system would be capable of shooting down no more than a couple of dozen warheads. The rationale for this limited system is the fear that North Korea, Iran, or Iraq might soon acquire the ability to threaten the United States with long-range missiles.

Despite its limited capabilities, the Clinton system has come under sharp attack abroad for potentially fueling a new arms race. Moscow rebuffed the administration's proposal to modify the Anti-Ballistic Missile Treaty to allow for deployment, arguing that the treaty is a cornerstone of strategic stability. Beijing has been an even more bitter critic for a very simple reason: if the Clinton system works, it would in theory render China's force of some 20 long-range missiles obsolete. European capitals have also been hostile. They dismiss the threat from North Korea, fear the start of a new arms race, and worry that they will become a more tempting target for attack.

The Clinton administration's system is proving to be increasingly controversial at home as well. The domestic coalition that pushed a reluctant president to embrace missile defense is fraying. Some missile defense proponents agree with the administration's decision to pursue a limited defense but argue that it has chosen the wrong architecture. They call for developing boost-phase interceptors that shoot missiles down shortly after launch before they can deploy any countermeasures. Other proponents dismiss the Clinton system as too limited. They favor larger defenses that could defeat a Chinese attack or handle a large-scale accidental launch from Russia. And still others cling to Ronald Reagan's vision of building an anti-missile shield that would render nuclear weapons "impotent and obsolete."

So the real debate over missile defense is just beginning. Arms control advocates hope to frame the debate as a question of whether to build defenses at all. But that is not likely to be the debate, notwithstanding North Korea's suddenly more moderate behavior. Both Al Gore and George Bush accept the need for missile defense in principle, though they differ sharply on the specifics, and the problem of missile proliferation is not going to fade away. Just as important, the Cold War is over. Washington and Moscow are no longer mortal enemies, and there is room to rethink the role of defense in American security. Russian President Vladimir Putin conceded this point himself with his proposal last June in the wake of the Moscow summit that Russia and NATO work together to develop a defense against the growing missile threat.

That is not to say that missile defense technology is ready today, that all defenses make sense, or that defensive deployments can be done cavalierly. Quite the contrary. The difficulties plaguing the Clinton administration's limited anti-missile system—it flunked two of its first three tests—show that the Pentagon has a long way to go in perfecting defenses against even very small attacks. For that reason, talk about defenses that will negate the nuclear balance of terror or do away with mutual assured destruction is wildly premature.

Even if more ambitious defenses become practical faster than anyone expects, they still may not be desirable. The effort to build a defense against China is unlikely to produce any lasting U.S. advantage and could well undermine U.S. security. Beijing is technologically and financially capable of developing missiles that could penetrate any American defense, and it could become more disagreeable on other issues (such as nuclear proliferation) that matter to the United States. Proposals to build ambitious defenses to handle a large-scale Russian accidental launch are of similarly dubious value. Building anything other than a clearly limited defense risks derailing efforts to make deep cuts in offensive forces because at some point Russia will need to keep more offensive weapons to preserve its nuclear deterrent. In short, it is simpler, cheaper, and far less destabilizing to work with Russia to cut its arsenal, to lower alert rates, and to strengthen its command and control and early warning systems.

Washington should also take the diplomacy of missile defense very seriously. The wisest course of action would be to negotiate modifications of the ABM Treaty with Moscow and possibly even conduct joint programs with Russia. The reason for so doing is not that the ABM Treaty is sacred but that formal agreement reassures Moscow about American intentions and substantially reduces the diplomatic costs of deployment. After all, Europe can hardly object to a missile defense if Moscow doesn't.

Of course, Moscow may prove intransigent on missile defense and leave the United States with no choice but to withdraw from the treaty. But if so, Washington should still seek to allay Russian concerns. At a minimum, it should pursue a tacit arms control policy that keeps Moscow informed of its plans and unilaterally accept intrusive verification procedures. No one should be under any illusion, however, that tacit arms control will be easy to establish. Not only is treaty abrogation an inauspicious foundation on which to build a new relationship with Moscow, but also domestic political support for tacit arms control could prove elusive. Critics will ask why the United States is sharing sensitive information with countries that target American cities and that are under no legal obligation to open their own nuclear arsenals up for inspection. The net result might be no arms control at all. Both Washington and Moscow should keep this in mind as they discuss the future of the ABM Treaty.

James M. Lindsay is a senior fellow in the Brookings Foreign Policy Studies program and the author of Congress and Nuclear Weapons *(Johns Hopkins, 1991) and* Congress and the Politics of U.S. Foreign Policy *(Johns Hopkins, 1994).*

Unit 6

Unit Selections

Key Points to Consider

- Itemize the products you own that were manufactured in another country.
- What recent contacts have you had with people from other countries? How was it possible for you to have these contacts?
- Identify nongovernmental organizations in your community that are involved in international cooperation.
- What are the prospects for international governance? How would a trend in this direction enhance or threaten American values and constitutional rights?
- How can the conflict and rivalry between the United States and Russia be transformed into more meaningful cooperation?

DUSHKIN ONLINE Links — www.dushkin.com/online/

26. **American Foreign Service Association**
    http://www.afsa.org/related.html
27. **Carnegie Endowment for International Peace**
    http://www.ceip.org
28. **Commission on Global Governance**
    http://www.cgg.ch
29. **OECD/FDI Statistics**
    http://www.oecd.org/statistics/
30. **U.S. Institute of Peace**
    http://www.usip.org

These sites are annotated on pages 4 and 5.

As the conference convened in Rome on June 15, it was beset by disagreement. The most divisive questions revolved around the precise definition of the crimes to be within the court's jurisdiction, the breadth of that jurisdiction and just who would determine which cases should be brought. The U.S. went in with goals that allied it uncomfortably with China, Russia and India, as well as Libya and Algeria, but put it at odds with most of its usual friends who gathered among the so-called Like-Minded Nations seeking a strong and independent Court. "We are not here," said Washington's U.N. ambassador, Bill Richardson, "to create a court that sits in judgment on national systems." The U.S. is concerned that its many soldiers serving overseas could become involved in confrontations that would make them vulnerable to what an Administration official called "frivolous claims by politically motivated governments."

The Washington negotiators—who rejected universal jurisdiction, subjecting any state, signatory or not, to the court's remit—agreed that the court should have automatic jurisdiction in the case of genocide, giving it the ability to prosecute individuals of any country that had signed the treaty. But they sought a clause allowing countries to opt out of the court's jurisdiction on war crimes and crimes against humanity for 10 years. The agreed statute allows states to opt out of the court's jurisdictions only on war crimes and only for seven years. It also includes the crime of "aggression" within the court's jurisdiction, subject to a precise definition of aggression. Washington had also wanted to give only the Security Council and states party to the agreement the right to bring cases to the court. The statute, however, also empowers the prosecutor to initiate cases. The U.S. did manage to get a compromise, promoted by Singapore, allowing the Security Council to call a 12-month renewable halt to investigations and prosecutions included in the text. "If states can simply opt in or out when they want, the court will be unworkable," said a senior official in the German delegation. Without an independent prosecutor, he added, "crimes will be passed over for political reasons."

Although conference chairman Philippe Kirsch of Canada had already successfully chaired at least eight international conferences—brokering agreements on issues such as terrorism and the protection of war victims—all his undoubted mediation skills failed to resolve the disputes. As Washington became increasingly isolated, a copy of U.S. "talking points" circulated among the delegations, suggesting that if the court did not meet U.S. requirements Washington might retaliate by withdrawing its troops overseas, including those in Europe. Although few believed in that possibility and the Administration downplayed it, State Department spokesman Jamie Rubin explained that "The U.S. has a special responsibility that other governments do not have."

After all the wrangling, what emerged was a court to be located in The Hague—where the International Court of Justice already deals with cases brought on a civil basis by states against other states. It is to contain four elements: a Presidency with three judges; a section encompassing an appeals division, trial and pre-trial divisions; a Prosecutor's office; and a Registry to handle administration. The court, which will act only when national courts are "unwilling or unable genuinely" to proceed, will confine its maximum penalty to life imprisonment.

How the court will fare without the support of the U.S. is unclear. Washington has provided vital political backing for the Yugoslav and Rwanda tribunals and continues to be their leading financier. "We have shown that the only way to get war criminals to trial is for the U.S. to take a prominent role," said one Administration official last week. "If the U.S. is not a lead player in the creation of this court, it doesn't happen."

Nevertheless, the fact that a court with teeth has actually been created was an unprecedented move by the world community to make the rule of law finally prevail over brute force—a step towards fulfilling Secretary-General Annan's pledge that "At long last we aim to prove we mean it when we say 'Never Again.' "

Enforcing Human Rights

Karl E. Meyer

In the century's surprising finale, human rights in its many guises has become a pervasive global cause, culminating in the most unusual of modern wars, the NATO intervention in Kosovo. As never before, the foreign news is seemingly dominated by demands for basic political rights and protests against internal repression. Stories involving human rights, or their absence, flow from lands of every description, ranging from the Vale of Kashmir to tiny East Timor in Asia, from every region of Africa, and from almost every ex-Soviet republic from the Baltic to the Caspian Sea. So strong is the tide that human rights offenses long past are being tried anew, either in British courts in the case of Chile's General Augusto Pinochet, or in American films and academic treatises in the case of African slavery.

Politics and technology help explain this development. Public diplomacy abhors a void, and with the end of the Cold War, there has been a palpable hunger for a unifying doctrine. Thus, the long ignored and most blatantly flouted of international covenants, the Universal Declaration of Human Rights, adopted by the United Nations in 1948, has assumed a robust second life. Its principles are advanced by an aggressive phalanx of nongovernmental organizations, notably Amnesty International, Doctors Without Borders, and Human Rights Watch. With an assist from pop stars and British royals, most Westerners are now conversant with the current vocabulary of human rights: boat people, "ethnic cleansing," Free Tibet, land mines, Live Aid, female mutilation, and that most misleading media mantra, the "international community." For Westerners, what happened in Kosovo was a good deal more than "a quarrel in a far away country between people of whom we know nothing," as Neville Chamberlain said of Czechoslovakia in 1938 (a phrase echoed by Secretary of State Warren Christopher, speaking about Bosnia in 1993).

For non-Westerners stifled by authoritarian regimes, human rights have acquired a different resonance. They provide a weapon of opposition that can generate foreign attention and even in some cases (Kosovo, for example) trigger intervention. On its face, prospects for moving forward appear promising. Earlier debates on the alleged conflict between "Asian values" and the U.N. declaration have abated, and the consensus on universal norms seems broad and hopeful. The failure of communism has given widespread and practical luster to such democratic values as free speech, civil society, the rule of law, and electoral accountability. Propitiously, new technologies have bored holes in closed frontiers. Fax machines, cellular telephones, and the Internet now feed the agitation against the hard-line ayatollahs of Iran and the Burmese jailers of Aung San Suu Kyi.

Yet however welcome to human rights activists, these favorable developments have raised expectations that cannot plausibly be realized. The American role is critical. No forward movement is possible without Washington's support and leadership, but the very exercise of such leadership stirs an outcry against U.S. hegemony abroad and a backlash from left and right

---

Karl E. Meyer has written extensively on human rights as a member of the New York Times *Editorial Board, 1979–98. He is the author, with Shareen Brysac, of* Tournament of Shadows: The Great Game and Race for Empire in Central Asia, *published in November by Counterpoint.*

 From *World Policy Journal,* Fall 1999, pp. 45-50.

at home. In truth, American policy has neither direction nor strategy but is a melange of bromidic phrases. At a recent panel discussion in New York, a Peruvian human rights worker confessed he could not understand why the Clinton administration, having uttered the right sentiments about repression in his country, went on to help finance a draconian narcotics sweep by the hated security police, bent U.S. laws to sell advanced warplanes to the all-too powerful military, and gave its blessing to fiscal measures that punish the poor and undermine Peruvian democracy. Asked what he most sought from Washington, he offered a one-word answer: "Coherence."

Wilsonian Trappings in the Real World

The rebuke is valid, but in the circumstances, inescapable. There is no "international community" in any meaningful sense, only its simulacrum in the form of an enfeebled (and insolvent) United Nations and a toothless World Court. Despite all the Wilsonian trappings, the world today substantially resembles that of 1900: one global superpower (America, in place of Britain), a dozen or so pivotal powers (Britain, Germany, France, Russia, China, Japan, India, Brazil, Indonesia, Israel, Turkey, Pakistan, and South Africa), and upward of 150 lesser entities, most of them poor and dependent. Granted, the old colonial empires have melted away, but from the human rights vantage, this is not always a plus. For reasons of crass self-interest, colonial powers maintained a monopoly on the use of force, put down regional and ethnic separatists, and imposed a rough Hobbesian peace. As we have seen in Rwanda, Bosnia, and Somalia, the "international community" has failed to devise a more acceptable, and effective, substitute.

In the nineteenth century, it is worth recalling, a "power" was defined as a country strong enough to resist foreign intervention. The distinction still holds. It is highly unlikely, putting it mildly, that the "international community" would ever intervene forcibly on human rights grounds against any of the pivotal powers. To be sure, sanctions of various degrees of severity are feasible, and can have teeth, as in the case of South Africa during the apartheid era. But this was an exception. In the post—Cold War era, pivotal powers generally get a human rights pass: consider Turkey and the Kurds, China and the Tibetans, Russia and the Chechens. Thus, harsher measures invariably apply to the weak, the poor, and the pariah (Serbia and Iraq). There is no equal justice under world law.

All this is known to policymakers. As the writer David Rieff usefully reminds us, officials reserve their lofty phrases for the public pulpit, and in private employ terms that Bismark would have no trouble understanding.[1] In that realistic spirit, one should attempt to sort out the policy choices for the United States in the coming decades. In my view, they boil down to three. Washington could dispense with cant and unilaterally proclaim a Pax Americana, dispatching Marines or cruise missiles, when necessary, to rush in humanitarian aid, prevent massacres, and punish tyrants. A second option would be to heed George Kennan's advice: abjure interventionist meddling, address our own neglected ills, and lead by moral example. Or Washington could, for the first time, make a serious commitment to collective action, building on structures that already exist, and thereby give some meaning to the hollow phrase "international community."

The perils of the first course were apparent in the Clinton administration's punitive air strikes in 1998 against presumed terrorists in Afghanistan and Sudan. The suspicion that President Clinton was trying to change the subject during the impeachment proceedings against him sharpened when the Pentagon could not confirm that a factory it destroyed in Khartoum actually produced chemical weapons. To the peril of seeming cynical and incompetent when operations misfire is added the peril of seeming a hegemonic bully when missions succeed. In any case, unilateral military adventures are easier to initiate than to end. Previous American "police actions" in Haiti, the Dominican Republic, and Nicaragua turned into occupations that endured through six American administrations, from William Howard Taft to Franklin D. Roosevelt (who is still remembered in Latin America as the good neighbor who pulled out the Marines).

The problem with George Kennan's prescription is its unfeasibility in a multiethnic democracy in which legislators play so important a role in foreign policy. One may sympathize with Kennan's distaste for moralizing bombast from members of Congress, but that is the price of popular democracy. Indeed, examined more closely, our melting-pot diplomacy, whatever its periodic excesses, has also had its triumphs. While serving as secretary of state, Henry Kissinger deplored the Jackson-Vanik Act that attached human rights conditions to most-favored-nation trade benefits, and he was at best lukewarm about the human rights provisions in the 1975 Helsinki Accords that gave all signatories the right to inquire into and judge compliance—yet both helped to legitimize internal opposition to Soviet repression. We tend as well to forget that in enacting economic sanctions against South Africa, Congress overrode President Reagan's veto—an instance in which a legislative measure palpably fostered peaceful change in another country. All these measures were attributable to human rights agitation and melting-pot politics, and all involved the kind of moralizing intervention that George Kennan too indiscriminately deplores.

If popular involvement in foreign policy is integral to our system, why not turn this to advantage? Why not tap the undoubted reserves of American goodwill and generosity, as evidenced in the continuing vitality of the Peace Corps? For starters, the next president could reverse course and support the 1998 Rome Statute creating an International Criminal Court, ending the need for ad hoc tribunals to try accused war criminals. Why not take the braver course—sign the statute and address its shortcomings while moving forward to full ratification? It is hard to believe that Americans lack the legal wit to safeguard U.S. troops from frivolous prosecutions—cited by the Clinton administration as a major reason for refusing to sign. Had Harry Truman heeded similar warnings from lawyers, to whom every precedent is a slippery slope, the Nuremberg Tribunal would never have been established. (Indeed, a British initiative to give the tribunal permanent status was among the sadder political casualties of the Cold War.)

Additionally, the next president could call upon the country to join with willing foreign partners, notably Canada and the Netherlands, finally to establish a voluntary standby force under the United Nations capable of responding swiftly when genocidal disasters threaten. Of the regrettable features of the NATO intervention in Kosovo, two stand out: the reliance on massive air power to avoid NATO casualties, thus all but destroying the country that was to be saved, and the use of a regional military alliance to bypass authorization by the U.N. Security Council. These were precedents far graver than any of the claimed pitfalls in the Rome Statute, and it would require courage for a presidential contender to say as much. But absent that kind of courage, it is hard to see how anything like a real "international community" will ever emerge.

Washington's Frosty Response

In George Kennan's telling phrase, American support for human rights has been declaratory in nature, not contractual. This was so from the outset. The Truman administration was delighted when Eleanor Roosevelt gained unanimous General Assembly approval in 1948 for the Universal Declaration of Human Rights (48 in favor, none opposed, two absent, and eight abstentions, mostly Soviet bloc delegates). As the first chairman of the U.N. Human Rights Commission, Mrs. Roosevelt adroitly coaxed support for language that emphasized individual rights, while it also recognized social and economic rights. Article One paraphrases Jefferson's Declaration, *sans* Creator: "All human beings are born free and equal in dignity and rights. They are endowed with reason and conscience and should act toward one another in the spirit of brotherhood."

Yet when Mrs. Roosevelt, "the First Lady of the World," pressed for ratification of implementing covenants, she met with a frosty response in Washington. As the writer Michael Ignatieff has remarked, American human rights policy is distinctive and paradoxical, "a nation with a great rights tradition that leads the world in denouncing human rights violations but which behaves like a rogue state in relation to international legal conventions."[2] The Senate has refused to approve, or has imposed demeaning reservations on, nearly every important U.N. covenant with respect to human rights. The U.S. Senate, typically enough, deliberated for nearly four decades before ratifying, with qualifying conditions, the 1948 Genocide Convention. (It needs adding that Sen. William Proxmire for three years took the floor daily to express his dismay at this shaming lassitude.)

To be sure, the constitutional requirement of a two-thirds vote for ratifying treaties gives inordinate leverage to a Senate minority. Granted as well, during the Cold War's glacial phase, the United Nations fell so far in American esteem that a Reagan administration delegate invited the organization to sail into the sunset (a geographic impossibility from New York harbor), a sentiment seconded by Mayor Ed Koch, a Democrat. Many Americans, not all of them conservatives, found it unconscionable to be lectured on human rights by members of the Soviet bloc and the Third World majority in the General Assembly. This is now history. The Soviet Union no longer exists, the General Assembly has rescinded its resolution equating Zionism with racism, most of the basic fiscal and management reforms demanded by Washington have been undertaken—yet the Clinton administration and the U.S. Congress still regard the United Nations as something like an unfriendly foreign power, unworthy of real trust, or even indeed of its $1.6 billion in treaty-mandated back dues and assessments.

The result, in the words of Brian Urquhart, is a weak, divided and underfinanced international system, on which the world must prayerfully count to prevent wars (internal and regional), genocide, nuclear proliferation, and environmental calamities. Urquhart, a former undersecretary general of the United Nations, offers a gloomy but accurate summary of what this means: "More than ever it is clear that there is a large hole in this ramshackle international structure—the absence of consistent and effective international authority in vital international matters. The very notion of international authority is anathema to many governments, great and small, until they are looking disaster in the face, by which time it is usually too late for useful international action.[3]

The next president has a history-given opportunity to treat Americans as grownups, by stating plainly that this country has neither the wit nor the resources to be the world's sheriff, that sharing global obligations makes political and fiscal sense, that a new administration wishes to work with others to clear out land mines everywhere, that it welcomes proposals for training international police, and indeed would even consider (as David Rieff suggests) some form of long-term authority in places like Kosovo, where creating stable political arrangements may take a generation.

A specific and useful proposal is already on the table: the creation of a multinational standby force that could be rapidly deployed to check genocidal massacres. No matter that such crises are infrequent: when they occur, the aftershocks endure for decades. Interestingly, when such a force was first proposed in 1992, it was endorsed by candidate Bill Clinton: "We should explore the possibility of creating a standby, voluntary U.N. rapid deployment force to deter aggression against small states and to protect humanitarian relief shipments."

The standby proposal originated in "An Agenda for Peace," a report to the Security Council by Egypt's Boutros Boutros-Ghali, a smart, abrasive, and unpopular U.N. secretary general. As he was at pains to emphasize, he was not suggesting the formation of a U.N. army but instead asking as many nations as possible to make available troops on a standby basis, so operations could get underway in days, not months. Such a force was envisioned in Article 43 of the U.N. Charter, under which all members "undertake to make available to the Security Council, on its call and in accordance with a special agreement...armed forces, assistance, and facilities, including rights of passage, necessary for the purpose of maintaining international peace and security."

Fatal Timing

Boutros-Ghali's proposal had merit, but his timing was fatal. In 1993, the untested Clinton team inherited from the Bush administration a muddled humanitarian mission in Somalia meant to feed a stricken people without taking sides in a civil war. Although nominally under U.N. auspices, Operation Restore Hope was directly controlled by the United States, which provided most of the troops. On October 3, 1993, eighteen U.S. Rangers were killed in a skirmish, a shaken President Clinton pulled back and out, and hopes for a multinational standby force died in the mean streets of Mogadishu.

The need for such a force was underscored with horrific finality in April 1994, with the outbreak of ethnic massacres in Rwanda. A small U.N. force of 2,500 troops was instantly withdrawn from the Rwandan capital, Kigali, and Washington blocked Security Council authorization for a stronger force, among the gravest foreign affairs mistakes by the Clinton White House. Around 800,000 Rwandans were slain; the slaughter was followed by the exodus of 2.5 million refugees and a cycle of violence in Central Africa whose end is not in sight. In his memoirs, Boutros-Ghali recalls a White House meeting in May 1994 at which, to his surprise, the president all but shrugged off Rwanda to discuss the appointment of an inspector general at the United Nations and the naming of his candidate as the director of the United Nations International Children's Emergency Fund (UNICEF). (Years later, it should be noted, President Clinton more creditably acknowledged American culpability in failing to respond to the Rwanda genocide.)

The Canadian commander of the U.N. force in Kigali, Gen. Romeo Dallaire, asserts that even with two or three thousand troops he could have substantially limited the killings—a judgment supported by Scott R. Fell in a report to the Carnegie Commission on Preventing Deadly Conflict. Fell estimates that a trained force of 5,000 soldiers, deployed in April 1994 could have significantly reduced the toll.[4]

In its indifference to the United Nations, the Clinton administration expressed Washington's abiding bipartisan distaste for multilateral operations in any form, unless there is clear demonstration of American national interest (for example, the Desert Storm operation against Iraq) or an American is in charge (as at the World Bank and UNICEF). Even so, the case for a standby force has gained converts in Washington. In 1998, the Department of Defense quietly won approval for providing $200,000 as seed money for a fund to finance a rapid deployment mission headquarters under Bernard Miyet, the undersecretary general for peacekeeping.

The fund grows out of a Canadian proposal in 1995 for the establishment of such a force, a suggestion strongly seconded by the Dutch. Interestingly, as of July 1999, 85 countries, ranging from Argentina to Zambia, have officially expressed willingness to participate in standby arrangements. The French and the British have offered to make available 5,000 and 10,000 troops respectively. Participants would be obliged to train and pay costs while the forces remained on standby, with the U.N. providing reimbursements after the deployed troops left their country. Of the 85 volunteers, 24 states have already signed a memorandum of understanding with the United Nations, 14 have provided planning data, 23 (including the United States) have listed their capabilities, and 24 have expressed a willingness to take part. Adding the first three groups together, the United Nations on paper could mobilize 84,000 reserves, 56,700 support troops, 1,600 military observers, and 2,050 civilian police.

This is not a standing U.N. army. Its American equivalent is a trained volunteer fire department, able to respond quickly in emergencies. Deployment would be subject to approval of the Security Council, whose five permanent members—the United States,

Russia, China, Britain, and France—each wield a veto. Even so, given America's resistance to multilateral operations, winning approval for such a volunteer standby army would require a fair measure of presidential imagination, persuasiveness, and courage.

How refreshing it would be if the next chief executive reported to Americans on the world as it really is, warned human rights activists that frustration and disappointments were unavoidable, acknowledged that double standards exist and that the "international community" has yet to be created, added that the most likely threats to peace and human rights will arise from civil strife within sovereign frontiers, that to deal with this threat the world needed both regional and international standby reserves, that Washington would do what it could to help, and that as a first step he or she would seek to persuade Americans that it was in their interest to pay the dues owed an organization inspired by American ideals and located in the world's most ethnically diverse city. How refreshing, and how necessary

Notes

1. See David Rieff, "A New Age of Liberal Imperialism?" *World Policy Journal,* vol. 16 (summer 1999).
2. Michael Ignatieff, "Human Rights: The Midlife Crisis," *New York Review of Books,* May 20, 1999.
3. Brian Urquhart, "Looking for the Sheriff," *New York Review of Books,* July 16, 1998.
4. See *Preventing Genocide: How the Early Use of Force Might Have Succeeded in Rwanda,* which is available, along with the Carnegie Commission's final report on Rwanda, at http://www.ccpdc.org. For Boutros Boutros-Ghali's version of the U.S. response to Rwanda, see his memoir, *Unvanquished: A United States-United Nations Saga* (New York: Random House, 1999). For the pros and cons of the Rome Statute, see the monograph, *Toward an International Court* (New York: Council on Foreign Relations, 1999).

Ecotourism without tears

Sylvie Blangy

From Ecuador to Namibia, indigenous communities are striking up innovative partnerships with tour operators to promote ecotourism on their own terms—a strategy to bring in revenue and protect their culture and environment

In the heart of Ecuador's rain forest, forty-five minutes by foot away from their own village, a small group of Huaorani, an Amazon indigenous people, built a palm-thatched roof cabin for eight. Fearing that too much tourism could disrupt their traditional hunter-gatherer lifestyle and bring in unwelcome consumer habits, the Huaorani only accept one group of visitors per month, for two to six days.

But during this time, they are given full attention. Community representatives greet visitors upon their arrival and discuss some of their people's social and environmental concerns. During this first meeting, a per-night fee is paid to the head of the community for each visitor and the money is distributed evenly among all the families. Salaries for the various jobs (guides, maintenance, canoe paddlers etc) are calculated by doubling what a person would earn as a labourer for an oil company, the main alternative source of income. Huaorani guides accompany visitors on hikes and teach them about medicinal plants, the rainforest's ecology, their spiritual relationship with the environment, and local handicrafts. At the end of their trip, visitors are invited to raise awareness in their own countries about the Huaorani's efforts to defend their land and culture. This initiative has led to donations that have financed training workshops, high frequency radios and solar panels.

The fact that such a vulnerable population living in a region prone to outside encroachment—from unscrupulous jungle tour operators to petroleum companies—managed to set up a project that won a prize for the best ecotourism programme at the 1998 Berlin Tourism Expo is not a product of chance. It took nine months of planning and orientation meetings for the Huaorani to finetune a tourism strategy, a task carried out hand in hand with TROPIC Ecological Adventures, a tour operator with a long experience in working with indigenous communities, notably on bringing the Huaorani's problems with the oil industry to international attention. Not only has this community defined its own rules for tourism, but it has gained indispensable exposure on the international travel market through a fruitful business partnership.

Sylvie Blangy is responsible for the ecotourism department at Seca, a French consulting firm specializing in the protection and management of natural sites

Reprinted with permission from the *Unesco Courier,* July/August 1999, pp. 32-33.

A strong conservationist slant

Just as importantly, the Huaorani have opted for a self-managed community-based activity that represents a potential economic alternative to oil and logging. Many indigenous communities see ecotourism as the most rational way of protecting the rainforest, creating jobs for the young and generating revenue for education, community health and transportation. They also see it as a way of maintaining their cultural integrity. Ecuador is a veritable laboratory for community-based ecotourism, with some environmentalists contending that revenues earned from tourism in the Amazon rainforest could eventually outstrip oil earnings.

The tourist is a child of the 20th century who only travels to comfort his prejudices.

Joaquín Luna

Spanish journalist

The Cofan indigenous people have developed a fairly sophisticated management system in Zabalo, under the guidance of Randy Borman, the son of an American missionary who grew up with the Cofan and has played a leading role in resisting the efforts of oil companies to prospect on their territory. In 1992, Borman established a community-run company in Zabalo with ten Cofan associates who invested their labour in building guest cabins. Other community members are paid for doing various jobs while a small co-operative craft store also brings in income.These various initiatives provide the Cofan of Zabalo with an estimated $500 annually per person.The project also has a strong conservationist slant: the community has defined separate zones for hunting and ecotourism, with fines levied on members for taking certain species such as toucans and parrots (particularly coveted by tourists), or for exceeding quotas in the hunting zones.

Besides the need for a close relationship with a partner who has a sound knowledge of the travel market and a sensitivity toward indigenous communities, such projects need at least five years before they can become commercially viable. Training is the backbone of any succcessful enterprise. Even though these trips are no-frills experiences, some basic notions such as punctuality and hygiene in food preparation have to be understood by the community. Just as important, if a real exchange is to happen during the trip, guides have to know how to speak to visitors about their lifestyle and natural surroundings, and realize that they may have to slow down their pace when leading hikes along rainforest trails. All this requires dialogue and a community that is united around a respected leader. Although NGOs have also assisted communities in developing tourism projects, experience shows that they often lack contacts on the travel market to make these initiatives viable.

'Unlike oil, tourism is sustainable'

Other countries and continents are also boosting their presence on this niche market which is attracting more and more North American and European travellers. Take the case of Venezuela. Here, one indigenous group, the Pemons, does not flinch at accepting 100 tourists a day who fly in from a beach resort on Margarita Island to visit Salto Angel, the world's highest waterfall, in the southeast of the country. Besides accompanying visitors to the falls and serving them a meal, the Pemons have also built a village (an hour by road away from their own) of ten traditional cabins for overnight groups. Tourism revenue (the Pemons receive about $25 per day per visitor, the total package costing $70) has served to set up a school and a health dispensary and make up for declining state subsidies. Another group, the Ye'Kuanas, won rights from the government to manage land-use of a forest reserve. Part of it, beyond a natural barrier formed by a waterfall over the Caura river, is off limits to visitors, while in another, they have built guest cabins and developed itineraries for tourists in partnership with Natura Raid, an operator based in Caracas.

As awareness of environmental issues has spread over the past decade, a growing number of travellers are looking into how the adventure/discovery-style trips they choose benefit communities. In response, the latter are joining forces in an effort to better promote their projects and design common standards. In Ecuador, the CONFENIAE, a confederation of indigenous groups from the Amazon basin, has published guidelines for managing ecotourism.The Ecuadorian Ecotourism Association has designed tools for evaluating the environmental policies of tour operators, which are now used in other Latin American countries. In Africa, Namibia formed a national association for community-based tourism (NACOBTA) in 1995 which groups 41 communities from a range of ethnic groups. It provides advice and training to communities seeking to start up projects, but also keeps a high profile in international travel fairs. Many experts see NACOBTA as one of the most rational ways for promoting and defending this tourism, which by nature, is small in scale and highly personalized.

The challenge today lies in designing national strategies that put the accent on training, access to markets and capital, and safety norms—issues that will be on the agenda of the Ecotourism Society's general assembly, to be held in December 1999 in Quito, upon the invitation of the Ecuadorian government. Clearly, this gesture is another sign that indigenous groups have gained a voice at national level, and tourism is just one way in which they are being heard. As one Ecuadorian ecotourism operator put it, "Unlike oil, tourism is sustainable."

✚• • •

- **Megan Epler-Wood,** ***Meeting the Global Challenge of Community Participation in Ecotourism: Case Studies and Lessons from Ecuador,*** **USAID, The Nature Conservancy, 1998**
- **Judy Karwacki, "Indigenous Ecotourism: Overcoming the Challenge," The Ecotourism Society Newsletter, first quarter 1999**
- **The Nacobta Community Based Tourism Association at nacobta@ iafrica.com.na,**
- **Andy Drumm,** ***New Approaches to Community-based Ecotourism Management; Learning from Ecuador, Ecotourism, A Guide for Planners and Managers,*** **vol. 2. The Ecotourism Society 1998.**

TRIBES UNDER THE MICROSCOPE

Genetic researchers view the world's indigenous cultures as "living laboratories"—but what happens when new science clashes with ancient beliefs?

by Vida Foubister

Patauaki is my sacred mountain

Rangitaiki is my sacred river. Ngati Awa is my tribe, Ngati Pahipoto my sub-tribe, and Kokohinau my meeting place. Mataatua is the canoe whose genealogy binds me to my tribe, the nine tribes of my region and the other tribes of the North whose genealogy stems from the same ancestors as mine."

This traditional Maori introduction, translated by Aroha Te Pareake Mead, manager of Cultural Heritage and Indigenous Issues for the Ministry of Maori Development in Wellington, New Zealand, reveals his identity and standing in the world as it is interpreted by his people.

The Maori, the indigenous people of New Zealand, have a detailed genealogy that traces back to their account of creation, in which Ranginui, the Sky Father, and Papatuanuku, the Earth Mother, sacrifice their deep love for each other and separate because their earthly embrace is suffocating their children, the Maori.

The Maori's belief in this epic love story is strong, and Western notions of evolution and genetic inheritance, despite being presented as scientific fact, do not compete as credible alternatives. Likewise, other indigenous peoples throughout the world hold just as strongly to their own traditional cosmologies.

It is against this backdrop that science, especially gene-based medical research, finds itself increasingly viewed with suspicion by the very populations that would make perfect "living laboratories"—indigenous tribes and other isolated groups whose members share common ancestors and, thus, many distinct genetic traits.

For example, as the Human Genome Project, the publicly funded international effort to sequence or "map" the human genetic code known as DNA (deoxyribonucleic acid), nears its completion, researchers are becoming increasingly interested in the genetic variations between populations. They theorize that analyzing these small differences will help them to identify which genes or genetic mutations put some people at risk for specific diseases, which could lead to medical breakthroughs. Such differences are easier to isolate if the study groups have their genetic homogeneity largely intact.

But here is where science clashes with traditional beliefs. To begin with, such analysis requires genetic sampling, usually by obtaining small amounts of blood, hair or saliva from the subjects. These procedures are simple, but loaded with cultural implications in the case of subjects who identify themselves not just as individuals, but—often more strongly—as members of a tribe or other distinct group.

"There's a basic ideological conflict when it comes to DNA and genes and parts of the body in general," says Debra Harry, executive director of the Indigenous Peoples Council on Biocolonialism in Nixon, Nevada, USA, and a member of the Northern Paiute tribe of American Indians.

"From an indigenous perspective, we are not the owners of our DNA," she says. "We don't have a right to change it and fix it and manipulate it or sell it because it belongs to our future generations. We also have spiritual beliefs about the body, that you don't take a piece of somebody's body from them because it also has a part of their spirit."

Says Barbara Burns McGrath, RN, PhD, a medical anthropologist at the University of Washington in Seattle: "Genetic research is based on Western ideas of improvement and progress and the benefits of science. We're going headstrong into this new biology without really recognizing the fact that not all people, not all cultures, share these values to the same extent."

Mead adds that the whole empirical concept of "true or false" carries little weight where deep-seated cultural beliefs are concerned. "Those who dispel the Maori view, or any indigenous cosmological view, don't seem to realize that the main message of any knowledge system is not whether it is true or false," he says. "It's not about ideas being proven or unproved. The purpose of any people's evolutionary framework is, and always will be, the social, cultural and ethical values that it promotes among its members."

Another problem is that current ethics protocols for obtaining informed consent from study subjects may not address the implications that genetic research can have on family members or the extended cultural group.

"As soon as you say 'Navajo' [an American Indian tribe], then you're talking about not just that person, but a nation," explains Brett Lee Shelton, an attorney in Boulder, Colorado, USA, and a member of the Oglala Lakota tribe. "That person can't speak for the nation, so their sample can't stand for the nation unless the nation agrees."

Such concerns led to opposition that essentially derailed the Human Genome Diversity Project (HGDP), an international effort launched in 1993 to determine the origins and migration patterns of the world's populations. Currently, the HGDP is collecting genetic samples only in China and Southwest Asia and lacks the funding to do so in North America.

But private companies, eager to develop gene-based medicines, are picking up where the HGDP left off.

"Now that the commercial importance of this information is becoming much bigger, that's where all the research is going on," says Julie Delahanty, researcher and program manager for the Rural Advancement Foundation International (RAFI) in Winnipeg, Manitoba, Canada.

Several genomics companies that have sprung up in the past decade are pioneering this research, often in partnership with major pharmaceutical companies.

"Most of the genetic research that's done in isolated communities is driven by companies," agrees Bernard Zinman MD, a senior scientist at Mount Sinai Hospital's Samuel Lunenfeld Research Institute in Toronto. "Sometimes they have agreements [with the study groups], and sometimes they just take the DNA and they do what they want."

This push to study genetic variation is bringing some scientists into contact with indigenous groups for the first time, driving the issue of cultural sensitivity to the forefront.

"There are researchers who work with Native American populations their whole lives and who are very sensitive to their needs," says George J. Annas, a health law professor at Boston University School of Public Health. "There are others who really haven't thought about Native Americans at all and they have no understanding of Native American history or culture or values."

These scientists not only need to overcome indigenous people's concerns about genetic research, but to meet their cultural expectations as well.

William L. Freeman, MD, MPH, director of the U.S. Indian Health Service research program in Rockville, Maryland, USA, says many Native American automatically place a visiting medical researcher in the same category as their own traditional healers, often highly esteemed and respected members of the group, which can lead to misunderstandings if expectations aren't met. "They expect a caring relationship, and if the researcher falls into that role without even knowing it and doesn't meet the demands of that role, then people can get very upset about it," he says.

Researchers often are unaware of any cultural blunders they might have made during a project. Often equally unaware is the office or committee set up to monitor ethics protocols.

One relatively simple solution to the problem is to proactively involve the communities in the research projects. One approach, called "community consultation," strives to educate the target community about the nature and significance of the project and invites local input, increasing the likelihood that the project will fulfill cultural expectations and garner willing participation.

"We can be more than people landing in the village square announcing the research project and, when it's over, leaving without a trace," says Timothy F. Murphy, PhD, head of Medical Humanities at the University of Illinois at Chicago.

Other models go further by requiring official community consent for members to participate. Though there's considerable debate about whether or not community leaders should have the right to decide who takes part in certain research projects, tribal governments in the United States already have this jurisdiction on reservation land. Federally recognized tribes are considered sovereign nations within a sovereign nation, and people who choose to live there respect the power of their elected leaders.

"As a native woman, what my elders have said is what I'm doing, and that's protecting the DNA of my people," says Judy Gobert, who serves as the spokeswomen on genetic research for the Confederated Salish and Kootenai Tribes of the Flathead Reservation in Montana. "As tribal members, we have an obligation to our people. It's our people first and ourselves second."

"As tribal members, we have an obligation to our people. It's our people first and ourselves second."

While genetic research holds tremendous promise, and many experts expect the anticipated high-tech breakthroughs will soon change the way medicine is practiced, some question its relevance to the indigenous groups—very often low-income people who even now lack access to basic health care and nutrition.

"The concern that I have is that the cures they're looking for are not going to benefit all of humankind," Gobert said, referring to the fact that much of the research is to combat diseases prevalent in the Western world, not among the populations being studied.

For example, Rural Advancement Foundation International recently cited a Columbia University study conducted in a remote Pakistani village with a high incidence of a genetic disease that leaves men and women completely hairless. The researchers were seeking a genetic cure for baldness, a condition for which consumers in the United States alone spend an estimate $7 billion annually in hair replacement therapies, drugs and other treatments.

"What they're really looking at are diseases of affluent Americans willing to pay for therapies that have nothing to do with health," Delahanty says.

Another widely cited case occurred a few years ago, when the U.S. National Institutes of Health took out a patent on the "cell line" of a study subject who was a member of the Hagahai tribe of Papua New Guinea. A cell line is a family of cells derived from a single parent cell that will replicate indefinitely under the right laboratory conditions, a trait that makes it a valuable commodity in the research world. Some laboratory animals, such as rodents, yield cell lines easily, but establishing cell lines from human tissue is considered difficult.

International pressure from human rights groups and foreign governments, which charged that informed consent had not been sought or given by the Hagahai subject, led the NIH to drop the patent in 1996. The Hagahai cell line, however, remains commercially available through the American Type Culture Collection, a nonprofit organization that authenticates and distributes biological resources worldwide.

In general, however, the odds of finding a lucrative commercial use for any genetic finding are "in the nature of a lottery ticket," says attorney Hank Greely, co-director of the Stanford University program in genomics, ethics and society.

But there's increasing recognition that communities still should have the right to share in the commercial potential, however remote. At the very least, some ethicists contend, scientists should ensure that the communities receive some benefit from participating in research projects.

"Some of us do that by hiring members from the community to be part of the research team," Dr. McGrath says. "This has the dual benefit of sharing some research funds with the community, as well as recognizing their expertise."

Other options include the funding of special health clinics or developing health promotion and disease prevention programs tailored to the community.

An example of a successful collaboration between researchers and their study group is a diabetes project involving the Sandy Lake First Nation, a community of Oji-Cree people in remote, northwestern Ontario, Canada. The partnership began nearly a decade ago when the tribe's chief and council, concerned about the community's unusually high rate of diabetes—five times the national average—invited medical researchers from Toronto to investigate. The project led to the discovery of a genetic mutation—a specific change in the DNA related to diabetes—that places the people at greater risk for the disease.

Originally, the mutation likely was a survival mechanism that evolved hundreds of years ago, when the tribe was a hunting-and-gathering society, explains Dr. Zinman of Toronto's Mount Sinai Hospital. It allowed them to store calories to survive seasonal feast-and-famine cycles. But the mutation became a liability in recent generations as the tribe developed a more settled lifestyle with regular access to commercial food.

The agreement between the researchers and the tribe guaranteed Sandy Lake a 20 percent share of any commercial value that resulted from the study. That hasn't happened yet, but the discovery itself has prompted an aggressive public health and awareness campaign that has convinced many in the community to adopt more healthful lifestyles. The local grocery store now uses Oji-Cree icons to identify low-fat products. Walking trails have been built to encourage exercise, and elementary school children now receive culturally appropriate lessons in healthful living.

"We started with very little understanding about the problem," says Sandy Lake Deputy Chief Harry Meekis. "Consultation and participation have opened our eyes and the minds of those who for years have accepted diabetes as a problem without hope."

The Sandy Lake agreement appears to have succeeded in helping both science and the community, but if it had gone awry, the Oji-Cree would have had little recourse beyond filing a lawsuit, a situation which puts many money-strapped

"Researchers have a moral obligation to respect the values and interests of communities . . . "

tribal governments at a distinct disadvantage.

"That places all of the burden of policing it on the tribes," says Gobert, of the Flathead Reservation in Montana. "No responsibility is laid on the researchers."

That's why Charles Weijer, MD, PhD, a bioethicist at Dalhousie University in Halifax, Nova Scotia, Canada, wants to see the Belmont Report, the U.S. government's ethics blueprint for medical research involving human subjects, amended to include a "respect for communities" clause.

Meanwhile, groups such as RAFI are pushing several international bodies, including the United Nations Human Rights Commission, the World Health Organization and the United Nations Educational, Scientific and Cultural Organization's International Bioethics Committee, to regulate genetic diversity research as it applies to indigenous populations.

Until such protections are in place, indigenous peoples likely will continue to be wary of gene-based research and its effects on their traditions, beliefs and status as culturally distinct populations.

Says Dr. Weijer: "Researchers have a moral obligation to respect the values and interests of communities and, wherever possible, protect communities in research from harm."

A Canadian citizen, Vida Foubister is a healthcare journalist and freelance writer based in Chicago. She holds a bachelor's degree in cell biotechnology and a master's degree in biochemistry.

Child Labour: Rights, risks, and realities

by Carol Bellamy

"Dust from the chemical powders and strong vapours in both the store-room and the boiler room were obvious . . . We found 250 children, mostly below 10 years of age, working in a long hall, filling in a slotted frame with sticks. Row upon row of children, some barely five years old, were involved in the work."

The description could come from an observer appalled at the working conditions endured by children in the 19th century in British mills and factories.

But the quote is from a report on the matchstick-making industry of modern day Sivakasi, in India.

Similar descriptions of children at work in hazardous conditions can be gathered from countries across the world. In Malaysia, children may work up to 17-hour days on rubber plantations, exposed to insect- and snakebites. In the United Republic of Tanzania, they pick coffee beans, inhaling pesticides. In Portugal, children as young as 12 are subject to heavy labour and the myriad dangers of the construction industry. In Morocco, they hunch at looms for long hours and little pay, knotting the strands of luxury carpets for export. In the United States, children are exploited in garment-industry sweatshops. In the Philippines, young boys dive in dangerous conditions to help set nets for deep-sea fishing. Statistical data on child labour is scarce, but our most reliable estimates indicate about 250 million child labourers (ages 10–14) in developing countries alone.

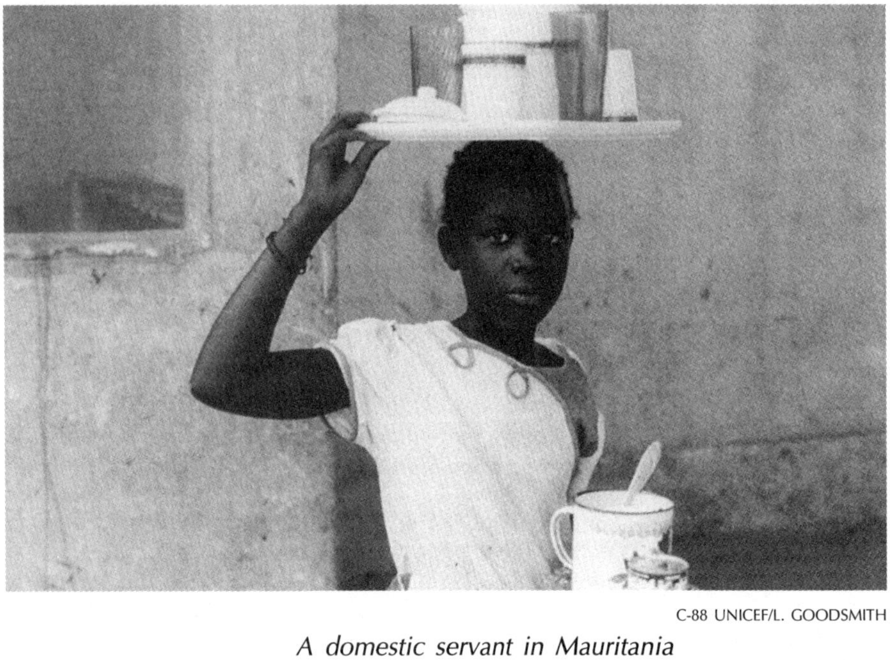

C-88 UNICEF/L. GOODSMITH

A domestic servant in Mauritania

The world should, indeed, have outgrown the many forms of abuse that labouring children endure. But it hasn't, although not for lack of effort. Child labour was one of the first and most important issues addressed by the international community, resulting in the 1919 Minimum Age Convention of the International Labour Organization.

Early efforts were hobbled, in part, because campaigners struggling to end child labour appealed to morality and ethics, values easily sidelined by the drive for profit and hard realities of commercial life.

From *The Rotarian,* September 1997, pp. 26-29. Adapted from *The State of the World's Children* by Carol Bellamy. © 1997 by Oxford University Press. Reprinted by permission.

86-147 UNICEF/YANN GAMBLIN

Herding cattle in Kenya

Child labourers were objects of charity and humanitarian concern, but they had no rights.

Today's world is somewhat different. Children have rights established in international laws, not least in the Convention on the Rights of the Child, which has now been ratified by 191 countries—all but the U.S. and Somalia—making it the most universally embraced human rights instrument in history. One provision—Article 32—obligates governments to protect children "from economic exploitation and from performing any work that is likely to be hazardous or to interfere with the child's education, and/or to be harmful to the child's health or physical, mental, spiritual, moral, or social development."

Children's exploitation in work also contravenes many more of the rights enshrined in the Convention, among them children's rights to parental care, to compulsory and free primary education, to the highest attainable standard of health, to social security, and to provisions for rest and recreation.

Looking at children's work through the lens of the Convention on the Rights of the Child offers not only new ways of understanding the problem of child labour, but also provides new impetus and direction to the movement against it.

Child labour is often a complex issue. Powerful forces sustain it, including many employers, vested interest groups, economists proposing that the market must be free at all costs, and traditionalists who believe that the low caste or class of certain children denudes them of rights.

The overriding consideration must always be the best interests of the child. It can never be in the best interests of a child to be exploited or to perform heavy and dangerous forms of work. No child should labour under hazardous and exploitative conditions, just as no child should die of causes that are preventable.

Work that endangers children's physical, mental, spiritual, moral, or social development must end. Hazardous child labour is a betrayal of every child's rights as a human being and is an offence against civilization.

Most children who work do not have the power of free choice. They do not choose between career options with varying advantages, drawbacks, and levels of pay. A fortunate minority have sufficient material means behind them to be pulled toward work as an attractive option offering them even more economic advantages.

But the vast majority are pushed into work that is often damaging to their development for three reasons: the exploitation of poverty, the absence of education, and the restrictions of tradition.

The exploitation of poverty

The most powerful force driving children into hazardous, debilitating labour is the exploitation of poverty. Where society is characterized by poverty and inequity, the incidence of child labour is likely to increase, as does the risk that it is exploitative.

For poor families, the small contribution of a child's income or assistance at home that allows the parents to work can make the difference between hunger and a bare sufficiency. Survey after survey makes this clear. A high proportion of child employees give all their wages to their parents. Children's work is considered essential to maintaining the economic level of the household.

If employers were not prepared to exploit children, there would be no child labour. The parents of child labourers are often unemployed or underemployed, desperate for secure employment and income. Yet it is not they but their children who are offered the jobs. Why? Because children can be paid less, of course. (In Latin America, for example, children ages 13 to 17 earn on average half the pay of a wage-earning adult with seven years of education.) Because children are more malleable, they will do what they are told without questioning authority. Because children are largely powerless before adults, they are less likely to organize against oppression and can be physically abused without striking back.

Put simply, children are employed because they are easier to exploit.

Exploitation of the poor and the powerless not only means that adults are denied jobs that could better have sustained their families. It not only means that children are required to work in arduous, dangerous conditions. It also means a life of unskilled work and ignorance not only for the child, but often for the children of generations to come. Any small, short-term financial gain for the family is at the cost of an incalculable long-term loss. Poverty begets child labour begets lack of education begets poverty.

A serious attack on poverty will reduce the number of children vulnerable to exploitation at work. Social safety nets are essential for the poor, as are access to credit and income-generating schemes, technology, education, and basic health services. Budgetary priorities need to be re-examined in this light.

Tackling the exploitation itself does not have to wait until some future day when world poverty has been brought to an end. Hazardous child labour provides the most powerful of arguments for equality and social justice. It can and must be abolished here and now.

The lack of relevant education

Cuts in social spending worldwide have hit education—the most important single factor in ending child labour—particularly hard.

In all regions, spending per student for higher education fell during the 1980s, and in Africa and Latin America, spending per pupil also fell for primary education.

A pilot survey, sponsored by the United Nations Educational, Scientific, and Cultural Organization (UNESCO) and the United Nations Children's Fund (UNICEF) and carried out in 1994 in 14 of the world's least-developed countries, reinforced concerns about the actual conditions of primary schools. In half of these countries, classrooms for the equivalent of first grade have sitting places for only four in 10 pupils. Half the pupils have no textbooks and half the classrooms have no chalkboards. Teachers commonly have to attempt

88-002 UNICEF/ASLAK AARBUS

Picking cotton in El Salvador

to handle huge classes—an average of 67 pupils per teacher in Bangladesh and nearly 90 per teacher in Equatorial Guinea. In 10 of the 14 countries, most children are taught in a language not spoken at home. And most homes, of course, have no books or magazines in any language.

Education everywhere is clearly underfunded, but the school system as it stands in most developing countries of the world is blighted by more than just a lack of resources. It is often too rigid and uninspiring in approach, promoting a curriculum that is irrelevant to and remote from children's lives.

Education has become part of the problem. It has to be reborn as part of the solution.

Traditional expectations

The economic forces that propel children into hazardous work may be the most powerful of all. But traditions and entrenched social patterns play a part, too.

In industrialized countries, it is now almost universally accepted that if children are to develop normally and healthily, they must not perform disabling work. In theory at least, education, play and leisure, friends, good health, and proper rest must all have an important place in their lives. This idea emerged only relatively recently. In the early decades of industrialization, work was thought to be the most effective way of teaching children about life and the world. Some residue of this notion remains in the widespread expectation that teenage children should take on casual jobs alongside school, both to gain an understanding of the way the world functions and to earn spending money of their own.

There is a darker side to the expectations about children's work. The harder and more hazardous the jobs become, the more they are likely to be considered traditionally the province of the poor and disadvantaged, the lower classes, and ethnic minorities. In India, for example, the view has been that some people are born to rule and to work with their minds while others, the vast majority, are born to work with their bodies. Many traditionalists have been unperturbed about lower-caste children failing to enroll in or dropping out of school. And if those children end up doing hazardous labour, it is likely to be seen as their lot in life.

Understanding all the various cultural factors that lead children into work is essential. But deference to tradition is often cited as a reason for not acting against intolerable forms of child labour. Children have an absolute, unnegotiable right to freedom from hazardous labour—a right now established in international law and accepted by every country that has ratified the Convention on the Rights of the Child. Respect for diverse cultures should not deflect us from using all the means at our disposal to make every society, every economy, every corporation, regard the exploitation of children as unthinkable.

Mobilizing society

Nongovernmental organizations, such as Rotary International, have a vital role to play both in raising levels of public concern and in protecting children. You can monitor the conditions in which children work and help launch the long, indispensable process of changing public attitudes.

R.I. President Glen W. Kinross has asked Rotarians this year to "strike out at the root causes of child abuse and abandonment and child labour. Children are our most precious treasure and the future belongs to them." And we know that today many Rotary clubs are working to improve the lives of children by striving to fight poverty and hunger, provide education, and prevent child abuse and exploitation. On behalf of the world's children, thank you, Rotarians, for your concern and actions.

As we step into the next millennium, hazardous child labour must be left behind, consigned to history as completely as those other forms of slavery that it so closely resembles.

• *Carol Bellamy is Executive Director of the United Nations Children's Fund (UNICEF).*

Unit 7

Unit Selections

Key Points to Consider

- Comment on the idea that it is naive to speak of international politics and economics in terms of ethics. What role can governments, international organizations, and the individual play in making the world a more ethical place?
- The consumption of resources is the foundation of the modern economic system. What are the values underlying this economic system, and how resistant to change are they?
- How easily are the values of democracy transferred to new settings such as Russia?
- What are the characteristics of leadership?
- In addition to the ideas presented here, what other new ideas are being expressed, and how likely are they to be widely accepted?
- How do the contemporary arts reflect changes in the way humanity views itself?
- How will the world be different in the year 2030? What factors will contribute to these changes? What does your analysis reveal about your own value system?

DUSHKIN ONLINE Links

www.dushkin.com/online/

31. **Human Rights Web**
    http://www.hrweb.org
32. **InterAction**
    http://www.interaction.org

These sites are annotated on pages 4 and 5.

Values and Visions

The final unit of this book considers how humanity's view of itself is changing. Values, like all other elements discussed in this anthology, are dynamic. Visionary people with new ideas can have a profound impact on how a society deals with problems and adapts to changing circumstances. Therefore, to understand the forces at work in the world today, values, visions, and new ideas in many ways are every bit as important as new technology or changing demographics.

Novelist Herman Wouk, in his book *War and Remembrance*, observed that many institutions have been so embedded in the social fabric of their time that people assumed that they were part of human nature. Slavery and human sacrifice are two examples. However, forward-thinking people opposed these institutions. Many knew that they would never see the abolition of these social systems within their own lifetimes, but they pressed on in the hope that someday these institutions would be eliminated.

Wouk believes the same is true for warfare. He states, "Either we are finished with war or war will finish us." Aspects of society such as warfare, slavery, racism, and the secondary status of women are creations of the human mind; history suggests that they can be changed by the human spirit.

The articles of this unit have been selected with the previous six units in mind. Each explores some aspect of world affairs from the perspective of values and alternative visions of the future.

New ideas are critical to meeting these challenges. The examination of well-known issues from new perspectives can yield new insights into old problems. It was feminist Susan B. Anthony who once remarked that "social change is never made by the masses, only by educated minorities." The redefinition of human values (which, by necessity, will accompany the successful confrontation of important global issues) is a task that few people take on willingly. Nevertheless, in order to deal with the dangers of nuclear war, overpopulation, and environmental degradation, educated people must take a broad view of history. This is going to require considerable effort and much personal sacrifice.

When people first begin to consider the magnitude of contemporary global problems, many often become disheartened and depressed. Some ask: What can I do? What does it matter? Who cares? There are no easy answers to these questions, but people need only look around to see good news as well as bad. How individuals react to the world is not solely a function of so-called objective reality but a reflection of themselves. Different people react differently to the same world.

As stated at the beginning of the first unit, the study of global issues is the study of people. The study of people, furthermore, is the study of both values and the level of commitment supporting these values and beliefs.

It is one of the goals of this book to stimulate you, the reader, to react intellectually and emotionally to the discussion and description of various global challenges. In the process of studying these issues, hopefully you have had some new insights into your own values and commitments. In the presentation of the allegory of the balloon, the third color added represented the "meta" component, all of those qualities that make human beings unique. It is these qualities that have brought us to this "special moment in time," and it will be these same qualities that will determine the outcome of our historically unique challenges.

Are Human Rights Universal?

Shashi Tharoor

The growing consensus in the West that human rights are universal has been fiercely opposed by critics in other parts of the world. At the very least, the idea may well pose as many questions as it answers. Beyond the more general, philosophical question of whether anything in our pluri-cultural multipolar world is truly universal, the issue of whether human rights is an essentially Western concept—ignoring the very different cultural, economic, and political realities of the other parts of the world—cannot simply be dismissed. Can the values of the consumer society be applied to societies that have nothing to consume? Isn't talking about universal rights rather like saying that the rich and the poor both have the same right to fly first class and to sleep under bridges? Don't human rights as laid out in the international convenants ignore the traditions, the religions, and the socio-cultural patterns of what used to be called the Third World? And at the risk of sounding frivolous, when you stop a man in traditional dress from beating his wife, are you upholding her human rights or violating his?

This is anything but an abstract debate. To the contrary, our is an era in which wars have been waged in the name of human rights, and in which many of the major developments in international law have presupposed the universality of the concept. By the same token, the perception that human rights as a universal discourse is increasingly serving as a flag of convenience for other, far more questionable political agendas, accounts for the degree to which the very ideas of human rights is being questioned and resisted by both intellectuals and states. These objections need to be taken very seriously.

The philosophical objection asserts essentially that nothing can be universal; that all rights and values are defined and limited by cultural perceptions. If there is no universal culture, there can be no universal human rights. In fact, some philosophers have objected that the concept of human rights is founded on an anthropocentric, that is, a human-centered, view of the world, predicated upon an individualistic view of man as an autonomous being whose greatest need is to be free from interference by the state—free to enjoy what one Western writer summed up as the "right to private property, the right to freedom of contract, and the right to be left alone." But this view would seem to clash with the communitarian one propounded by other ideologies and cultures where society is concieved of as far more than the sum of its individual members.

Who Defines Human Rights?

Implicit in this is a series of broad, culturally grounded objections. Historically, in a number of non-Western cultures, individuals are not accorded rights in the same way as they are in the West. Critics of the universal idea of human rights contend that in the Confucian or Vedic traditions, duties are considered more important than rights, while in Africa it is the community that protects and nurtures the individual. One African writer summed up the African philosophy of existence as: "I

 From the *World Policy Journal,* Winter 1999/2000, pp. 1-6.

am because we are, and because we are therefore I am." Some Africans have argued that they have a complex structure of communal entitlements and obligations grouped around what one might call four "r's": not "rights," but respect, restraint, responsibility, and reciprocity. They argue that in most African societies group rights have always taken precedence over individual rights, and political decisions have been made through group consensus, not through individual assertions of rights.

These cultural differences, to the extent that they are real, have practical implications. Many in developing countries argue that some human rights are simply not relevant to their societies—the right, for instance, to political pluralism, the right to paid vacations (always good for a laugh in the sweatshops of the Third World), and, inevitably, the rights of women. It is not just that some societies claim they are simply unable to provide certain rights to all their citizens, but rather that they see the "universal" conception of human rights as little more than an attempt to impose alien Western values on them.

Rights promoting the equality of the sexes are a contentious case in point. How, critics demand, can women's rights be universal in the face of widespread divergences of cultural practice, when in many societies, for example, marriage is not seen as a contract between two individuals but as an alliance between lineages, and when the permissible behavior of womenfolk is central to the society's perception of its honor?

And, inseparable from the issues of tradition, is the issue of religion. For religious critics of the universalist definition of human rights, nothing can be universal that is not founded on transcendent values, symbolized by God, and sanctioned by the guardians of the various faiths. They point out that the cardinal document of the contemporary human rights movement, the Universal Declaration of Human Rights, can claim no such heritage.

Recently, the fiftieth anniversary of the Universal Declaration was celebrated with much fanfare. But critics from countries that were still colonies in 1948 suggest that its provisions reflect the ethnocentric bias of the time. They go on to argue that the concept of human rights is really a cover for Western interventionism in the affairs of the developing world, and that "human rights" are merely an instrument of Western political neocolonialism. One critic in the 1970s wrote of his fear that "Human Rights might turn out to be a Trojan horse, surreptitiously introduced into other civilizations, which will then be obliged to accept those ways of living, thinking and feeling for which Human Rights is the proper solution in cases of conflict."

In practice, this argument tends to be as much about development as about civilizational integrity. Critics argue that the developing countries ofren cannot afford human rights, since the tasks of nation building, economic development, and the consolidation of the state structure to these ends are still unfinished. Authoritarianism, they argue, is more efficient in promoting development and economic growth. This is the premise behind the so-called Asian values case, which attributes the economic growth of Southeast Asia to the Confucian virtues of obedience, order, and respect for authority. The argument is even a little more subtle than that, because the suspension or limiting of human rights is also portrayed as the sacrifice of the few for the benefit of the many. The human rights concept is understood, applied, and argued over only, critics say, by a small Westernized minority in developing countries. Universality in these circumstances would be the universality of the privileged. Human rights is for the few who have the concerns of Westerners; it does not extend to the lowest rungs of the ladder.

The Case for the Defense

That is the case for the prosecution—the indictment of the assumption of the universality of human rights. There is, of course, a case for the defense. The philosophical objection is, perhaps surprisingly, the easiest to counter. After all, concepts of justice and law, the legitimacy of government, the dignity of the individual, protection from oppressive or arbitrary rule, and participation in the affairs of the community are found in every society on the face of this earth. Far from being difficult to identify, the number of philosophical common denominators between different cultures and political traditions makes universalism anything but a distortion of reality.

Historically, a number of developing countries—notably India, China, Chile, Cuba, Lebanon, and Panama—played an active and highly influential part in the drafting of the Universal Declaration of Human Rights. In the case of the human rights covenants, in the 1 1960s the developing world actually made the decisive contribution; it was the "new majority" of the Third World states emerging from colonialism—particularly Ghana and Nigeria—that broke the logjam, ending the East–West stalemate that had held up adoption of the covenants for nearly two decades. The principles of human rights have been widely adopted, imitated, and ratified by developing countries; the fact that therefore they were devised by less than a third of the states now in existence is really irrelevant.

In reality, many of the current objections to the universality of human rights reflect a false opposition between the primacy of the individual and the paramountcy of society. Many of the civil and political rights protect groups, while many of the social and economic rights protect individuals. Thus, crucially, the two sets of rights, and the two covenants that codify them, are like Siamese twins—inseparable and interdependent, sustaining and nourishing each other.

Still, while the conflict between group rights and individual rights may not be inevitable, it would be native to pretend that conflict would never occur. But while groups may collectively exercise rights, the individuals within them should also be permitted the exercise of their rights within the group, rights that the group may not infringe upon.

A Hidden Agenda?

Those who champion the view that human rights are not universal frequently insist that their adversaries have hidden agendas. In fairness, the same accusation can be leveled against at least some of those who cite culture as a defense against human rights. Authoritarian regimes who appeal to their own cultural traditions are cheerfully willing to crush culture domestically when it suits them to do so. Also, the "traditional culture" that is sometimes advanced to justify the nonobservance of human rights, including in Africa, in practice no longer exists in a pure form at the national level anywhere. The societies of developing countries have not remained in a pristine, pre-Western state; all have been subject to change and distortion by external influence, both as a result of colonialism in many cases and through participation in modern interstate relations.

You cannot impose the model of a "modern" nation-state cutting across tribal boundaries and conventions on your country, appoint a president and an ambassador to the United Nations, and then argue that tribal traditions should be applied to judge the human rights conduct of the resulting modern state.

In any case, there should be nothing sacrosanct about culture. Culture is constantly evolving in any living society, responding to both internal and external stimuli, and there is much in every culture that societies quite naturally outgrow and reject. Am I, as an Indian, obliged to defend, in the name of my culture, the practice of suttee, which was banned 160 years ago, of obliging widows to immolate themselves on their husbands' funeral pyres? The fact that slavery was acceptable across the world for at least 2,000 years does not make it acceptable to us now; the deep historical roots of anti-Semitism in European culture cannot justify discrimination against Jews today.

The problem with the culture argument is that it subsumes all members of a society under a cultural framework that may in fact be inimical to them. It is one thing to advocate the cultural argument with an escape clause—that is, one that does not seek to coerce the dissenters but permits individuals to opt out and to assert their individual rights. Those who freely choose to live by and to be treated according to their traditional cultures are welcome to do so, provided others who wish to be free are not oppressed in the name of a culture they prefer to disavow.

A controversial but pertinent example of an approach that seeks to strengthen both cultural integrity and individual freedom is India's Muslim Women (Protection of Rights upon Divorce) Act. This piece of legislation was enacted following the famous Shah Banu case, in which the Supreme Court upheld the right of a divorced Muslim woman to alimony, prompting howls of outrage from Muslim traditionalists who claimed this violated their religious beliefs that divorced women were only entitled to the return of the bride price paid upon marriage. The Indian parliament then passed a law to override the court's judgment, under which Muslim women married under Muslim law would be obliged to accept the return of the bride price as the only payment of alimony, but that the official Muslim charity, the Waqf Board, would assist them.

Many Muslim women and feminists were outraged by this. But the interesting point is that if a Muslim woman does not want to be subject to the provisions of the act, she can marry under the civil code; if she marries under Muslim personal law, she will be subject to its provisions. That may be the kind of balance that can be struck between the rights of Muslims as a group to protect their traditional practices and the right of a particular Muslim woman, who may not choose to be subject to that particular law, to exempt herself from it.

It needs to be emphasized that the objections that are voiced to specific (allegedly Western) rights very frequently involve the rights of women, and are usually vociferously argued by men. Even conceding, for argument's sake, that child marriage, widow inheritance, female circumcision, and the like are not found reprehensible by many societies, how do the victims of these practices feel about them? How many teenage girls who have had their genitalia mutilated would have agreed to undergo circumcision if they had the human right to refuse to permit it? For me, the standard is simple: where coercion exists, rights are violated, and these violations must be condemned whatever the traditional justification. So it is not culture that is the test, it is coercion.

Not with Faith, But with the Faithful

Nor can religion be deployed to sanction the status quo. Every religion seeks to embody certain verities that are applicable to all mankind—justice, truth, mercy, compassion—though the details of their interpretation vary according to the historical and geographical context in which the religion originated. As U.N. secretary general Kofi Annan has often said, the problem is usually not with the faith, but with the faithful. In any case, freedom is not a value found only in Western faiths: it is highly prized in Buddhism and in different aspects of Hinduism and Islam.

If religion cannot be fairly used to sanction oppression, it should be equally obvious that authoritarianism promotes repression, not development. Development is about change, but repression prevents change. The Nobel Prize–winning economist Amartya Sen has pointed out in a number of interesting pieces that there is now a generally agreed-upon list of policies that are helpful to economic development—"openness to competition, the use of international markets, a high level of literacy and school education, successful land reforms, and public provision of incentives for investment, export and industrialization"—none of which requires authoritarianism; none is incompatible with human rights. Indeed, it is the availability of political and civil rights that gives people the opportunity to draw attention to their needs and to demand action from the government. Sen's work has established, for example, that no substantial famine has ever occurred in any independent and democratic country with a relatively free press. That is striking; though there may be cases where authoritarian societies have had success in achieving economic growth, a country like Botswana, an exemplar of democracy in Africa, has grown faster than most authoritarian states.

In any case, when one hears of the unsuitability or inapplicability or ethnocentrism of human rights, it is important to ask what the unstated assumptions of this view really are. What exactly are these human rights that it is so unreasonable to promote? If one picks up the more contentious covenant—the one on civil and political rights— and looks through the list, what can one find that someone in a developing country can easily do without? Not the right to life, one trusts. Freedom from torture? The right not to be enslaved, not to be physically assaulted, not to be arbitrarily arrested, imprisoned, executed? No one actually advocates in so many words the abridgement of any of these rights. As Kofi Annan asked at a speech in Tehran University in 1997: "When have you heard a free voice demand an end to freedom? Where have you heard a slave argue for slavery? When have you heard a victim of torture endorse the ways of the torturer? Where have you heard the tolerant cry out for intolerance?"

Tolerance and mercy have always, and in all cultures, been ideals of government rule and human behavior. If we do not unequivocally assert the universality of the rights that oppressive governments abuse, and if we admit that these rights can be diluted and changed, ultimately we risk giving oppressive governments an intellectual justification for the morally indefensible. Objections to the applicability of international human rights standards have all too frequently been voiced by authoritarian rulers and power elites to rationalize their violations of human rights—violations that serve primarily, if not solely, to sustain them in power. Just as the Devil can quote scripture for his purpose, Third World communitarianism can be the slogan of a deracinated tyrant trained, as in the case of Pol Pot, at the Sorbonne. The authentic voices of the Third World know how to cry out in pain. It is time to heed them.

The "Right to Development"

At the same time, particularly in a world in which market capitalism is triumphant, it is important to stress that the right to development is also a universal human right. The very concept of development evolved in tune with the concept of human rights; decolonization and self-determination advanced side by side with a consciousness of the need to improve the standards of living of subject peoples. The idea that human rights could be ensured merely by the state not interfering with individual freedom cannot survive confrontation with a billion hungry, deprived, illiterate, and jobless human beings around the globe. Human rights, in one memorable phrase, start with breakfast.

For the sake of the deprived, the notion of human rights has to be a positive, active one: not just protection from the state but also the protection of the state, to permit these human beings to fulfill the basic aspirations of growth and development that are frustrated by poverty and scarce resources. We have to accept that social deprivation and economic exploitation are just as evil as political oppression or racial persecution. This calls for a more profound approach to both human rights and to development. Without development, human rights could not be truly universal, since universality must be predicated upon the most underprivileged in developing countries achieving empowerment. We can not exclude the poorest of the poor from the universality of the rich.

After all, do some societies have the right to deny human beings the opportunity to fulfill their aspirations for growth and fulfillment legally and in freedom, while other societies organize themselves in such a way as to permit and encourage human beings freely to fulfill the same needs? On what basis can we accept a double standard that says that an Australian's need to develop his own potential is a right, while an Angolan's or an Albanian's is a luxury?

Universality, Not Uniformity

But it is essential to recognize that universality does not presuppose uniformity. To assert the universality of human rights is not to suggest that our views of human rights transcend all possible philosophical, cultural, or religious differences or represent a magical aggregation of the world's ethical and philosophical systems. Rather, it is enough that they do not fundamentally contradict the ideals and aspirations of any society, and that they reflect our common universal humanity, from which no human being must be excluded.

Most basically, human rights derive from the mere fact of being human; they are not the gift of a particular government or legal code. But the standards being proclaimed internationally can become reality only when applied by countries within their own legal systems. The challenge is to work towards the "indigenization" of human rights, and their assertion within each country's traditions and history. If different approaches are welcomed within the established framework—if, in other words, eclecticism can be encouraged as part of the consensus and not be seen as a threat to it—this flexibility can guarantee universality, enrich the intellectual and philosophical debate, and so complement, rather than undermine, the concept of worldwide human rights. Paradoxical as it may seem, it is a universal idea of human rights that can in fact help make the world safe for diversity.

Note

This article was adapted from the first Mahbub-ul-Haq Memorial Lecture, South Asia Forum, October 1998.

Shashi Tharoor is Director of Communications and Special Projects in the Office of the Secretary General of the United Nations. The views expressed here are the author's own and do not necessarily reflect the positions of the United Nations.

The Grameen Bank

A small experiment begun in Bangladesh has turned into a major new concept in eradicating poverty

by Muhammad Yunus

Over many years, Amena Begum had become resigned to a life of grinding poverty and physical abuse. Her family was among the poorest in Bangladesh—one of thousands that own virtually nothing, surviving as squatters on desolate tracts of land and earning a living as day laborers.

In early 1993 Amena convinced her husband to move to the village of Kholshi, 112 kilometers (70 miles) west of Dhaka. She hoped the presence of a nearby relative would reduce the number and severity of the beatings that her husband inflicted on her. The abuse continued, however—until she joined the Grameen Bank. Oloka Ghosh, a neighbor, told Amena that Grameen was forming a new group in Kholshi and encouraged her to join. Amena doubted that anyone would want her in their group. But Oloka persisted with words of encouragement. "We're all poor—or at least we all were when we joined. I'll stick up for you because I know you'll succeed in business.

Amena's group joined a Grameen Bank Center in April 1993. When she received her first loan of $60, she used it to start her own business raising chickens and ducks. When she repaid her initial loan and began preparing a proposal for a second loan of $110, her friend Oloka gave her some sage advice: "Tell your husband that Grameen does not allow borrowers who are beaten by their spouses to remain members and take loans." From that day on, Amena suffered significantly less physical abuse at the hands of her husband. Today her business continues to grow and provide for the basic needs of her family.

Unlike Amena, the majority of people in Asia, Africa and Latin America have few opportunities to escape from poverty. According to the World Bank, more than 1.3 billion people live on less than a dollar a day. Poverty has not been eradicated in the 50 years since the Universal Declaration on Human Rights asserted that each individual has a right to:

> A standard of living adequate for the health and well-being of himself and of his family, including food, clothing, housing and medical care and necessary social services, and the right to security in the event of unemployment, sickness, disability, widowhood, old age or other lack of livelihood in circumstances beyond his control.

Will poverty still be with us 50 years from now? My own experience suggests that it need not.

After completing my Ph.D. at Vanderbilt University, I returned to Bangladesh in 1972 to teach economics at Chittagong University. I was excited about the possibilities for my newly independent country. But in 1974 we were hit with a terrible famine. Faced with death and starvation outside my classroom, I began to question the very economic theories I was teaching. I started feeling there was a great distance between the actual life of poor and hungry people and the abstract world of economic theory.

I wanted to learn the real economics of the poor. Because Chittagong University is located in a rural area, it was easy for me to visit impoverished households in the neighboring village of Jobra. Over the course of many visits, I learned all about the lives of my struggling neighbors and much about economics that is never taught in the classroom. I was dismayed to see how the indigent in Jobra suffered because they could not come up with small amounts of working capital. Frequently they needed less than a dollar a person but could get that money only on extremely unfair terms. In most cases, people were required to sell their goods to moneylenders at prices fixed by the latter.

This daily tragedy moved me to action. With the help of my graduate students, I made a list of those who needed small amounts of money. We came up with 42 people. The total amount they needed was $27.

I was shocked. It was nothing for us to talk about millions of dollars in the classroom, but we were ignoring the minuscule capital needs of 42 hardworking, skilled people next door. From my own pocket, I lent $27 to those on my list.

Still, there were many others who could benefit from access to credit. I decided to approach the university's bank and try to persuade it to lend to the local poor. The branch manager said, however, that the bank could not give loans to the needy: the villagers, he argued, were not creditworthy.

I could not convince him otherwise. I met with higher officials in the banking hierarchy with similar results. Finally, I offered myself as a guarantor to get the loans.

In 1976 I took a loan from the local bank and distributed the money to poverty-stricken individuals in Jobra. Without exception, the villagers paid back their loans. Confronted with this evidence, the bank still refused to grant them loans directly. And so I tried my experiment in another village, and again it was successful. I kept expanding my work, from two to five, to 20, to 50, to 100 villages, all to convince the bankers that they should be lending to the poor. Although each time we expanded to a new village the loans were repaid, the bankers still would not change their view of those who had no collateral.

Because I could not change the banks, I decided to create a separate bank for the impoverished. After a great deal of work and negotiation with the government, the Grameen Bank ("village bank" in Bengali) was established in 1983.

From the outset, Grameen was built on principles that ran counter to the conventional wisdom of banking. We sought out the very poorest borrowers, and we required no collateral. The bank rests on the strength of its borrowers. They are required to join the bank in self-formed groups of five. The group members provide one another with peer support in the form of mutual assistance and advice. In addition, they allow for peer discipline by evaluating business viability and ensuring repayment. If one member fails to repay a loan, all members risk having their line of credit suspended or reduced.

The Power of Peers

Typically a new group submits loan proposals from two members, each requiring between $25 and $100. After these two borrowers successfully repay their first five weekly installments, the next two group members become eligible to apply for their own loans. Once they make five repayments, the final member of the group may apply. After 50 installments have been repaid, a borrower pays her interest, which is slightly above the commercial rate. The borrower is now eligible to apply for a larger loan.

The bank does not wait for borrowers to come to the bank; it brings the bank to the

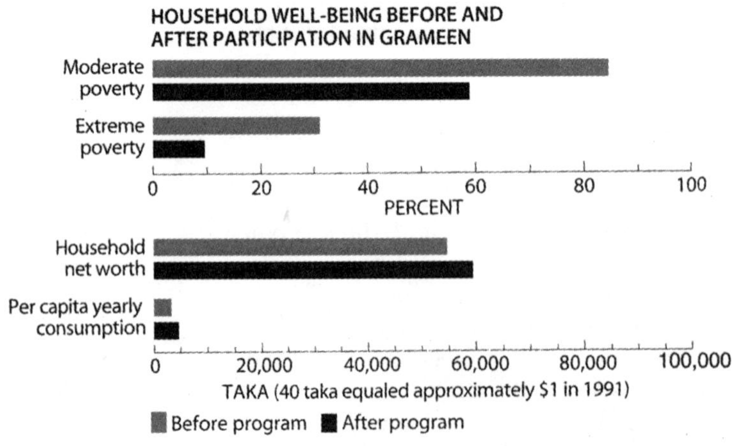

people. Loan payments are made in weekiy meetings consisting of six to eight groups, held in the villages where the members live. Grameen staff attend these meetings and often visit individual borrowers' homes to see how the business—whether it be raising goats or growing vegetables or hawking utensils—is faring.

Today Grameen is established in nearly 39,000 villages in Bangladesh. It lends to approximately 2.4 million borrowers, 94 percent of whom are women. Grameen reached its first $1 billion in cumulative loans in March 1995, 18 years after it began in Jobra. It took only two more years to reach the $2-billion mark. After 20 years of work, Grameen's average loan size now stands at $180. The repayment rate hovers between 96 and 100 percent.

A year after joining the bank, a borrower becomes eligible to buy shares in Grameen. At present, 94 percent of the bank is owned by its borrowers. Of the 13 members of the board of directors, nine are elected from among the borrowers; the rest are government representatives, academics, myself and others.

A study carried out by Sydney R. Schuler of John Snow, Inc., a private research group, and her colleagues concluded that a Grameen loan empowers a woman by increasing her economic security and status within the family. In 1998 a study by Shahidur R. Khandker an economist with the World Bank, and others noted that participation in Grameen also has a significant positive effect on the schooling and nutrition of children—as long as women rather than men receive the loans. (Such a tendency was clear from the early days of the bank and is one reason Grameen lends primarily to women: all too often men spend the money on themselves.) In particular, a 10 percent increase in borrowing by women resulted in the arm circumference of girls—a common measure of nutritional status—expanding by 6 percent. And for every 10 percent increase in borrowing by a member the likelihood of her daughter being enrolled in school increased by almost 20 percent.

Not all the benefits derive directly from credit. When joining the bank, each member is required to memorize a list of 16 resolutions. These include commonsense items about hygiene and health—drinking clean water, growing and eating vegetables, digging and using a pit latrine, and so on—as well as social dictums such as refusing dowry and managing family size. The women usually recite the entire list at the weekly branch meetings, but the resolutions are not otherwise enforced.

Even so, Schuler's study revealed that women use contraception more consistently after joining the bank. Curiously, it appears that women who live in villages where Grameen operates, but who are not themselves members, are also more likely to adopt contraception. The population growth rate in Bangladesh has fallen dramatically in the past two decades, and it is possible that Grameen's influence has accelerated the trend.

In a typical year 5 percent of Grameen borrowers—representing 125,000 families—rise above the poverty level. Khandker concluded that among these borrowers extreme poverty (defined by consumption of less than 80 percent of the minimum requirement stipulated by the Food and Agriculture Organization of the United Nations) declined by more than 70 percent within five years of their joining the bank.

To be sure, making a microcredit program work well—so that it meets its social goals and also stays economically sound—is not easy. We try to ensure that the bank serves the poorest: only those living at less than half the poverty line are eligible for loans. Mixing poor participants with those who are better off would lead to the latter dominating the groups. In practice, however, it can be hard to include the most abjectly poor, who might be excluded by their peers when the borrowing groups are being formed. And despite our best efforts, it does sometimes happen that the

LISA BURNETT

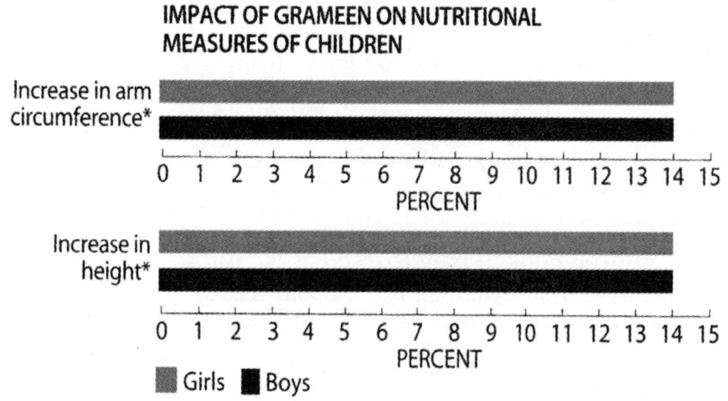

Bars reflect changes accompanying a 10 percent increase in credit to women.

money lent to a woman is appropriated by her husband.

Given its size and spread, the Grameen Bank has had to evolve ways to monitor the performance of its branch managers and to guarantee honesty and transparency. A manager is not allowed to remain in the same village for long, for fear that he may develop local connections that impede his performance. Moreover, a manager is never posted near his home. Because of such constraints—and because managers are required to have university degrees—very few of them are women. As a result, Grameen has been accused of adhering to a paternalistic pattern. We are sensitive to this argument and are trying to change the situation by finding new ways to recruit women.

Grameen has also often been criticized for being not a charity but a profit-making institution. Yet that status, I am convinced, is essential to its viability. Last year a disastrous flood washed away the homes, cattle and most other belongings of hundreds of thousands of Grameen borrowers. We did not forgive the loans, although we did issue new ones, and give borrowers more time to repay. Writing off loans would banish accountability, a key factor in the bank's success.

Liberating Their Potential

The Grameen model has now been applied in 40 countries. The first replication, begun in Malaysia in 1986, currently serves 40,000 poor families; their repayment rate has consistently stayed near 100 percent. In Bolivia, microcredit has allowed women to make the transition from "food for work" programs to managing their own businesses. Within two years the majority of women in the program acquire enough credit history and financial skills to qualify for loans from mainstream banks. Similar success stories are coming in from programs in poor countries everywhere. These banks all target the most impoverished, lend to groups and usually lend primarily to women.

The Grameen Bank in Bangladesh has been economically self-sufficient since 1995. Similar institutions in other countries are slowly making their way toward self-reliance. A few small programs are also running in the U.S., such as in innercity Chicago. Unfortunately, because labor costs are much higher in the U.S. than in developing countries—which often have a large pool of educated unemployed who can serve as managers or accountants—the operations are more expensive there. As a result, the U.S. programs have had to be heavily subsidized.

In all, about 22 million poor people around the world now have access to small loans. Microcredit Summit, an institution based in Washington, D.C., serves as a resource center for the various regional microcredit institutions and organizes yearly conferences. Last year the attendees pledged to provide 100 million of the world's poorest families, especially their women, with credit by the year 2005. The campaign has grown to include more than 2,000 organizations, ranging from banks to religious institutions to nongovernmental organizations to United Nations agencies.

The standard scenario for economic development in a poor country calls for industrialization via investment. In this "topdown" view, creating opportunities for employment is the only way to end poverty. But for much of the developing world, increased employment exacerbates migration from the countryside to the cities and creates low-paying jobs in miserable conditions. I firmly believe that, instead, the eradication of poverty starts with people being able to control their own fates. It is not by creating jobs that we will save the poor but rather by providing them with the opportunity to realize their potential. Time and time again I have seen that the poor are poor not because they are lazy or untrained or illiterate but because they cannot keep the genuine returns on their labor.

Self-employment may be the only solution for such people, whom our economies refuse to hire and our taxpayers will not support. Microcredit views each person as a potential entrepreneur and turns on the tiny economic engines of a rejected portion of society. Once a large number of these engines start working, the stage can be set for enormous socioeconomic change.

Applying this philosophy, Grameen has established more than a dozen enterprises, often in partnership with other entrepreneurs. By assisting microborrowers and microsavers to take ownership of large enterprises and even infrastructure companies, we are trying to speed the process of overcoming poverty. Grameen Phone, for instance, is a cellular telephone company that aims to serve urban and rural Bangladesh. After a pilot study in 65 villages, Grameen Phone has taken a loan to extend its activities to all villages in which the bank is active. Some 50,000 women, many of whom have never seen a telephone or even an electric light, will become the providers of telephone service in their villages. Ultimately, they will become the owners of the company itself by buying its shares. Our latest innovation, Grameen Investments, allows U.S. individuals to support companies such as Grameen Phone while receiving interest on their investment. This is a significant step toward putting commercial funds to work to end poverty.

I believe it is the responsibility of any civilized society to ensure human dignity to all members and to offer each individual the best opportunity to reveal his or her creativity. Let us remember that poverty is not created by the poor but by the institutions and policies that we, the better off, have established. We can solve the problem not by means of the old concepts but by adopting radically new ones.

The Author

MUHAMMAD YUNUS, the founder and managing director of the Grameen Bank, was born in Bangladesh. He obtained a Ph.D. in economics from Vanderbilt University in 1970 and soon after returned to his home country to teach at Chittagong University. In 1976 he started the Grameen project, to which he has devoted all his time for the past decade. He has served on many advisory committees: for the government of Bangladesh, the United Nations, and other bodies concerned with poverty, women and health. He has received the World Food Prize, the Ramon Magsaysay Award, the Humanitarian Award, the Man for Peace Award and numerous other distinctions as well as six honorary degrees.

Further Reading

GRAMEEN BANK: PERFORMANCE AND SUSTAINABILITY. Shahidur R. Khandker, Baqui Khalily and Zahed Khan. World Bank Discussion Papers, No. 306. ISBN 0-8213-3463-8. World Bank, 1995.

GIVE US CREDIT. Alex Counts. Times Books (Random House), 1996.

FIGHTING POVERTY WITH MICROCREDIT: EXPERIENCE IN BANGLADESH. Shabidur R. Khandker. Oxford University Press, 1998.

Grameen Bank site is available at www.grameenfoundation.org on the World Wide Web.

Why Environmental Ethics Matters to International Relations

"Environmental ethics [should] not be seen as an add-on to be approached after the important issues of security and economics have been settled. Instead, we [should] recognize that all our important social choices are inherently about the 'natural' world we create."

JOHN BARKDULL

JOHN BARKDULL *is an associate professor of political science at Texas Tech University. His research interests include international political theory, international ethics, and environmental policy.*

What challenge does environmental ethics pose for international relations? International relations is usually understood as the realm of power politics, a world in which military might and the quest to survive dominate. In this world, moral concern for other human beings, much less nature, is limited or entirely lacking. Environmental ethics—a set of principles to guide human interaction with the earth—calls on us to extend moral consideration beyond humans to other living things and to natural "wholes" such as bioregions and ecosystems. Is it possible to introduce environmental ethics' far-reaching moral claims into the competitive, militarized, economically unequal world political system?

Although explorations in environmental ethics now have a long resumé, the dialogue over the human debt to the natural environment has proceeded largely without reference to international politics, to international relations theory, or even to the literature on international ethics. Practical politics is thus often removed from consideration. And scholars of international relations have barely considered the relationship between their studies and environmental ethics.

Bringing the two fields into the same conversation is possible. International political theory has profound implications for understanding how humans ought to relate to the environment. Realism and liberal institutionalism (the mainstream of international relations theory), by suggesting what political, economic, and social goals are desirable, also imply what environmental values should prevail. They indicate what kind of world humans should or can create and thus tell us how we should relate to the environment. The question then is not whether environmental ethics should matter in world politics, but in which way: which environmental ethic does in fact matter, which should, and what obstacles prevent needed changes in political practices from being made?

WHICH ENVIRONMENTAL ETHICS?

Environmental ethics can be anthropocentric, biocentric, or ecocentric. Anthropocentric ethics is about what humans owe each other. It evaluates environmental policies with regard to how they affect human well-being. For example, exploitation of natural resources such as minerals can destroy forests on which indigenous peoples depend. Moral evaluation of the environmental destruction proceeds in terms of the rights, happiness, or just treatment of all human parties, including the displaced tribes and the consumers who benefit from the minerals. Anthropocentric environmental ethics generally calls for more environmental protection than we now undertake; current unsustainable resource-use patterns and conversion of land to agricultural or urban uses mean that existing practices do more harm to humans than good, especially when future generations are considered. Still, many observers find anthropocentric environmental ethics unsatisfactory because it appears not to recognize other creatures' inherent right to share the planet and considers only their value to human beings.

Biocentric environmental ethics seeks to correct this deficiency by according moral standing to non-human creatures. Humans have moral worth but only as one species among many living things that also have moral standing. The grizzly bear's right to sufficient domain for sustaining life and reproduction has as much moral weight (if not more) as a logging company's desire to make a profit in that domain. Even if maintaining the grizzly bear's habitat means some humans must live in somewhat less spacious homes, the loss of human utility by no means cancels the animal's moral claim to the forest. In short, animals have rights. Which animals have moral standing and whether plants do as well remain matters of dispute among biocentric theorists. Nonetheless, biocentric theory expands the moral realm beyond humans and hence implies greater moral obligations than anthropocentric ethics.[1]

Ecocentric theory tackles a problem at the heart of biocentric theory. In reality, ecosystems work on the principle of eat and be eaten. We may accord the grizzly "rights" but the bear survives by consuming salmon, rodents, and

The gap between what environmental ethics calls for and what international political theory postulates may find its bridge in the land ethic.

so forth, thus violating other living creatures' right to life. Humans are simply part of a complex food chain or web of life. Given this, ecocentric theory asserts that moral status should attach to ecological wholes, from bioregions to the planetary ecosystem (sometimes called Gaia). Ecocentric theorists are not concerned about particular animals or even species, but with the entire evolutionary process. Evolution involves the "land" broadly understood to include all its organic and nonorganic components. To disrupt or destroy the evolutionary process, reducing the diversity of life and the stability and beauty of the natural system, is unethical. As Aldo Leopold, the environmental philosopher who first developed the land ethic, put it in his 1949 book, *A Sand County Almanac and Sketches Here and There,* "A thing is right when it tends to preserve the integrity, stability, and beauty of the biotic community. It is wrong when it tends otherwise." The emphasis here is on the word "community."

Each of these approaches suggests the need for change in the practice of international politics. Anthropocentric environmental ethics implies the least extensive reform, although these still could be far-reaching, especially with regard to current economic arrangements. Developed industrial economies rely heavily on the global commons for "free" natural services, such as areas to dispose of pollutants. For example, reliance on fossil fuels leads to increases in CO_2 in the atmosphere, and in turn to global warming. Developing countries undergoing industrialization will draw on the atmosphere's capacity to absorb greenhouse gases. The added load, along with already high levels of emissions from developed countries, could push the environment beyond a critical threshold, setting off catastrophic climate changes because of global warming. These climatic upheavals could lead to crop failures and destructive storms battering coastal cities. What is fair under these circumstances? Should developed countries make radical changes—such as decentralizing and deindustrializing—in their economic arrangements? Should they refrain from adding the potentially disastrous increment of greenhouse gases that will push the climate over the threshold of climatic catastrophe? If yes, then anthropocentric environmental ethics calls for far-reaching social and economic reform.

Biocentric environmental ethics also implies considerable economic reform. If animals have moral standing, then killing them or destroying their habitat for human benefit is unacceptable. In particular, the massive species loss resulting from deforestation is a moral failure even if humans profit. Likewise, agricultural practices that rely on pesticides and fertilizers that harm nonhuman species should be curtailed. Warfare's effects on nonhuman living things would also need to be evaluated. Just-war theory generally evaluates collateral damage's significance in the context of civilians killed or injured due to military operations. Yet collateral damage also kills and injures animals that have even less stake and less say in the conflict than civilians. Should their right to life be considered? Biocentric ethics would say yes. If so, virtually the entire practice of modern war might be held as inherently immoral.

Ecocentric ethics implies the strongest critique of current practices. Disrupting the ecological cycle or the evolutionary process is morally unacceptable. Most current economic or military practices would not pass muster. Indeed, in its strong form, ecocentric ethics would require a major reduction in the human population, since the 6 billion people now on earth are already disrupting the evolutionary process and will continue to do so as world population grows to 10 billion or more. Political institutions must be replaced, either with one-world government capable of implementing ecocentric environmental policy, or with ecologically based bioregional political units (ecocentric theorists hold differing views on whether authoritarian government or more democracy is needed to make ecocentrism effective in practice). If bioregionalism were adopted, world trade would come to a halt since each bioregion would be self-sustaining. Wasteful resource use would be curtailed. Long-term sustainability in harmony with the needs of other living things would be the desired end. For some ecocentric thinkers, the model is a hunter-gatherer society or a peasant agriculture society.

Environmental ethics in each form carries important implications for the practice of international politics. Yet the environmental ethics literature usually pays little attention to obvious features of the international system. This is not to say that environmental ethics bears no relationship to political realities. If realism (the theory of power politics) and liberal institutionalism (the theory emphasizing interdependence and the possibilities for cooperation) both contain implicit environmental ethics, then environmental ethics contains implicit political theory. Yet without explicit attention to international political theory, environmental ethics lacks the basis to determine which of its recommendations is feasible, and which utopian.

Bridging the Gap

The gap between what environmental ethics calls for and what international political theory postulates may find its bridge in the land ethic. The land ethic, as formulated by J. Baird Callicott, recognizes that environmental obligations are only part of our moral world.[2] Although the land ethic implies significant change in existing practices, it does not necessarily call for abandoning the sovereign state, relinquishing national identity or authority to a world government, or even abolishing capitalism. Rather, it asks for balance between human needs and the requisites of preserving the diversity of life flowing from the evolutionary process. The land ethic simply states that which enhances the integrity, stability, and beauty of the land is good, and that which does not is bad. Human intervention can serve good purposes by this standard. (Indeed, Aldo Leopold was himself a hunter, and found no contradiction between that pursuit and his commitment to the land ethic.) Presumably, human-induced changes to the landscape must be evaluated in context, assessing positive and negative effects.

Yet if the land ethic is to provide guidance for international politics, it needs to identify the other values that must be balanced with its requirements. In international politics, these can be determined in terms of mainstream international political theory, realism and liberal institutionalism. Realism and liberal insitutionalism capture much about how the international system works and what values shape international political practices. Thus we can observe the world for clues as to what international theory entails for the kind of world we should create. Although the verdict is not positive for existing practices, this does not foreclose the possibility of change within either paradigm. But how specifically does realism and liberal institutionalism see the relationship of humans to nature?

Realism and the Environment

Realism is generally understood to be amoral. States do as they must to survive. Survival can justify breaking agreements, lying, deception, violence, and theft. Those who fail to play the game disappear. Those who are best at the game dominate the others. Morality, when invoked, is usually a cover for state interests. Certainly, some prominent realists have said otherwise. Hans Morgenthau recognized the moral content of foreign policy, as did E. H. Carr and Reinhold Niebuhr. Nonetheless, realists usually observe the human capacity for "evil" when the stakes are high.

But this negative perspective on morality obscures realism's highly moral claims. Realism asserts that humans naturally form groups, which experience conflicts of interest because resources are scarce. Maintaining the group's autonomy and freedom is the highest good. On it depends the ability of a people to work out their destiny within the borders of the state. Implicitly, this moral project justifies the extreme measures states undertake. Environmental ethics must recognize this as an extremely powerful moral claim. At the same time, international relations theory must recognize that staking this claim, which superficially appears to be a social question, implies a view of how humans should relate to the natural world.

Realism assumes that the state system, or at least some form of power politics involving contending groups, will characterize human relations as long as humans inhabit the planet. The possibilities for environmental (or any other) ethics are limited by this evidently permanent institutional arrangement. Virtually every state action must be evaluated in terms of the relative gains it offers with other states. The struggle for survival and dominance is an endless game in which any minor advantage today could have profound consequences tomorrow. Moreover, as Machiavelli observed, chance plays such a large role in human affairs that immediate advantage is all the prudent policymaker can consider. Thus, to think about long-term environmental trends, for example, is impractical, because an actor that sacrifices present advantage for future gains may not be around to enjoy the fruits.

Perhaps the most significant implication of realism lies in its emphasis on military security. Military imperatives dictate that states develop and deploy the most effective military technology available. The effects on the land of the particular choices made are little considered. No military technology could be more environmentally damaging than nuclear weapons, but these weapons confer maximum national power. Thus the environmental effects of producing, storing, deploying, and dismantling them (not to mention the effects they would have on the environment if ever used) are considered secondary. Here we see how realism as an international political theory is at the same time an implicit environmental ethic: land has little or no moral worth. This is a choice about how humans are to relate to the natural world, not only a choice about how states (or humans) are to relate to one another. A similar argument could be made about the entire range of military technologies, from cluster bombs to napalm to defoliants to biological weapons.

According to realism, the economic institutions of a society must support the most effective military establishment. Societies that attempt to structure economic relations along other lines, such as long-term sustainability, will soon find themselves overwhelmed by other states that make choices geared toward military dominance. States that wish to survive will emulate the most successful economic systems of other states and constantly seek economic innovations that will give them the edge. Capitalism as practiced in the United States and other major Western nations seems to be most compatible with military preponderance.

Realism thus implicitly endorses capitalism, albeit only because it is the most successful economic system at present for enhancing national power (as the former Soviet Union discovered). Capitalism has put the United States at the top of the international order. Others fail to emulate the United States at their peril. Moreover, realism would suggest that because economic growth facilitates military preparedness, autonomous economic growth should override other goals, including environmental protection. Saving a wetland will not contribute as much to national security as producing goods for export. Consequently, realism's emphasis on security leads to embracing the market in its most environmentally heedless form.

Realism's attitude toward the land is that it is territory, an asset of the state, a form of property. The land's status is as a mere resource with no moral standing apart from human uses. It has no life of its own. Prudent management is the most that is morally required. Hence realism shares the modern notion of nature as a spiritless "other" that humans can rightfully manipulate to serve their own ends.

We see that realism's strong moral claim—that a people's right to determine their own destiny, to define and develop their own idea of freedom and the good society, without interference from others—contradicts the institutional arrangements that realism produces. In practice, few alternatives are available. A people who decide that their destiny is to live in harmony with the land, to follow the land ethic's central precept, would quickly lose the freedom to do so through conquest and domination by other states. Aside from the evident fact that many environmental problems require cooperation across political jurisdictions, the competitiveness of the state system ensures that environmental consciousness will not long guide state policy.[3] Realism thus implies an environmental ethic; unfortunately, it is a most pernicious one. Equally unfortunate for environmental ethics is that realism is an undoubtedly incomplete, but not inaccurate, description of how the international system works.

Yet realism's historical and social argument rests on the moral claim that the group is the highest value: that it is within the group that some conception of the good society can be pursued. But surely a good society is one that fosters environmental values, a goal that suffers when nations pursue national security at all costs. As environmental crises mount, the contradiction at the heart of realist ethics becomes more obvious. Perhaps this can lead to changed conceptions of morality.

Ethical standards change. Nationalism, which underpins today's state system, has not driven human behavior for all history (nationalism, for example, had little influence in feudal Europe). Humans can change their view of how best to pursue a vision of the good society. To the extent that the land ethic becomes part of the moral dialogue, institutional change to bring about a healthier human-environment relationship is possible. Nonetheless, realism reminds us that the road to ethical change toward a land ethic likely will be long and hard.

Liberal Institutionalism and the Environment

Liberal institutionalism is far more ready to accept that universal values such as respect for the land exist. Unlike realism, the liberal perspective considers human rights standards to apply across boundaries and cultures. Individuals are the moral agents and moral objects of liberal thought. Individuals have rights that exist regardless of their cultural heritage.

Furthermore, liberalism asserts that these individuals have a particular character. Partly self-interested and partly altruistic, individuals are aware of their dependence on collective action to obtain the good life. The liberal individual also acts, or should, through enlightened self-interest, which is the best way to secure the means of life and protection against bodily harm. Liberal individuals are predisposed to make certain choices. But would they choose a different way of life, namely, one more in harmony with the land?

The question becomes pertinent because it is not at all clear that liberal society is sustainable. Liberalism as manifested in practice is strongly committed to the market system. Indeed, the entire point of liberal institutional international political economy is to find the means to open the world economy to free trade and investment. From this perspective, environmental problems become unintended side-effects of otherwise desirable industrialization and economic growth. The problem for liberalism is simply managing these unfortunate consequences in ways that maintain the open economy. But as the modern market system encompasses more of the globe and penetrates deeper into social life, profound social choices occur, the result of the incremental effects of countless discrete, uncoordinated individual actions. Liberals are comfortable with this way of making social choices due to their faith in progress; the mounting ecological catastrophe might speak against this optimistic view.

Liberal institutionalism cannot escape its entanglement with and commitment to the capitalist market system. In effect, this means that liberal institutionalism can only with difficulty critique that system as it has developed in history. Hence liberal institutionalism will continue to see normal diplomacy and statecraft, the operations of multinational corporations, the growth of free trade and investment, and rising interdependence as progress toward a better world. This in turn exhibits liberal institutionalism's environmental ethic: managerial, limited to mitigation of the market's worst effects, and committed to economic growth and development. The world we should build is on display. It is embodied in the more enlightened liberal states, those that combine commitment to individual liberty, representative democracy, and free enterprise with some degree of environmental awareness. It is industrialized, or postindustrial. It is technologically advanced. It provides a wide range of goods and services to consumers. Environmental concerns enter by way of interest groups devoted to the "issue" rather than as fundamental values that determine which practices to retain and which to abandon.

Like realism, liberal institutionalism captures a large part of the truth about how contemporary international politics operates. It suggests emphasizing certain trends in the hope of dampening others; strengthening the forces for globalization to reduce the impact of military competition. But its commitment to the predominant global economic institutions leaves little room for a land ethic. Liberal institutionalism's anthropocentrism and consequent emphasis on economic growth leads to a relative lack of concern for the stability, integrity, and beauty of the land. Nonetheless, liberal institutionalism is far more open to the possibility of value change and political transformation than is realism. Liberal theory's faith in progress can imply that liberalism itself eventually will be transcended in favor of more earth-centered ethics. Yet current liberal international theory does not recognize or embrace this possibility. To the extent that theory is practice, liberal international theory contributes to the worsening environmental crisis rather than offering a way out.

A NEW DIALOGUE

Both realism and liberal institutionalism are implicitly environmental ethics. They tell us the relationship humans should have with nature, even if they largely base their claims not on ethical choice but on what we must do under existing circumstances. But humans can make conscious choices about what kind of international order to create and maintain. The realist imperative to play the game of power politics or be eliminated from the system depends on a prior choice about ethics and practice. It precludes the possibility of collaboratively engaging the "other" in democratic dialogue aimed at discovering different social practices that do not, for example, lead to environmentally heedless arms races. The "other" must always remain other in realist thought, an assumption that is far from proven. Likewise, liberalism's imperative to rely on the market if we are to achieve individual liberty and social progress is open to question. If the individual is constituted in community—that is, by social practices—then the self-definition of the community can change. Acquisitive individualism and consumerism need not define the individuals.

How is change to come about? More authentic democracy, based on unforced, open discourse, affords the opportunity to choose consciously the kind of world we are to build. The choice need not come about indirectly, as the result of more immediate decisions on how to achieve national security, nor need it occur unintentionally as individuals make the best of circumstances not of their choosing. Engaging in this dialogue will require abandoning the notion that nature and the social are distinct. The social and the natural are inextricable. We constitute nature through our practices at the same time that we constitute the social world. Thus an ecologically informed political discourse will be one that recognizes the environmental ethics embedded in all political worldviews.

Environmental ethics will not be seen as an add-on to be approached after the important issues of security and economics have been settled. Instead, we will recognize that all our important social choices are inherently about the "natural" world we create. We will consciously raise the question of what this particular action means for that world, and we will recognize that it is our responsibility, not something external to us.

Notes

1. For more on anthropocentric and biocentric ethics, see J. Baird Callicott, *In Defense of the Land Ethic: Essays for Environmental Philosophy* (Albany: State University of New York Press, 1989).
2. See Callicott, *In Defense of the Land Ethic.*
3. This competition also influences the abilities of states to cooperate to deal with transnational environmental problems. States are expected to attempt to free ride or otherwise exploit the global "commons." If environmental cooperation occurs, it is likely due to a hegemonic power or small group of large powers imposing an international regime. Of course, the Hobbesian use of power to make and enforce law is the antithesis of democratic decision making (which could well be a major element of the society's vision of the good life). But because states are and must be shortsighted and self-interested, no alternative to coercive imposition of regimes exists. Whether such regimes would conform to the requisites of long-term environmental sustainability—much less to the integrity, beauty, and stability of the land—is doubtful.

Will Globalization Make You Happy?

Thanks to globalization, human beings are wealthier and freer than at any time during our long climb from the top of the evolutionary food chain to the highest rung of the corporate ladder. But are we happier? Put down that cellphone, ignore that incoming e-mail, and consider the evidence.

By Robert Wright

Robert Wright is a visiting scholar at the University of Pennsylvania and author of The Moral Animal *(New York: Vintage Books, 1995) and* Nonzero: The Logic of Human Destiny *(New York: Pantheon Books, 2000).*

For all the discord over globalization, virtually everyone agrees on two of its properties. First, globalization is very hard to stop. Ever since card-carrying progressive William Greider titled his 1997 book *One World, Ready or Not,* even the left has increasingly viewed globalization as something to be tamed, not killed. Second, globalization makes the world—on balance, at least—more prosperous. The critique of globalization isn't that it fails to churn out ever more stuff, but that churning out more stuff has lots of drawbacks, especially given the way the stuff gets distributed.

These two properties are related: Globalization is almost unstoppable precisely because it is driven by lots of people hellbent on increasing their prosperity. Nike stockholders want to boost profits by holding down production costs, which means manufacturing overseas. Indonesian workers want to elevate their income by moving from farm fields to Nike factories. Nike customers want, well, they want a shoe that has not just the generic "Air Sole" (old hat) but a "Tuned Air unit in the heel and Zoom Air in the forefoot"—not to mention "Optimal Motion flex grooves."

As all these people try to upgrade their standard of living, the invisible hand obliges by enmeshing them in an ever larger, ever denser web of investment and production. Human nature itself—the deep desire to amass resources, to keep up with the Joneses, and, if possible, to leave them in the dust—drives the engine that is transforming the world.

Unfortunately, human nature has a spotty record in the driver's seat. The one realm where even a cynic might think human nature excels—helping people selfishly pursue their own well-being—is an area of frequent failure. Humanity is famous for pursuing things, such as power and riches, that don't bring lasting happiness. Are those Nike stockholders really happier behind the wheel of a Mercedes-Benz SUV than they would be driving a Hyundai Accent? Might some Indonesian factory workers be better off if they had never left the farm and the time-test folkways that govern life there? Couldn't a weekend athlete find enduring contentment even without Optimal Motion flex grooves?

This question—Does globalization bring happiness?—is the $64,000 question. Although it underlies much of the globalization debate and is sometimes tossed out rhetorically, it is seldom seriously addressed, perhaps because of its presumed elusiveness. But psychologists actually have amassed a lot of data about what does and doesn't make people happy. This data doesn't come just from undergraduate volunteers on U.S. campuses: Several massive cross-cultural surveys have been completed over the past two decades. And it is becoming clearer which economic and political circumstances lead people to feel satisfied with their lot in life.

When you combine this data with what we know about globalization's economic and political effects, it becomes possible to take a preliminary shot at the big question: Is globalization good or bad? If you were God (and a utilitarian), would you adopt a hands-off policy, leaving transnational capitalism on autopilot, or would you intervene? And what form might intervention take? How, if at all, should globalization be governed? Psychology's happiness database doesn't answer these questions, but it helps us ponder them. In the process, it also helps overturn some conventional wisdom about who benefits and who suffers under globalization's advance.

THE GLOBAL PURSUIT OF HAPPINESS

Does money bring happiness? Psychologists have gone to dozens of nations, rich and poor, and asked people

> Once your nation attains a fairly comfortable standard of living, more income brings little, if any, additional happiness.

how satisfied they are with their lives. The upshot is that, while poor nations seem to breed unhappiness, very rich nations don't necessarily breed happiness. There is, on the one hand, a clear connection between a nation's per capita gross domestic product (GDP) and the average happiness of its citizens. But the strength of that connection—in most studies, at least—comes almost entirely from nations in the bottom three fourths of the income scale. Once your nation attains a fairly comfortable standard of living, more income brings little, if any, additional happiness. In the United States between 1975 and 1995, real per capita GDP grew by 43 percent, but the average happiness of Americans didn't budge.

The point where more wealth ceases to imply more happiness is around $10,000 per capita annually—roughly where Greece, Portugal, and South Korea are now. Above that point, additional dollars don't seem to cheer up nations, and national differences in happiness hinge on the intangibles of culture. The Irish are appreciably happier than the Germans, the Japanese and the British, though less wealthy than all of them. And Scandinavia's extraordinary happiness (Who would have guessed?) isn't traceable to any economic edge over other developed countries. (One possible explanation: Nations with high levels of trust tend to be happier, and Scandinavians, according to surveys, are inordinately trusting.)

This fact alone—that making poor nations less poor seems to raise the level of happiness, but making rich nations richer doesn't—is worth contemplating in light of globalization. Before contemplating it, we have to ask whether this fact is really as methodically sturdy as it sounds.

First, all these studies rely on self-reported satisfaction with life. You could debate for weeks whether that is a reliable index of true happiness without exhausting all related psychological, sociological, and epistemological conundrums. Is there any other kind of evidence that lends credence to these reports?

Yes. Consider, for example, the extraordinary gloom pervading the former Soviet bloc. In 1994, when the World Values Study Group published a ranking of 41 nations' self-reported "life satisfaction," the least satisfied nations were, in order: Bulgaria, Russia, Belarus, Latvia, Romania, Estonia, Lithuania, and Hungary. But couldn't this just be a Communist-induced measurement error? Could decades of official denunciations of selfishness have discouraged people from admitting to being happy?

As it happens, psychologists Martin Seligman and Gabriele Oettingen shed light on this question during the 1980s. They observed West and East Berliners as they went about their everyday lives. West Berliners smiled and laughed more often than East Berliners and had more upright and open postures. Clearly, East Germans didn't suffer merely from a culturally ingrained reluctance to admit their gaiety to pollsters. What's more, studies in various nations have shown that self-reported happiness correlates well not just with this objectively observed demeanor, but with the evaluations of friends and relatives and with survey questions that get at happiness more obliquely (for example, by determining how many pleasant memories a person can summon).

The second big methodological question is whether economic output masks other variables that are the real source of happiness. Are the keys to happiness really just things that money can buy—more food, cleaner drinking water, better healthcare, more comfortable housing? As William Easterly of the World Bank showed in a study published last year, richer nations, compared to poor ones, tend to have "more democracy, less corruption . . . more rule of law, and higher bureaucratic quality . . . more civil liberties, less abuse of human rights." Indeed, if you just forget about GDP and plot national happiness levels against various indexes of freedom, you'll see a clear relationship. Ed Diener, one of psychology's leading happiness researchers, notes that it will take further, more focused study to separate the effect of wealth from the effect of human rights and democracy. The correlation between economic and political variables is so strong, and the number of data points so small, that statistically disentangling the influences isn't yet possible.

Then again, the very strength of this correlation may render the question moot. If, indeed, economic development not only improves diet, medicine, and shelter, but also goes hand in hand with more democracy and human rights, then one way or another, economic development will probably make people in poor nations happier. And judging by recent anecdotal evidence from Mexico, South Korea, and Taiwan, economic development does indeed improve political life. (Although, as Easterly notes, the end of the Cold War has also seen democracy come to poorer nations.)

THE RICH (AND THE POOR) GET RICHER

The potential for prosperity—one way or another—to markedly increase the happiness of poor nations may seem to cast the current era in an ironic light. After all, according to one common view, globalization showers prosperity on rich nations, often at the expense of poor nations. Union leader Jay Mazur has written that "globalization has dramatically increased inequality between and within nations," and Lori Wallach, the oft-quoted antiglobalization activist, concurs. Even Laura D'Andrea Tyson, former national economic adviser to President Bill Clinton, wrote recently that "as globalization has intensified, the gap between per capita incomes in rich and poor countries has widened."

These observations are misleading at best. First, in absolute terms, poor nations have become less poor. Even if some of them have shown alarming stagnation, the economic output of the average poor nation has grown in recent decades. Of course, Mazur and Wallach and Tyson are talking about relative income—and it's true that the gap between the richest and poorest nations has grown. But it's hard to argue that globalization is the problem. As economists Jeffrey Sachs and Andrew Warner showed years ago, and as other economists have since confirmed, developing nations with the most open economies—the nations most thoroughly plugged into the global market system—grow the fastest. The most stubbornly poor nations, it seems, are so poor because they are underglobalized. This theory helps explain why East and Southeast Asia, with their embrace of global markets, have massively reduced poverty, while sub-Saharan Africa, featuring more statist economies and an unappetizing political environment for foreign investment, has been less successful.

Some would claim that the rising level of prosperity among the more open developing nations is misleading because their poorer citizens are being left behind. Certainly, nations sometimes do grow more economically stratified as they get richer. But notwithstanding the confident assertions of Mazur and Wallach, economists have found no general tendency for economic growth to exacerbate income inequality. And this past spring, World Bank economists David Dollar and Aart Kraay released a study that looked not just at the effects of economic growth but specifically at the impact of globalization. Tracking nations with the most open, most globalized economies over the last several decades, they found that, as national income grew, the fraction of the economic pie going to the bottom fifth of the income scale didn't shrink. The rising tide indeed seemed to lift all boats.

There is one final reason that plaints about growing income inequality among nations are misleading. Nations differ in size, and those stubbornly poor, underglobalized nations that account for the growing gap between rich and poor nations tend to be small, while some of the poor nations that are getting richer (such as China) are quite large. If you look at the world as a utilitarian God would—just ignore political boundaries and focus on the total number of souls—the picture looks brighter. Bernard Wasow of the Century Foundation has calculated that between 1965 and 1997, the poorest 10 percent of the world's population increased its share of world income from 0.3 percent to 0.5 percent. Of course, 0.5 percent seems pathetically low—especially given that the richest 10 percent meanwhile expanded its share from 50.6 percent to 59.6 percent. Still, the fact remains that in 1965 the average income of the top 10 percent was 160 times the average income of the bottom 10 percent, and by 1997 that ratio had fallen to 127 times. And that calculation includes those poor nations with closed, underglobalized economies.

To put the progress against poverty in slightly less abstract terms, according to a report issued in June by a squadron of multilateral agencies—the United Nations, the World Bank, the Organisation for Economic Co-operation and Development, and the International Monetary Fund—the number of people who live on less than a dollar a day dropped by 100 million between 1990 and 1998. The number remains astoundingly high—1.2 billion—but bear in mind that the drop came even as the population of poor nations grew by hundreds of millions.

In short, the rule of thumb for the world's poor people seems to be that they're getting less poor in absolute terms and, by some measures, less poor in relative terms. And the more globalized that poor nations become, the better their people do in both absolute and relative terms.

If you put these findings together with the happiness data, the implication is a bit perverse. A common stereotype of globalization is that it's something done by the rich, for the rich, and to the poor. It's certainly true that the world's affluent peoples make the big decisions about how capital is deployed and make lots of money off globalization. Yet, in terms of psychological payoff—in terms of actual happiness—the benefits of globalization would seem to go overwhelmingly to the world's lower classes, to nations with a per capita annual income under $10,000. Only at that level of national income does money reliably bring happiness.

Indeed, richer nations not only fail to get happier as national income grows; even as their average level of happiness stays constant, the small fraction of the population suffering from serious psychopathology expands. More people become chronically depressed, and the suicide rate often rises.

Thus, it appears that what is now a major chunk of conventional wisdom in some political circles—that globalization is good for the rich, bad for the poor—is not just wrong, but wrong by 180 degrees. Globalization, at least to judge by its effect on income and the effect of income on happiness, is good for the poor and, if anything, bad for the rich.

FASTER, JOHN Q. PUBLIC—CONSUME! CONSUME! CONSUME!

It makes you wonder: Why do the rich work so hard at getting richer if it isn't making them any happier and is making a few of them crazier? In a sense, their behavior is not as irrational as it sounds. Understanding this fact is the first step to fathoming the paradoxical engine that drives globalization. It is also the first step to deciding

> Consultants and lawyers and corporate execs spread their time among so many nations that they almost cease to have a homeland.

whether globalization, given its manifest benefits to the poor, should simply be left on autopilot.

Within nations, as among them, there is a link between income and happiness. The link is not terribly strong—and certainly not as strong as we make ourselves believe. Most if not all of the thrill of a pay raise we worked hard for wears off quickly, leaving us hungry for more. What's more, as with national happiness, there is a per capita income level beyond which more money brings declining utilitarian bang per buck. (In the United States, the point is a bit shy of $20,000.) Still, the bang per buck doesn't quite level off to zero. Affluent Americans are a bit happier than their middle-class compatriots, and much happier than the poor. Of course, this link between money and happiness could just mean that upbeat people are more likely to make money than perennially sad people. But almost no one who has studied the question thinks that the causality works only in that direction. Making more money stands a good chance of making people at least somewhat happier.

So if individual Americans get happier as they get richer, why doesn't the United States collectively get happier as it gets richer? The answer favored by some psychologists and championed by the economist Robert Frank in his book *Luxury Fever* is simple: Much of what gratifies people about higher income is that it boosts their relative standing in society. To the extent that this is true—that our happiness comes from comparing our station in life with that of other people—then within a society, one person's gain is another person's loss.

Consider the late Greek shipping magnate Aristotle Onassis, who insisted that the faucets on his yacht be made of solid gold, and that the yacht's bar stools be covered with the ultrasoft foreskin of a whale's penis (I'm not making this up). Let us stipulate, for thought-experiment purposes, that Onassis impressed people enough to raise his social status, his serotonin level, and his sense of well-being. To the extent that he succeeded, he lowered the relative social standing of rival shipping magnate and yachtsman Stavros Niarchos. (And, needless to say, the whale's well-being suffered, too.) In Greek society as a whole, there was no net utilitarian gain.

This theory makes sense in light of evolutionary psychology. As Frank notes, the human mind was designed by natural selection in the context of small hunter-gatherer societies back when social status was correlated with reproductive success. One's goal, in Darwinian terms, was to be higher on the totem pole than one's competitors—that is, one's neighbors. Of course, there is only one top spot on the totem pole, and one number two spot, and so on; social status is a finite resource, and anyone's gain must come at someone else's expense. The modern legacy of our brains' having been built to play this game is that, within the United States or Japan or France, pursuing happiness through monetary gain is essentially a zero-sum game. That's why riches can elevate the level of happiness for a given American while failing to do so for the United States as a whole.

Within poor nations, by contrast, this game is partly non-zero-sum. To be sure, the link between individual income and individual happiness that is found in rich nations also holds within poor nations—if anything, it is stronger there. And no doubt some of that happiness comes from one-upmanship. Still, because a poor nation's growing GDP does bring markedly more happiness, the game among citizens is not entirely zero-sum. As people struggle to raise their standard of living, they are attaining things—decent nutrition, healthcare—that raise their happiness level without reducing anyone else's. Moreover, these upwardly mobile citizens are moving the nation as a whole toward more human rights, more political freedom, even more democracy—the political ingredients of national happiness.

For that matter, the relationship between the poor nations and the rich nations is non-zero-sum. Upper-middle-class Americans, in scrapping for income and status, in working overtime to afford that forest-green Ford Explorer, may be jostling for pieces of a more-or-less finite happiness pie. But at least some of that car was built in a developing country, so some of the dollars they paid for it went to a place where money actually can buy more national happiness. Net happiness is created by U.S. status seeking—even if none of the happiness winds up in the United States. A utilitarian God, indifferent to national boundaries, would be pleased.

Or would he (or she)? It is wonderful that globalization brings happiness by reducing poverty. But reducing poverty isn't all that globalization does, and income isn't the only ingredient of happiness. Globalization also affects the texture of life, sometimes the very structure of life, and on these things much of our happiness depends.

Bear in mind that those cross-national correlations between happiness and GDP tell us nothing about the "real-time" effects of modernization. The nations at the high-income, high-happiness end of the spectrum are mostly nations—in North America and Western Europe—that underwent the transition from agrarian to industrial society long ago and have had time to catch their breath. To be sure, it's auspicious that more recent modernizers, such as South Korea and Taiwan, show pretty high levels of happiness, too. Still, for all we know, the current pace of transition may give many modernizing nations a degree of disorientation that neutralizes much of the happiness brought by growing income.

The early 20th century American sociologist William Ogburn had this type of problem in mind when he coined the term "cultural lag." Cultural lag happens when material culture changes so fast that immaterial culture (government, social norms, moral strictures) falls dangerously behind. Some of globalization's examples of cultural lag are vivid and much discussed. For example, the pollution that envelops a Mexico City or a Bangkok can race ahead of the government's capacity or will to solve the problem. Other aspects of "cultural lag" are less tangible, but at least as important.

Take family and friends. Strong and intimate social bonds are deeply conducive to happiness. In a U.S. survey, respondents who could list at least five people with whom they had discussed matters of personal significance within the last six months were 60 percent more likely to say they felt "very happy" than people who could list none. People with close friends and kin also handle stress, illness, and career setbacks better.

Moving from an agrarian to an industrial society can upset the social structures in which social bonds are embedded, a fact now evident across the developing world. In Brazil, a worker in the "informal sector" gets up each day, takes a bus out to an industrial area, then starts walking back towards his slum, stopping at work sites along the way in hopes of landing a few hours of labor. If he succeeds, he may spend the day among strangers; if he fails, he spends it alone. In India, journalist Robert Kaplan writes of "polluted, grimy factory encampments" where tens of millions of migrants no longer tethered to the norms of the rural village, are "assaulted by the temptations of the pseudo-Western city—luxury cars, night clubs, gangs, pornographic movies."

Of course, the modernized nations underwent a roughly comparable transition—and lived to tell about it. In the United States at the end of the 19th century and the beginning of the 20th, as young men and women moved from farm to city and workplaces became larger and more impersonal, there was a palpable sense of social crisis. The examples from Brazil and India are reminiscent of the United States' turn-of-the-century working-class slums, where rural migrants, remote from their families, tried to scratch out a living amid disease, corruption, and new forms of temptation. Yet by World War II, Americans had at least partly succeeded in weaving a new social fabric—building stable urban neighborhoods and founding social clubs and civic groups.

Still, today's developing nations are facing this adjustment in fast forward: Some are starting out more agrarian than the United States was in the late 19th century and are being asked to move not just into the industrial age, but into the electronic age—an age that even "modern" nations are struggling to cope with. In the United States, television has been famously blamed by political scientist Robert Putnam (author of *Bowling Alone*) for helping to fray that recently woven industrial-age social fabric and eroding everything from civic participation to picnic attendance. (People who watch lots of TV, by the way, are unusually unhappy, though that could be because unhappiness leads people to watch TV.)

On paper, the newer electronic technologies—microcomputers, modems—might seem just what the doctor ordered. Unlike TV, they are tools of communication, even long-distance friendship. But there are reasons to doubt that they will bring widespread bliss to any part of the world at any time soon.

One reason is that cybercafes were not part of the environment in which Homo sapiens evolved. We most naturally get social gratification from face-to-face contact, not from sentences on a computer screen. What's more, we seem to have evolved in a context of small and intimate communities that offered the chance for long-term social bonds; what we need isn't just "friends" in the sense of "acquaintances" or even "colleagues," but actual friends. (To an evolutionary psychologist, it is no surprise that U.S. soldiers placed in 12-person teams with stable membership wind up mentally healthier and happier about their jobs than soldiers assigned to large groups with fluid membership.) And information technology, while offering the potential for intimate communication, often fails to deliver.

Just look at all the names in your e-mail address book. My, but you're well connected! But "well connected" doesn't mean "deeply connected." It means widely and shallowly connected. You communicate with many people along narrow channels of common interest, and you get to know few of them well. Of course, different people use technology differently, and your mileage may vary. But for many people, at least, e-mail only sustains the trend—which David Riesman described in his 1950 book *The Lonely Crowd*—away from a solid grounding in kin and trusted friends and toward the superficiality of broad and efficient social networks. It is in the world described by Riesman that rates of depression and suicide have grown.

Information technology also abets the much-noted transience of the modern workplace. Deft communication makes it easier for companies to find temporary workers, easier for slightly underpaid executives to find their full market value at another firm—easier, in general, for economic efficiency to trump social stability. According to a study published by the consulting firm McKinsey & Company, the number of companies the average executive has worked for grew over the last decade from three to five. And many people don't work for companies in the traditional sense at all—they just contract with them. The resulting "free-agent" culture has made many people richer (especially people at income levels where money doesn't make you much happier anyway) by making their social environment less solid.

On the cusp of globalization is the ultimate in high-tech transience—the consultants and lawyers and corporate execs who spread their time among so many nations that they almost cease to have a homeland. This is the class dubbed "the cosmocrats" in *A Future Perfect,* the recent book on globalization by John Micklethwait and Adrian Wooldridge. I have always had trouble working up sympathy for people who seldom fly coach, and reading this book's description of the cosmocrats—"an anxious elite" who face "the perils of placelessness"—failed to wrench a single tear from my eye. Still, it is true that many cosmocrats live in a vast and fluid web of facile connections. We don't yet know whether this can bring long-term happiness, but we do know that this isn't the way human beings were designed to live.

It is important to guard against overextrapolating from these information-age trends. In many cases, there is little point in extrapolating at all. The information age and globalization are still young. As the World Wide Web goes broadband, making real-time video more practical, rendering "tele-presence" more and more realistic, the Web could well become a more gratifying medium, allowing even "placeless" elites to stay deeply in touch with a core of intimates.

But there is one rule about evolving information technology that is sure to hold, however broad the band—and this rule underscores the perils of "cultural lag." As more and more powerful means of communication become cheaper and cheaper, groups of people with common interests will find it easier and easier to organize. In most cases this will be wonderful—or, at least, not bad. But in an age when rapid social transformation is giving some groups deep grievances, this new capacity for mobilization will also lead to trouble.

In fact, leave aside the many new and coming grievances. There are enough groups with long-simmering grievances—Kurds, Basques, Chinese Muslims, various Indonesian minorities—for real havoc to ensue, given the growing access to potent technologies of organization and potent munitions. When you add in the backlashes fomented by globalization—among militias in the U.S. heartland, rabid nationalists in Russia and Germany, and alienated religious fundamentalists worldwide—the picture only gets spookier.

To be sure, the threat that information technologies pose to entrenched, centralized powers very often serves just causes, notably freedom and democracy. But even political improvement can be deeply unsettling when it is sudden. The lowest national happiness level ever recorded anywhere was in the Dominican Republic in 1962, not long after the assassination of the dictator Rafael Trujillo—which, in retrospect, was the first in a series of steps toward democracy. And, leaving survey data aside, when political turmoil brings widespread death, as it often does, lots of people forever cease to be happy.

TAKE IT DOWN A NOTCH

The author Dorothy Parker, when asked if she enjoyed writing, supposedly replied, "No. I enjoy having written." So it sometimes is with historical progress. It could well turn out that having globalized is more fun than globalizing. Though the ends of globalization are fundamentally good—reducing poverty, nurturing democracy and freedom—the process of globalizing can be quite costly in human terms, especially when it moves at high velocity.

How to proceed when the destination is good but the journey dicey? One approach is to just get it over with. Certainly a good piece of advice to Parker would have been: Sit down and get the thing written and quit wallowing in the agony of creativity! But there is a difference. Writing isn't massively more painful when fast than when slow. But globalizing can be. With technological and social change, there can be discontinuities of consequence; above a critical velocity, the negative fallout may grow by orders of magnitude.

One reason is the growing access to catastrophic technologies, most notably biological and nuclear weapons. But even past eras with lower-tech forms of slaughter attest to the toll that history can take when it's on fast forward. As the Industrial Revolution, having matured fairly gradually in westernmost Europe, swept rapidly eastward in the late 19th century, it brought extreme social dislocation to German lands and to Russia. It is not crazy, indeed, to see both the virulent German nationalism of the 20th century and Stalin's reign of terror as long-run consequences of this disruptive change. By extension, it is not crazy to see the current suffering in the former Soviet bloc—the unhappiest place on Earth—as the stubborn legacy of overly rapid 19th-century globalization.

So what would a utilitarian God advise? I doubt that the advice would be to systematically slow down globalization. Trying to fine-tune the velocity of history seems beyond our mortal capacity. Still, maybe we should look with increased sympathy on policy ideas that have plausible internal logic and may have the side effect of slightly slowing down globalization.

Consider Robert Frank's plan for dampening luxury fever. By Frank's analysis, remember, people in affluent nations who pursue happiness via money and status are playing a zero-sum game. But that doesn't mean that pursuing happiness by any means would be zero-sum; if you spend more time with friends, you and the friends feel better and no one need suffer.

Ah, Frank asks, but where does the ardent happiness maximizer find the time to spend with friends? After all, if you cut back on your work hours, your income and status might slip; you could lose an increment of happiness to a rival. That is the paradox: If everyone in an affluent society cut back on their work so their relative incomes didn't change, they could all spend more time with friends—and the society's overall happiness would grow. Yet it may not be in the best interest of any one person to take the initiative. What we need, says Frank, is a way to halt the individually rational but collectively futile status-seeking arms race and use the time to pursue happiness more wisely. He proposes a progressive consumption tax that would, among other virtues, discourage 60-hour workweeks.

No doubt such a tax would cut demand for some products made in the developing world. It would, in that sense, subdue globalization. But when globalization is already moving at a mildly scary pace, this slowdown is not necessarily an indictment of the proposal.

So too with various initiatives that might otherwise be shouted down because they slightly slow the wheels of commerce. If a fossil fuel tax designed to fight global warming has the side effect of dampening demand for cars, that needn't be considered a flaw. You could say much the same about putting environmental and labor accords in trade agreements. On the one hand, we shouldn't pretend that such accords won't slightly reduce the rate at which globalization boosts the standard of living in developing countries. But neither should we ignore the possibility that, given globalization's eerie velocity, this sedative effect would have an upside. If such accords help solve environmental problems or help soften the resentment toward globalization felt by low-wage workers in affluent nations, so much the better.

If you find yourself losing sleep over the idled Sri Lankan factory workers that a slightly slowed globalization implies, there are ways to ease your anxiety: Donate money to charities that provide food and medicine to the world's poorest. Unless you are yourself poor, you weren't getting much joy out of those few dollars anyway. Besides, one psychologist found that performing altruistic acts gives people a psychological lift. And another found that teenagers who were especially concerned with the welfare of others were especially happy. Apparently, giving things to people can be a non-zero-sum game. Human nature is full of ironies.

Globalization, given enough time, could itself bring one final irony. Suppose that, as technology continues to shrink distances, the world truly becomes a "global village," and a sense of common belonging suffuses all humankind. Wouldn't that be wonderful? Maybe not. To the extent that happiness depends on how your social station compares with that of your neighbors, the happiness of poor nations might suffer. Upon seeing rich nations up close and personal, people in the developing world could start using them as a reference point and then feel deflated by the comparison.

Indeed, one psychologist, Michael Hagerty, has speculated that the global telecommunications web is already becoming dense enough for these "comparison effects" to take a toll. And telecommunications aside, as more cosmocrats conspicuously roam more cities in more developing nations, the toll could grow. The world's poor may soon acquire a strong—and increasingly collective—sense of envy and resentment toward the world's collective rich.

On the other hand, as economic development proceeds, and both the poor and the rich in developing nations become better off, this very sort of transnational class consciousness could begin to deter war among nations. One effective antiwar activity is networking among national elites—from the United States to China to Botswana. A similar connectedness among the world's lower socioeconomic classes could have the same effect; the more people have in common with kindred spirits abroad, and the more conscious of this commonality they become, the less prone they will be to a purely nationalist fervor.

Such a supranational class conflict would always hold the threat of turning violent. But assuming the world's upper classes have the presence of mind to minimize resentment with ameliorative economic and social policies, any such warfare is unlikely to be as destructive as the 20th century's wars among nations were. It is also unlikely to match the horrors of current ethnically based civil wars (which, you will note, tend to afflict nations not deeply and richly embedded in the global economy). Given the alternatives, a certain degree of class conflict on a global scale is a problem we should be happy to face.

Want to Know More?

The state-of-the-art volume on the study of happiness is ***Well-being: The Foundations of Hedonic Psychology*** (New York: Russell Sage Foundation, 1999), edited by Daniel Kahneman, Ed Diener, and Norbert Schwarz. A less academic but still reliable treatment is ***The Pursuit of Happiness: Who is Happy—and Why*** (New York: W. Morrow, 1992) by David G. Myers. In ***Modernization and Postmodernization: Cultural, Economic, and Political Change in 43 Societies*** (Princeton: Princeton University Press, 1997), Ronald Inglehart presents findings from the ***World Values Surveys*** and summarizes his theory that modernization fosters "post-materialist values."

Among the recent books that examine the failure of money to make affluent societies happier are Robert H. Frank's ***Luxury Fever: Why Money Fails to Satisfy in an Era of Excess*** (New York: Free Press, 1999), and Robert E. Lane's ***The Loss of Happiness in Market Democracies*** (New Haven: Yale University Press, 2000). A recent book that touches intermittently on the psychological rewards and burdens of globalization is ***A Future Perfect: The Challenge and Hidden Promise of Globalization*** by John Micklethwait and Adrian Wooldridge (New York: Times Books, 2000). William Greider's ***One World, Ready or Not: The Manic Logic of Global Capitalism*** (New York: Simon & Schuster, 1997) focuses at length on globalization's dislocating effects.

David Dollar and Aart Kraay challenge the widely held belief that economic growth exacerbates income inequality in their report **"Growth Is Good for the Poor"** (Washington: World Bank, 2000). Ruut Veenhoven, editor of the new ***Journal of Happiness Studies,*** has started a database on comparative national levels of happiness.

For links to relevant Web sites, as well as a comprehensive index of related FOREIGN POLICY articles, access **www.foreignpolicy.com.**

A group of "Latin intellectuals and left-leaning politicians" is determined to put Latin America on a new course to prosperity and equality. "The group's goal of rolling back the Washington Consensus and ushering in a model based on productive investment and a democratized economy sounds like a pipe dream. But time and trouble may be on its side."

A Fourth Way? The Latin American Alternative to Neoliberalism

LUCY CONGER

Latin America weathered fairly well the initial financial shock from the Asian turbulence that began last fall, primarily because Brazil spent $8 billion to defend its currency and thereby kept the region's largest economy on course. In subsequent months, Latin America suffered a trade shock as the Asian tsunami lapped at its shores, gouging prices of key Latin commodity exports such as oil and copper and creating stiffer competition for Latin products in markets like the United States.

Hopes that the region could withstand the buffeting from Asia were dashed when Russia devalued the ruble and defaulted on its debt this August. In the last hellish week of that month, Latin American stock markets sank as much as 10 percent on investor concerns about Russia, and some of the region's leading economies suffered attacks on their currencies. Still licking their wounds, the large Latin nations were hammered again on September 3 when Moody's, the international credit-rating agency, downgraded the ratings of Brazilian and Venezuelan debt and placed Mexico and Argentina on a "watch" for a possible debt downgrade.

Financial markets voted no confidence in Latin America despite the sweeping reforms most of the region's countries had implemented in an attempt to meet the demands of international investors. In the past decade, most Latin governments have adopted what is called the "Washington Consensus": reforms backed by the IMF and the United States Treasury Department that include lifting restrictions on trade and foreign investment, privatizing state enterprises, stabilizing local currencies, and clamping down on government spending to achieve balanced budgets.

The reforms have created a dramatic turnaround in Latin American economies, ending the state-dominated populist and protectionist regimes. Yet implementing the policy package that Latins call "neoliberalism" has been costly: millions have lost jobs because of privatization, public services including health care and education have been sharply reduced, and in many countries the number of people living below the poverty line has increased. Benefits have accrued to the reformed countries as trade and foreign investment have increased and sound finances have spurred growth. But, as the August rout proves, Latin America remains subject to recurrent crises.

POINTING TO AN ALTERNATIVE

Well before the weakness in Asia drove home the vulnerability of Latin American economies, a group of Latin intellectuals and left-leaning politicians had begun to debate an alternative program that would promise development for their

 Reprinted with permission from *Current History*, November 1998, pp. 380-384.

countries. By November 1997, after 18 months of meetings, they had forged a consensus and launched a platform called the "Latin American Alternative" (Alternative Latinoamericana). The group is spearheaded by Jorge Castañeda, a Mexican political scientist (and *Current History* contributing editor), and Roberto Mangabeira Unger, a Brazilian and professor at Harvard Law School. They have been joined in the debate by some two dozen Latin politicians, including two presidential candidates from Brazil and presidential hopefuls from Argentina, Chile, and Mexico, as well as former finance ministers, senators, governors, and mayors from throughout the region.

The alternative model endorsed by this group accepts the market economy, global economic integration, free trade, and privatization of state companies—all central tenets of the Washington Consensus. But the model proposes radical new policy directions to achieve sustained economic growth, link the poor to national and global economies, and encourage greater democratic political participation. "We can reform the market economy to tighten the link between savings and production and make money more complicit in the real economy," says Unger, who complains that the "financial casino" of stock markets and currency trading dissipates savings worldwide, and especially in emerging market countries.

A guiding principle of the alternative model is to combat the social and economic dualism that pervades life in Latin America. The region can claim the most inequitable income distribution in the world and rigid barriers to social mobility. The model would raise taxes to increase government funding for social services and education, which would improve the productive capacity of the workforce. Locally based credit institutions would be promoted to fund the upgrading and expansion of undercapitalized small businesses, which employ the majority of Latin Americans. Incentives for savings would be established to reduce the dependence of the region's emerging markets on volatile foreign capital inflows. Referendums and recall elections would be used to circumvent political impasses that blocked passage of reforms.

This effort to create a program for leftist politicians and generate an alternative to the neoliberal model is ambitious. Winning a hearing for the Latin group's vision and implementing its program will be uphill battles. "The basic objective is to establish in Latin America a movement of ideas, a current of opinion to get at economic orthodoxy and economic populism," says Unger.

Most of the politicians in the group predictably take a more optimistic and pragmatic view, believing they can win office and govern better with some of these ideas. They are also motivated by the need to build center-left political alliances strong enough to defeat the center-right elected regimes that predominate and then enact an alternative economic program. "The center-left is in a boom period" in Latin America, says Senator Carlos Ominami of Chile, a former economy minister. Others in the group advocate the alternative model with all of its ideas, including some that may seem unrealistic. "If you ask me do we have to put forward maximum utopias, I say yes," says Graciela Fernández Meijide, a former human rights activist and now the likely presidential candidate for Argentina's center-left alliance. "You have to propose a lot to get what you get."

The group's goal of rolling back the Washington Consensus and ushering in a model based on productive investment and a democratized economy sounds like a pipe dream. But time and trouble may be on its side. "The present world financial crisis has strengthened the need for such a debate and ultimately strengthened the readiness to hear this message," argues Unger. Certainly, the Asian crisis puts the IMF's credibility to the test and may overturn the conventional wisdom favoring unrestricted movements of capital. For market watchers willing to open their minds to other doubts, here are the ideas that these Latin Americans propose.

BUILDING THE MODEL

Supporters of the Latin American Alternative aim to correct the errors of both neoliberalism and populism. Neoliberalism has failed in Latin America, they argue, because it has not achieved sustained economic growth and it condemns large parts of the population to social and economic misery. The social programs of neoliberalism are inadequately funded and cannot reduce inequities because they are combined with orthodox economic structures that reinforce the highly unequal distribution of income that typifies Latin economies. Populism, meanwhile, is "merely distributive" and has failed to spawn deep reforms of the productive structure, says Unger.

"Alternative Latinoamericana" promises a democratized market economy that would bridge the gap between technologically advanced industries and undercapitalized, inefficient small and microbusinesses; it also promises a strong federal government with increased revenues that would support social and educational services to narrow the chasm separating the rich from the poor (who make up 40 percent of the population in many Latin countries).

A basic underpinning of the model is an increase in taxes and tax collection so that state revenues top 30 percent of gross domestic product. "In no country in the world has it been possible to generate solid social equilibrium with [government] spending levels below 30 percent of GDP," according to Alternative Latinoamericana. This poses an enormous challenge in Latin America, where tax collection averages about 12 percent of GDP and tax evasion is a national pastime. The increase in revenues would come from raising taxes on consumption, known as a value-added tax. At the outset, an increase in income taxes is not foreseen. The tax hike to all consumers, rich and poor alike, would be compensated for by social spending that would redistribute income and opportunities. In addition, the proceeds from the privatization of state companies would be used to pay off domestic public debt and reduce domestic interest rates to levels competitive with those in the industrialized nations.

To combat social inequities, state spending would guarantee equal access to quality education for all citizens and would provide meals and medical care to all children. Workers' salaries would be increased so that they made up a greater percentage of national income.

The group argues that speculative short-term capital flows threaten the sovereignty of states.

The model would attempt to reduce the predominance of what Unger dubs the "financial casino." The group proposes to adopt controls on short-term capital flows by imposing taxes or requiring reserve deposits. The controls would help stimulate domestic savings and create incentives to channel investment to productive uses. "Financial logic tends to impose itself over productive logic," the group's proposal notes. The group argues that speculative short-term capital flows threaten the sovereignty of states because international financial markets pressure governments to lift regulations and throw open their borders to stateless private capital. They have gained some powerful allies on their point recently. In late September, IMF officials indicated that the fund may encourage the use of controls on short-term volatile capital flows.

Alternativa Latinoamericana also proposes that savings be increased to exceed 30 percent of the national economy; this would be accomplished principally by creating private pension funds. To encourage the use of these savings for productive purposes, special investment funds would be set up, and incentives would be created for investing in undercapitalized small and medium-sized firms. The investment funds are meant to offer an alternative to conventional stock market and banking investments that fuel the financial sector but fail to create employment or goods and services for unskilled and poor workers. A key would be to make financial services, especially credit, available to all citizens. The traditional financial system should expand its coverage through the formation of credit unions, savings and loans, microcredit lending groups, and other locally based finance agencies scattered throughout the countryside.

The model must attempt to overcome the separation between the productive niches Unger calls the "vanguard" and the "rear guard." The vanguard includes innovative, technologically sophisticated, internationally competitive industries; in most emerging markets they capture a huge share of profits but represent a small slice of employment and the production of goods and services consumed by the poor domestically. The rear guard includes the legions of unproductive, undercapitalized small and medium-sized firms and cottage industries that work with obsolete technology and are not linked to the global economy. In Latin America, most employment is generated by firms in the rear guard, and typically the jobs lack social benefits for the workers.

Bridging the gulf between the vanguard and the rear guard would require a new type of linkage between government and private industry to allow flexible and decentralized coordination with small and medium-scale firms at a local level. The alternative model proposes to group small firms together in networks to gain access to investment funds, public and private bank credits, and assistance programs. These relationships would create channels to transmit vanguard practices, especially permanent innovation, reduction of the layers of hierarchy among personnel, and the mixing of cooperation and competition, to the rear guard.

The model would make big business play by the rules of market competition instead of reaping benefits from government support and protection. Policy reform to level the playing field in Latin market economies would include reorienting government support programs toward small and medium-sized companies, advancing stiff antimonopoly laws, ensuring protection for minority shareholders, and eliminating nonvoting shares in companies. The principle of "free trade without dogma" would include adopting selective temporary tariffs to encourage long-term, high-risk investment and reduce the favoritism often shown to big business.

The left also argues that political institutions must be modified so that frequent change is easier. The model proposes giving presidents and congresses the power to call a new election for both executive and legislative branches when reform is blocked. Presidents would be granted "fast-track" procedures to speed decisions on strategic issues.

DEMOCRACY: A KEY INGREDIENT

Deepening democracy in Latin America is a pillar of the model to bridge the region's social and economic divide. Honest elections and constant civic mobilization are but the first steps to this goal. Unger takes a dim view of recent constitutional changes in several Latin countries that allow for the reelection of the president. The reforms have given a second term to Carlos Menem in Argentina and Alberto Fujimori in Peru and returned Brazil's Fernando Henrique Cardoso to power in elections in October. "The development of the reelection system threatens to return Latin America to the era of civilian caudillos," or strongmen, says Unger.

Additional proposals aim to reduce the influence of money in politics through public financing of campaigns, disclosure of private contributions, and the expansion of free access to television for political parties and social movements. To hold governments accountable for their acts, instruments must be created that allow citizens and legislators to call bureaucrats to task. These instruments would include popularly initiated recall votes, referendums, congressional oversight of government agencies, independent accounting offices to combat corruption, and citizen selection and supervision of public works projects.

Democratization of information is also required in the vision of a strengthened society and a transparent government. Practical means must be found to inform constituents of their rights as citizens, as men and women, and as members of ethnic groups, and to encourage them to defend their rights. Private monopolies that control the policy and content of mass media, especially television, must be broken up by limiting the concentration of concessions or frequencies. Television cries out most urgently for this reform because across Latin America it is the leading source of news for most people. In Brazil, for example, 80 percent of adults never read newspapers. The power of Latin media magnates and the ongoing wave of privatizations of media-related industries such as telecommunications companies combine to create strong allegiances between the information industry and government, says Unger.

PUTTING THE PLAN TO THE POLITICAL TEST

While some elements of this model may seem far-fetched, more than a few are gaining currency among economists and government and development officials. "What seemed fringe ideas two to three years ago are becoming more mainstream," Castañeda observes. In particular, creating controls to regulate flows of short-term capital seems like an idea whose time has come. To reduce the volatility that afflicts emerging markets, controls on short-term capital have been endorsed since the Asian crisis by prominent figures including billionaire hedge fund investor George Soros, World Bank chief economist Joseph Stiglitz, and Goldman Sachs managing director E. Gerald Corrigan. Stiglitz condemns free movement of capital, citing economic research that shows there is no relationship between unrestricted capital flows and economic growth.

Long a taboo in Latin America, tax reform designed to increase government revenues by raising taxes and broadening the tax base is being put before legislatures across the region. Latin governments, the World Bank, and regional development banks such as the Inter-American Development Bank are now taking a closer look at poverty. There is a growing consensus that attacking poverty requires broad social programs beyond the transfer payments and slim subsidies widespread today. Finally, Castañeda points out, the dangers of maintaining an overvalued currency and monetary instability are widely accepted in financial circles.

PROMISING RESULTS

The politicians in the group have led innovative programs with successful results that show how the model could work. In Brazil, Workers' Party leader Tarso Genro is a case in point. While serving as mayor of the southern city of Porto Alegre, he established a partnership between the municipal government and the private sector to finance a fund to make small loans to small-scale businesses. He created participatory budgeting by dividing the city into 16 districts, each with an elected council that set priorities on public works projects such as schools, community health clinics, and roads. Citizen groups managed the budget and supervised the construction of projects in their neighborhoods. The result: money was spent carefully and about one-third more projects than usual were completed. Genro also raised municipal revenues by 25 percent by taxing undeveloped urban land being held for speculation and placing a levy on urban services. At the end of his four-year term in 1997, he boasted a 75 percent approval rating.

Vicente Fox, the governor of Guanajuato state in central Mexico and presidential hopeful from the conservative National Action Party, is promoting microlending. He used $5 million from state funds and raised an equal amount from the private sector to create the initial capital for the nonprofit Banco Santa Fé de Guanajuato. Modeled after the Grameen Bank of Bangladesh, the bank grants microcredits of as little as $100 to tiny enterprises such as pig-raising in a backyard stable and sidewalk food-stands. The bank has made many loans to working women who often are the mainstay of the family, since Guanajuato sends many migrant workers to the United States.

Also in Mexico, a recent referendum on national economic issues has strengthened the opposition mandate to hold the government accountable for federal spending. Opposition politicians have seized on a government bank bailout scheme—which would have cost taxpayers $65 billion in public debt—to mobilize citizen demands for greater control over the budget. Andrés Manuel López Obrador, president of the left-wing Democratic Revolution Party (PRD), led the referendum, which drew more than 3 million votes nationwide on August 31. The PRD referendum marked the first time since the economic reforms began that the citizenry has been consulted on economic policy. More than 95 percent of those voting opposed the government's proposal to assume bad bank loans as public debt.

The referendum provided overwhelming support for PRD proposals to audit large corporate loans, which make up about half the bad debt; provide aid to small debtors; and restrict foreign investment in banks. Although government and banking officials discredited the referendum, saying it was skewed to favor PRD positions, it nevertheless strengthened the opposition mandate to demand that banks shoulder more of the burden of the bailout.

The mechanisms for combating neoliberalism and the possibilities of forming center-left alliances will vary with each country. But there is agreement that the Alternativa group provides a prized function as a forum for exchanging ideas and practical experiences to improve Latin American societies. "It can contribute to the formation of a bloc that is political, democratic, anti-neoliberal, and is occupying spaces in Latin America," Brazil's Genro said in a recent interview. This group is preparing to influence regional issues, in particular to set an agenda for labor and social issues in the negotiations of the Free Trade Area of the Americas, the hemisphere-wide free trade area that is to be set up in the next seven years. The debate over center-left alliances has been maturing with the group's deliberations. "Our countries require great transformations [that] cannot be made without wide citizen backing and that require alliances, and that requires pluralism," said Gabriel Gaspar, a research fellow at Flacso, a research institution in Santiago, Chile.

It was not possible to build such an alliance for the October 4 presidential race in Brazil, the first of a wave of elections in Latin America between now and mid-2000. "That was not due to the impotence of the group, it was due to objective conditions of the Brazilian political process," says Genro. Brazil's Workers' Party backed its two-time presidential candidate, Luis Inácio "Lula" da Silva, because the traditional left within his party resisted an alliance with centrist Ciro Gomes and hoped to win congressional seats on Lula's coattails.

In other countries, however, the chances for center-left alliances are strong and the coalitions might defeat neoliberal regimes in coming elections. In El Salvador, the guerrilla force turned political party, the Farabundo Martí National Liberation Front, is seen as the front-runner in the March 1999 presidential race it will run in an alliance with a range of civic organizations. In Argentina, the Alianza, a political grouping made up of the Frepaso and Unión Cívica Radical parties, is a strong contender in the 1999 presidential race. In Chile, the ruling center-left coalition is expected to keep the presidency in December 1999 elections with front-runner candidate Ricardo Lagos, a moderate socialist, backed by the Christian Democrats. The Mexican election in July 2000 is too far off to call, but the Alternative's meetings have provided a setting for dialogue between the two most likely opposition candidates, Mexico City mayor Cuauhtémoc Cárdenas and Vicente Fox.

The model has yet to be adopted by Latin America's conventional leftist parties. However, it is gaining ground as left-wing and center politicians search for a program to offer constituents in the postcommunist era. For some leftist parties in Latin America, the model fuels splits that were already brewing by providing ideas for those who have accepted the inevitability of globalization. The aim of Alternativa Latinoamericana is to stimulate a process of gradual economic, political, and societal change to combat a destiny that the continent does not deserve.

LUCY CONGER *is a writer based in Mexico City covering Latin American finance and economy. She is a correspondent for* Institutional Investor *magazine and writes for* U.S. News and World Report *and other publications. Some of the material in this article was originally reported for* Institutional Investor *and is included with permission.*

DEMOCRACY IN RUSSIA

How free is free?

On paper, Vladimir Putin's Russia is a splendidly democratic place. But there are increasingly ominous signs

MOSCOW

DEPENDING on where you stand, you can be elated by Russia's democratic progress since the collapse of the Soviet Union a decade ago, or depressed by its shortcomings; or even both at once. By Soviet standards, Russia is incomparably freer than it used to be. By the standards of western democracies, there is some cause for concern; and those concerns are growing, rather than diminishing.

Begin with celebration. After 70 years of one-party rule, isolation, repression and bouts of mass murder, Russia is now governed not by Communist ideologues but by rulers who profess democracy. Compared with the Soviet era, most people can choose where they work and live, travel abroad, meet foreigners, try to get rich without being punished for it, worship freely, set up political parties, and complain individually or with others about most of the country's plentiful problems. Some can even send their children to private schools. For anyone familiar with the horrors of the past, it is a cause for great rejoicing.

But historical perspective does not answer the most important question: what is happening to Russian democracy now? Are its current ills—menaced media, fixed elections, an over-mighty security service, harassment of the opposition, xenophobia and racism, to name just a few—just temporary wobbles, or do they mark a slide towards something new and nasty?

Start with the way Russia runs its elections. These are free and multi-party, and it is hard to argue that the man who emerged from the last round of parliamentary and presidential elections, Vladimir Putin, was not the candidate most Russians wanted. Mr Putin was his predecessor's nominated heir; but so, too, were John Major and Al Gore. What is more worrying is that the most important bits of the media—state-controlled television stations—were biased in his favour. As in the current batch of local elections, the Kremlin also used the courts, the tax police, and blackmail against its opponents: many of whom, admittedly, would have done just the same given the chance.

The Chechen war helped too. Some Russian journalists and politicians suspect that the authorities had a hand in the mysterious bombs, in the autumn of 1999, that were its ostensible justification. There is no hard evidence either way: Mr Putin calls the very suggestion "immoral". But the media's exaggerated portrayal of the war as righteous self-defence against international Islamic terrorism certainly helped Mr Putin, who was then an obscure, newly appointed prime minister, to gain popularity quickly.

The *Moscow Times*, an English-language daily, recently published a lengthy investigation into ballot-rigging in the presidential election in March. Few doubt that Mr Putin, with all his other advantages, would have anyway beaten his lacklustre Communist opponent in the run-off. But it may have been phantom voters, forgeries and other fraud that helped him win a narrow outright victory in the first round. According to the *Moscow Times* report, about 1.3m extra voters mysteriously appeared on the election rolls in the three months before the election; and it seems strange, to say the least, that Chechnya went so heavily for Mr Putin.

There was no response to this report. No other news organisation picked up the story. The few Russians who heard about it shrugged cynically. No official bothered to refute the details. Contrast that with the current fuss in Florida, and it highlights another problem. Democracy is not just about elections: it is also about how wrongs are righted. In a healthy system, politicians, courts, journalists, independent officials and trade unions are strong and interlocking. A scandal broken by a newspaper may well be raised in parliament, persuade the public prosecutor to take action, lead to a public inquiry and prompt a resignation or a new law.

In Russia, these institutions, groups and processes are weak. At best, the watchdogs bark. They rarely if ever bite. As a result, human rights are easily abused. On paper, Russia sub-

From *The Economist*, November 25, 2000, pp. 23-24, 26.

scribes to all the international norms. In practice, it is often a different story.

Muffled voices

The press in Russia has all the appearance of being free. It is not difficult to start a website, or a small newspaper: something unthinkable ten years ago. But the more effectively you criticise the authorities, the more difficult life becomes. In the provinces, your competitors will be subsidised, either through cheap paper and premises, or directly. Officials may stop talking to your journalists. You risk regular, disruptive investigations by the tax, hygiene, fire or labour inspectors. You may be sued for defamation, with little chance of acquittal. You may find distributing your paper and selling advertising very difficult.

At national level, the Kremlin tolerates, more or less, independent newspapers and magazines (which typically sell a few tens of thousands of copies, in a country of 140m). But it does not like national television channels that it cannot control. Two leading tycoons, Boris Berezovsky and Vladimir Gusinsky, who had built up powerful media interests, are now in exile, facing fraud charges. Other tycoons with equally questionable records, but better relations with the Kremlin, are flourishing unhindered.

It is important not to exaggerate the immediate effects of this. Mr Gusinsky's television station is still broadcasting, and still much better than its competitors. Things are much worse in most of the rest of the former Soviet Union. The Russian authorities' hostility to the idea of a free and effective press is only a shadow of the treatment meted out to publishers of *samizdat* in the Soviet Union. Russian media proprietors are not comparable to the heroic dissidents of the past, who used their television channels ruthlessly to fight their political battles. Russian journalism is often indefensibly sensationalist and corrupt.

But as Mr Putin consolidates power, the likelihood of greater state control of the media is growing. The government is toying with a law that would restrict the operations of foreign-owned media in Russia, such as the Russian language services of Reuters, a news agency, or Radio Liberty, a broadcaster financed by the American government. In a healthy democracy, annoying the authorities is how many journalists make their careers. In Russia, it is a good way to become unemployable; many of Mr Gusinsky's journalists hastily left for other jobs when he got into trouble.

The authorities' motives in all this are mixed. Partly it is just convenience, or the belief that such measures are temporarily necessary. Partly it reflects Russia's continuing obsession with national security. A critic is often portrayed as a saboteur, and one with foreign friends is a spy. When he was president, Boris Yeltsin muffled the xenophobic reflexes of the Soviet system. Under Mr Putin, they seem to be returning.

As head of the FSB (the domestic-security successor to the Soviet KGB), Mr Putin bluntly dismissed environmental groups as fronts for foreign intelligence gathering. He has also worried publicly about "unauthorised" contacts with foreigners. It has now become quite risky to be a foreign researcher or businessman in Russia if your field of interest includes anything that a spy-catcher could possibly construe as secret. Recent practical examples include civil-military relations, arms exports and pollution by the armed forces.

The victims are still very few: one American businessman is currently on trial on flimsy-sounding espionage charges. A handful of Russians are in a similar pickle. Grigory Pasko, an environmentalist, told Japanese television about the navy's mishandling of nuclear waste. After a court decision on November 21st, he faces a new bout of pre-trial detention. Another American businessman is also currently in jail, on trial in a different case. Mr Pasko's charge that the "spy mania"' is sweeping the country sounds overblown. But once you start blaming outsiders for your problems, it may be difficult to stop.

Second-class citizens

This whiff of xenophobia is matched by racism. Although Mr Putin had a well-publicised lunch with the doyen of Soviet-era Jewish *refusniks*, Natan Sharansky, anti-Semitism in Russia provokes rather mild official objections. In September, masked right-wing extremists stormed into a Jewish school in Ryazan, terrifying the children and breaking furniture. The police have done next to nothing. The recently elected governor of the Kursk region, Alexander Mikhailov, said his fight against Jewish "filth" was supported by the president. The Kremlin rebuked him, but merely for "foolishness". Mr Putin's own local representative said he was convinced the remarks were not Mr Mikhailov's "ideological position".

Jews in fact enjoy considerable religious freedom in Russia. For other religions, especially smaller and foreign-sounding ones, official obstruction is an increasing nuisance. The Salvation Army, for example, which feeds around 6,000 hungry Russians every month in the winter, has had to waste tens of thousands of dollars in legal fights over registration, and the Catholic church has had trouble getting visas for its foreign clergy.

For ethnic minorities in Russia that lack the Jews' powerful allies abroad, life is often difficult. In official rhetoric, the words "Islamic" and "terrorist" are interchangeable. Efforts by non-Russian nationalities to preserve their languages and cultures risk denunciation as "separatism". When the Chechen war started, thousands of Chechen residents of Moscow were simply rounded up and thrown out of the city. Anyone with a dark skin (as plenty of foreigners have found to their cost) risks harassment from the police that can range from a tiresome document check to detention, or worse.

The Chechen war itself, now 15 months old and with no end in sight, overshadows all other problems with Russia's democracy. Of course, democracies do fight wars, sometimes very bloody ones. Anyone wanting to stress the uniqueness of Russian crimes in Chechnya needs to bear in mind comparisons both geographical (Turkey and the Kurds) and historical (France in Algeria), as well as the Chechens' own kidnap industry.

For all that, Russia's conduct of the war, especially in the treatment of prisoners and refugees, has been revolting and counter-productive. A lengthy new report by Human Rights Watch catalogues the tortures inflicted on Chechen detainees, including women, young people and the elderly. Many Chechens are arrested and abused for no better reason than to extract a ransom. "If it were possible to gain access to Chechens detained in Russia one would probably have a list of political prisoners running into the thousands," says Alex Anderson of Amnesty International, a pressure group.

The underlying problem is that Russia has not considered—or really even started discussing—what sort of country it wants to be. Is the Russian Federation basically a Russian empire, with a few non-Russians living in it as second-class citizens? In that case, conflicts with resentful or ambitious non-Russian nationalities are all but inevitable. Or can it become a multinational country where Russian just happens to be the main language and culture, but where Tatars, Kalmyks, and others, who make up more than a sixth of the population, can feel equally at home and respected—like, say, Latinos in America or the Swedish minority in Finland?

That might well have a better chance of working eventually, although even the most advanced and liberal democracies, including the United States, have made quite a hash of assimilating people of different races. In any case, most Russians, used to being the unquestioned top dogs in the Soviet Union, find it hard to take ethnic minorities seriously.

A second big shortcoming of the Russian political system highlighted by the war in Chechnya is the weakness of civilian oversight of the armed forces. Although the elected Duma, through its committees, and the media have some power to oversee and comment on abuses, the army, in many respects, is a law unto itself. Corruption is rampant.

This may improve a bit under the ambitious military reform plans announced earlier this month by Mr Putin. But—as with many other reforms—improvements are coming thanks to narrowly conceived orders from the top, rather than the popular will channelled through the political system. Mr Putin's main complaint about the army is that it is wasteful and ineffective, not that it is brutal and lawless.

Reform of government is a similar example. Again, it is commendable that this is happening at all. Clearly, something had to be done about the corrupt and incompetent people running Russia's provinces. Mr Putin's answer, shortly after taking power, was to appoint seven prefects, each in charge of a dozen or so regions. These men, five of them with a military or security background, are meant to keep a strict eye on the governors, especially when they have imposed local laws that differ from federal ones.

The seven presidential representatives are proving quite good at biffing local tyrants. But they are showing little interest in putting something more democratic in their place. There is little contact with the public, no encouragement of independent media. The biffing is very selective: the city of Moscow, for example, has managed so far to maintain its unconstitutional system of residence permits, a huge source of graft and unfairness. The result may prove more orderly, and better for business. But it will not make Russia's regions more democratic.

Few checks, few balances

All Russia's problems of human rights and democracy come back to three things: the legislature, the executive and the judiciary. None works as well as it should. Parliament passes laws in a hurry, and has neither the ability nor the will to call high officials to account. State officials abuse human rights (either on their own, or on orders from on high) and work with remarkable slowness and disorganisation. The courts almost completely fail in their role as the ultimate safeguard of freedom and order.

Russian parliamentarians largely see their job as voting the way they are told (or paid), rather than dealing with their voters' grievances. The only post-Communist countries that have managed to build a decent state administration and the rule of law are those which had them before 1945. Russian bureaucrats behave very rationally: almost everywhere, the rewards for honesty and efficiency are tiny. So are the penalties for graft and laziness.

Judges are ill-trained, badly paid and under heavy outside pressure. Almost all criminal cases end in a conviction. There are jury trials in only nine of Russia's 89 regions. Sergei Pashin, a prominent judicial reformer and judge, was sacked last month for criticising the conduct of the trial of a conscientious objector, and for giving out his telephone number during a radio programme. The Moscow board of judges said that his behaviour was "not fitting".

There is very little sign of this changing. If anything, the consolidation of power in the past year has made it worse. "We wanted a stronger state to make bureaucrats obey the law, but Mr Putin sees a stronger state as meaning a stronger bureaucracy," says Ludmila Alexeyeva, who heads a big human-rights organisation in Moscow.

The blame rests not only with Russia's rulers. It also reflects public attitudes and behaviour. First, Russians themselves, quite understandably, think that many of their laws are bad and feel no compunction about breaking them. Second, they have little faith in formal ways of complaining. As a result, they seldom use them. "We have no tradition of living by the law," says Mrs Alexeyeva. "Faced with a problem, people try bribes, personal connections or force."

After decades of totalitarianism and centuries of autocracy, it would be silly to expect Russia to sprout a strong civil society and independent institutions like mushrooms. There are plenty of countries that are unpleasantly tough with pushy foreigners, ethnic minorities and the political opposition, but have a reasonably stable and competent government and manage to get a bit freer and more prosperous every year. Many Russians would think that sounded pretty good. It may well be what Mr Putin wants too. If he delivers it, many foreign countries would heave a sigh of relief.

Yet Russia's current economic stability is perilously balanced on the high oil price. Most of the economy is still largely in ruins after the Soviet collapse and botched reform. Some Russians have been speculating that the government may be planning to move to a "mobilisation economy" in the event of a downturn, which would mean a much greater degree of planning and controls. If that happened, political as well as economic freedoms would suffer.

Second, the danger of silencing critics is that bad policies continue and frustration mounts. Harassing greens, rather than listening to them, means even less chance of salvaging Russia's devastated environment. The difficulties put in the way of independent trade unions will keep Russian industrial workplaces in an awful state. Ethnic minorities that see their language and culture dying tend to start letting off bombs if no one listens to them.

Authoritarian temptations

Third, heavy-handed habits tend to grow on rulers, especially in countries where the bureaucracy is very incompetent. In general, Mr Putin seems keen to avoid the appearance of authoritarianism. "Our big hope is that Mrs Putin likes having tea with the Empress of Japan," jokes one of Mr Gusinsky's editors. "He won't do anything that risks a scandal abroad." Certainly Mr Putin delights in international respectability. On specific issues, such as Chechnya, he seems to choose to brazen out criticism from abroad, rather than overrule his own hard men. But he shows some sign of learning on the job, and, even if he has authoritarian instincts, they may be checked by experience.

In sum, there is a respectable case for optimism about Russia; but there is a case for pessimism too. When push comes to shove—at a time, for example, of national emergency—the gains of the past ten years will have to guarantee Russian democracy. "It is not so gloomy, because of what happened in the last ten years," says Mrs Alexeyeva, a veteran of Soviet-era dissent. "Society can defend itself." Cross your fingers.

One battle after another

Women fought for their rights throughout the twentieth century. In the past several decades, their struggle has truly become global, but all is far from won

Sophie Bessis

We often hear that this will be the century of women, in light of the tremendous strides that have been made in the past thirty years or so. Although it is far too soon to confirm this prediction, it can safely be asserted that the twentieth century was marked by their struggle to leave the home, where they were confined by the ancestral division of roles along gender lines. Around the world, women have campaigned to win the rights they have been denied and to build, side-by-side with men, the future of the planet.

True, such struggles had already been waged in the past, although they were deliberately shunned in official historical accounts. But the brief revolts of this special "minority", which accounts for over half of humanity, did not change the place of women in their societies. They may have ruled the roost, sometimes enjoying undeniable respect, but nevertheless they were still born to serve men and bring their husbands' descendants into the world.

Education: their first struggle

Yet, at the start of the twentieth century, the traditional distribution of roles, seemingly legitimised by every religion and frozen in a "natural" order, began to crumble under the two-pronged assault of modernisation and women's struggle for their collective emancipation. They waged many battles to gradually obtain, despite setbacks, a change in their status—which is still far from achieved.

The first struggle of the twentieth century was for education. In 1861, a young woman graduated in France with a baccalaureate, a highschool leaving exam, for the first time. In 1900, the first female university was founded in Japan. The same year, girls won the right to secondary education in Egypt and the first girls' school opened in Tunisia. Young women who could made the most of these new educational opportunities, not only to become better household managers and good educators for their children, as the main discourse of the period suggests, but also to do something unprecedented: to enter the forbidden spheres of public life, to exercise citizenship and to participate in politics.

> **For a long time I have hesitated to write a book on women. The subject is irritating, especially to women; and it is not new.**
>
> Simone de Beauvoir,
> French writer (1908–1986)

Throughout the twentieth century, women waged a battle on two fronts: by fighting for their own rights and taking part in the major social and political emancipation movements. In 1917, the Russian Bolshevik Alexandra Kollontaï became the world's first woman cabinet minister. African American Rosa Parks triggered the civil rights movement by refusing to give up her seat to a white man on an Alabama bus in 1955. Djamila Boupacha was a heroine of Algeria's war for independence. Women were entirely committed to the goals of these movements but seldom received anything in return for participating in them. Once their countries' new masters took power, they often found themselves sent back to the kitchen. But they continued fighting for their own rights, and it is on this front that they achieved their greatest victories.

The earliest feminist movements, which first appeared in the West in the late nineteenth century, focused on workplace and civil rights issues. Industry needed women's labour, which was underpaid in comparison

Reprinted from the *Unesco Courier*, June 2000 by Sophie Bessis. Reprinted by permission.

with that of their male counterparts. 'Equal pay for equal work!' demanded American and European women, who began setting up their own trade unions and organizing strikes. They made unquestionable strides, but after more than one century of struggle, most women around the world still earn less pay for equal work.

The right to vote

The second objective of the twentieth century's pioneers was participation in public life, which hinged first and foremost on having the right to vote. The struggle was long and sometimes violent, as shown by the British "suffragettes" who demonstrated in the streets or Chinese women who made their demands heard by invading their country's new parliament in 1912. Everywhere, the fierce resistance of the political world progressively yielded to determined women's movements.

Scandinavia is where women first won the right to vote and to run for election, with Finland leading the way in 1906. The First World War thrust them into the forefront, with most European women winning the right to vote in 1918 and 1919, although French and Italian women had to wait until after the Second World War to at last be recognized as citizens. Outside the West, women also organized to demand their rights. Groups were founded in Turkey, Egypt and India. In 1930, the first congress of women from the Near and Middle East gathered in Damascus to demand equality. Throughout this period, women everywhere declared that, outside of motherhood, they had the right to be just like men, and that men could not deny them this right.

Control over their own bodies

For a while, women's rights movements took a back seat to the Second World War and liberation struggles in the European colonies. The fight against fascism and, after 1945, colonialism, mobilized all their energy. Women distinguished themselves in these struggles, but that did not suffice to establish their rights as a gender. However, the world continued to change. With independence, many women in the South won access to schooling, salaried employment and, in a few exceptional cases, the closed world of politics. In Western countries, the postwar period saw them enter the work force on a massive scale. The gap between social reality and the discriminatory laws defended by exclusively male power structures grew wider.

In the West, the second generation of feminists emerged in the wake of the libertarian movements of 1968. Picking up where their elders left off, they broadened the scope of their demands, for late-twentieth century feminists no longer aspired to the right to be "just like men". Challenging the claim of the "white male" to represent universality, their goal was to achieve equality while remaining distinct as women. The women's liberation movement that first emerged in the American middle-class claimed the right to control one's own body. Feminists fought for contraception and abortion rights in many countries where one or both were against the law, and for autonomy and equality within the couple. "The personal is political," proclaimed women inspired by Marxism and psychoanalysis. "Workers of the world, who washes your socks?" chanted demonstrators in the streets of Paris in the 1970s. In France, the Veil law legalizing abortion unleashed emotional debate in 1974.

Many Third World women could not identify with the struggles being waged in the West and insisted on leading their own battles at their own pace. However, these Western feminist movements breathed new life into the cause. Recognizing the changes and proclaiming their intention to accelerate them, the United Nations declared 1975 "International Women's Year" and organized the first international women's conference in Mexico City.

Already proclaimed in the Universal Declaration of Human Rights in 1948, sexual equality was reasserted in 1979 by the Convention on the Abolition of All Forms of Discrimination Against Women, which became a precious emancipation tool in the North as well as the South. At UN conferences in Copenhagen in 1980, Nairobi in 1985 and Beijing in 1995, women from both hemispheres found common ground, demanding the right to "have a child if I want it, when I want it," rejecting Malthusian principles and claiming their place in political bodies that until then had decided the world's future without them, struggling against religious fundamentalism that jeopardizes their modest gains.

Misogyny of the political class

Of course, the struggle of Kuwaiti women against those who have denied them the right to vote or Indian women against the forced abortion of female fœtuses is not the same as American women's battle against their own fundamentalists or French women's campaign against the misogyny of the political class. Women's movements take different approaches depending on the continent and do not necessarily have the same priorities, but the struggle has nonetheless become global during the past several decades. In the last twenty-five years, women have gradually increased their presence in public life, although it can hardly be said that the doors are wide open for them. From Africa to Asia, women's organizations have multiplied and acquired experience.

But their victories remain incomplete and the future is uncertain. From the nightmare of Afghan women to the ways in which equality is resisted in the so-called most advanced countries, the obstacles show that there is still a long way to go. Will women see the end of the struggle in this century that has just begun, the one which supposedly belongs to them?

World Map

This map has been developed to give you a graphic picture of where the countries of the world are located, the relationship they have with their region and neighbors, and their positions relative to the superpowers and power blocs. We have focused on certain areas to more clearly illustrate these crowded regions.

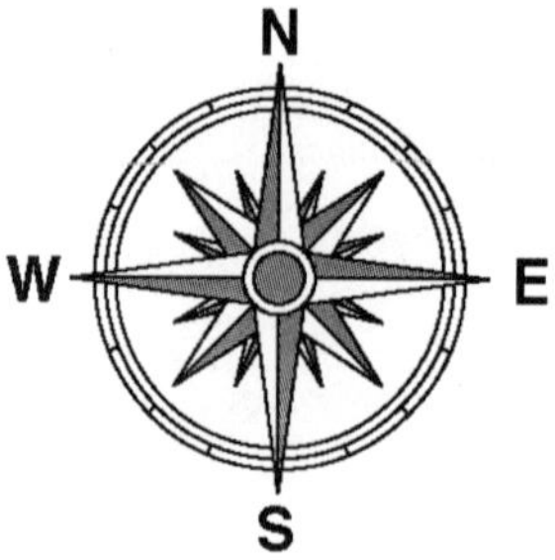

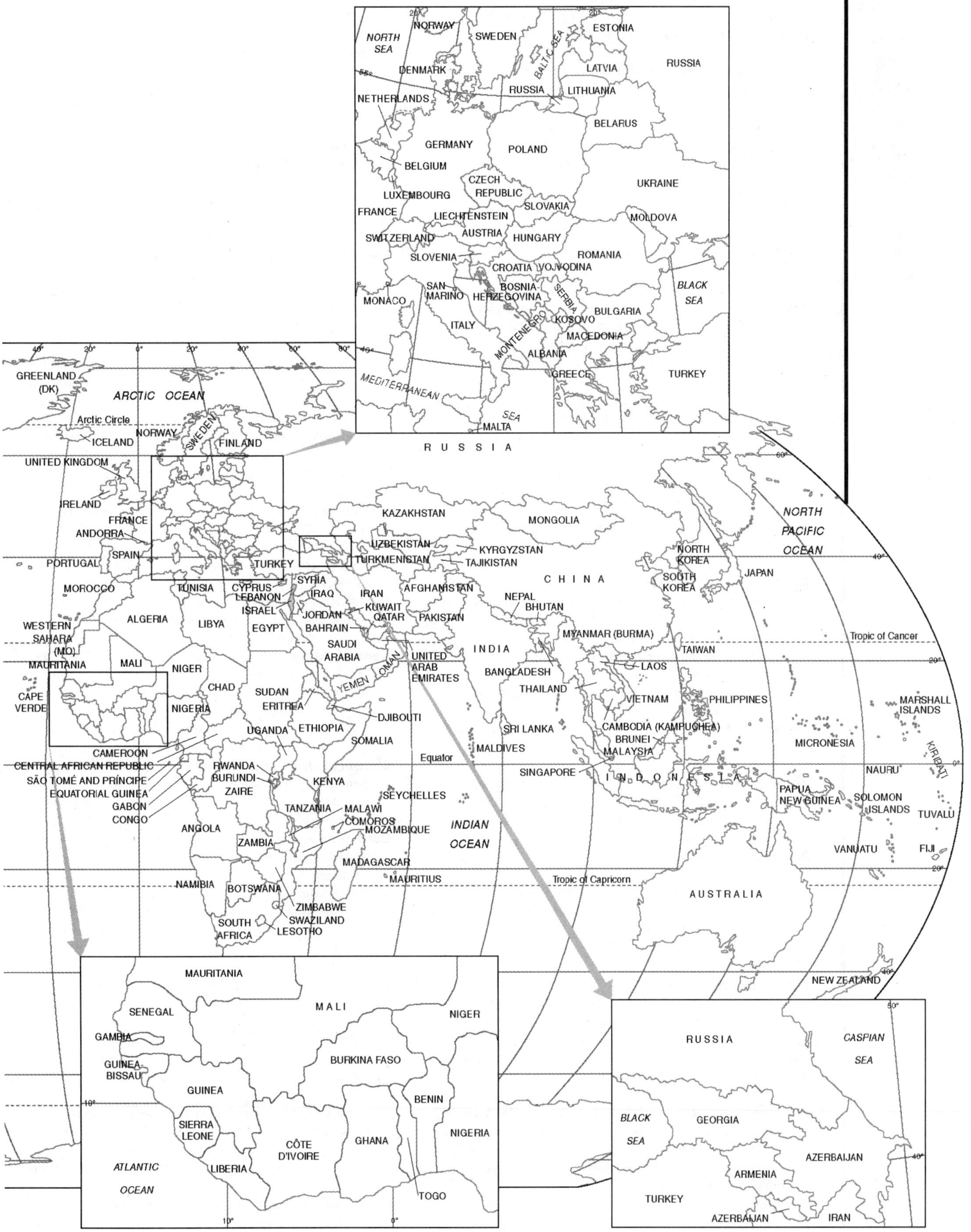
NORTH SEA
NORWAY
SWEDEN
BALTIC SEA
ESTONIA
RUSSIA
DENMARK
LATVIA
NETHERLANDS
RUSSIA
LITHUANIA
BELARUS
GERMANY
POLAND
BELGIUM
CZECH REPUBLIC
UKRAINE
LUXEMBOURG
SLOVAKIA
FRANCE
LIECHTENSTEIN
MOLDOVA
SWITZERLAND
AUSTRIA
HUNGARY
SLOVENIA
ROMANIA
CROATIA
VOJVODINA
SAN MARINO
BOSNIA-HERZEGOVINA
SERBIA
BLACK SEA
MONACO
BULGARIA
KOSOVO
ITALY
MONTENEGRO
MACEDONIA
ALBANIA
GREECE
TURKEY
MEDITERRANEAN SEA
MALTA
GREENLAND (DK)
ARCTIC OCEAN
Arctic Circle
ICELAND
NORWAY
SWEDEN
FINLAND
R U S S I A
UNITED KINGDOM
IRELAND
FRANCE
ANDORRA
SPAIN
PORTUGAL
MOROCCO
TUNISIA
CYPRUS
LEBANON
ISRAEL
TURKEY
SYRIA
IRAQ
JORDAN
KAZAKHSTAN
MONGOLIA
UZBEKISTAN
TURKMENISTAN
KYRGYZSTAN
TAJIKISTAN
NORTH KOREA
SOUTH KOREA
JAPAN
NORTH PACIFIC OCEAN
C H I N A
IRAN
AFGHANISTAN
NEPAL
BHUTAN
KUWAIT
QATAR
BAHRAIN
PAKISTAN
WESTERN SAHARA (MO)
ALGERIA
LIBYA
EGYPT
SAUDI ARABIA
MYANMAR (BURMA)
Tropic of Cancer
TAIWAN
MAURITANIA
MALI
NIGER
UNITED ARAB EMIRATES
I N D I A
OMAN
YEMEN
BANGLADESH
LAOS
CAPE VERDE
CHAD
SUDAN
ERITREA
THAILAND
VIETNAM
PHILIPPINES
MARSHALL ISLANDS
NIGERIA
DJIBOUTI
ETHIOPIA
UGANDA
SOMALIA
SRI LANKA
CAMBODIA (KAMPUCHEA)
BRUNEI
MALAYSIA
MICRONESIA
KIRIBATI
CAMEROON
CENTRAL AFRICAN REPUBLIC
SÃO TOMÉ AND PRÍNCIPE
EQUATORIAL GUINEA
GABON
CONGO
RWANDA
BURUNDI
ZAIRE
KENYA
MALDIVES
Equator
SINGAPORE
I N D O N E S I A
NAURU
SEYCHELLES
PAPUA NEW GUINEA
SOLOMON ISLANDS
TUVALU
TANZANIA
MALAWI
COMOROS
MOZAMBIQUE
INDIAN OCEAN
ANGOLA
ZAMBIA
VANUATU
FIJI
MADAGASCAR
MAURITIUS
Tropic of Capricorn
NAMIBIA
BOTSWANA
A U S T R A L I A
ZIMBABWE
SWAZILAND
SOUTH AFRICA
LESOTHO
NEW ZEALAND
MAURITANIA
M A L I
SENEGAL
NIGER
GAMBIA
BURKINA FASO
GUINEA-BISSAU
GUINEA
BENIN
SIERRA LEONE
CÔTE D'IVOIRE
GHANA
NIGERIA
LIBERIA
ATLANTIC OCEAN
TOGO
R U S S I A
CASPIAN SEA
BLACK SEA
GEORGIA
AZERBAIJAN
ARMENIA
TURKEY
AZERBAIJAN
IRAN

Glossary

Actors (international) Individuals or organizations that play a direct role in the conduct of world politics.

Adjudication The legal process of deciding an issue through the courts.

African, Caribbean, and Pacific Countries (ACP) Seventy-one countries associated with the European Community.

African National Congress (ANC) South African organization founded in 1912 in response to the taking of land from Africans and the restrictions on their employment and movement.

Andean Group Consisting of Bolivia, Colombia, Ecuador, Peru, and Venezuela, this community's main objective is to eliminate trade barriers within the group.

Antiballistic Missile (ABM) Treaty This 1971 treaty placed stringent limits on U.S. and Soviet efforts to build a ballistic missile defense (BMD) system.

Apartheid A system of laws in the Republic of South Africa that segregated and politically and economically discriminated against non-European groups.

Arab Maghreb Union (AMU) An organization whose members include the North African states of Algeria, Libya, Mauritania, Morocco, and Tunisia. Created to provide an alternative framework for dealing with regional political, economic, and security issues among Maghreb countries.

Arms control Any measure limiting or reducing forces, regulating armaments, and/or restricting the deployment of troops or weapons.

Asian-Pacific Economic Cooperation (APEC) A regional trade organization founded in 1989 and including 18 countries.

Association of Caribbean States (ACS) Created to advance greater cultural, economic, political, scientific, social, and technological cooperation among the Caribbean peoples, governments, and countries.

Association of Southeast Asian Nations (ASEAN) A regional regrouping made up of Brunei, Indonesia, Laos, Malaysia, Myanmar, Philippines, Singapore, Thailand, and Vietnam.

Autarky Establishing economic independence from external sources.

Balance of payments A figure that represents the net flow of money into and out of a country due to trade, tourist expenditures, sale of services (such as consulting), foreign aid, profits, and so forth.

Balance of trade The relationship between imports and exports.

Bantustans Ten designated geographical areas or "homelands" that were created for each African ethnic group under the apartheid government of South Africa.

Barrel A standard measure for petroleum, equivalent to 42 gallons or 158.86 liters.

Big emerging markets Countries or regions that are starting to develop; countries that are geographically large, have significant populations, and strong growth potential for most manufactured products.

Bilateral diplomacy Negotiations between two countries.

Bilateral (foreign) aid Foreign aid given by one country directly to another.

Biological and Toxins Weapons Convention (BWC) Held in 1972, the convention was directed toward general and complete disarmament, including the prohibition and elimination of all types of bacteriological (biological) weapons of mass destruction. Of the 159 signatories, 141 countries ratified the agreement.

Biosphere The environment of life and living processes at or near Earth's surface, extending from the ocean floor to about 75 kilometers into the atmosphere. It is being endangered by consequences of human activities such as air and water pollution, acid rain, radioactive fallout, desertification, toxic and nuclear wastes, and the depletion of nonrenewable resources.

Bipolar system A world political system in which power is primarily held by two international actors.

Bretton Woods system The international monetary system that existed from the end of World War II until the early 1970s; named for a 1944 international economic conference held in Bretton Woods, New Hampshire.

Camp David Agreements/Accords Agreements signed in September 1978, at Camp David—a mountain retreat for the U.S. president in Maryland—by President Anwar al-Sadat of Egypt and Prime Minister Menachem Begin of Israel, and witnessed by President Jimmy Carter.

Capitalism An economic system based on the private ownership of real property and commercial enterprise, competition for profits, and limited government interference in the marketplace.

Caribbean Community (CARICOM) All Commonwealth Caribbean countries are members of this group, which is aimed at stimulating and promoting economic political integration.

Caribbean Free Trade Association (CARIFTA) Created in 1967 as a limited free trade agreement, it was superseded by 1973 CARICOM (Caribbean Community).

Carrying capacity The number of people that an environment can feed, provide water for, and otherwise sustain.

Cartel An international agreement among producers of a commodity that attempts to control the production and pricing of that commodity.

Central American Common Market (CACM) Started in 1960 (by treaty) between Guatemala, Honduras, Nicaragua, El Salvador, and later Costa Rica, the group has made advances toward economic integration. It has been judged more successful at lowering trade barriers than any other Latin American grouping.

Chemical Weapons Convention (CWC) Treaty Signed in 1993 (effective in 1995), the treaty requires signatories to pledge to eliminate all chemical weapons by the year 2005 and to submit to rigorous inspection.

Cold war A condition of hostility that existed between the United States and the Soviet Union in their struggle to dominate the world scene following World War II. It ended with the collapse of the Soviet Union in 1991.

Collective security The original theory behind UN peacekeeping. It holds that aggression against one state is aggression against all and should be defeated by the collective action of all.

Combined Joint Task Force Structures (CJTFS) A 1994 NATO-approved concept for coordinated military operations outside the territory of NATO members. CJTFS will permit NATO or Western European Union forces to form ad hoc coalitions of willing countries.

Commodity The unprocessed products of mining and agriculture.

Common foreign and security policy (CFSP) Established by the Maastricht Treaty in 1993, and revised by the Amsterdam Treaty in 1997, the treaty creates a security and common defense policy for the Euopean Union.

Common Heritage of Mankind A 1970 UN declaration that states that the "seabed and ocean floor, and the subsoil thereof, beyond the limits of national jurisdiction . . . , as well as the resources of the area, are the common heritage of mankind."

Common Market A customs union that eliminates trade barriers within a group and establishes a common external tariff on imports from nonmember countries.

Commonwealth of Independent States (CIS) In December 1991 the Soviet Union was dissolved and 15 independent countries were formed: Armenia, Azerbaijan, Byelorussia (Belarus), Estonia, Georgia, Kazakhstan, Kirghizia (Kyrgyzstan), Latvia, Lithuania, Moldavia (Moldova), Russia, Tadzhikistan (Tajikistan), Turkmenistan, Ukraine, and Uzbekistan. Some of the republics have since changed their names. CIS represents a collective term for the group of republics.

Comprehensive Test Ban Treaty (CTBT) The three main purposes of the treaty were to curb proliferation; to end the contamination and destruction of fragile environments from nuclear explosions; and to halt the arms race by preventing new and modernized weapons from being added to the nuclear arsenals.

Concessional loans Loans given to less developed countries that can be repaid in soft (nonconvertible) currencies and with nominal or no interest over a long period of time.

Conditionality A series of measures that must be taken by a country before it could qualify for loans from the International Monetary Fund.

Conference on Security and Cooperation in Europe (CSCE) Series of conferences among 51 NATO, former Soviet bloc, and neutral European countries (52 counting Serbia or rump Yugoslavia). Established by 1976 Helsinki Accords.

Consensus In conference diplomacy, a way of reaching agreements by negotiations and without a formal vote.

Counterforce The use of strategic nuclear weapons for strikes on selected military capabilities of an enemy force.

Countries in transition (CITs) Former communist countries such as Russia whose economies are in transition from socialism to capitalism.

Cultural imperialism The attempt to impose your own value systems on others, including judging others by how closely they conform to your norms.

Current dollars The value of the dollar in the year for which it is being reported. Sometimes called inflated dollars. Any currency can be expressed in current value. *See* Real dollars

Decision making The process by which humans choose which policy to pursue and which actions to take in support of policy goals.

Dependencia model The belief that the industrialized North has created a neocolonial relationship with the South in which the LDCs are dependent on and disadvantaged by their economic relations with the capitalist industrial countries.

Deployment The actual positioning of weapons systems in a combat-ready status.

Détente A relaxation of tensions or a decrease in the level of hostility between opponents on the world scene.

Deterrence Persuading an opponent not to attack by having enough forces to disable the attack and/or launch a punishing counterattack.

Developed countries (DCs) Countries with relatively high per capita GNP, education, levels of industrial development and production, health and welfare, and agricultural productivity.

Developing countries (also called less developed countries) These countries are mainly producers of raw materials for export with high growth rates and inadequate infrastructures in transportation, educational systems, and the like. There is, however, a wide variation in living standards, GNPs, and per capita incomes among less developed countries.

Development The process through which a society becomes increasingly able to meet basic human needs and ensure the physical quality of life of its people.

Disinformation The spreading of false propaganda and forged documents to confuse counterintelligence or to create political confusion, unrest, and scandal.

Dumping A special case of price discrimination, selling to foreign buyers at a lower price than that charged to buyers in the home market.

Duty Special tax applied to imported goods, based on tariff rates and schedules.

East-West axis The cold war conflict between the former Soviet Union and its allies and the United States and its allies.

Economic Cooperation Among Developing Countries (ECDC) Also referred to as intra-South, or South-South cooperation, it is a way for less developed countries to help each other with appropriate technology.

Economic statecraft The practice of states utilizing economic instruments, such as sanctions, to gain their political ends. Economic statecraft is closely related to "mercantilism," or the use of political power to advance a country's economic fortunes.

Economically developed countries (EDCs) The relatively wealthy and industrialized countries that lie mainly in the Northern Hemisphere (the North).

Escalation Increasing the level of fighting.

Euro The single European currency among the majority of European Union members.

Eurodollars U.S. dollar holdings of European banks; a liability for the U.S. Treasury.

Euromissiles Shorthand for long-range theatre nuclear forces stationed in Europe or aimed at targets in Europe.

European Community (EC) This Western European regional organization was established in 1967 and included the European Coal and Steel Community, the European Economic Community, and the European Atomic Energy Community. *See also* European Union

European Currency Unit (ECU) The common unit of valuation among the eight members of the European Monetary System.

European Economic Community (EEC) The regional trade and economic organization established in Western Europe by the Treaty of Rome in 1958; also known as the Common Market.

European Free Trade Association (EFTA) Austria, Finland, Iceland, Liechtenstein, Norway, Portugal, Sweden, and Switzerland. Each member keeps its own external tariff schedule, but free trade prevails among the members.

European Political Cooperation (EPC) In 1970 members of the European Economic Community (Belgium, France, Germany, Italy, Luxembourg, and the Netherlands), joined together to strengthen their solidarity on major international issues through their diplomatic services.

European Union The Western European regional organization established in 1983 when the Maastricht Treaty went into effect. The EU encompasses the still legally exisiting European Community (EC). When the EC was formed in 1967 it included the European Coal and Steel community, the European Economic Community, and the European Atomic Energy Community.

Exchange rate The values of two currencies relative to each other, for example, how many yen equal a dollar or how many lira equal a pound.

Export subsidies Special incentives, including direct payments to exporters, to encourage increased foreign sales.

Exports Products shipped to foreign countries.

Foreign direct investment (FDI) Buying stock, real estate, and other assets in another country with the aim of gaining a controlling interest in foreign economic enterprises.

Foreign policy The sum of a country's goals and actions on the world stage. The study of foreign policy is synonymous with state-level analysis and examines how countries define their interests, establish goals, decide on specific policies, and attempt to implement those policies.

Foreign portfolio investment (FPI) Investment in the stocks and the public and private debt instruments (such as bonds) of another country below the level where the stock- or bondholder can exercise control over the policies of the stock-issuing company or the bond-issuing debtor.

Fourth World A term used to designate collectively the indigenous (aboriginal, native) people of the countries of the world.

Free trade The international movement of goods unrestricted by tariffs or nontariff barriers.

Free Trade Area of the Americas (FTAA) The tentative name given by the countries that met in 1994 at the Summit of the Americas to the proposed Western Hemisphere free trade zone that is projected to come into existence by the year 2005.

Functional relations Relations that include interaction in such usually nonpolitical areas as communication, travel, trade, and finance.

Functionalism International cooperation in specific areas such as communications, trade, travel, health, or environmental protection activity. Often symbolized by the specialized agencies, such as the World Health Organization, associated with the United Nations.

General Agreement on Tariffs and Trade (GATT) Created in 1947, this organization is the major global forum for negotiations of tariff reductions and other measures to expand world trade. It has grown to a membership of over 100.

General and complete disarmament (GCD) Total disarmament.

General Assembly The main representative body of the United Nations, composed of all member states.

Generalized System of Preferences (GSP) A system approved by GATT in 1971, which authorizes developed countries to give preferential tariff treatment to less developed countries.

Global Pertaining to the world as a whole; worldwide.

Global commons The Antarctic, the ocean floor under international waters, and celestial bodies within reach of planet Earth. All of these areas and bodies are considered the common heritage of mankind.

Global negotiations A new round of international economic negotiations started in 1980 over raw materials, energy, trade, development, money, and finance.

Golan Heights Syrian territory adjacent to Israel, which has occupied it since the 1967 war. Several Syrian-Israeli peace talks have attempted (unsuccessfully) to resolve border questions and water sharing rights.

Gross domestic product (GDP) A measure of income within a country that excludes foreign earnings.

Gross national product (GNP) A measure of the sum of all goods and services produced by a country's nationals, whether they are in the country or abroad.

Group of Seven (G-7) The seven most economically developed countries: Canada, France, Germany, Italy, Japan, United Kingdom, and United States.

Group of 77 Group of 77 countries of the South that cosponsored the Joint Declaration of Developing Countries in 1963 calling for greater equity in North-South trade. This group has come to include more than 120 members and represents the interests of the less developed countries of the South.

Hard currency Currencies, such as dollars, marks, francs, and yen, that are acceptable in private channels of international economics.

Hegemonism Any attempt by a larger power to interfere, threaten, intervene against, and dominate a smaller power or a region of the world.

Hegemony Domination by a major power over smaller, subordinate ones within its sphere of influence.

Helsinki Agreement. *See* Conference on Security and Cooperation in Europe.

Highly Indebted Poor Countries (HIPC) Countries that have such extreme poverty and financial insolvency that they are marked for a special kind of despair and economic isolation.

Horn of Africa The northeast corner of Africa that includes Ethiopia, Djibouti, and Somalia. It is separated from the Arabian peninsula by the Gulf of Aden and the Red Sea. It is plagued with tribal conflicts between Ethiopia and Eritrea, and between Ethiopia and Somalia over the Ogaden desert. These conflicts have generated a large number of refugees who faced mass starvation.

Human rights Rights inherent to human beings, including but not limited to, the right of dignity; the integrity of the person; the inviolability of the person's body and mind; civil and political rights (freedom of religion, speech, press, assembly, association, the right to privacy, habeas corpus, due process of law, the right to vote or not to vote, the right to run for election, and the right to be protected from reprisals for acts of peaceful dissent); social, economic, and cultural rights. The most glaring violations of human rights are torture, disappearance, and the general phenomenon of state terrorism.

Idealists Analysts who reject power politics and argue that failure to follow policies based on humanitarianism and international cooperation will result in disaster.

Ideological or theological principles A set of related ideas in secular or religious thought, usually founded on identifiable thinkers and their works, that offers a more or less comprehensive picture of reality.

IFOR (Implementation Force) The NATO-led Implementation Force formed in December 1995 to police the Dayton Agreement for Peace in Bosnia. This new NATO-led task force was originally composed of about 100,000 men and women involved in all aspects of the police operation from 29 countries.

Imports Products brought into a country from abroad.

Inkatha Freedom Party (IFP) A Zulu-based political and cultural movement that is one of the main rivals of the African National Congress in South Africa.

Innocent passage In a nation's territorial sea, passage by a foreign ship is innocent so long as it is not prejudicial to the peace, good order, or security of the coastal state. Submarines must surface and show their flag.

Inter-American System (IAS) Formal, multipurpose, regional (Western Hemisphere-wide) organization among the American states that originated in 1889 and has evolved to the present day.

Interdependence (economic) The close interrelationship and mutual dependence of two or more domestic economies on each other.

Intergovernmental organizations (IGOs) International/transnational actors composed of member countries.

Intermediate-range nuclear forces Nuclear arms that are based in Europe with a deployment range that easily encompasses the former USSR.

Intermediate-range Nuclear Forces Treaty (INF) The treaty between the former USSR and the United States that limits the dispersion of nuclear warheads in Europe.

Intermestic The merger of *inter*national and do*mestic* concerns.

International Between or among sovereign states.

International Atomic Energy Agency (IAEA) An agency created in 1946 by the UN to limit the use of nuclear technology to peaceful purposes.

International Court of Justice (ICJ) The World Court, which sits in The Hague with 15 judges and which is associated with the United Nations.

International Development Association (IDA) An affiliate of the World Bank that provides interest-free, long-term loans to developing countries.

International Energy Agency (IEA) An arm of the Organization of Economic Cooperation and Development (OECD) that attempts to coordinate member countries' oil imports and reallocate stocks among members in case of disruptions in the world's oil supply.

International Finance Corporation (IFC) Created in 1956 to finance overseas investments by private companies without necessarily requiring government guarantees. The IFC borrows from the World Bank, provides loans, and invests directly in private industry in the development of capital projects.

International Monetary Fund (IMF) The world's primary organization devoted to maintaining monetary stability by helping countries fund balance-of-payments deficits. Established in 1947, it now has 170 members.

International political economy (IPE) A term that encapsulates the totality of international economic interdependence and exchange in the political setting of the international system. Trade, investment, monetary relations, transnational business activities, aid, loans, and other aspects of international economic interchange (and the reciprocal impacts between these activities and politics) are all part of the study of IPE.

Interstate International, intergovernmental.

Intifada (literally, resurgence): A series of minor clashes between Palestinian youths and Israeli security forces that escalated into a full-scale revolt in December 1987.

IRA (Irish Republican Army) Organized in 1916, this secret military organization (the military wing of the Sinn Fein party) seeks to unite the independent country of Ireland with Northern Ireland. It declared a cease-fire in 1995 when Sinn Fein participated in talks with Great Britain.

Islamic fundamentalism Early nineteenth-century movements of fundamentalism sought to revitalize Islam through internal reform, thus enabling Islamic societies to resist foreign control. Some of these movements sought peaceful change, while others were more militant. The common ground of twentieth-century reform movements and groups is their fundamental opposition to the onslaught of materialistic Western culture and their desire to reassert a distinct Islamic identity for the societies they claim to represent.

KGB Security police and intelligence apparatus in the former Soviet Union, engaged in espionage, counterespionage, antisubversion, and control of political dissidents.

Kiloton A thousand tons of explosive force. A measure of the yield of a nuclear weapon equivalent to 1,000 tons of TNT (trinitrotoluene). The bomb detonated at Hiroshima in World War II had an approximate yield of 14 kilotons.

League of Nations The first true general international organization. It existed between the end of World War I and the beginning of World War II and was the immediate predecessor of the United Nations.

Least developed countries (LLDCs) Those countries in the poorest of economic circumstances. Frequently this term includes those countries with a per capita GNP of less than $400 in 1985 dollars.

Less developed countries (LDCs) Countries, located mainly in Africa, Asia, and Latin America, with economies that rely heavily on the production of agriculture and raw material and whose per capita GNP and standard of living are substantially below Western standards.

Lisbon Protocol Signed in 1992, it is an agreement between ex-Soviet republics Kazakhstan and Belarus to eliminate nuclear weapons from their territories.

Lome Convention International aid and trade agreements between the European Union and the ACP countries (African, Caribbean, and Pacific countries), to gain comprehensive self-sustained development.

Maastricht Treaty Signed by the European Community's 12 member countries in December 1991, the Maastricht Treaty outlines steps toward further political/economic integration.

MAD *See* Mutual Assured Destruction

MERCOSUR (Southern Common Market) MERCOSUR is made up of Argentina, Brazil, Paraguay, and Uruguay. This group negotiates free trade deals with key countries in South America and with the Economic Union.

Microstate A small country, usually with a population of less than one million, that cannot economically survive unaided or that is inherently so militarily weak that it is an inviting target for foreign intervention.

Missile Technology Control Regime (MTCR) A series of understandings that commit most of the countries capable of producing extended-range missiles to a ban on the export of ballistic missiles and related technology and that also pledge MTCR adherents to bring economic and diplomatic pressure to bear on countries that export missile-applicable technology.

Monetary relations The entire scope of international money issues, such as exchange rates, interest rates, loan policies, balance of payments, and regulating institutions (for example, the International Monetary Fund).

Most favored nation (MFN) In international trade agreements, a country grants most-favored-nation status to another country in regard to tariffs and other trade regulations.

Multilateral (foreign) aid Foreign aid distributed by international organizations such as the United Nations.

Multinational corporations (MNCs) Private enterprises doing business in more than one country.

Multinational states Countries in which there are two or more significant nationalities.

Multipolar system A world political system in which power primarily is held by four or more international actors.

Multistate nationalities Nations whose members overlap the borders of two or more states.

Munich analogy A belief among post-World War II leaders, particularly Americans, that agression must always be met firmly and that appeasement will only encourage an agressor. Named for the concessions made to Hitler by Great Britain and France at Munich during the 1938 Czechoslovakian crisis.

Mutual Assured Destruction (MAD) The basic ingredient of the doctrine of strategic deterrence that no country can escape destruction in a nuclear exchange even if it engages in a preemptive strike.

National Intelligence Estimate (NIE) The final assessment of global problems and capabilities by the intelligence community for use by the National Security Council and the president in making foreign and military decisions.

Nation-state A political unit that is sovereign and has a population that supports and identifies with it politically.

NATO (North Atlantic Treaty Organization) Also known as the Atlantic Alliance, NATO was formed in 1949 to create an alliance committed to mutual defense. It originally started with 12 independent nations; 4 more European nations joined between 1952 and 1982; and in 1999 they were joined by the Czech Republic, Hungary, and Poland. The 19 member countries of the alliance are: Belgium, Canada, the Czech Republic, Denmark, France, Germany, Greece, Hungary, Iceland, Italy, Luxemborg, Netherlands, Norway, Poland, Portugal, Spain, Turkey, United Kingdom, and the United States.

Nautical mile 6,076.115 feet (1,852 meters).

Neocolonialism A perjorative term describing the economic exploitation of less developed countries by the industrialized countries, in particular through the activities of multinational corporations.

New International Economic Order (NIEO) A term that refers to the goals and demands of the South for basic reforms in the international economic system.

Newly industrializing countries (NICs) Less developed countries whose economies and whose trade now include significant amounts of manufactured products. As a result, these countries have a per capita GDP significantly higher than the average per capita GDP for less developed countries.

Nonaligned movement (NAM) A group of less developed countries interested in promoting economic cooperation and development.

Nongovernmental organizations (NGOs or INGOs) Transnational (international) organizations made up of private organizations and individuals instead of member states.

Nonproliferation of Nuclear Weapons Treaty (NPT) Signed by nuclear weapon states, who pledge not to transfer nuclear explosive devices to any recipient and not to assist any nonnuclear weapon state in the manufacture of nuclear explosive devices.

Nontariff barriers (NTB) Subtle, informal impediments to free trade designed for the purpose of making importation of foreign goods into a country very difficult on such grounds as health and safety regulations.

Normalization of relations The reestablishment of full diplomatic relations, including de jure recognition and the exchange of ambassadors between two countries that either did not have diplomatic relations or had broken them.

North (as in North-South dialogue): (a) A shorthand, nongeographic term for the industrialized countries of high income, both East and West; (b) Often means only the industrialized, high-income countries of the West.

North American Free Trade Agreement (NAFTA) A 1994 economic agreement among the United States, Canada, and Mexico that will eliminate most trade barriers between the countries by 2009 and will also eliminate or reduce restrictions on foreign investments and other financial transactions among the NAFTA countries.

North Atlantic Cooperation Council (NACC) Consists of 37 members, including all members of NATO, the former Warsaw Pact members, and former Soviet republics (Russia, Ukraine, Belarus, Georgia, Moldova, Armenia, Azerbaijan, Kazakhstan, Uzbekistan, Kyrgyzstan, Turkmentistan, and Tajikstan), the Czech Republic, Slovakia, Poland, Hungary, Romania, Bulgaria, Estonia, Latvia, Lithuania, and Albania.

North Atlantic Treaty Organization *See* NATO

North-South Axis The growing tension that is developing between the few economically developed countries (North) and the many economically deprived countries (South). The South is insisting that the North share part of its wealth and terminate economic and political domination.

NPT Extension Treaty An agreement to extend the nonproliferation treaty indefinitely without additional restrictions was approved by unanimous consent in May 1995 at an international conference held in New York. In exchange for the consent of nonnuclear nations agreeing to forgo development of nuclear weapons, the nuclear powers pledged to terminate atmospheric tests by 1996.

Nuclear Nonproliferation Treaty (NPT) A treaty that prohibits the sale, acquisition, or production of nuclear weapons.

Nuclear terrorism The use (or threatened use) of nuclear weapons or radioactive materials as a means of coercion.

Nuclear Utilization Theory (NUT) Advocates of this nuclear strategy position want to destroy enemy weapons before the weapons explode on one's own territory and forces. The best way to do this, according to this theory, is to destroy an enemy's weapons before they are launched.

Nuclear-free zone A stretch of territory from which all nuclear weapons are banned.

Official Development Aid (ODA) Government contributions to projects and programs aimed at developing the productivity of poorer countries. This is to be distinguished from private, voluntary assistance, humanitarian assistance for disasters, and, most importantly, from military assistance.

On-site inspection (OSI) An arms control verification technique that involves stationing your or a neutral country's personnel in another country to monitor weapons or delivery vehicle manufacturing, testing, deployment, or other aspects of treaty compliance.

Organization for Economic Cooperation and Development (OECD) An organization that has existed since 1948 (and since 1960 under its present name) to facilitate the exchange of information and otherwise to promote cooperation among the economically developed countries. In recent years, the OECD has begun to accept as members a few newly industrializing and former communist countries in transition.

Organization for Security and Cooperation in Europe Series of conferences among 34 NATO, former Soviet bloc, and neutral European countries that led to permanent organization. Established by 1976 Helsinki Accords.

Organization for the Prohibition of Chemical Weapons (OPCW) Established at the Chemical Weapons Convention to oversee compliance with the Convention's ban on all chemical weapons.

Organization of Arab Petroleum Exporting Countries (OAPEC) Established in 1968 to promote cooperation and ties between member countries in activities related to the oil industry. Algeria, Bahrain, Egypt, Iraq, Kuwait, Socialist People's Libyan Arab Jamahiriya, Qatar, Saudi Arabia, Syrian Arab Republic, and United Arab Emirates are members.

Organization of Economic Cooperation and Development (OECD) An organization of 24 members that serves to promote economic coordination among the Western industrialized countries.

Organization of Petroleum Exporting Countries (OPEC) A producers' cartel setting price floors and production ceilings of crude petroleum. Member countries are: Algeria, Indonesia, Islamic Republic of Iran, Iraq, Kuwait, Nigeria, Qatar, Saudi Arabia, Socialist People's Libyan Arab Jamahiriya, United Arab Emirates, and Venezuela.

Palestine "Palestine" refers to the historical and geographical entity administered by the British under the League of Nations mandate from 1918 to 1947. It also refers to a future entity in the aspirations of Palestinians who, as was the case of the Jews before the founding of the State of Israel, are stateless nationalists. Whether Palestinians will have an autonomous or independent homeland is an ongoing issue.

Palestine Liberation Organization (PLO) A coalition of Palestinian groups united by the goal of a Palestinian state through the destruction of Israel as a state.

Partnership for Peace Program A U.S.-backed policy initiative for NATO formulated by the Clinton administration in 1994. The proposal was designed to rejuvenate the Atlantic Alliance and contribute to the stability of recent independent countries in Eastern Europe and the former Soviet Union. No NATO security guarantees or eventual membership in the alliance are specifically mentioned.

Peacekeeping Occurs when an international organization such as the United Nations uses military means to prevent hostilities, usually by serving as a buffer between combatants. This international force will remain neutral between the opposing forces and must be invited by at least one of the combatants. *See* Collective security

Petrodollars U.S. dollar holdings of capital-surplus OPEC countries; a liability for the U.S. Treasury.

Physical Quality of Life Index (PQLI) Developed by the Overseas Development Council, the PQLI is presented as a more significant measurement of the well-being of inhabitants of a geographic entity than the solely monetary measurement of per capita income. It consists of the following measurements: life expectancy, infant mortality, and literacy figures that are each rated on an index of 1–100, within which each country is ranked according to its performance. A composite index is obtained by averaging these three measures, giving the PQLI.

Polisario The liberation front of Western Sahara (formerly Spanish Sahara). After years of bitter fighting over Western Sahara, Polisario guerrillas signed a cease-fire agreement with Morocco in 1990. The UN has yet to conduct a referendum in Western Sahara on whether the territory should become independent or remain part of Morocco.

Postindustrial Characteristic of a society where a large portion of the workforce is directed to nonagricultural and nonmanufacturing tasks such as servicing and processing.

Precision-guided munitions (PGM) Popularly known as "smart bombs." Electronically programmed and controlled weapons that can accurately hit a moving or stationary target.

Proliferation Quick spread, as in the case of nuclear weapons.

Protectionism Using tariffs and nontariff barriers to control or restrict the flow of imports into a country.

Protocol A preliminary memorandum often signed by diplomatic negotiators as a basis for a final convention or treaty.

Quota Quantitative limits, usually imposed on imports or immigrants.

Rapprochement The coming together of two countries that had been hostile to each other.

Real dollars (uninflated dollars) The report of currency in terms of what it would have been worth in a stated year.

Regionalism A concept of cooperation among geographically adjacent states to foster region-wide political, military, and economic interests.

Reprocessing of nuclear waste A process of recovery of fissionable materials among which is weapons-grade plutonium.

Resolution Formal decisions of UN bodies; they may simply register an opinion or may recommend action to be taken by a UN body or agency.

Resolution 242 Passed by the UN Security Council on November 22, 1967, calling for the withdrawal of Israeli troops from territories they had captured from Egypt (Sinai), Jordan (West Bank and East Jerusalem), and Syria (Golan Heights) in the 1967 war, and for the right of all nations in the Middle East to live in peace in secure and recognized borders.

Resolution 435 Passed by the UN Security Council in 1978, it called for a cease-fire between belligerents in the Namibian conflict (namely SWAPO, Angola, and other front-line states on the one side, and South Africa on the other) and an internationally supervised transition process to independence and free elections.

Resolution 678 Passed by the UN in November 1990 demanding that Iraq withdraw from Kuwait. It authorized the use of all necessary force to restore Kuwait's sovereignty after January 15, 1991.

SALT I The Strategic Arms Limitation Treaty that was signed in 1972 between the United States and the former Soviet Union on the limitation of strategic armaments.

SALT II This Strategic Arms Limitation Treaty was signed in 1979, but it was withdrawn from the U.S. Senate by President Carter before ratification in response to the (1979) Soviet invasion of Afghanistan.

Secretariat (a) The administrative organ of the United Nations, headed by the secretary-general; (b) An administrative element of any intergovernmental organization (IGO); this is headed by a secretary-general.

Security Council The main peacekeeping organ of the United Nations. The Security Council has 15 members, including 5 permanent members.

Solidarity Independent, self-governing trade union movement started in Poland in 1980. It was terminated in December 1981 after radical members of its Presidium passed a resolution calling for a national referendum to determine if the communist government of Poland should continue to govern.

South (as in North-South Axis): A shorthand, nongeographic term that includes economically less developed countries, often represented by the Group of 77.

Sovereignty The ability to carry out laws and policies within national borders without interference from outside.

Special drawing rights (SDRs) Also known as paper gold. A new form of international liquid reserves to be used in the settlement of international payments among member governments of the International Monetary Fund.

START I *See* Strategic Arms Reduction Talks Treaty I

START II *See* Strategic Arms Reduction Talks Treaty II

START III *See* Strategic Arms Reduction Talks Treaty III

State Regarding international relations, it means a country having territory, population, government, and sovereignty; for example, the United States is a state, while California is not a state in this sense.

State terrorism The use of state power, including the police, the armed forces, and the secret police, to create fear among the population regarding any act of dissent or protest against a political regime.

"Stealth" A code name for an "invisible" aircraft, supposedly not detectable by hostile forces, that is the main U.S. strategic fighter-bomber.

Strategic Arms Reduction Talks (START I, Treaty I) A nuclear weapons treaty signed by the Soviet Union and the United States in 1991 and later re-signed with Belarus, Kazakhstan, Russia, and Ukraine that will limit Russia and the United States to 1,600 delivery vehicles and 6,000 strategic explosive nuclear devices each, with the other three countries destroying their nuclear weapons or transferring them to Russia.

Strategic Arms Reduction Talks (START II, Treaty II) A nuclear weapons treaty signed by the Soviet Union and the United States in 1993, which establishes nuclear warhead and bomb ceilings of 3,500 for the United States and 2,997 for Russia by the year 2003 and which also eliminates some types of weapons systems. Russia's Duma ratified the agreement in April 2000.

Strategic Arms Reduction Talks (START III, Treaty III) Basic elements of START III, as agreed by Presidents Clinton and Yelsin during the March 1997 Helsinki Summit Meeting: By December 31, 2007, conterminous with START II, the United States and Russia will deploy no more than 2,000 to 2,500 strategic nuclear warheads each on intercontinental ballistic missiles (ICBMs), submarine-launched ballistic missiles (SLBMs), and heavy bombers; both countries will negotiate measures relating to strategic nuclear warhead inventories and the destruction of these warheads as well as other jointly agreed technical and organizational measures to promote the irreversibility of deep reductions; and both countries will resolve issues related to the goal of making the current START treaties unlimited in duration.

Strategic Defense Initiative (SDI) A space-based defense system designed to destroy incoming missiles. It is highly criticized because the technological possibility of such a system is questionable, not to mention the enormous cost.

Strategic minerals Minerals needed in the fabrication of advanced military and industrial equipment. Examples are uranium, platinum, titanium, vanadium, tungsten, nickel, chromium, and so on.

Strategic nuclear weapons Long-range weapons carried on either intercontinental ballistic missiles (ICBMs) or submarine-launched ballistic missiles (SLBMs) or long-range bombers.

Strategic stockpile Reserves of certain commodities established to ensure that in time of national emergency such commodities are readily available.

Structural Adjustment Program *See* Conditionality

Superpowers Countries so powerful militarily (the United States and Russia), demographically (Pacific Rim countries), or economically (Japan) as to be in a class by themselves.

Supranational organization Organization that is founded and operates, at least in part, on the idea that international organizations can or should have authority higher than individual states and that those states should be subordinate to the supranational organization.

Sustainable development The ability to continue to improve the quality of life of those in the industrialized countries and, particularly, those in the less developed countries while simultaneously protecting Earth's biosphere.

Tariff A tax levied on imports.

Territorial sea The territorial sea, air space above, seabed, and subsoil are part of sovereign territory of a coastal state, except that ships (not aircraft) enjoy right of innocent passage. As proposed, a coastal state's sovereignty would extend 12 nautical miles beyond its land territory.

Terrorism The systematic use of terror as a means of coercion.

Theatre In nuclear strategy, it refers to a localized combat area, such as Europe, as opposed to global warfare that would have involved the United States and the former Soviet Union in a nuclear exchange.

Third World A term once commonly used to designate the countries of Asia, Africa, Latin America, and elsewhere that were economically less developed. The phrase is less often used since the end of the cold war, although some analysts continue to employ it to designate the less developed countries.

Tokyo Round The sixth round of General Agreement on Tariffs and Trade (GATT) trade negotiations, begun in 1973 and ended in 1979. About 100 nations, including nonmembers of the GATT, participated.

Torture The deliberate inflicting of pain, whether physical or psychological, to degrade, intimidate, and induce submission of its victims to the will of the torturer. It is a heinous practice used frequently in most dictatorial regimes in the world, irrespective of their ideological leanings.

Transnationalism Extension beyond the borders of a single country; applies to a political movement, issue, organization, or other phenomenon.

Trilateral countries The United States and Canada, Japan, and the Western European countries.

Unilateral One-sided, as opposed to bilateral or multilateral.

UN Conference on Population and Development (UNCPD) A UN-sponored conference that met in Cairo, Egypt, in 1994 and was attended by delegates from more than 170 countries. The conference called for a program of action to include spending $17 billion annually by the year 2000 on international, national, and local programs to foster family planning and to improve the access of women in such areas as education.

UN Conference on Trade and Development (UNCTAD) A coalition of disadvantaged countries that met in 1964 in response to their effort to bridge the standard-of-living gap between themselves and developed countries.

UN Development Programme (UNDP) An agency of the UN established in 1965 to provide technical assistance to stimulate economic and social development in the economically less developed countries. The UNDP has 48 members selected on a rotating basis from the world's regions.

UN Industrial Development Organization (UNID) A UN specialized agency established in 1967, currently having 165 members, that promotes the industrialization of economically less developed countries.

Vietnam analogy An aversion to foreign armed intervention, especially in less developed countries involving guerrillas. This is an attitude that is especially common among those who were opposed to U.S. participation in the Vietnam War or who were otherwise influenced by failed U.S. efforts there and the domestic turmoil that resulted.

Visegrad Group Term used to refer to Poland, Hungary, Slovakia, and the Czech Republic. These countries were subject to the same conditions and status in their recent application to participate in NATO's Partnership for Peace initiative.

Warsaw Pact or Warsaw Treaty Organization Established in 1955 by the Soviet Union to promote mutual defense. It was dissolved in July 1991. Member countries at time of dissolution were the Soviet Union, Bulgaria, Czechoslovakia, Hungary, Poland, and Romania.

West (as in the East-West conflict): Basically the market-economy, industrialized, and high-income countries that are committed to a political system of representative democracy. The three main anchors of the West today are North America, Western Europe, and Japan, also known as the Trilateral countries. Australia and New Zealand are also parts of the West.

Western European Union An arrangement among European countries to permit modest military operations that do not involve the United States. The main force of this military arm of the European Union was originally composed of Franco-German troops, but now includes Belgian and Spanish troops. This force was initially envisioned as the framework for a "European defense identity," but it was integrated into NATO Combined Joint Task Force Structures (CJTFS) by the end of 1995.

World Bank (International Bank for Reconstruction and Development [IBRD]): Makes loans, either directly to governments or with governments as the guarantors, and through its affiliates, the International Finance Corporation and the International Development Association.

Xenophobia A dislike, fear, or suspicion of other nationalities.

Zionism An international movement for the establishment of a Jewish nation or religious community in Palestine and later for the support of modern Israel.

SOURCES

World Politics: International Politics on the World Stage, Third Edition, 2000, McGraw-Hill/Dushkin.

International Politics on the World Stage, Seventh Edition, 1999, McGraw-Hill/Dushkin.

Global Studies: Africa, Eighth Edition, 1999, McGraw-Hill/Dushkin.

Global Studies: Russia, The Eurasian Republics, and Central/Eastern Europe, Eighth Edition, 2000, McGraw-Hill/Dushkin.

Global Studies: The Middle East, Eighth Edition, 2000, McGraw-Hill/Dushkin.

Index

Test Your Knowledge Form

We encourage you to photocopy and use this page as a tool to assess how the articles in ***Annual Editions*** expand on the information in your textbook. By reflecting on the articles you will gain enhanced text information. You can also access this useful form on a product's book support Web site at ***http://www.dushkin.com/online/.***

NAME: DATE:

TITLE AND NUMBER OF ARTICLE:

BRIEFLY STATE THE MAIN IDEA OF THIS ARTICLE:

LIST THREE IMPORTANT FACTS THAT THE AUTHOR USES TO SUPPORT THE MAIN IDEA:

WHAT INFORMATION OR IDEAS DISCUSSED IN THIS ARTICLE ARE ALSO DISCUSSED IN YOUR TEXTBOOK OR OTHER READINGS THAT YOU HAVE DONE? LIST THE TEXTBOOK CHAPTERS AND PAGE NUMBERS:

LIST ANY EXAMPLES OF BIAS OR FAULTY REASONING THAT YOU FOUND IN THE ARTICLE:

LIST ANY NEW TERMS/CONCEPTS THAT WERE DISCUSSED IN THE ARTICLE, AND WRITE A SHORT DEFINITION:

We Want Your Advice

ANNUAL EDITIONS revisions depend on two major opinion sources: one is our Advisory Board, listed in the front of this volume, which works with us in scanning the thousands of articles published in the public press each year; the other is you—the person actually using the book. Please help us and the users of the next edition by completing the prepaid article rating form on this page and returning it to us. Thank you for your help!

ANNUAL EDITIONS: GLOBAL ISSUES 01/02

ARTICLE RATING FORM

Here is an opportunity for you to have direct input into the next revision of this volume. We would like you to rate each of the 38 articles listed below, using the following scale:

1. Excellent: should definitely be retained
2. Above average: should probably be retained
3. Below average: should probably be deleted
4. Poor: should definitely be deleted

Your ratings will play a vital part in the next revision. So please mail this prepaid form to us just as soon as you complete it. Thanks for your help!

RATING	ARTICLE
	1. A Special Moment in History
	2. The Many Faces of the Future
	3. World Prisms: The Future of Sovereign States and International Order
	4. The American Way of Victory: A Twentieth-Century Trilogy
	5. The Big Crunch
	6. Breaking *Out* or Breaking *Down*
	7. The Misery Behind the Statistics: Women Suffer Most
	8. Grains of Hope
	9. The Global Challenge
	10. Climatic Changes That Make the World Flip
	11. The Energy Question, Again
	12. Invasive Species: Pathogens of Globalization
	13. We *Can* Build a Sustainable Economy
	14. The Complexities and Contradictions of Globalization
	15. Dueling Globalizations: A Debate Between Thomas L. Friedman and Ignacio Ramonet
	16. The Crisis of Globalization
	17. Globalization and American Power
	18. Reality Check: The WTO and Globalization After Seattle
	19. Where Have All the Farmers Gone?
	20. Beyond the Transition: China's Economy at Century's End
	21. What Pacific Century?
	22. Life After Pax Americana
	23. An Anachronistic Policy: The Strategic Obsolescence of the "Rogue Doctrine"
	24. Europe at Century's End: The Challenge Ahead
	25. Ethnic Conflict: Think Again
	26. The Nuclear Agenda
	27. Justice Goes Global
	28. Enforcing Human Rights
	29. Ecotourism Without Tears
	30. Tribes Under the Microscope
	31. Child Labour: Rights, Risks, and Realities
	32. Are Human Rights Universal?
	33. The Grameen Bank
	34. Why Environmental Ethics Matters to International Relations
	35. Will Globalization Make You Happy?
	36. A Fourth Way? The Latin American Alternative to Neoliberalism
	37. Democracy in Russia: How Free Is Free?
	38. One Battle After Another

(Continued on next page)

ANNUAL EDITIONS: GLOBAL ISSUES 01/02

NO POSTAGE NECESSARY IF MAILED IN THE UNITED STATES

BUSINESS REPLY MAIL

FIRST-CLASS MAIL PERMIT NO. 84 GUILFORD CT

POSTAGE WILL BE PAID BY ADDRESSEE

McGraw-Hill/Dushkin
530 Old Whitfield Street
Guilford, CT 06437-9989

ABOUT YOU

Name ______________________ Date ________

Are you a teacher? ☐ A student? ☐

Your school's name ______________________

Department ______________________

Address ______________ City ________ State ____ Zip ____

School telephone # ______________________

YOUR COMMENTS ARE IMPORTANT TO US !

Please fill in the following information:

For which course did you use this book? ______________________

Did you use a text with this *ANNUAL EDITION*? ☐ yes ☐ no

What was the title of the text? ______________________

What are your general reactions to the *Annual Editions* concept? ______________________

Have you read any particular articles recently that you think should be included in the next edition? ______________________

Are there any articles you feel should be replaced in the next edition? Why? ______________________

Are there any World Wide Web sites you feel should be included in the next edition? Please annotate. ______________________

May we contact you for editorial input? ☐ yes ☐ no

May we quote your comments? ☐ yes ☐ no